THE ZOO BOOK

A GUIDE TO AMERICA'S BEST

ALLEN W. NYHUIS

Foreword by
Dr. Lee G. Simmons,
Director of Omaha's Henry Doorly Zoo

CAROUSEL PRESS

Copyright ©1994 Allen W. Nyhuis

Published by: **CAROUSEL PRESS**
                 P.O. Box 6061
                 Albany, CA 94706-0061
                 (510) 527-5849

Distributed to the book trade by Publishers Group West

Nyhuis, Allen W., 1957-
        The zoo book : a guide to America's best / Allen W. Nyhuis.
                p.   cm.
        "Includes best foreign zoos."
        Includes bibliographical references (p.   ) and index.
        ISBN 0-917120-13-2 : $14.95
        1. Zoos--United States--Guidebooks. 2. Zoos--Guidebooks.
    I. Title.
    QL76.5.U6N94   1994
    590' .74'473--dc20

                                              93-46925
                                              CIP

Published in the United States of America

10 9 8 7 6 5 4 3 2 1

Although the author and publisher have made every effort to ensure that the information in this book was correct at press time, the author and publisher do not assume, and hereby disclaim, any liability to any party for any loss or damage caused by errors, omissions, or any potential travel disruption due to labor or financial difficulty, whether such errors or omissions result from negligence, accident, or any other cause.

To my children,
Jeremy, Mandy, Becky, and Millie.

Acknowledgments

This book is the result of thousands of miles of traveling, hundreds of hours spent walking through zoos, and thousands of hours spent writing. Yet even with all of the hard work on my part, this book would not have been completed without the help of many people from across the country.

I would like to thank all of the zoo employees, from secretaries to zoo directors, at the more than 80 zoos nationwide who provided me with important information and photographs. A special thanks to Dr. Lee Simmons, Director of Omaha's Henry Doorly Zoo, for writing the foreword, and to Jim Marlett in Wichita, Mike Morgan in Washington, and Suzanne Braun in Indianapolis for their personalized attention and help.

I express my gratitude to the friends, relatives, and family across the country who toured zoos with me, gave me a place to stay, and helped me in other important ways. These special people include my Uncle Paul and Aunt Gayle in Minnesota, my sister-in-law Karen in Buffalo, my sister Amy in Wisconsin, my Aunt Judy and the Armerdings in San Diego, the Muckells in New York, and the Copps in Maryland. My brother and sister-in-law, David and Jennifer of Tacoma, deserve special thanks for getting me to three zoos, for helping me review my early drafts, and especially for their early encouragement. My in-laws, Owen and Shirley Wald, also deserve a special thanks. It was my father-in-law, Owen, who first believed in my ability to write this book. I posthumously acknowledge my Uncle Dave, not only for being a personal mentor, but also for providing important information about the San Diego Zoo.

My close friends Earl Miller and Dave Nelson, both of Indianapolis, were vital in helping me formulate my ideas. Special thanks to my friend and colleague, Ann Hendrich, for her help and for making it possible for me to get to many of the zoos. I also greatly appreciate all of my church friends, especially the Wisemans, for their help and prayers.

Of course, I very much appreciate my publisher, Carole Terwilliger Meyers, for her help, for her confidence in me, and especially for her willingness to take a chance on me.

My lifelong gratitude goes to my parents, Wayne and Lois of Wisconsin, for their love and care for me over the years. They also took me to my first zoo so many years ago.

My childhood love of zoos probably would not have re-emerged if my wonderful children Jeremy, Mandy, Becky, and Millie had not come into my life. Seeing life through their eyes made me see what a special place a zoo is, especially for families. My children toured many of the zoos with me and provided the best company anyone could ask for. A big hug and thank-you goes to each.

Most of all, thanks to my wife Kathy. It was no small chore for her to stay home alone with four kids while I was off touring zoos. Kathy provided invaluable help with proof-reading, and also gave me encouragement when I needed it most.

Finally I thank my God and Creator for the ability and opportunity He has given me to put this book together.

Credits

Editor: Carole Terwilliger Meyers
Typesetting, Layout, and Cover Design: Betsy Joyce
Computer Wizardry: Gene Meyers
Printing: McNaughton & Gunn, Inc.

Photos: p.13: (Arabian Oryx) Neal Johnston, Los Angeles Zoo; p.14: (Mandrill) Susan Reich, The Lincoln Park Zoo Society; (Bonobos) San Diego Zoo; (Cheetahs) Oklahoma City Zoo; p.15: (Colobus Monkeys) Neal Johnston, Los Angeles Zoo; (Gerenuk) Robert Cabello, Dallas Zoo; (Japanese Macaques) Indianapolis Zoo; p.16: (Koalas) F.D. Schmidt, Zoological Society of San Diego; (Ring-Tailed Lemurs) Neal Johnston, Los Angeles Zoo; p.17: (Snow Leopard) Mike Greer, Chicago Zoological Society; (Emperor Tamarins) Underwood, San Francisco Zoo; (Meerkats) New York Zoological Society; p.18: (Naked Mole-Rat) Cincinnati Zoo; (Okapi) Ron Austing, Cincinnati Zoo; (Pronghorn) Neal Johnston, Los Angeles Zoo; p.19: (Red Panda) Cincinnati Zoo; (Sumatran Rhino) Neal Johnston, Los Angeles Zoo; (Malayan Tapirs) New York Zoological Society; p.20: (Vampire Bat) Sedgwick County Zoo; (Bulka Walrus) Jim Schulz, Chicago Zoological Society; (Wart Hog) Neal Johnston, Los Angeles Zoo; p.21: (White Bengal Tiger) Cincinnati Zoo; (Crowned Crane) Cincinnati Zoo; (Black-and-White Casqued Hornbill) San Francisco Zoo; p.22: (King Vulture) Fort Worth Zoo; (Gharial) Bronx Zoo/Wildlife Conservation Park; p.23: (Komodo Dragon) Jessie Cohen, National Zoological Park; (Leaf-Cutter Ants) Cincinnati Zoo; p.31: (Woodchuck Habitat) Jane Ballentine, The Baltimore Zoo; p.34: (Indian Rhinos) New York Zoological Society; p.35: (Zoo Center) New York Zoological Society; p.38: (African Lion) Filip R. Caruso, Buffalo Zoo; p.41: (Sea Lion Pool) Central Park Zoo; p.45: (Giant Panda) Jessie Cohen, National Zoological Park; p.49: (Camel) Oglebay's Good Children's Zoo; p.53: (Jaguar) Steve Walker, Philadelphia Zoo; p.56: (Panther Chameleon) Burnet Park Zoo; p.71: (Gorillas) Blair Callicutt, North Carolina Zoo; p.72: (Elephant Habitat) Jim Page, North Carolina Zoo; p.75: (Flamingos) Riverbanks Zoo; p.80: (Manatee) Lowry Park Zoo; p.84: (White Alligator and Sumatran Tigers) Audubon Park & Zoo; p.91: (Children's Zoo) Robert Cabello, Dallas Zoo; p.95: (Bald Eagle) Fort Worth Zoo; p.98: (King Cobra hatchling) Gladys Porter Zoo; p.103: (Bottlenosed Dolphin) Oklahoma City Zoo; p.109: (Tropical Tour) San Antonio Zoo & Aquarium; p.110: (Polar Bear) Tulsa Zoo and Living Museum; p.116: (White-Handed Gibbon) Binder Park Zoo; p.118: (African Spoonbill) Mike Greer, Chicago Zoological Society; p.119: (Humboldt Penguin) Mike Greer, Chicago Zoological Society; p.126: (Macaw) Cleveland Metroparks Zoo; p.134: (Polar Bear) Indianapolis Zoo; p.144: (Hippo) The Toledo Zoo; p.147: (Bighorn Sheep) James Terlechi, John Ball Zoo; p.153: (Sun Bear) Minnesota Zoo; p.155: (Takin) Minnesota Zoo; p.170: (Mountain Lion) Arizona-Sonora Desert Museum; p.177: (Reticulated Giraffes) Denver Zoo; p.180: (Mexican Wolf) Dick George, The Phoenix Zoo; p.182: (Seals & Sea Lions Exhibit) Rio Grande Zoo; p.185: (Black and White Ruffed Lemur) Wildlife World Zoo; p.188: (Grevy's Zebras) The Living Desert; p.190: (Condor chick) Los Angeles Zoo; p.192: (Rocky Mountain Goats) Neal Johnston, Los Angeles Zoo; p.195: (Francois Leaf Monkey) Michael Durham, Metro Washington Park Zoo; p.198: (Sand Tiger Shark) Point Defiance Zoo & Aquarium; p.200: (Tour Bus) Ron Garrison, Zoological Society of San Diego; p.201: (Corn Snake) Ron Garrison, Zoological Society of San Diego; p.209: (Pygmy Marmosets) Woodland Park Zoo; p.214: (Wildlife Viewing Drive) Fossil Rim Wildlife Center; p.220: (Sea Otter) Monterey Bay Aquarium; (Belukha Whale) Paul J. Horton, Mystic Marinelife Aquarium; p.223: Tennessee Aquarium; p.226: (Adelies Penguins) Sea World Inc.; p.227: (American Crocodile) Florida's Silver Springs; p.228: (Raccoons) Florida's Silver Springs; p.230: (Orangutan) Metro Toronto Zoo; back cover: (Author Allen W. Nyhuis at the Indianapolis Zoo) Susie Wiseman

Contents

Zoo Reviews:

Foreword

What is a zoo?

Ask ten different people—visitors, zoo professionals, educators, etc.—for a concise definition of a zoo, and you are liable to get ten different answers. Each seemingly diverse opinion is likely to be valid from the perspective of the individual's age, background, education, or professional discipline.

Because of this diversity of opinion, it is virtually impossible to rank zoos in numerical order from best to worst. Happily, Allen Nyhuis does not fall into the trap of attempting to do this. He has taken the list of zoos generally accepted by the zoological community as major zoos, by virtue of their size and the scope of their programs, and has attempted to identify each zoo's strong features. Particular attention is paid to identifying unique features and diversities to be found in each institution. Since most visitors find it nearly impossible to see all of a major zoo on a single visit, this book's summaries of the scope and orientation of the zoo's collection, of its major exhibits, and of its "must see" exhibits provide a very useful and easy-to-use guide to help visitors extract the most out of a 2-, 3-, or even 5-hour visit.

In reading through this information for many of the zoos about which I have firsthand knowledge, I was impressed by the consistency in which the high points, and the exhibitry with which I mentally associate these zoos, is pointed out. Additionally, many features and exhibits are highlighted which even I, as a visiting professional with either a director or curator as a guide, had managed to miss, or which had slipped into the recesses of my memory. The amount of research and attention to detail exhibited by Allen Nyhuis is impressive. I suspect this book will quickly find a place in zoo libraries as a welcome reference guide.

The diversity of the exhibits and collections described in this book is a visible manifestation of the diversity of the natural world and of the zoo world's evolving role in conservation. Evidence of this evolution is demonstrated by the fact that the traditional definition of "wild animals" versus "captive animals" is no longer really valid. IN TODAY'S WORLD THERE ARE ONLY CAPTIVE ANIMALS! Some are captive in state-of-the-art zoos where husbandry and management programs have insured, or are being developed to insure, both the individual's well-being and the long-term survival and genetic health of the total captive population. Some are captive in well-managed "wild" sanctuaries and protected habitats that are large enough to support genetically viable populations and keep them relatively secure from stochastic events such as hurricanes, earthquakes, forest fires, etc. Some, unfortunately, are captive in "wild habitats" that are either too small to support a genetically viable population, too poorly managed or funded to supply adequate resources, or too poorly protected to prevent the poaching of ivory, rhino horns, tiger bones, rare orchids, etc. for the illegal black market.

The zoo world's role in the conservation strategy to preserve species, habitats, and ecosystems has, of necessity, evolved to the point where the old boundaries of "captive breeding and management" versus "wildlife management" are blurred or non-existent. This blurring of traditional boundaries is the result not only of a dramatic expansion of the scope of interests, disciplines, and activities of zoo professionals, but of the evolving recognition that individual zoos and the world zoo community have both the ability and the responsibility to serve as conservation entities that go far beyond just providing collections for the entertainment and enlightenment of their visiting public.

Acting collaboratively with a roster of thousands of zoologists, veterinarians, reproductive physiologists, geneticists, educators, nutritionists, conservation biologists, and other relevant disciplines, the world zoo community is uniquely qualified to fill this conservation role.

It is a fact that change in public attitudes comes about primarily as a result of the public's awareness of the need for change. Zoos are in the position of having a unique opportunity to inform and educate, and thereby influence, local, regional, and world awareness and attitudes on conservation issues. It is estimated that, worldwide, over 600 million people visit these institutions annually. The effect of this influence can already be seen in the modification of individual practices and, perhaps more importantly, in the influence an informed public has on the decisions made by government and private policy makers.

A more immediately recognizable conservation role is the zoo world's efforts in formal public education programs and in captive breeding and species survival programs (SSPs). Many of these SSPs will ultimately provide the genetic base from which to restock populations back into their native habitat. Today zoo professionals work not only in their individual zoos, but also as part of inter-zoo teams on collaborative regional projects and as part of large multi-disciplinary, long-term team efforts on international projects—such as a black-footed ferret project in North America, a Sumatran tiger project in Indonesia, a hornbill workshop in Singapore, a primate project in Thailand or Vietnam, or a Siberian tiger project in the Russian Far East. Perhaps the best indicator of the changing role of zoos in conservation is that zoo professionals are often found working in the wild side-by-side with more traditional field and wildlife biologists.

Last, but not least, for many of the world's species that have simply run out of living space in their native habitats, the zoos of the world may well serve as essential temporary sanctuaries—providing the husbandry and management to preserve genetic diversity until safe, natural habitats once again exist. It is from these zoological sanctuaries that the gene pools for reintroduction or re-enforcement of "wild" populations will spring.

— Dr. Lee G. Simmons
Director of Omaha's Henry Doorly Zoo

Introduction

It is well documented that every year zoos in the United States attract more visitors than all spectator sports combined. Of these millions of visitors, out-of-town tourists are usually only a small minority. A few exceptions exist. The San Diego Zoo is competitive with Disneyland and other major southern California tourist attractions. The Arizona-Sonora Desert Museum, located just outside of Tucson, is the second most popular tourist attraction in that state (the Grand Canyon is first). For the most part, the rest of America's zoos are visted primarily by local school children and families.

A common misconception about zoos is that they are all alike. This erroneous belief keeps many people from adding zoos to their travel itineraries. The fact is that each zoo is different, and some are entirely unique: the Minnesota Zoo, the North Carolina Zoo, and the Point Defiance Zoo in Tacoma, Washington. Some exhibits, such as the Lied Jungle (at Omaha's Henry Doorly Zoo in Nebraska) and Tropic World (at the Brookfield Zoo near Chicago) are unparalleled. Koalas, okapis, Komodo dragons, and even beavers are displayed at very few zoos, and the National Zoo in Washington, D.C. is the only U.S. zoo with a giant panda permanently on display. So a visit to any zoo offers an experience that is different than going to your local zoo.

I have visited all of the 53 major zoos within the last 3 years, and I have been to most more than once. I have visited these zoos as a tourist, often with my small children accompanying me, and have taken careful note of what would interest a typical visitor. My hope is that this book will inspire you to visit more of our country's zoos.

Current Trends at U.S. Zoos

Zoo Origins

The first zoos in the United States opened in Philadelphia, New York, and Chicago just after the Civil War. By 1900, more than 20 public zoos were in operation, one as far west as Seattle. During the 20th century, a large zoo became a major source of community pride for nearly every large city, as well as for many medium and small cities. Putting together a zoo was like assembling a coin collection—displaying one or two of as many different "items" as possible was the goal. The emphasis in these menageries was on quantity, not quality.

Exhibiting a maximum number of animals meant squeezing in as many cages as the available space would allow, with little regard to the amount of room for animals inside. Outdoor cages featured thick iron bars and concrete floors. Inside the great animal houses of the day, cages were equipped with tile walls and either tile or concrete floors; they were fronted with either iron bars or glass. The small cage size enabled visitors to get a very close look at exotic animals. Tile walls and concrete floors made the exhibits easy to clean, a benefit for zoo employees and, it was thought, the animals as well. The rationale of the day was: "A clean exhibit makes a healthy animal." Research had not yet shown that the animals' pacing and silent staring were not natural behaviors.

Breeding

Until the 1960s, breeding was not a high priority for zoos. If a popular animal died, the zoo would simply purchase a new one captured from the wild. Suddenly, things were not so simple. Political instabilities and a desire to protect their natural heritage prompted many nations to close their borders to animal collectors. Zoos were then forced to acquire new animals from other zoos or to breed them themselves.

Another problem soon came to the attention of both zoos and the public. Popular animals such as tigers, cheetahs, rhinos, gorillas, and elephants were quickly becoming rare in the wild, with some dangerously close to extinction. By 1962, the population of Arabian oryxes in the world fell to single digits. The world's zoos banded together and saved this animal from extinction. Similar efforts saved the Pere David's deer and Mongolian wild horse. With so many other animals in a similar predicament, the zoological world initiated the Species Survival Plans (SSPs). These organized efforts use all of the zoos' resources to save the most endangered animals. Today more than 60 mammals, birds, reptiles, amphibians, and invertebrates are a part of the SSP program. Most of these animals, though very rare in the wild, are increasingly common in zoos. This is why so much attention is paid to such otherwise unknown species as Chinese alligators, addax, and Guam rails.

Today baby gorillas, elephants, rhinos, chimpanzees, and many other baby animals are common sights on a zoo visit, though still always a highlight. However, until 1956 gorillas had never reproduced in any zoo, and it had been nearly 40 years since an elephant calf had been seen by zoo visitors. Zoos putting an emphasis on saving species and breeding rare animals gives visitors today this opportunity to see many baby animals.

Getting wild animals to mate and reproduce in zoos didn't just happen. Important changes had to be made. Most important was pairing up reproductive males and females of the various species. As part of the SSP plans, genetic research is used to match mating partners that will produce the genetically best possible offspring for the continuation of the species.

Habitats

Another change necessary to encourage breeding was upgrading the animals' homes. The iron and concrete cages created a bare, sterile environment. This plus the gawking of thousands of visitors prevented animals from performing natural behaviors, including mating. Animal research showed that if animals felt like they were in their native home, they would also act like they were. With this in mind, zoos began to build wonderful natural habitats for their animals.

Across the country, zoos constructed habitats that simulated the African savanna, the North American prairie, the rocky Pacific coastline, the ice flows of the Arctic and Antarctic Circles, and most notably, the tropical rain forests of the world. One of the most important features of these re-created habitats was the use of living plants, preferably from the native habitat. When a zoo's climate forbade the use of exotic native plants, clever use was made of "look-alike plants." Natural habitats are appreciated by both animals and zoo visitors, and today the word "cage" is almost a dirty word in zoos.

As mentioned, the rain forest has become a very popular environment to simulate. In 1974, the Topeka Zoo opened their *Tropical Rain Forest* building under a large acrylic dome. Three years later, Wichita's Sedgwick County Zoo, also in Kansas, opened the larger and lusher *Jungle* building. Since then huge rain forest buildings have been springing up across the nation, culminating with the opening of Omaha's astonishing *Lied Jungle* in 1992. All of these remarkable buildings are filled with palm, fig, banana, bamboo, and other tropical trees, plus ferns, flowering plants, waterfalls, flowing streams, free-flying colorful birds, and a variety of animals.

The rain forest buildings are examples of the exciting concept of multi-species exhibits, which display many types of animals together in the same space just as they live in the wild. Most African savanna exhibits now have giraffes, zebras, antelope, ostriches, and other mammals and birds roaming the open veldt together. Of course the meat-eating predators, such as lions and cheetahs, cannot be mixed directly with the zebras and antelope, their natural prey, but zoos have made it "seem" to happen. So-called "predator/prey" exhibits utilize a hidden deep moat to separate natural enemies, while making them appear to be together in the same exhibit.

Watching animals in today's zoos is like being a part of a *National Geographic* wildlife special. Americans can now experience a realistic tour of the African savanna, an Amazon rain forest, or the Himalayan highlands. A new concept called "landscape immersion" puts people into the animals' home rather than vice versa. Modern technology has provided fog machines, convincing artificial rocks and trees, and recordings of wildlife noises that allow visitors not only to see animals in a realistic rain forest setting, but also to feel as if they are actually in the rain forest themselves. The exhibits look, feel, sound, and even smell like the real thing.

Technology Provides a Better View

The major drawback of these incredible natural habitats is that the animals were sometimes difficult to see in the dense vegetation or rocky crevices. Steps have been taken to remedy this problem. Heated rocks, watering holes, and viewing caves are used to keep the animals in view.

Modern advances in glass-making have provided larger, stronger, and even curved panels that give visitors unique views of the world's aquatic animals. Underwater viewing galleries are being built in nearly every major zoo. Visitors can now see seals and sea lions, walruses, dolphins, polar bears, penguins, otters, crocodiles, tapirs, and even hippos swimming and diving underwater. In the Toledo Zoo's beautiful *Hippoquarium,* underwater hippo births have been witnessed by humans for the first time.

Many zoos are going "barless" and removing all visible barriers between the animals and visitors. Animals are exhibited on islands or separated from viewers only by a moat, stream, or pond. Some of the animals that cannot be exhibited in this manner, such as birds and large cats, are restrained by ultra-thin harp (or piano) wire. This strong wire is thin enough so that most cameras can focus it away for a clear, barless picture.

The Conservation Message

The parent organization that officially accredits the nation's zoos and aquariums is the American Zoo and Aquarium Association (AZA). To receive a highly coveted accreditation, a zoo must pass a site visit from an AZA representative. One of the most important items checked is the zoo's educational programs.

Today's zoo is more than a source of entertainment or a refuge for endangered animals. It is also a major educational center that hosts thousands of school children every year. So most exhibits now are enhanced by attractive graphics that provide visitors with animal names and both important and trivial information about the animals. Many exhibits, especially in children's zoos, are equipped with hands-on activities that encourage learning by doing. Some compare human abilities with those of various animals. Also, most animal shows presented in zoos are now called "demonstrations" and are primarily educational.

Today zoos also have a very specific message to preach. By introducing the public to the world's enormous variety of animals and their native habitats, they hope that people will better appreciate the animals and want to help preserve them. Visitors are encouraged to recycle and conserve, and they are advised not to pollute and not to buy exotic animal products.

Visitors: The Bottom Line

In the last 10 years, America's zoos have spent more than $1 billion on upgrading and improvements. While most zoos get some government financial support, very few would survive without a growing attendance rate and strong support from their community. Quite simply, zoos need visitors.Some zoos are attempting to attract them some with theme park-like rides such as monorails and sky rides. All in all, the incredible variety of animals, exhibits, scenery, rides, and shows is causing many zoos to become popular destinations for vacationers, business travelers, and local residents alike.

Going To The Zoo

Planning Ahead

Many zoos in the United States are massive and can be overwhelming if you are unprepared. One way to prepare for a visit is to call or write to the zoo in advance. Request a map and brochure about the zoo, along with the current hours and admission fees. Most zoos are glad to oblige. Then, using the map, plan a route through the zoo. Show children animal pictures in the brochures to encourage excitement about their upcoming "safari."

Also, look over the zoo's review in this book. Make note of the exhibits and animals listed as "Don't Miss." Read through the narrative portion of the review, noting what interests each member of the family. Re-read the review on the way to the zoo as a reminder of what everyone wants to see.

What To Bring

Once on the zoo grounds, just about anything you might need is available—for a price. Because the price can be steep, it is important to think about what to bring along.

A full day of walking zoo trails, especially at the larger zoos, can cause very tired feet. Small children can become cranky and spoil everyone's fun. So do bring along a stroller or rent one at the zoo. Wagons can also be rented at many zoos and are becoming increasingly popular because more than one child, and older children, can ride. Also pack a few bandages for possible blisters.

While refreshments and meals from zoo snack bars and restaurants can be costly, they are also convenient and fun. If you want to save money by bringing your own picnic, check first to determine whether the zoo allows food to be brought in. Most, but not all, zoos have designated picnic areas. Others provide picnic tables directly outside the entrance.

In summer, protection from the ill effects of the sun is a priority. Bring sun hats, visors, and sunscreen to shield faces and limbs.

If you bring along a camera or camcorder, don't forget to bring extra film, tapes, and batteries. Binoculars are also handy to have along. Some exhibits are so massive that a lot is missed using just the naked eye.

Finally, some consideration should be given to what you wear on your zoo visit. Check the weather forecast and dress accordingly. If unsure, bring extra clothes in the car—just in case. Comfortable walking shoes are, of course, essential.

When To Go

In summer it is important to arrive early. This gets you to the zoo when the crowds are thinnest, the temperatures are coolest, and the animals are most active.

Summer, however, is not the only time to go. Many people think that the zoo is not an enjoyable place unless the weather is warm and sunny. What they do not realize is that the zoo can be just as much fun, maybe even more so, during bad weather. Inclement weather reduces the crowds. You won't have to strain then to see over people. Also, with smaller crowds and cooler weather, animals tend to be more active.

It is true that when the temperature is cold, fewer animals from Africa and tropical Asia will be outside (though it can be surprising how tough some of these animals are). Then again, when else but in winter can you see a polar bear or a Siberian tiger playing in a fresh blanket of snow? Many zoos (particularly the northern zoos) have numerous warm indoor exhibits (which are air-conditioned in the summer). These buildings are, of course, not affected by the weather and are especially delightful when relatively empty.

Starting Your Tour

When entering the zoo, get everyone in your party a guide map. Children especially enjoy having their own map and might even pick up a few map-reading skills.

Determine what each person wants to see most. Mark those exhibits on the map and then plan a route that leads to all of them. If the zoo has a circular layout, it's a good idea to go "against the flow," that is to see the zoo in a counter-clockwise direction (most people tend to go clockwise). Some crowd buildup can be avoided this way.

When checking over the guide map, note the times of any animal shows or feedings that sound interesting. Adjust your route to lead to these exhibits at the specified times.

Rules and Manners

Everyone should be aware of two simple rules. First, the animals should not be teased or intentionally disturbed. Some visitors like to tap on the glass or throw rocks at the animals to get their attention; both actions are forbidden. Second, visitors should not feed the animals—not even grass—unless the zoo makes it very clear that it is all right to do so. Zoo animals are on special diets designed for their optimal health. Violating either of these rules may harm the animals, cause embarrassment to the violators and their companions, and possibly result in the violators being asked to leave.

Shows

Most zoos offer animal shows, but their appeal varies greatly. Some are of the caliber found at major theme parks, such as Sea World, while others are simple, informal demonstrations. One way to gauge the potential appeal of a show is to look at the size of its amphitheater. If it has a large seating capacity, it is probably popular. Almost any show featuring dolphins, sea lions, or elephants will be good. (The best animal shows are mentioned in the Entertainment section of each Zoo Review.)

When taking very small children to a show, try to sit near the exit. Even the best entertainment can be boring to toddlers and babies, so you might need to make a fast getaway.

Dining

Many zoo restaurants offer seating with a captivating view of wild animals. For example, Omaha's Henry Doorly Zoo has a 400-seat restaurant with glass panels overlooking the amazing *Lied Jungle*. A more simple, though almost as pleasing, experience can be had in the outdoor seating area of the Indianapolis Zoo's *Cafe on the Commons*, where the lunchtime entertainment features gibbons on one side and lemurs on the other.

Fun is sometimes on the menu, too. Dolphin-shaped French fries or a "Happy Meal" with a zoo theme are exciting choices for children. Sometimes soft drinks are served in colorful plastic souvenir cups that make great mementos for zoo-loving kids.

Zoo Membership

Since numerous visits to the zoo can get to be quite expensive, consider buying a zoo membership. It usually pays for itself in just two or three visits. Besides free admission, most zoos offer their members other advantages such as inclusion in special events and discounts at the gift shop. Also, a reciprocity program among most zoos allows members to enter other zoos across the country free with their membership card. Zoos that participate in this program are so noted in the Admission Fees section of each Zoo Review.

WHEN CHILDREN ARE ALONG

Educational Fun

It is no accident that many schools plan field trips to the zoo. Observing animals is educational. Even more can be learned by reading informative signs that not only identify the animals, but also tell where they come from, what they eat, and what is unusual about them. Read these signs to, or with, your children. An 8-year-old who knows that a koala is not a bear is one step ahead of the general population. Because children appreciate snow leopards more when they actually see how they are similar to their pet cat, and because they are impressed by the great size difference between a 9-foot-tall grizzly bear and a 4-foot-tall sun bear, not all learning requires reading signs.

Many zoos take extra steps to make learning an enjoyable experience. At the Brookfield Zoo's *Tropic World* and the North Carolina Zoo's *R. J. Reynolds Forest Aviary*, a card or flyer with pictures of all the creatures in the exhibit is given to each visitor, who is then challenged to find as many of the animals as possible. At the Washington Park Zoo (in Portland, Oregon), the *Africa Rain Forest* features a *Kongo Ranger Station*. This very authentic African camp displays a jeep and animal skins, and at times even has a native African on hand to talk about his homeland. (Extra-special educational offerings such as these are highlighted in each Zoo Review.)

Games and Activities

Another way to make a zoo visit educational and at the same time keep children from becoming bored is to engage them in games and activities such as these:

Animal Alphabet. Each child writes the alphabet, one letter per line, on a sheet of lined paper. On their tour of the zoo, children look for animals to write down for each letter (for example: Z—zebra). At the end of the day, the child with the most animals written down wins.

Post Card Search. This easy activity for younger children starts with a stop at the gift shop upon entering the zoo. Each child picks out five post cards depicting their favorite zoo animals. Their task is to find the animals that are on their post cards. The first child to find all of their animals wins. Make this activity more difficult by having the adult select post cards depicting unfamiliar animals.

Zoo Grid. Using one sheet of paper per child, draw a grid with seven rows and four columns. Head the four columns "Mammals," "Birds," "Reptiles," and "Amphibians." On the far left of the seven rows, list the world's seven continents: Africa, Asia, Australia, Europe, North America, South America, Antarctica. Children then have 28 boxes to fill in with specific types of animals from each of the world's continents. At the end of the zoo visit, the child with the most boxes filled in wins. Make this game more challenging by dividing "Mammals" into "Primates," "Cats," "Bears," and other classes of mammals.

Modify these activities, or make up your own, so as to best suit your children.

Rides

To a child, a zoo trip can be the best part of an entire vacation. A child visiting New York City might enjoy a day at the Bronx Zoo far more than a day at the Statue of Liberty. Keep this point of view in mind when considering whether a ride on that little train is worth the money. It may not look so important through adult eyes, but it can look like a ride at Disneyland through 5-year-old eyes.

If your budget is tight, do let the kids pick out at least one ride to enjoy. A ride on an elephant or camel, though very short in duration, is long remembered by children.

Sky rides and monorails are offered at only a few zoos, and they are every bit as fun as most theme park rides. Don't miss the opportunity to enjoy them.

Souvenirs

In the rush to get tired bodies home, don't overlook one of the highlights of a zoo visit for many children—selecting a souvenir at the gift shop. A lot of money isn't required to buy children something special that will serve as a comforting memento of a good time. A plastic animal figurine, an animal-shaped eraser, or even a few post cards depicting their favorite animals can be very special, even though they cost very little.

Should you decide to spend more and purchase a plush stuffed animal, consider making it one of the exotic animals that you viewed at the zoo. Instead of a bear or a bunny, select a stuffed red panda or a black and white Malayan tapir.

An excellent, yet inexpensive, keepsake is the souvenir guidebook sold at many zoos. It will be a reminder of your happy day at the zoo and can also serve as a great animal reference book.

The money you spend on these souvenirs is often going to a good cause. Many zoos depend on their gift shop profits for their very survival.

A souvenir that costs no money is the zoo map. It can be fun to form a collection of them, or to pin them onto your child's bedroom wall.

Going Home

An important, but often ignored, rule is don't overdo it. When planning an outing to your local zoo, consider that a few short visits are often more enjoyable than one long one. Potentially wonderful days at the zoo have been ruined by parents who insisted on seeing everything. When the children are worn out, call it a day and be thankful for the memories already made. If exhibits are missed that someone still wants to see, come back another day.

Interesting Animals to Look For

Most zoo visitors are quite familiar with zebras, giraffes, elephants, gorillas, seals, lions, tigers, and bears. These animals are very popular and, therefore, expected. Many other zoo animals are not nearly so well-known to the average zoo-goer.

This chapter is devoted to the more unusual, interesting, and rare animals that you might see. They are, as this chapter is titled, "interesting animals to look for."

MAMMALS

Arabian Oryxes

Sometimes called the "desert unicorn," this endangered antelope is found in the hot, dry deserts of the Arabian peninsula. Due to hunting parties using jeeps and automatic weapons, the oryxes were nearly extinct by 1962. Then "Operation Oryx" rounded up the nine remaining Arabian oryxes and sent them to the Phoenix Zoo for safe breeding. By 1979, the world herd numbered 68 oryxes. Today, with over 1,000 oryxes spread among zoos and with a few reintroduced into their native range, the program can be called a success.

BEST EXHIBITS: *Gladys Porter Zoo, The Living Desert.*

Mandrill

Baboons

Of the eight species of baboons, five can be found in American zoos. Primarily ground dwellers, most are found in stony regions of eastern or southern Africa. The Hamadryas baboons are found in Egypt and Arabia. Baboons are best known for their muzzle faces, long canine teeth, and behavior of grooming each other. Mandrills are the largest and most unique of the baboons, with bright blue-and-scarlet faces. Drills look like black-faced mandrills and are the most endangered of all primates. Gelada baboons are easily recognized by their bright red chests. Male geladas have long manes, and when excited, will bare their fearsome teeth.

BEST EXHIBITS: *Bronx Zoo, Phoenix Zoo, Brookfield Zoo.*

Bonobos (Pygmy Chimpanzees)

Better known as pygmy chimpanzees, bonobos are a distinct species and not just a smaller version of common chimpanzees. They are roughly the same size as com-

mon chimps, though with a slimmer build, and are rare in both American zoos and in their native rain forests of central Africa. Their method of walking, mating habits, and intelligence make bonobos the most human-like of all primates.

BEST EXHIBITS: *San Diego Zoo, Milwaukee Zoo, Cincinnati Zoo.*

Cheetahs

Crowned the world's fastest land animal, cheetahs can run up to 70 m.p.h. during short hunting spurts. They are perhaps the most unusual cat, with a sleek, slender build resembling a greyhound and a vocal bark like that of a dog. Once used by Indian royalty for hunting, they are now nearly extinct in Asia and found mainly in the savannas of

eastern and southern Africa. The status of cheetahs is very grave due to poaching and a severe lack of genetic diversity.

BEST EXHIBITS: *National Zoo, Columbus Zoo, Cincinnati Zoo.*

Colobus Monkeys

Among the most beautiful of primates, these large black monkeys from central and western African forests are distinguished by their flowing white manes and tails. They are extremely agile in treetops and are good jumpers. They feed mainly on leaves, including some that are toxic to other animals. Their adorable babies are completely white when born.

BEST EXHIBITS: *Central Park Zoo, Miami Metrozoo.*

Gerenuks

Of all the interesting African antelope varieties, the slender gerenuk may be the most engaging. Common in the dry, thornbush regions of East Africa, gerenuks have extremely long necks and legs, which they use to their advantage for feeding. In order to nibble at leaves several feet above them, gerenuks will stand up on their hind legs and maintain this stance for several minutes.

BEST EXHIBIT: *Los Angeles Zoo.*

Japanese Macaques (Snow Monkeys)

Macaques (pronounced mah-KAKs) are among the most common types of monkeys in American zoos. Japanese macaques are better known as snow monkeys due to their ability to thrive in cold, snowy climates. Native to Japan's Honshu Island, these water-loving monkeys are the most northerly primates in the world. They live in close-knit troops with a dominant male,

a few other protective males, and a core of females and juveniles.

BEST EXHIBITS: *Central Park Zoo, Indianapolis Zoo, Milwaukee Zoo, Minnesota Zoo.*

Koalas

Koalas are not bears but are, in fact, closely related to kangaroos. Found in the forests of eastern Australia, they are marsupials. This means that baby koalas spend their first 6 months in their mother's pouch, where they are nursed. Koalas eat only leaves from eucalyptus trees and are very fussy about *which* leaves. Zoos outside of Florida or California have to fly in fresh eucalyptus leaves for them every other day.

BEST EXHIBITS: *San Diego Zoo, Los Angeles Zoo, Minnesota Zoo.*

Lemurs

There are more than 15 species of lemurs seen in zoos, and all of them are native only to Madagascar—the large island off the east coast of Africa. Lemurs, which are primates, have a dog-like snout and are good tree-climbers. Ring-tailed lemurs have a long raccoon-like tail and are the most common type seen in zoos. Beautiful ruffed lemurs can be either red or black and white. Tiny mouse lemurs are the smallest primates.

BEST EXHIBITS: *Gladys Porter Zoo, Cincinnati Zoo, Omaha's Henry Doorly Zoo, Indianapolis Zoo.*

Ring-Tailed Lemurs

Leopards

Found throughout most of Africa and Asia, leopards are classified into three different species. The familiar common leopards are divided into subspecies that include African leopards, Persian leopards, Chinese leopards, and many more. These large, spotted cats hunt at night and will often, after a kill, store their prey in a tree for a later meal. Black leopards (a color phase) are often called panthers. Snow leopards (a separate species) are native to the cold Himalayan regions of Asia. Their thick, beautiful fur coat serves to keep them warm but also makes them a prime poaching target. They are also well-known for their extremely long tails and incredible leaping ability. Clouded leopards, the smallest of the big cats, live and hunt in the trees of Southeast Asia. These 50-pound cats are considered by many to be the most beautiful of the cat family.

BEST EXHIBITS: *Memphis Zoo, Bronx Zoo, Denver Zoo, Houston Zoo, Lincoln Park Zoo.*

Snow Leopard

Emperor Tamarins

Marmosets and Tamarins

There are over 30 kinds of squirrel-sized marmosets and tamarins. They live almost entirely in the trees of the Central and South American rain forests. Pygmy marmosets, weigh only 4 1/2 ounces, are the smallest of all monkeys. Golden lion tamarins, which are bright orange with a lion-like mane, are common in zoos today because their native Brazilian jungle habitat has been decimated. Other attractive species include cotton-top and emperor tamarins.

BEST EXHIBITS: *National Zoo, Bronx Zoo, Lincoln Park Zoo.*

Meerkats

Hailing from the grassy woodlands of southern Africa, meerkats are related to mongooses. Because of their appearance and the complex burrow systems in which they live, they are often mistaken for prairie dogs by zoo-goers. They have a fascinating behavior of standing erect on their hind legs on top of their burrow, scanning the horizon for predators. Being a part of a meerkat family means taking turns at both look-out duty and babysitting duty, while the rest of the pack goes hunting for scorpions, snakes, and insects.

BEST EXHIBITS: *Los Angeles Zoo, San Diego Zoo, Dallas Zoo, Toledo Zoo, Brookfield Zoo.*

Naked Mole-Rats

These gerbil-sized rodents from the arid regions of East Africa live in burrow systems that can sometimes occupy the space of six football fields. With large buck teeth and almost hairless bodies, naked mole-rats are ugly. They have an interesting insect-like social structure in which only a single female—the "queen"—does all of the breeding. They feed on underground tubers.

BEST EXHIBITS: *Brookfield Zoo, Cincinnati Zoo, Philadelphia Zoo.*

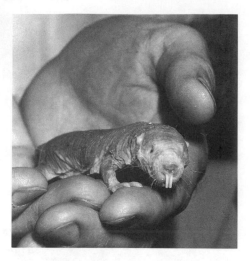

Okapis

Unknown to the Western world until 1901, okapis (pronounced oh-KAH-pees) are native to the dense jungles of the Congo. Related to giraffes, they have a similar long tongue which they use to strip leaves off of branches. With their zebra-striped legs, brown horse-like body, and giraffe-like head, okapis are oddly beautiful.

BEST EXHIBIT: *Dallas Zoo.*

Pronghorns

Pronghorns are native to the plains and deserts of North America. They are neither antelope nor deer, yet they are the "antelope" that play with the deer at "home on the range" in the well-known song. These graceful animals can run at speeds exceeding 60 m.p.h., making them second only to the cheetah in running speed. Like bison, their long-time prairie companions, pronghorns have returned from the brink of extinction.

BEST EXHIBIT: *Minnesota Zoo.*

Red Pandas

While most zoo-goers wish they could see giant pandas more often, the similar red (or lesser) pandas are fairly common in large zoos and are just as adorable. They are similar in that both types are native to the high bamboo forests of China, both feed primarily on bamboo shoots, and both have that familiar sad face. The main difference is that giant pandas are actually bears, while the tree-dwelling red pandas are related to raccoons.

BEST EXHIBITS: *Bronx Zoo, Cincinnati Zoo.*

Sumatran Rhinoceroses

The shaggy-coated Sumatran rhino, which measures only 5 feet high, is the smallest of the rhinos. It is found in isolated rain forests in Southeast Asia. These rhinos are vocal, docile, very friendly, and extremely endangered.

ONLY EXHIBITS: *Cincinnati Zoo, San Diego Zoo, Los Angeles Zoo.*

Tapirs

The most unfamiliar of the large pachyderms, tapirs come in four species. Brazilian, Baird's, and hairy mountain tapirs are native to South and Central America. The black and white Malayan tapirs are found from Southeast Asia down to Indonesia. All tapirs have a flexible, elongated snout that they use to forage for swamp vegetation. Babies are born with a dark coat dotted with white spots and stripes.

BEST EXHIBITS: *San Diego Zoo, Omaha's Henry Doorly Zoo, Bronx Zoo.*

Malayan Tapir and Baby

Vampire Bats

Bats are the only true flying mammals. Thanks to folklore, the most famous bats are the small vampire bats found from Argentina to northern Mexico. True to legend, vampire bats do feed exclusively on blood—from pigs, cattle, horses, and sometimes humans. Contrary to their image, they do not suck blood but rather lap it from the small, painless wounds they inflict on their sleeping victim. The only real danger vampires present is the possibility of transmitting rabies.

BEST EXHIBITS: *Houston Zoo, Philadelphia Zoo, Milwaukee Zoo.*

Vampire Bat Drinking Blood

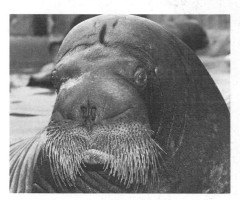

Bulka Walrus

Walruses

Members of the seal family, walruses are best known for their upper tusks (which can grow up to 3 feet long) and their stiff-bristled beard. Found on islands in the icy waters of the Arctic Circle, males can weigh as much as $1\frac{1}{2}$ tons. They feed mainly on shellfish and fish.

ONLY EXHIBITS: *Point Defiance Zoo, Brookfield Zoo, Cincinnati Zoo, and the Sea World parks.*

Wart Hogs

Described as "so ugly they're cute," wart hogs do have grotesque, warty bumps on their faces along with large, sharp tusks. Though they are common in the savanna regions of sub-Saharan Africa, they are rare in American zoos because of import restrictions designed to protect the U.S. pork industry from diseases.

BEST EXHIBITS: *Phoenix Zoo, Los Angeles Zoo, Cleveland Zoo.*

White Bengal Tigers

Four tiger subspecies are exhibited in zoos, and all four are endangered. White tigers are a rare color phase of Bengal tigers from India. These beautiful cats have brown or gray stripes and blue eyes. Their color makes it virtually impossible for them to hunt effectively, and thus to survive, in the wild.

BEST EXHIBITS: *Cincinnati Zoo, Miami Metrozoo, Omaha's Henry Doorly Zoo.*

BIRDS

Cranes

Long-legged cranes are some of the largest flying birds in the world and among the most endangered. Of the world's 15 crane species, the rarest are Siberian white cranes and North America's whooping cranes. (After being reduced to only 21 in the 1950s, the whooping cranes now number around 200.) Sandhill cranes, also from North America, are frequently displayed in zoos, but African crowned cranes are the most common and most beautiful.

BEST EXHIBITS: *San Antonio Zoo, International Crane Foundation.*

Crowned Crane

Black-and-White Casqued Hornbill

Hornbills

Found mostly in forests from India to Southeast Asia, hornbills are so-named for their enormous bill with a protruding casque. Females lay their eggs in a tree cavity and are imprisoned there for nearly 3 months. The male seals up the cavity with mud, passing food in through a small slit. The largest and most imposing hornbills are the great Indian hornbills, rhinoceros hornbills, and the ground hornbills from the plains of Africa.

BEST EXHIBITS: *Audubon Zoo, San Diego Zoo, Bronx Zoo.*

King Vultures

Of all the many birds of prey, few are as colorful as the king vultures, found from South America to Mexico. Like other vultures, they feed on carrion, but they also prey on reptiles and cattle. Unlike other vultures, they rely on their sense of smell to locate food and have an extremely strong beak.

BEST EXHIBITS: *Fort Worth Zoo, Los Angeles Zoo.*

REPTILES

Gharials

One of the rarest and most unusual members of the alligator family called crocodilians, gharials are found in the rivers of eastern India and Bangladesh. They are best known for their extremely long and slender, but still very toothy, snout. Because of this snout, they feed mainly on fish. Similar-looking false gavials are also seen in zoos.

BEST EXHIBIT: *Bronx Zoo.*

Komodo Dragons

Komodo dragons are the largest of the world's lizards. Measuring up to 10 feet long and weighing up to 310 pounds, they are found only on a few remote islands of

Indonesia. They prey on deer, pigs, and other medium-sized mammals, and sometimes on humans.
ONLY EXHIBITS: *Cincinnati Zoo, National Zoo, San Diego Zoo.*

INVERTEBRATES

Leaf-Cutter Ants

Energetic leaf-cutter ants live in the tropical rain forests of South America in enormous underground colonies of up to 5 million ants. Worker ants come to the surface in search of certain types of leaves. They use their scissor-like jaws to cut chunks out of the leaves, then carry the chunks to an underground chamber where they chew them into a pulp. (They use the pulp to grow a particular fungus on which they feed.) Some leaf-cutter ant exhibits use miniature video cameras to provide close views of the queen, soldier, and worker ants.
BEST EXHIBITS: *Cincinnati Zoo, Central Park Zoo.*

MORE BEST EXHIBITS

Beavers: *Minnesota Zoo.*
Bison: *Bronx Zoo, Minnesota Zoo.*
Camels: *Minnesota Zoo.*
Elephants: *Woodland Park Zoo, Metro Washington Park Zoo.*
Giraffes: *Cheyenne Mountain Zoo, Rio Grande Zoo.*
Gorillas: *Zoo Atlanta, Woodland Park Zoo, Columbus Zoo, Dallas Zoo, Lincoln Park Zoo.*
Hippos: *Toledo Zoo.*
Kangaroos: *Oklahoma City Zoo, Indianapolis Zoo.*

Lions: *Topeka Zoo, Minnesota Zoo.*

Penguins: *Metro Washington Park Zoo, Indianapolis Zoo, Detroit Zoo, Milwaukee Zoo, Central Park Zoo.*

Polar Bears: *Central Park Zoo, Metro Washington Park Zoo, Lincoln Park Zoo.*

Sea Lions: *Rio Grande Zoo, Oklahoma City Zoo, Denver Zoo, Indianapolis Zoo.*

Wolves: *Minnesota Zoo, Columbus Zoo, Milwaukee Zoo.*

Zebras: *North Carolina Zoo, Woodland Park Zoo.*

How To Use This Book

There are nearly 400 institutions in the United States that can be classified as a "zoo." Only the top 53 so deemed by a media survey are extensively detailed in this book. Among them are the 31 zoos that the American Automobile Association's *TourBooks* rate as "of exceptional interest and quality." Twenty-nine additional zoos are briefly described in the "Best of the Rest" sections.

Zoo Reviews

To assist you in finding the best zoos along a particular trip route, Zoo Reviews are divided into seven geographic regions.

At the beginning of each Zoo Review is the zoo's official name, address, and phone number. Information in the **Hours** and **Admission Fees** sections should be used as guidelines; hours can change and fees will almost certainly increase in the future. Zoos that admit members of other zoos free of charge under the reciprocity program are noted here.

Directions are meant to guide visitors to the zoo from major interstate highways. When available, interstate exit numbers are provided. If the zoo is conveniently accessible from a mass transit system, this is also mentioned.

The listing of exhibits, shows, and rides in the **Don't Miss** section is designed to aid visitors who are short of time but want to see the highlights. Attractions are listed in descending order according to their entertainment value and uniqueness. Those marked with an asterisk (*) are of special interest to children.

In **Touring Tips** are hints that make touring the zoo easier and more efficient. Step-saving tram and train rides are mentioned. Restaurants or snack bars that provide interesting menu selections, or an especially delightful or unique dining atmosphere, are also included, as are special picnic sites, gift shops, and nearby attractions.

Most zoos offer entertaining animal shows. These shows are listed in the **Entertainment** section, sometimes with a brief description. Show times are usually available at the zoo's entrance gate. Scheduled animal feedings are also listed in this section.

In each zoo's description, the first paragraph or two are devoted to discussing interesting and important facts about the zoo, including its history.

Featured Exhibits contains a detailed, you-are-there description of the best exhibits listed in the "Don't Miss" section. The names of the exhibits are **boldfaced** when first introduced. The smaller exhibits that are a part of the main exhibits are named in *italics*.

The remainder of the zoo's major exhibits are covered briefly in **Other Exhibits**. Names are boldfaced or italicized as above.

Special children's zoos and their youth-oriented displays, activities, playgrounds, petting areas, and rides are described in **For the Kids**.

In **New at the Zoo**, any new exhibits or changes made at the zoo since 1992 are described. Exhibits scheduled to open during the next few years are also briefly discussed here.

Other Information

Innovative new exhibits are discussed in the Zoo Reviews. More information about the new ways that zoos are displaying their animals can be found in the "Current Trends at U.S. Zoos" chapter. For interesting facts about some of the lesser-known animals that zoos feature, see the "Interesting Animals to Look For" chapter. It also tells where the best exhibits of popular animals can be found.

The best of the wildlife parks, aquariums, specialized zoos, aquatic parks, and animal-displaying theme parks in the United States are covered briefly in "More Places to See Animals." The top zoos in Canada, Mexico, and the rest of the world are highlighted in "Foreign Zoos."

"The Top Ten Zoo Lists" provides some perspective on how U.S. zoos compare to each other. The lists tell which zoos have the very best displays in 16 different categories. Another appendix lists the "Top 25 U.S. Zoo Exhibits."

ZOO

REVIEWS

Eastern Zoos

The Baltimore Zoo

Druid Hill Park
Baltimore, Maryland 21217
(410) 396-7102 or 366-LION

Hours: *10-4 daily; extended hours in summer. Closed on Christmas Day.*
Admission Fees: *Adults $6.50, 63+ and 2-15 $3.50. Participates in reciprocity program. Zoo Tram 25¢, ZooChoo $1, Victorian Carousel $1.*
Directions: *From I-83, take Exit 7A West to Druid Park Lake Drive, then follow signs to zoo.*
Don't Miss: *Children's Zoo, African Zoogeographic Region exhibits, Reptile House.*
Touring Tips: *The **Zoo Tram**, which stops at all major exhibits, provides basic transportation within this 158-acre zoo. Ticket-holders can ride all day. The new Village Green restaurant is convenient to the Children's Zoo.*
Entertainment: *African elephant demonstrations are presented daily at 2:30 p.m. in their exhibit. Live animal shows are sometimes offered in the Farmyard amphitheater. Animal feedings include Kodiak bears and penguins.*

Opened in 1876, The Baltimore Zoo is the third-oldest zoo in the nation. Until recently, it was clearly showing its age. Since 1984, many new exhibits have opened, moving this zoo into the modern era. With its new, top-rated Children's Zoo, it has moved out of the shadow of Washington's National Zoo—located just 40 miles away—and has established an image of its own.

FEATURED EXHIBITS

Besides the Children's Zoo, the most attractive area here is a group of exhibits in the **African Zoogeographic Region**. A new **African Watering Hole**, framed by kopje rock outcrops, is the centerpiece. The Safari Trail boardwalk provides views of 6 acres of grassland and the white rhinos, zebras, sable antelope, gazelles, ostriches, and pelicans that live there. The watering hole can be viewed up close from a pavilion that houses two interactive learning exhibits. A mesh-enclosed, walk-through aviary allows visitors to see some of Africa's prettiest birds, including Egyptian geese, violet touracos, and lesser flamingos.

Vultures and sitatunga marsh antelope peek through tall grass near a cascading 15-foot waterfall in the **African Waterfall** exhibit. Across the boardwalk, Nile hippos submerge in their deep pool. The 2-acre **African Plains** features giraffes and lions separated by only an invisible moat. A glass-enclosed aviary with colorful African birds is in the **Giraffe House**. A spacious 3-acre **African Elephant Exhibit**, which includes two separate yards with large pools, is best viewed from the high observation deck. Members of the nation's largest colony of African black-footed penguins are usually visible in the waters of the deep moat around **Rock Island**.

OTHER EXHIBITS

While cages in the **Main Valley** are not impressive, the variety of caged carnivores is. Among the interesting animals seen here are jaguars, pumas, leopards, sloth bears, spectacled bears, aardwolves, red pandas, and arctic foxes. Hyenas live in the zoo's oldest structure, which dates from 1874. Kodiak bears can be seen in two massive grottoes, but the valley's highlight is the *Siberian Tiger Exhibit*, where a special viewing window allows face-to-face encounters with the tigers. Other exhibits include tropical bird cages, eight species of cranes, a prairie dog town, and polar bears with a large blue swimming pool.

This zoo is well known for the breeding success of its endangered lion-tailed macaques, occupants in the **Monkey House**. Spider monkeys, Diana monkeys, and various guenons and tamarins also dwell in this old building, as do some interesting non-primates, such as rock hyraxes, meerkats, aardwolves, exotic squirrels, and armadillos. At the zoo's highest elevation, Axis deer, yaks, and kangaroos live in open yards, and bald and golden eagles perch in moderate-size flight cages.

The **Hippo House** offers indoor poolside viewing of Nile hippos, pygmy hippos, and capybaras.

FOR THE KIDS

Very few zoos count their **Children's Zoo** as their premier exhibit, but this is definitely one that does. The best in the U.S., this 8-acre children's zoo has 48 interactive exhibits that give children the opportunity to jump, climb, and crawl like one of the animals on display. More than 100 different species represent the wildlife of Maryland. The *Lyn P. Meyerhoff Maryland Wilderness* occupies a previously untouched wilderness area.

The Discovery Path starts with a boardwalk to the *Marsh Aviary*—a walk-through enclosure with herons and snowy egrets. Nearby, kids can climb into gourd-shaped oriole's nests, sit in a heron's nest, and hop across a stream on king-sized lily pads—providing a great photo-op for parents. At the *Otter Pond*, a few steps lead down into an underwater acrylic tunnel where river otters can be viewed swimming above. Black bears are seen in the natural *Black Bear Falls* habitat. Behind the waterfall, the path leads into *Wilderness Cave*, where bats, owls, and poisonous snakes are exhibited among realistic stalactites and stalagmites, and a jungle gym shaped like a woolly mammoth skeleton beckons. Across a swinging rope bridge, the man-made *Giant Tree* houses a spiral staircase and close-up exhibits of a skunk, saw whet owls, and other tree animals. Adventurous children can exit the tree down a fast slide through a hollowed-out limb. Wildflowers fill the *Meadow*, where kids can climb through a maze of underground tunnels to pop-up plastic domes positioned in the middle of the woodchuck habitat.

In the *Farmyard*, goats and other pettable farm animals live in fenced corrals. A demonstration dairy with a mechanical cow is in the barn, which also has a silo slide from the second floor. A blacksmith's shop, a brooder for hatching chicks, and pony rides are also featured.

The ZooChoo train ride and Victorian Carousel are popular attractions in the **Village Green** concession area, and the **African Village** provides a herd of pygmy goats to pet.

Woodchuck Habitat

NEW AT THE ZOO

Outside the zoo grounds, a short walk from the main entrance, is the **Reptile House**. It reopened in 1993 after many years of renovation. Crocodile lizards, bearded dragons, dwarf caimans, gila monsters, and king cobras are some of the reptiles housed in 24 accurate reproductions of the world's natural habitats.

Exciting changes in the future include **Leopards' Lair**, **Chimpanzee Forest**, **International Valley** (where natural habitats will replace the old cages), a **South American region** with a thatched-roof canoe tour, and **Austral-Asia**, which will be viewed from a new **Orient Express** train.

Bronx Zoo/
Wildlife Conservation Park

185th Street & Southern Boulevard
Bronx, New York 10460
(212) 367-1010

Hours: *10-5 Monday-Friday, 10-5:30 Saturday-Sunday and holidays, March-October; 10-4:30 daily, rest of year.*

Admission Fees: *Adults $5.75, 2-12 $2; free on Wednesdays. Children's Zoo (April-October) $1.50; Bengali Express monorail (May-October) $1.50, on Wednesdays $2; Skyfari aerial tram (April-October) $1.50; Zoo Shuttle (April-October) $1.50; camel ride $2. World of Reptiles, World of Darkness, JungleWorld: 50c each on Wednesdays. Combination ticket (includes admission, Children's Zoo, monorail, aerial tram, and shuttle): adults $10.60, 65+ and 2-12 $7.60. Parking $5.*

Directions: *From the Bronx River Parkway, take Exit 7 (Bronx Zoo) or Exit 6 (Fordham Road). Zoo is accessible via subway, train, or bus routes. Call for directions.*

Don't Miss: *JungleWorld, Bengali Express monorail (Wild Asia), Children's Zoo, Skyfari aerial tram, Africa Plains (especially the Baboon Reserve), World of Darkness, Himalayan Highlands, World of Birds, Zoo Center, World of Reptiles, MouseHouse*.*

Touring Tips: *Park in the zoo's protected parking lot; the surrounding neighborhood is not safe. Arrive early to enjoy as much of this huge zoo as possible. If children are a part of your group, don't plan to see everything. The tractor-train Zoo Shuttle offers transportation between Wild Asia and the Children's Zoo.*

Entertainment: *Informal talks featuring live animals are presented regularly during the summer at the **Wild Asia Theatre** and the **Children's Theatre**. Schedules are posted at these outdoor amphitheaters. Animal feedings include penguins, pelicans, crocodiles, and sea lions.*

In the largest city in the United States, it seems only natural to have the nation's largest urban zoo. The Bronx Zoo is situated on 265 acres in New York's northernmost borough. Its enormous size provides many of its animal residents with more than enough room to roam, while its human visitors have a near impossible task if they wish to see everything in one day. With over 4,300 animals, this zoo also has the country's largest wild animal population, and the 674 different species represent the third-most diverse collection in the nation.

Chartered in 1895 and opened in 1899, this historic zoo offers the best of the old and new. Many of the buildings in the central Astor Court area are classic turn-of-the-century structures. Some are presently empty, with designated plans for future exhibits, but most of these original buildings have ultra-modernized interiors for the comfort of both residents and visitors. This zoo has always been a leader, and its innovative exhibits have been imitated by many other zoos throughout the nation.

The Bronx Zoo is the hub of NYZS/The Wildlife Conservation Society—a zoological society that also operates three other New York City zoos (including Central Park), the New York Aquarium, and the St. Catherine's Wildlife Survival Center (a breeding center off the coast of Georgia). It is also involved in 150 conservation projects in over 40 countries worldwide. The Society hopes the more than 2 million annual visitors to the Bronx Zoo will leave with an appreciation for its efforts in preserving and protecting the world's wildlife.

FEATURED EXHIBITS

This zoo is most famous for its remarkable Asian exhibits and is rated in this book as the nation's top zoo for displaying Asian animals.

One of the most popular exhibits is the nearly 1-acre **JungleWorld** building. As visitors pass through the temple-like entrance, which features hanging Burmese banners, there is a feeling that this is a mystical place. The 783-foot wooden pathway passes through three distinct jungles (the Indonesian Scrub Forest, Mangrove Jungle of Borneo, and the Southeast Asian Rain Forest), each dense with both real and man-made trees, vines, and other exotic plants. One of the artificial trees is the largest ever made by man. Behind the lush foliage, a lifelike mural makes the view seem farther than it is. Five waterfalls drop into jungle streams and pools, while a fog machine fills the air with steamy humidity.

Within the three jungles, various jungle birds, marsh crocodiles, a water monitor lizard, small-clawed otters, Malayan tapirs, and silvered leaf langurs can be viewed. The nation's only colony of proboscis monkeys (named for their long floppy noses) is among the most memorable animals in the entire zoo. Sleek black leopards seem dangerously close to the path, but thick glass keeps them in their enclosure. At the end of a deep cascading river is a seating area where visitors can relax and watch gharials from both above and below water. Above them, the trees are filled with Indian fruit bats, gibbons, and great hornbills. The three jungle habitats are separated by galleries where native reptiles, amphibians, fish, insects, and small mammals are displayed.

The award-winning JungleWorld is one part of the **Wild Asia** exhibit. The *Asia Plaza* includes an outdoor amphitheater, a snack bar, camel rides, and the **Bengali Express** monorail ride. The specially designed one-sided monorail cars seat riders facing out towards the animals—providing superb viewing. The 2-mile, 25-minute tour crosses the Bronx River to the 38-acre Wild Asia preserve. Siberian tigers, Asian elephants, Indian rhinos, gaurs (wild cattle), and a variety of Asian deer and antelope are just some of the rare animals from Asia's forests and plains that the monorail silently passes. The Formosan sika deer seen here are now extinct in the wild, and the herd of sambars is the only one in North America.

The wildlife of Asia's mountains are presented in the 2-acre **Himalayan Highlands**, which is probably the nation's most convincing mountain habitat. An uphill trail winds around large boulders, crosses bridges over ravines, and passes Tibetan signposts to the red pandas and beautiful Temminck's tragopan pheasants.

Indian Rhinos and Bengali Express Monorail

Endangered snow leopards, often with cubs, can be seen from many vantage points, some protected by nearly invisible harp wire.

The African area is also impressive. At the opening of the **Africa Plains,** tall walls of pointed sticks are on both sides. The circular trail is enhanced with simulated lava flows and termite mounds. Animals seen from the trail include lions, cheetahs, and several antelope species such as nyalas, slender-horned gazelles, and Arabian oryxes. The **Carter Giraffe Building** is home to a colony of playful meerkats and is winter quarters for the zebras and Baringo giraffes.

The highlight of the trail is the award-winning new **Baboon Reserve**. This 5-acre exhibit simulates the Ethiopian highlands home of the gelada baboons. The male geladas are especially stunning with their bright red chests. Sharing the exhibit with nearly 20 baboons are Nubian ibexes (wild goats with large curved horns). A viewing cave allows visitors to get up close, and mounted telescopes are nearby. Adjacent to the reserve, the **African Market** has a pygmy goat corral, a gift shop, and a snack bar with an outdoor terrace from which diners can watch the baboons.

When it opened, the **World of Darkness** was the first exhibit of its kind. Inside this tall, black C-shaped building, deep red lighting is used to convince over 300 nocturnal animals that it is nighttime—their most active period. The sound of chirping crickets helps human visitors imagine the same. Some of the highlights are a swamp where raccoons and skunks appear to share the exhibit with alligators, an open cave with fluttering bats, and a desert exhibit with cacti and ringtails from the American Southwest.

Zoo Center, a stately old structure in the middle of the zoo, is home to Asian

Elephant in Zoo Center

elephants and Malayan tapirs. All around this domed building jungle paths lead to lookout points.

The large, recently-renovated **World of Birds** is a strange-looking building. More than 500 birds of over 100 species are exhibited in naturalistic settings, many with nothing separating them from the viewers. Dazzling birds of paradise, cock-of-the-rocks, and pink pigeons are among the rarest birds seen here. The South American rain forest walk-through aviary features a towering waterfall.

The 1899 **World of Reptiles** building, renovated in 1991, is not a typical reptile house. A broad collection of snakes, lizards, turtles, frogs, and salamanders are housed in room-size habitats instead of rows of small terrariums. Among a notable collection of four endangered types of crocodilians are Chinese alligators.

Small mammals live in the **MouseHouse**. This building, which is especially favored by children, shelters one of the largest collections of rodents anywhere. Notable residents include zebra mice, flying squirrels, dwarf mongooses, giant cloud rats, and an overactive spotted skunk.

OTHER EXHIBITS

The top-rated, vast collection of birds is spread throughout the grounds. In the **Aquatic Bird House** are such favorites as spoonbills, kingfishers, and puffins, as well as the world's only exhibit of hoatzins from the Amazon. The gigantic walk-through **DeJur Aviary Seabird Colony** displays Magellanic penguins, cormorants, and assorted sea gulls in a most appealing seashore setting. **Cope Lake** has an attractive display of brown pelicans swimming in front of two islands where gibbons hang from willow branches. The **Birds of Prey** area has a row of large flight exhibits with Andean condors, bald eagles, king vultures, and owls. Another row of aviaries show off a colorful variety of pheasants. The **Wildfowl Marsh** offers visitors a peaceful stroll beside a self-sustaining marsh with rare and exotic ducks. Tall birds include cassowaries, flamingos, emus, storks, and a wide variety of cranes.

Most of the native North American animals are found in or near the area called **Holarctica**. Included are polar and Kodiak bears, timber wolves, coatis, river otters, California sea lions, and large herds of rare Pere David's deer and American bison. (The Bronx Zoo played a major role in saving the bison from extinction in the early 1900s.) The **Northern Ponds** exhibit has coin-operated mounted telescopes for close-up views of trumpeter swans, ruddy ducks, and other North American waterfowl.

The small **South America** area features Patagonian cavies, guanacos (related to llamas), and flightless rheas. Mongolian wild horses, now extinct in the wild, thrive in a large herd in the **Rare Animal Range**.

The old **Monkey House** is still very popular. In exhibits lush with greenery, the 14 species of small monkeys displayed include pygmy marmosets, highly endangered golden lion tamarins, and rare Goeldi's monkeys.

FOR THE KIDS

The recently renovated **Children's Zoo** is an award-winner and one of the nation's best. This 3-acre exhibit uses woodland, marsh, forest, and desert habitats to educate children about the homes, motion, defenses, and senses of animals. Children are encouraged to experience the animal world as they sit in a child-size heron's nest, pop out of a prairie dog burrow, scoot through a raccoon log, play on a spider web, hop like a wallaby on a pogo stick, climb a lemur's tree, smell a skunk, crawl in a turtle shell, escape like a lizard down a hollow tree slide, and listen like a fennec fox with simulated fox ears. Nearby, the animals watch the young humans imitating them. Before leaving this special place, children can pet or feed a variety of domestic animals.

A highlight for most kids is a ride on the **Skyfari** aerial tram. Riders get a panoramic view of the entire zoo from high above the Baboon Reserve. A camel ride is also available in Wild Asia Plaza.

NEW AT THE ZOO

In mid-1993 the *Naked City*, which is populated by naked mole-rats, opened in the World of Darkness. These unusual critters live in well-organized colonies in a complex subterranean tunnel system. Recently this zoo became the first on the East Coast to exhibit beautiful, rare okapis.

Future exhibit plans include the **Flooded Forest**—a re-creation of an Amazon rain forest in one of the vacant Astor Court buildings. The exhibit will likely include giant otters, bush dogs, small monkeys, big fish, caimans, and other reptiles. Also, the **Congo Forest** is being designed to include lowland gorillas, mandrill baboons, and other African primates. A large family of gorillas currently resides inside and outside of the outdated **Great Ape House**.

Buffalo Zoological Gardens

Delaware Park
Buffalo, New York 14214
(716) 837-3900

Hours: *Gates 10-5:30, buildings 10-6, grounds 10-6:30, daily Memorial Day-Labor Day; gates 10-4:30, buildings 10-5, grounds 10-6, rest of year. Closed Thanksgiving Day and Christmas Day.*

Admission Fees: *Adults $5, senior citizens $2, 4-16 $3. Participates in reciprocity program. Camel ride $2, carousel $1, kiddie train $1. Parking $3.*

Directions: *From Kensington Expressway, take Humboldt Parkway (Highway 198) to Delaware Park Exit. From I-190, take the Scajaquada Expressway (Exit N11, Highway 198) to the Parkside/Buffalo Zoo Exit. On Delaware Avenue, go west on Amherst Street to the zoo.*

Don't Miss: *Lowland Gorilla African Tropical Forest, Reptile House, Habicats.*

Touring Tips: *This small, 23-acre zoo is easy to get around in. A Visitor Guide map is essential, as the maze of pathways can be confusing. Guided tours are available by advance request. Many picnic tables are provided in park-like settings.*

Entertainment: *Volunteers frequently bring hawks, arctic foxes, and other animals out to meet the public up close in the **Visitor Center** area. Magic shows are presented throughout the summer in the Main Building's auditorium. Birds of prey shows are regularly scheduled as well. Other animal-related activities, including puppet shows, are available in the Children's Zoo.*

While western New York's main draw is Niagara Falls, the area's second largest tourist attraction is 15 miles south—the Buffalo Zoo. Exhibiting just a small herd of deer, this zoo officially opened in 1875, making it one of the oldest zoos in the country. Despite its small size, it has the feel of a large wooded park and offers an extensive selection of activities for children.

FEATURED EXHIBITS

Just inside the Main Entrance, a left turn leads into the **Main Building**—a long, horseshoe-shaped structure that is actually five animal houses connected together. The premier exhibit of this building—and of the entire zoo—is the **Lowland Gorilla African Tropical Forest.** The entrance foyer has a new *Diversity of Life* exhibit that includes attractive displays of insects, arthropods, and crustaceans, plus a burrowing owl in a desert setting. The gorillas live in a replicated rocky riverbank that extends into the visitor area, so that viewers seem to be in the same environment with the apes. High above the two family groups of gorillas, under a glass roof, a waterfall crashes down through the thick African broadleaf plants. Tall glass panels all around the habitat provide many viewing angles from which to watch the apes. Near the exit, the *African River Aquarium* has beautiful cichlid fish swimming in an equally beautiful pool with clear, glass walls. (Note that the gorillas are not exhibited on Mondays.)

The **Reptile House** is on the other end of the Main Building's horseshoe. When it first opened in 1942, Marlin Perkins (the zoo's Director from 1938 to 1944) called it the "finest Reptile House in America." Today it is still very good, with its glass-fronted natural habitats enhanced by realistic background murals. Some of the memorable reptiles in the main hall include rattlesnakes, cobras, and crocodile monitor lizards. A tropical bird exhibit is also here, as is the *Tropics Room* with an American alligator habitat and various exotic frogs and snakes.

African Lion

Outside, in the Main Building's Central Court, two natural **Habi-cats,** displaying lions and tigers, are across from each other. Their grassy yards are enhanced with pools, tree branches and boulders for climbing, and a waterfall for the tigers. The top celebrity is the white Bengal tiger, which may be viewed from 10 a.m. to 2 p.m. daily.

OTHER EXHIBITS

Between the gorilla habitat and Reptile House, the Main Building has three more animal houses—all with long bending rows of traditional exhibits. While these cages are not impressive, the collection of animals that they hold is. The **Primate House** features guenons, macaques, and mandrills. The **Small Mammal House,** which is probably the best of the three houses, has large collections of many interesting animals—sloths, rat kangaroos, prehensile-tailed porcupines, rock cavies, bushbabies, and both Geoffroy's and cottontop tamarins. The **Feline House** features clouded leopards, snow leopards, and cougars. The Main Building also has a small **South American Rain Forest** exhibit and the **George L. Wolff Gallery,** which displays over 90 Boehm porcelain wildlife figures.

Across the zoo, the **Asian Forest** is a large, wooded meadow that is grazed by always-spotted Axis deer, gaurs, and an Indian rhino. Other large, open yards contain the **African Hoofed Animals**—endangered addax, gemsbok, zebras, and one of the country's largest herds of roan antelope. All are within sight of their natural predators—the spotted hyenas. The **Domestic Work Animals** area has llamas, camels, and Scandinavian reindeer in open yards. Though the nearest mountains are hundreds of miles away, there is an excellent collection of mountain animals, including large flocks of bighorn sheep and markhor goats. It is fitting that Buffalo also has a fine herd of buffalo (or bison).

Two rings of cages exhibit an assortment of cranes, vultures, hawks, eagles, owls, and eagle owls. Andean condors are also exhibited, and five waterfowl ponds are populated with colorful water birds from five continents.

Small mammal grottoes contain red pandas, arctic foxes, and peccaries. Other notable exhibits include the popular **Prairie Dog Exhibit**, the **Giraffe House**, and the dens for polar, Kodiak, and spectacled bears.

FOR THE KIDS

The **Children's Zoo** has brick pathways and an 18th-century atmosphere. Exotic domestics such as zebu cattle, pygmy goats, karakul sheep, Shetland ponies, Sardinian donkeys, and guanacos are found in the supervised *Summer Contact Area*. The *Western New York Bird Walk* is a walk-through mesh aviary where ring-necked pheasants and other native birds can be viewed from an elevated walkway.

Camel rides are available during the summer, as are rides on a musical carousel and a kiddie train.

NEW AT THE ZOO

The elephants received a new and improved home in 1993. The large, naturalistic habitat includes trees, vines, and shrubbery, plus a 50-foot-diameter pool. The **World of Wildlife** building, constructed in 1992, is an educational complex with hands-on learning exhibits, touchable animal artifacts, and displays of interesting small creatures.

Central Park Wildlife Conservation Center (Central Park Zoo)

830 Fifth Avenue
New York, New York 10021
(212) 439-6500

Hours: *10-5 weekdays, 10:30-5:30 weekends and holidays, April-October; 10-4:30 daily, November-March.*
Admission Fees: *Adults $2.50, senior citizens $1.25, 3-12 50¢.*
Directions: *On the southeast corner of Central Park. Entrance is off Fifth Avenue at 64th Street. On-street parking is extremely limited. Access from the NYCTA subway system: Take the Broadway line to the Fifth Avenue Station, then walk 5 minutes uptown to the zoo.*
Don't Miss: *Tropic Zone, Polar Circle.*
Touring Tips: *This 5-acre zoo is small enough so that nothing needs to be skipped. The Zoo Cafe has a good menu selection and pleasant indoor and outdoor seating areas. No stroller rentals are available. Because of its small size and intimate exhibits, the zoo is a great place*

for one parent to take the children while the other enjoys the nearby Metropolitan Museum of Art or some other Manhattan attraction geared to adults.
Entertainment: *Sea lion and penguin feedings many times daily.*

Designed by famed architect Frederick Law Olmsted, Central Park is the most famous urban park in the United States. Its zoo, opened in 1864, is the nation's oldest. In 1980 the New York Zoological Society, which also operates the Bronx Zoo, took over the operation of the Central Park Zoo from the City of New York. By that time it had become a frequent target of critics, who complained about the rows of tired-looking iron and concrete cages. The Society closed down the animal houses in 1983; the zoo re-opened in 1988 with new natural habitat exhibits.

Today this progressive zoo is high-tech. Reminders of its historic architecture are visible in the glass-covered walkways, 2 elegant formal gardens, and 112 octagonal brick piers. Animals are well-organized into three climatic zones.

FEATURED EXHIBITS

With the 100-story skyscrapers of America's largest city visible from its entrance, the **Tropic Zone** begins with a beautiful toucan exhibit. Within this octagonal red brick building, a lush rain forest is re-created under a glass roof. It features free-flying colorful birds, tropical plants, and a 20-foot waterfall. Along the warm and humid tour is a stream populated with piranhas, tortoises, and caimans. In a side room, over 100,000 leaf-cutter ants can be watched in a super ant farm display. These hard-working ants can be seen face-to-face on one of three TV monitors hooked up to miniature cameras within the exhibit. Nearby a realistic bat cave has floor-to-ceiling glass that allows a great "you-are-there" illusion. Back in the jungle, always-active colobus monkeys live in a rocky cliff habitat seen through a wide 2-story-high glass wall. Next to a huge buttress-root tree, a stairway leads to a treetop jungle view and to the *Close-up Gallery*, where interesting exhibits include hanging parrots, water dragons, tiny tamarin monkeys, and many snakes. In the exit lobby, another excellent naturalistic exhibit features gila monsters and other desert lizards.

The **Polar Circle** represents a totally different climate with its exhibits of animals from the cold Arctic and Antarctic Circles. The zoo's largest animals—polar bears—inhabit a massive, multi-level rocky habitat with a deep pool and ten separate viewing areas. These ferocious white bears can be viewed from above, from a hidden viewing bay, or from underwater. Next to this spectacular exhibit is a similar display of harbor seals and arctic foxes. In the *Edge of the Ice Pack* building, two species of penguins can be seen either on the rocky beach of their Antarctic rookery or underwater in the depths of their icy pool. The dimly-lit, relaxing viewing area has many places to sit and is popular with Manhattan lunchers. Down the hall, a similar exhibit features tufted puffins from the Northern Hemisphere.

Sea Lion Pool

OTHER EXHIBITS

Between the earth's cold polar regions and hot equatorial tropics is the climatic region represented in the **Temperate Territory** exhibits. The area's highlight has waterfalls plunging into a large pool behind a rocky island that is home to a troop of playful Japanese macaques and graceful swans. Behind the macaques, the uphill path leading to a Northeastern pond exhibit of multi-colored ducks provides a dramatic view of the Manhattan skyline. A viewing pavilion extends into the habitat of cuddly red pandas, which can usually be seen in the trees or tall grass. Nearby, North American river otters have a stream to play in.

In the middle of the formal **Central Garden** is the **Sea Lion Pool**, the zoo's renowned meeting place. The pool of deep blue water is surrounded by glass walls that allow underwater viewing. The popular California sea lions are often seen basking on a tall boulder island.

Though it displays no live animals, the **Wildlife Conservation Center** has worthwhile exhibits demonstrating the Zoological Society's part in species-saving programs all around the world. The **Zoo Gallery** has rotating displays of wildlife art and photography.

FOR THE KIDS

While the zoo has no exhibits just for kids, almost all of the animals here are small and, therefore, appealing to children. Just up Fifth Avenue, another institution, the **Lehman Children's Zoo** features native and domestic animals that can be petted. It is closed indefinitely for renovation. A carousel is nearby in Central Park.

NEW AT THE ZOO

A beautiful Temminck's tragopan—a brilliantly-colored Himalayan pheasant—has replaced the snowy owl in the attractive exhibit at the Edge of the Ice Pack exit.

Franklin Park Zoo

Franklin Park Road
Boston, Massachusetts 02121
(617) 442-2002

Hours: *9-4:30 weekdays, 9:30-5 weekends, in summer; 9-4 daily, in winter. Closed New Year's Day, Thanksgiving Day, and Christmas Day.*
Admission Fees: *Adults $5; 60+, 4-11, students and military with I.D. $2.50. Participates in reciprocity program.*
Directions: *From I-93 (Southeast Expressway), take Exit 15 to Columbia Road. Go west to the third traffic light, where Columbia Road continues to the left. Follow through nine more lights (3 miles) to zoo. Using the MBTA mass transit system, take Bus #16 from either the Orange Line Forest Hills station or the Red Line Andrew station.*
Don't Miss: *African Tropical Forest, Birds World, Free Flight Cage, Waterfowl Pond.*
Touring Tips: *Scenic picnic spots are in attractive wooded settings. If time is short, park at the Pierpont Road gate, as the best exhibits are at this end. The zoo, with its many trees, is prettiest in autumn.*
Entertainment: *An outdoor theater in the Children's Zoo hosts Keeper of the Day talks. Three slide presentations depicting life in the rain forest are shown in the African Tropical Forest.*

As recently as 1989 the Franklin Park Zoo was listed as one of the "Ten Worst Zoos." At that time it was under state-controlled mismanagement and suffered from the state's severe economic problems. In 1991, with a new governor, the state began shifting control to a non-profit corporation. Since then, both attendance and revenues have increased significantly, and the zoo has regained the respect of the zoological community. While it has a long way to go before it will be considered a top U.S. zoo, it does have one of the country's top exhibits with its new African Tropical Forest.

FEATURED EXHIBITS

Nothing has boosted this zoo's reputation more than the magnificent **African Tropical Forest** that opened in 1989. With no internal upright supports, the 3-acre structure is the largest exhibit of its kind in North America. Under a 75-foot-high dome, more than 100 birds of over 25 tropical species, as well as fruit bats, fly freely through the trees. The lush tropical plants that fill the exhibit are the largest such collection in New England. A wandering jungle path encircles the large, rocky habitat of the lowland gorillas and leads to many open views of these large apes. All around the path, cliffside grottoes display dwarf crocodiles, small duiker antelope, bongos, saddle-billed storks, and pygmy hippos—all viewed across water moats. The hippos, along with cichlid fish, can be seen underwater from an aquatic theater. Hornbills and more primates—including mandrills, talapoin monkeys, and

DeBrazza's monkeys—are displayed behind wide, floor-to-ceiling windows in lush jungle habitats. The DeBrazza's monkeys even experience periodic artificial rainstorms. Other animals seen in glass-fronted jungle habitats include pythons, scorpions, Nile monitors, and a nocturnal exhibit of pottos (lemur-like primates). Four waterfalls crash down near the path—one into a pool of African bullfrogs and mud turtles. Both black and spotted leopards inhabit a dark, damp rain forest habitat behind thin harp wire. In the foyer areas space-age graphics explain the plight of the world's rain forests. Surrounding the huge structure, the gorillas and bongos enjoy natural outdoor habitats during warmer weather.

Behind a Japanese pagoda entrance, **Birds World** takes visitors to four different indoor environments. *A Swamp* features herons, spoonbills, scarlet ibises, and other water birds in a replicated cypress swamp with large tree trunks and cypress "knees." The plush visitor area and marshy pools are separated by a low glass divider. In *A Rain Forest*, a wooden walkway passes a towering cliff and waterfall where touracos, pied imperial pigeons, and other colorful birds fly freely. Cacti, rocks, and a mural background make *A Desert* seem real. Inca doves, noisy blacksmith plovers, and gila monsters are some of the inhabitants of this arid exhibit. A side exhibit of *A River Bank* has huge Burmese pythons and boa constrictors behind glass. In the tangled plants, blue-crowned motmots perch above exotic ducks swimming in a glass-fronted aquarium below.

In front of the Birds World building is the huge **Free Flight Cage**. An elevated walkway leads visitors through this long, high enclosure filled with tall trees and winding streams. Stanley cranes, golden pheasants, herons, and various teals and ducks are some of the free-roaming birds to look for.

Also in this avian area is an impressive **Waterfowl Pond**, with nature trails and seating areas providing panoramic views. Of the hundreds of waterfowl that can be observed here, bar-headed geese and whooper swans are the most notable.

OTHER EXHIBITS

Up on a hilltop, the **Hooves and Horns** area is bisected by a long path that passes fenced, spacious, grassy yards of camels, llamas, sable antelope, gazelles, brindled gnus, ostriches, and wallabies. Endangered species on this hill include addax and Grevy's zebras. Along the hillside slopes, mouflon sheep, Nubian ibexes, and Formosan sika deer live in open wooded yards.

FOR THE KIDS

The 3-acre **Children's Zoo** is highlighted by the *New England Farm*, where small petting corrals surround the animal barns. In the corrals, a Scotch highland cow, miniature donkeys, goats, sheep, rabbits, and turkeys can be petted. A chicken coop exhibits four different breeds, including Barred Plymouth Rock chickens. The small *Stuart B. Avery Reptile Exhibit* has geckos, boas, and other small creatures. Other enclosures contain coyotes, porcupines, prairie dogs, ring-tailed lemurs, and Japanese snow monkeys. The area also has a *Wetlands Exhibit*, *Woodlands Walk*, and small educational dioramas.

NEW AT THE ZOO

The newest residents in the African Tropical Forest are wart hogs. These rarely-exhibited, ugly creatures have their own mud wallow. Another new exhibit, *Poisons of the Tropics*, will open here soon. Outside, a new flight cage for Andean condors opened in 1993.

In coming years the zoo will fill some of its empty space with a **Plains of Africa** exhibit for lions and gazelles. The Children's Zoo will also be upgraded, and a new gift shop will be built.

National Zoological Park

3001 Connecticut Avenue, NW
Washington, DC 20008
(202) 673-4821

Hours: *Grounds 8-8 daily, mid-April to mid-October; 8-6, rest of year. Buildings 9-4:30 daily, year-round, unless otherwise posted.*
Admission Fees: *Free. Audio tour $2.50. Hourly parking rates.*
Directions: *From downtown, go 2 1/2 miles northwest on Connecticut Avenue. From Capital Beltway (I-495), take Exit 33, then go 4 1/2 miles south on Connecticut Avenue. Best idea: Take the Metro subway (Red line), getting off at either the Cleveland Park or Woodley Park-Zoo station.*
Don't Miss: *Panda House during feedings, Amazonia, Invertebrate Exhibit, Komodo dragons, Bird House, Small Mammal House, Cheetah Conservation Station, Wetlands Habitat.*
Touring Tips: *The entire zoo slopes downhill from its Connecticut Avenue entrance (where pedestrians and Metro riders enter) to its entrance near Lion-Tiger Hill and Harvard Street. Almost all of the animals are accessible from two connected paths:* **Olmsted Walk,** *which passes most of the indoor animal buildings, including the Panda House; and* **Valley Trail,** *which passes the bird and aquatic exhibits as well as Amazonia. Going up Olmsted Walk and down the steeper Valley Trail is the recommended route, except for late arrivers. This round-trip is a 2-mile hike. Maps are available at the information station at the bottom of the hill or in the* **Education Building** *at the top. To prevent crowding, the Reptile Discovery Center, Invertebrate Exhibit, and Amazonia have controlled access during busy times and also have shorter hours (check zoo map). An Audio Tour, with hand-held receivers that transmit interesting information about the animals, is available.*
Entertainment: *In summer, elephant and sea lion sessions are presented at their respective exhibits. Animal feedings include cheetahs, elephants, sea lions, seals, kiwis, pelicans, pandas, and more.*

Families from all across America come to Washington, D.C. to experience its rich educational opportunities. Many younger visitors do not fully appreciate the patriotic monuments, historic government structures, or vast museums. What many children do enjoy most about Washington is the National Zoo. Situated on 163 hilly acres along beautiful Rock Creek, the National Zoo has a name that implies that it is not just Washington's zoo, but one belonging to all Americans. Its 3 million annual visitors confirm this status. It is part of the well-known Smithsonian Institution, and is funded by our taxes.

The **American bison exhibit** is a tribute to this zoo's beginning. Ensuring the survival of these large animals was the motivation for establishing a national zoo back in 1889. Today it has become a national treasure in our capital city and is a must-see.

Many of the animal buildings were constructed over 50 years ago. They retain their exterior charm, but most have been renovated inside with modern naturalistic exhibits. These buildings are surrounded by outdoor animal enclosures that are easy to overlook, especially those behind the Reptile House and Great Ape House.

FEATURED EXHIBITS

Being our "national" zoo , it has become the main recipient of animal gifts to the American people from foreign governments. The most famous state gift arrived

in 1972, after President Nixon returned from China with the news that two giant pandas were on the way. Since this is the only zoo in the U.S. with a giant panda, which is the most popular of all zoo animals, many visitors come primarily to see him. Ling-Ling, the female, died in 1992, but her mate, Hsing-Hsing, lives on to delight the masses. The best time to visit the **Panda House** is during the 11 a.m. or 3 p.m. feeding, as Hsing-Hsing sleeps much of the rest of the day.

The **Bird House** is the centerpiece of the extensive bird collec-

Giant Panda

tion and is one of America's best bird buildings. Inside, many owls, toucans, and other tropical birds are behind nearly-invisible harp wire barriers. Notable exhibits include a walk-through aviary and a nocturnal exhibit of kiwis from New Zealand. (This is one of only five U.S. zoos displaying kiwis.)

Behind the Bird House, an impressive display of large birds includes ostriches, flamingos, various storks, rare cranes, goliath herons, and stunning double-wattled cassowaries from New Guinea. Down the hill, many more flight cages hold macaws, snowy owls, sea eagles, pelicans, and more.

The new **Wetlands Habitat** in front of the Bird House has a raised walkway over six ponds that provides a close-up view of waterfowl, frogs, turtles, and fish. Towering above are the famous 90-foot-tall **Great Outdoor Flight Cage** and a walk-in aviary housing bald eagles—our national birds.

Inside the **Reptile House** is a large and complete collection of snakes, lizards, and other reptiles. Behind the building is a swamp habitat where a boardwalk passes alligators and Cuban crocodiles, and leads to an exhibit of Komodo dragons. (These 10-foot-long, 200-pound lizards are seen at only three U.S. zoos.) In 1992 the zoo had 13 hatchlings emerge from their eggs—the first Komodo dragons born outside of Indonesia.

Also behind the Reptile House is the award-winning **Invertebrate Exhibit**. This unique indoor exhibit has a full range of often overlooked invertebrates on display, including crabs, anemones, jellyfish, a giant octopus, insects, and spiders. Interpreters are readily available to answer questions.

The **Small Mammal House** is the best building of its kind in the nation. Inside are naturalistic exhibits of many small, but fascinating, animals most people have never heard of, such as tiger quolls, dwarf mongooses, spiny mice, meerkats, tree shrews, and degus. The tiny monkeys, including pygmy marmosets, are very popular. An impressive forest habitat has a variety of small mammals living together.

OTHER EXHIBITS

Among the most celebrated projects here are the **free-ranging tamarins**, which have absolutely no barriers. These furry little orange monkeys have free range of the zoo, but usually stay in the trees and ropes near their nest box. During the summer a group of golden lion tamarins, which are nearly extinct in the wild, are trained for reintroduction to their native Brazilian home.

The rest of the large collection of primates is distributed primarily among two buildings and two outdoor exhibits. The **Great Ape House** displays gorillas and orangutans. Noisy gibbons and siamangs are found in a mesh enclosure nestled in a grove of maple trees at the new **Gibbon Ridge**. Attractive **Monkey Island** is a rocky home for playful Celebes crested macaques (black apes).

The zoo has had great success with the occupants of the **Red Panda Yard**. More than 100 have been born here. Other small mammals, which are particularly popular with children, are found in the spooky **Bat Cave** and in the prairie dog enclosure.

The 1¹/₂-acre **Lion-Tiger Hill** is a landmark. Its large cats are far from typical zoo animals. On one side are Atlas lions from North Africa, which are known for their long, thick manes. The other side has Sumatran tigers (the smallest, most colorful tigers) and a white Bengal tiger. Nearby are cages of leopards and servals.

One of the newer buildings, the **Australia Pavilion**, has a room-size Great Barrier Reef aquarium filled with brilliantly-colored saltwater fish. Outside, kangaroos, wallabies, emus, and black swans can be seen up close in the new *Australian Walkabout*. Nearby, at the very top of the zoo, are rare bongo antelope and Malayan tapirs.

In **Beaver Valley**, river otters, nutrias, and beavers swim, play, and build homes. The animals are most enjoyable when seen through underwater viewing panels. Other North American animals displayed nearby include deer, coatis, and endangered red wolves.

The recently renovated **Elephant House** is the home of Masai giraffes, African and Asian elephants, Indian rhinos, and Nile and pygmy hippos. The pygmy hippos here are direct descendants of the first pygmy hippo that was received in 1927. Bactrian camels are across the path.

FOR THE KIDS

On Fridays and weekends, hands-on learning labs are conducted for the entire family: **ZOOlab** (in the Education Building) and the **Bird Resource Center** (in the Bird House).

NEW AT THE ZOO

The new **Cheetah Conservation Station** is typical of this zoo's efforts to save endangered animals. In this miniature African savanna, the sleek cats chase a mechanical lure at up to 45 m.p.h. during daily exercise sessions. The cheetahs can be viewed from many different overlooks, with zebras grazing behind them.

The National Zoo plans a future as a "BioPark"—a place where art, culture, plants, and animals are blended together to re-create a holistic environment. The first major example of the BioPark design is the award-winning **Amazonia**, opened in late 1992. This indoor river and rain forest has a glass-domed roof and features 358 species of plants, including 50-foot trees that are native to the Amazon Basin. At the building's entrance, a crashing waterfall marks the beginning of the *flooded forest*. A 55,000-gallon cascading river aquarium displays an ever-changing exhibit of Amazon fish. Other animals seen on the lower level include titi monkeys and waterfowl. A re-created biologist's field station is also encountered in this warm, humid environment. Upstairs, visitors walk through a tropical forest where hummingbirds, otters, and sloths thrive. The *Education Gallery*, a high-tech museum with video displays and touch-screen computers, will open in the future.

Oglebay's Good Children's Zoo

Oglebay Park
Wheeling, West Virginia 26003
(304) 243-4030

Hours: *10-6 weekdays, 10-7 weekends, May-Labor Day; 11-5 daily, rest of year.*
Admission Fees: *Adults $4.25, 66+ $3.95, 2-17 $3.25, family $25. Participates in reciprocity program. C.P. Huntington Train Ride $1.*
Directions: *From I-70, take Exit 2A North, then turn right at the first traffic light (U.S. 40/National Road). Continue east to next traffic light (Highway 88/Bethany Pike), turn left and follow north 2 miles to Oglebay Park. Turn right past the park entrance and follow signs to zoo.*
Don't Miss: *Main Building exhibits (animals, model railroad), C.P. HuntingtonTrain Ride, Bear and Otter Exhibit, Deer Pen feeding, Red Wolf Den, Big Toy.*
Touring Tips: *The Nature Express gift shop has many inexpensive nature and animal-themed items for children. The zoo is part of Oglebay Park, an extensive family resort that also includes a deluxe hotel, family cabins, a nature center, three golf courses, miniature golf, indoor and outdoor pools, horse stables, tennis courts, museums, and more.*
Entertainment: *Attached to the Main Building, the 150-seat* **Benedum Natural Science Theater** *presents hourly films and programs. The theater has a 40-foot tilted dome that is used as a planetarium and for widescreen films. A list of its scheduled programs is provided at the gate.*

Located only a few miles off of I-70 (a connecting route between the East Coast and Midwest}, this small zoo is especially for children. Located just north of Wheeling in West Virginia's panhandle, it is an excellent place to take road-weary kids for a few hours.

The zoo opened in 1977 on 65 wooded, hilly acres. The name "Good" is a tribute to the memory of Philip Mayer Good, a 7-year-old nature-lover. His family donated the initial funds to start the zoo. Except for a few domestics, all creatures seen here are native to North America. The zoo's focus, however, is on providing a special time for children, especially small children.

FEATURED EXHIBITS

At the zoo's entrance is the **Main Building**, which looks like a giant rustic lodge. Walking down a long hallway, visitors pass an assortment of naturalistic habitats. An open marsh exhibit has herons and egrets, while an array of American songbirds are in a long glass enclosure. Many species of native snakes are exhibited in a rocky pine habitat located next to a desert exhibit featuring roadrunners and burrowing owls. Across the hall, a 3,000-gallon freshwater aquarium holds catfish, gars, and other native fish. On the ground floor, a 1,200-square-foot O-gauge miniature railroad exhibit depicts turn-of-the-century Wheeling. Children enjoy watching the trains and steamboats operate, while adults marvel at the incredible attention to detail.

The **Bear and Otter Exhibit** offers a chance to see popular black bears and river otters up-close in natural rocky habitats. The otters can be watched from underwater as they swim beneath a trickling waterfall.

The zoo is justly proud of its **Red Wolf Den.** Red wolves, which are among North America's most endangered mammals, are seen from an overlook as they prance through their tall grass yard or peek out of a rockpile den.

OTHER EXHIBITS

Bison Meadow, a spacious prairie yard, holds the zoo's largest animals. American bison and elk are seen best from the train.

Many large geese and swans swim on **Waterfowl Pond**, which features a peaceful resting area and a beautiful multi-step cascading waterfall.

FOR THE KIDS

While the entire zoo is for children, the most kid-oriented exhibit is the **Big Toy**—a large and unique wooden playground that features an immense log fort climbing structure with ropes and slides.

At the edge of the evergreen forest, the **Deer Pen** is a spacious, hilly yard with a herd of white-tailed deer. After purchasing deer food from coin-operated dispensers, children and adults are welcome to enter a fenced-in area to feed, pet, and chase the gentle deer.

The **C.P. Huntington Train Ride** is an 1863-vintage miniature railroad that takes riders on an interesting 1-mile tour through the middle of Bison Meadow, over a waterfall, behind Red Wolf Den, through a tunnel, and into a dense forest.

Situated around a big red barn, the **Barnyard Animals** area provides children with another petting opportunity. The contact yard has sheep,

Young Camel

pigs, and pygmy goats, while llamas, camels, miniature donkeys, and ponies are usually within reach in nearby corrals. A beehive and chicken coop are also in this area.

NEW AT THE ZOO

The Red Wolf Den, opened in 1989, is the newest major exhibit. Future plans include a prairie dog town.

Philadelphia Zoological Garden

3400 West Girard Avenue
Philadelphia, Pennsylvania 19104
(215) 387-6400

Hours: *9:30-5:45 weekdays, 9:30-6:45 weekends, April-October; 9:30-5:45 daily, March and November; 9:30-5:15 weekdays, 9:30-5:45 weekends, December-February. Shorter hours in Children's Zoo, all buildings, and Treehouse. Check Visitor's Guide for schedule.*
Admission Fees: *Adults $7, 66+ and 2-11 $5.50. Participates in reciprocity program. Camel ride $2, elephant picture $3, Treehouse $1. Safari Monorail: adults $4, 2-11 $3.50. Parking $4.*
Directions: *From I-76 take Exit 36 (Girard Avenue). The zoo is just off of the exit from either direction. From downtown, take the SEPTA #15 trolley, #38 bus, or #76 bus.*
Don't Miss: *Carnivore Kingdom, Treehouse*, Bird House, Bear Country, World of Primates, Rare Animal House, Reptile House, Tigers and Lions, Small Mammal House, Children's Zoo*.*
Touring Tips: *It is best to arrive before late afternoon, when some of the animals are put to bed. The open-air Safari Monorail provides a 20-minute narrated tour around the zoo perimeter.*
Entertainment: *Showtime!, a children's feature, is presented many times each day in the Treehouse. Live animal shows, cow milking, and wool spinning demonstrations are also presented many times each day in the Children's Zoo.* **Wildlife Theater** *shows are also presented frequently. Most shows are presented only during summer; check Visitor's Guide for schedule. Animal feedings include lions, tigers, and vampire bats.*

Referred to as "America's First Zoo," the Philadelphia Zoo was chartered in 1859. The Civil War delayed the opening day until 1874. Reminders of the zoo's illustrious history are seen throughout the park in the form of 19th century Victorian buildings, animal sculptures, statues, and fountains. Today it successfully maintains a delicate balance between preserving its historical heritage and exhibiting its impressive animal collection in the most modern and naturalistic habitats possible.

FEATURED EXHIBITS

A prime example of this balancing act is the **Bird House**. On the exterior it still has a 1916 Victorian charm, but inside it has been transformed into a *Jungle Bird Walk*. A long, winding path leads from one walk-through aviary to another—each lush with tropical plants, jungle streams, and waterfalls. Among the beautiful free-flying birds are Victoria crowned pigeons, paradise tanagers, and lorikeets from New Guinea. Some of the rarest and most spectacular specimens are kept in spacious wire mesh aviaries: Micronesian kingfishers, Guam rails, great hornbills, and quetzals (Guatemala's national bird).

The **Reptile House** is another stately old building with a magnificent interior. In themed galleries with names like *Aquatic Room*, *Desert Room*, *Defensive Behaviors*, and *Adaptations*, more than 190 species of reptiles and amphibians are displayed. (Only two U.S. zoos have more.) Featured exhibits offer the opportunity to compare the rarely-seen American crocodile with a Nile crocodile, and to see both Galapagos and Aldabra tortoises as well as the nation's only display of Chinese crocodile lizards.

The **Small Mammal House** is best known for the occupants of its nocturnal wing. Five different species of bats are exhibited, including the most popular—vampire bats. In another wing, pig-like aardvarks can be observed above ground or underground in their burrow. Also nearby are egg-laying echidnas (spiny anteaters from Australia), a colony of meerkats, and grass-climbing harvest mice.

The **Rare Animal House** is either the first or the last exhibit on a visitor's tour. This rather ordinary-looking building holds some of the zoo's most interesting and popular animals: naked mole-rats (living in what looks like a giant ant farm), chimpanzees, pygmy marmosets, dwarf mongooses, and ruffed lemurs.

Philadelphia joined the modern age of zoo exhibitry with its 1980 opening of **Bear Country**, which provides spacious, natural habitats for three fascinating types of bears. It is no surprise that the polar bears receive the most attention, especially at the underwater viewing area of their 200,000-gallon pool. The unusual spectacled and sloth bears are likewise very popular.

The new **World of Primates** is another exciting natural exhibit. The gorillas, orangutans, and gibbons are fascinating to watch on their island habitats, each of which sports an abundance of grass and trees that make the apes feel at home. Black-faced drill baboons, which are the world's most endangered primates, and an enclosure of ring-tailed lemurs are also nearby. Behind the four islands is a *Forest Walk* with viewing windows that allow excellent primate-watching opportunities.

OTHER EXHIBITS

On opposite ends of the zoo's old **Carnivore House** are huge, densely planted grottoes for the lions and Siberian tigers. The tigers are especially entertaining when they swim in their deep pool. The rest of this building is admittedly outdated, yet many visitors still enter to hear the lions and tigers roar, or to see the interesting residents, which include aardwolves, mouse lemurs, and weasel-like tayras.

The **Pachyderm House**, also old, has large open yards with water holes for the Indian rhinos, Malayan tapirs, Nile hippos, and African and Asian elephants.

The **African Plains** exhibits are part of the zoo's current effort to upgrade to natural habitats. *Phase I* is a replica of the arid African veldt, with sable antelope, zebras, giraffes, and ostriches living in a landscape dominated by a huge artificial baobob tree. *Phase II* simulates the African grasslands inhabited by fleet-footed antelope (springboks and blesboks) and a variety of African land birds.

The **Australian Outback** features red kangaroos, Bennett's wallabies, emus, and Cape Barren geese in an open pen. The animals of **South America** are displayed also, with two adjacent yards of giant anteaters, llamas, and capybaras (large aquatic rodents). The best opportunity to see North American animals is along **Penn's Woodland Trail**—a woodchip path through a forest filled with the wildlife of William Penn's 17th century Pennsylvania. Wild turkeys, porcupines, and bobcats are among the residents of this peaceful setting. Two new hillside habitats hold two of the most endangered meat-eaters of Africa—sleek cheetahs and fierce African hunting dogs.

The bird collection is scattered far beyond the famous Bird House. **Bird Valley** has a row of exotic waterfowl pools, with endangered Humboldt penguins being the most notable residents. Beautiful **Bird Lake**, which is overgrown with water plants and willow trees, is home to hundreds of ducks, geese, and swans. Other bird exhibits include large flight cages for Andean condors, rare hermit ibises, and bald eagles.

FOR THE KIDS

The **Children's Zoo** offers a wonderful variety of animal experiences, and shows and demonstrations are presented all day long. Crowds gather at the duck feeding pond, the pony ride, the farmyard, the sheep and goat contact yard, and *Backyard Bugs*—the summer insect zoo. When it gets hot, the *Ice Cream Parlor* just might be the most popular place of all.

The most memorable zoo exhibit for many children is the **Treehouse.** Kids don't just look at this unique exhibit, they become a part of it. Inside an 1877 building, fiberglass animals and animal artifacts are just the right size for curious kids to climb into. They can climb through a 27-foot beehive, peek out of a frog's mouth, and hatch out of a bird's egg—giving parents great photo opportunities. The centerpiece of this special place is a 4-story artificial fiscus tree that children love to climb.

In summer, children can ride a camel and have their picture taken on an elephant.

NEW AT THE ZOO

This is one of the nation's best zoos for viewing carnivores. In the new **Carnivore Kingdom** a winding path cuts around huge boulders to viewing points where visitors can observe many animals not displayed at most zoos. Natural habitats are provided for red pandas, jaguarundis, coatis, monitor lizards, snow leopards, clouded leopards, and jaguars. The exhibit's climax is a long cascading stream, where playful river otters can be watched through underwater windows.

Across the path a new habitat is being planned. **Lions Lookout** will be home not only to lions, but also to jackals and meerkats.

Jaguar in Carnivore Kingdom

The newest residents are white lions—the first in any zoo outside of South Africa. These rare felines arrived in mid-1993 and can be seen at the Carnivore House.

Pittsburgh Zoo

Highland Park, Hill Road
P.O. Box 5250
Pittsburgh, Pennsylvania 15206
(412) 665-3639

Hours: *10-6 daily, Memorial Day-Labor Day; 9-5, rest of year. Closed Christmas Day.*
Admission Fees: *Adults $5.75, 62+ and 2-13 $2.75. Participates in reciprocity program. Nature Trail Train $1, carousel 75¢.*
Directions: *From I-279, take Exit 15 (Route 28, Ohio Street) East. Follow Highway 28 along the river to the Highland Park Bridge (Route 130). Cross bridge, then turn right onto Butler Street and follow to zoo. From I-76 (Pennsylvania Turnpike), exit at Gate 5 and follow to Route 28 (Allegheny Valley Expressway) South. Follow south to the Highland Park Bridge, then refer to above directions.*
Don't Miss: *Tropical Forest, African Savanna, Aqua Zoo, Niches of the World, Asian Forest.*
Touring Tips: *Be prepared for some hill climbing. In the centrally-located **Visitor Plaza** food options range from pizza to Ice Cream Shoppe treats. Umbrella-shaded seating is available.*

Entertainment: *Farm demonstrations are given three times daily in the Children's Farm. Shark-diving and -feeding is presented on Saturdays in the Aqua Zoo. Other animal feedings include gorillas, bears, and penguins.*

The historic Pittsburgh Zoo, which opened in 1898, has quickly become one of America's most modern zoos. While some of the historic architecture still remains, most of the exhibits have either been built or renovated during the 1980s as part of an expansive master plan.

Located on Pittsburgh's northeast side, it is built on the steep slopes of the Allegheny River Valley. The resulting hilly terrain makes the new block-long moving walkways, which operate from the parking lot to the entrance gate, an appreciated amenity. Many children consider these giant escalators to be just one more exciting ride.

FEATURED EXHIBITS

The **Tropical Forest**, a 5-acre indoor/outdoor primate complex, is the crown jewel of the zoo. Just about every type of popular large or medium-sized primate can be found in tropical habitats that simulate their native homes. The great apes— orangutans and gorillas—are displayed in large, thickly-planted enclosures with plenty of branches to climb on. Lifelike background murals make the settings seem even more real. Another troop of gorillas can be viewed outside in a 1 1/2-acre grassy meadow. The rest of the primates are exhibited in separate 30-foot-tall habitats that are under a translucent roof in the center of the building. The floor of these natural habitats is a molded concrete likeness of a tropical riverbank. Animals in these central habitats include gibbons in a bamboo thicket; woolly monkeys, spider monkeys, and howler monkeys in South American palm forests; four African species—including mandrills and colobus monkeys—in lush broadleaf jungles; two types of lemurs from Madagascar; and a few non-primates such as rock hyraxes. The winding visitor hallway is nearly as lush with tropical greenery as the primate areas. Since it opened in 1991, the exhibit's best evidence of excellence is the primate "baby boom" it has experienced with many of its endangered species.

Also new, the **African Savanna** is the zoo's premier outdoor exhibit. Most of its animals—including African elephants, giraffes, zebras, bongos, and ostriches— are visible in the same sweeping panorama, which can be viewed from many forest clearing vantage points. White rhinos, like the elephants, dwell on their own island across a deep gulch from the visitors. Across the same gulch, a pride of lions can be seen from a covered viewing station. Other large African cats include spotted leopards in a lushly-vegetated enclosure and a cheetah. Flamingos, pelicans, and sacred ibises wade among the waters of an authentically planted African marsh.

As naturally landscaped as the African Savanna, the **Asian Forest** is the first exhibit area most visitors see. Siberian tigers prowl in a conifer forest with a waterfall crashing into a stream below. A marsh area exhibits white storks, cranes, other Asian waterfowl, and muntjacs (small Asian deer). Plush snow leopards are in a new enclosure.

This zoo has long been famous for its 2-story **Aqua Zoo**, which is one of the nation's best zoo aquariums. Its star, the Amazon dolphin (the only freshwater dolphin in North America), is in a shallow, solitary habitat that simulates its natural environment. Golden lion tamarins hide in a jungle setting above the dolphin pool. The *Living Coral Reef* is one of the few such exhibits in the U.S. Other interesting exhibits include a penguin display with underwater viewing, giant albino catfish, alligator gars, a large octopus tank, and a 90,000-gallon circular shark tank with giant sea turtles.

The long underground hallway of the old Reptile and Amphibian Building has been redesigned, renovated, and renamed **The Niches of the World**. The new exhibit presents a collection of fascinating, and often bizarre, nocturnal animals. More than 50 species of reptiles, amphibians, and small mammals live in their own "niches," or habitats—each with realistic rockwork, natural plantings, and beautiful mural backgrounds. Niche inhabitants include black-footed cats, emperor tamarins, meerkats, tiny dik-dik antelope, saltwater crocodiles (displayed at only one other U.S. zoo), bushmasters, and many other venomous and non-venomous snakes and lizards.

OTHER EXHIBITS

At the zoo's highest elevation, the **North America Exhibit** has a set of adjacent grassy yards inhabited by interesting hoofed animals that include bison, reindeer, elk, and pronghorn antelope. The focus of this area, however, is a pack of endangered red wolves.

Built into the valley below are four massive, rocky grottoes with deep pools. These **Bear Dens** are home to polar bears, Kodiak bears, sun bears, and black bears. Down another hill, the **Australia Exhibit** consists of a pool of black swans and a hillside yard of emus, scrub wallabies, and red kangaroos.

FOR THE KIDS

Surrounded by dense woods, the **Children's Farm** has outdoor corrals where children can pet some unusual domestic animals, such as a Scotch Highland cow sporting sizable horns and a Sardinian donkey, as well as the more common sheep, goats, and pigs.

Nearby, the **Nature Trail Train** is available for short, 10-minute nature trips into the woods. Riders can also pet fawns in a yard surrounded by the tracks. A carousel is also in this area.

NEW AT THE ZOO

The brand new *Insect Gallery* is the latest addition to the Aqua Zoo. Specimens range from butterflies to beetles, with an emphasis on native Pennsylvania species. One of the many interactive educational exhibits is a live terrarium with a joystick-controlled video bioscanner that gives visitors a super-magnified look at the tiny creatures.

A new **Education Complex** recently opened, and an improved **Children's Farm** will open soon. In the distant future, a **Small Animal Ecosystem** exhibit and an **Arctic Waters** exhibit can be expected.

BEST OF THE REST

Burnet Park Zoo
500 Burnet Park Drive
Syracuse, New York 13204
(315) 435-3774

After being closed for nearly 4 years, this zoo received a $13 million overhaul and reopened in 1986 with a uniquely themed arrangement. Exhibits that are all under the same roof include the nocturnal Adaptation exhibit; Antiquity—a cave with reptiles and amphibians; Diversity of Birds—a walk-through rain forest; and the Social Animals area featuring Asian lions, meerkats, mandrills, and other primates. Animals and People displays creatures that man has domesticated, from llamas and Asian elephants to American farm animals. The Wild North represents four different North American environments where bison, Rocky Mountain goats, mountain lions, lynx, brown bears, peccaries, and endangered red wolves can be seen from a raised boardwalk.

Panther Chameleon

Roger Williams Park Zoo
1000 Elmwood Avenue
Providence, Rhode Island 02907
(401) 785-9450

Many exciting new exhibits can be found in New England's oldest and most complete zoo. One of the newest is the Tropical America rain forest building where visitors are given a full-color, 24-page Field Guide to identify the various birds, reptiles, frogs, and monkeys. The Plains of Africa features elephants, giraffes, zebras, bongos, and cheetahs. Nearby, the African Fishing Village consists of a gift shop, restaurant, and indoor desert exhibit of hornbills, mongooses, and a naked mole-rat colony. The new Farmyard is the home of eight minor breeds, including Tunis sheep and Rhode Island red chickens. Polar bears, sea lions, penguins, prairie dogs, and red pandas are all nearby. The Wetlands Trail features native Rhode Island waterfowl and vegetation.

Staten Island Zoo
614 Broadway
Staten Island, New York 10310
(718) 442-3101

Located just south of the Statue of Liberty, this small zoo is famous for its focus on reptiles—primarily snakes. Its rattlesnake collection is one the largest and most complete in the country. A group of interconnected buildings house the Serpentarium, the modern Aquarium, and the walk-through South American Tropical Forest. Within this last building is one of the largest vampire bat exhibits in the country. In 1994, a fourth wing will become the African Savanna at Twilight. Popular small animals found in outside exhibits include prairie dogs, otters, raccoons, and porcupines. The Children's Center—a petting zoo set up to resemble a New England farm—is reached by crossing a covered bridge.

MORE ZOOS

Acadia Zoo *(Trenton, Maine)*
Attleboro Capron Park Zoo *(Attleboro, Massachusetts)*
Beardsley Zoological Gardens *(Bridgeport, Connecticut)*
Bergen County Zoological Park *(Paramus, New Jersey)*
Brandywine Zoo *(Wilmington, Delaware)*
Cape May County Park Zoo *(Cape May, New Jersey)*
Catoctin Mountain Zoological Park *(Thurmont, Maryland)*
Cohanzick Zoo *(Bridgeton, New Jersey)*
Elmwood Park Zoo *(Norristown, Pennsylvania)*
Erie Zoological Gardens *(Erie, Pennsylvania)*
Lake George Zoological Park *(Lake George, New York)*
Plumpton Park Zoo *(Rising Sun, Maryland)*
Popcorn Park Zoo *(Forked River, New Jersey)*
Queens Zoo/Wildlife Conservation Park *(Queens, New York)*
Ross Park Zoo *(Binghamton, New York)*
Salisbury Zoological Park *(Salisbury, Maryland)*

Seneca Park Zoo *(Rochester, New York)*
Space Farms Zoo and Museum *(New Castle, Pennsylvania)*
The Zoo at Forest Park *(Springfield, Massachusetts)*
Trailside Museum and Zoo *(West Point, New York)*
Trevor Zoo *(Millbrook, New York)*
Turtle Back Zoo *(West Orange, New Jersey)*
Utica Zoo *(Utica, New York)*
Walter D. Stone Memorial Zoo *(Stoneham, Massachusetts)*

Southern Zoos

Knoxville Zoological Gardens

3333 Woodbine Avenue
Knoxville, Tennessee 37914
(615) 637-5331

Hours: *9:30-6 daily, April-September; 10-4:30, rest of year.*
Admission Fees: *Adults $6.50, 62+ and 3-12 $4. Participates in reciprocity program. Zoo Choo train ride: adults $2, 62+ and 3-12 $1.50. Elephant ride $2. Parking $1.*
Directions: *From I-40, take Exit 392 (Rutledge Pike). Follow signs to Magnolia Avenue, Prosser Road, and zoo.*
Don't Miss: *Big Cat Country, Great Ape Exhibit, Reptile Complex, Marine Animal Complex, The Bird Show, Rhino Exhibit, Children's Zoo*, Zoo Choo train ride.*
Touring Tips: *All animals along the trail between the Reptile Complex and Big Cat Country will be seen twice. The rustic Tiger Tops Cafe is an excellent full-service restaurant with both indoor and outdoor seating that features views of the zoo and surrounding forest. The Safari Glen area has a picnic grove.*
Entertainment: *In the **Safari Glen** area, the new 300-seat outdoor **News-Sentinel Amphitheatre** presents **The Bird Show**, which features ten interesting species of birds, including parrots, macaws, hawks, owls, vultures, roadrunners, and even a red-legged seriema. These popular shows are held many times daily (except Mondays) in summer and on weekends in spring and fall. The seal and sea lion shows, held daily in the Marine Animal Complex, are both educational and fun.*

Not far from the Appalachians in Eastern Tennessee, the Knoxville Zoo takes full advantage of its natural terrain. Many exhibits are built along steep hillsides or are surrounded by thick forests. Panoramic views of the valleys and mountains in the distance are enjoyed from the grounds. The name, "Zoological Gardens," is evidenced in the many colorful flower beds and over 125 varieties of trees and shrubs. Located less than a mile off of I-40, this pretty zoo makes a great stop on a Smokey Mountain vacation.

FEATURED EXHIBITS

One of the nation's finest collections of big cats is found in the thick woods of **Big Cat Country.** At the start of the shaded trail is one of the highlights—a white Bengal tiger and her orange sister in a large forested yard. Up the trail, an Oriental-style gazebo provides a scenic overview of the exhibit. Siberian tigers are featured in the next woodland enclosure, viewed from an elevated boardwalk that protrudes into the exhibit. The tigers can sometimes be observed enjoying the diving platform and slide of the *Tiger Pool.* Rare snow leopards occupy another forest exhibit. Opened in 1991, *Cheetah Savannah* is a naturalistic 1-acre setting for the athletic cheetahs. Visitors can watch these fast cats from an overlook or through close-up viewing windows. Around the corner are lions, both African and Asian, in shaded grassy yards. (Knoxville has the only pure Asian lions in the United States. All others are hybrids.) Cougars, Canadian lynx, and a black leopard are displayed in smaller enclosures.

Visitors to the **Marine Animal Complex** walk along a raised platform and look down into four gigantic pools populated with polar bears, sea lions, harbor seals, and gray seals. On the lower level, the black-footed penguins' indoor habitat is seen through a long row of windows.

The white rhinos are among the zoo's premier animals. (They are seen here in greater numbers than at any other U.S. zoo.) The **Rhino Exhibit,** a large open field with many high overlooks, often boasts rhino calves.

With more than 400 reptiles of over 100 species, this zoo is justly proud of its **Reptile Complex**. This unique open-air exhibit displays cobras, vipers, rattlesnakes, skinks, small tortoises, and other reptiles in glass cylinders mounted in rows along the exterior of a stone building. Visitors can look over the plexiglas walls of the small, open enclosures of alligator snapping turtles, alligators, and poisonous gila monsters. In a much larger yard, giant Aldabra tortoises move slowly about. Most notable in the complex is the award-winning *Southern Appalachian Bog Exhibit,* where a successful breeding group of protected Tennessee bog turtles lives in a large man-made bog. A nearby cattail marsh has other native turtles on display.

OTHER EXHIBITS

Along the hillside path that connects the zoo's two main sections, a long row of aviaries displays a variety of colorful, exotic birds. A few of these aviary-like enclosures hold red pandas, one of this zoo's trademark animals. (The Knoxville Zoo is famous for its breeding success with these cuddly animals. It is second in the number of panda cubs born on site.)

The spacious, arid **African Plains**, viewable from two sides, is where giraffes, zebras, ostriches, sable antelope, and gazelles share a large water hole. Mounted, coin-operated binoculars are available for closer looks.

Starting at the zoo entrance, an S-shaped path leads uphill passing grottoes of hamadryas baboons, black bears, and drill baboons. More primates—endangered lion-tailed macaques and gibbons—are at the top of the hill. The **Elephant Exhibit** is also on this hill. (The first African elephant birth in the U.S. occurred here in 1978.)

Up in the woods, bald eagles and red wolves live in large mesh enclosures. Both of these animals have required major programs to avoid their extinction, and both species are being reintroduced into the wild in nearby Great Smokey Mountains National Park.

Other exhibits include **Tahr Mountain** (a rockpile "mountain" for Nilgiri tahrs and mouflon sheep), a deep hippo pool, Arabian oryxes, tiny blue duikers, a striped hyena, African hunting dogs, friendly binturongs, and endangered Andean condors.

FOR THE KIDS

Under a gigantic willow tree, corrals in the **Children's Zoo** hold donkeys, miniature ponies, and sheep, while small cages display owls and ravens. In the petting yard children can pet or feed pygmy goats, potbellied pigs, and llamas. Newborns needing special attention can be viewed in the *Animal Nursery*.

On the **Zoo Choo train ride**, passengers are taken on a 1-mile trip behind animal exhibits, through a forest, and over a high trestle. During warmer months, elephant rides are also offered.

NEW AT THE ZOO

Opened in 1993, the **Great Ape Exhibit** is an indoor/outdoor complex of natural habitats for gorillas and chimpanzees. Both of these popular great apes can be seen up close in their indoor homes through large viewing panels, or outside in mesh-covered courtyards. *Gorilla Valley* provides the gorillas with a 1-acre outdoor habitat that simulates their native African home. The chimps will soon have a similar natural outdoor habitat when the 2-acre *Chimpanzee Ridge* opens. In the future, island exhibits of lemurs and Diana monkeys will be added to this area.

Other future plans call for a new **Birds of the Tropics** walk-through aviary and expansions of the Reptile Complex and African Plains.

Louisville Zoological Garden

1100 Trevillian Way
Louisville, Kentucky 40213
(502) 459-2181

Hours: *10-5 daily, April-Labor Day; also to 8 p.m. Wednesdays and Thursdays, June-August; 10-4 daily, rest of year. Zoo closes 1 hour after gate closes.*
Admission Fees: *Adults $5.50, 61+ $3.50, 3-11 $2.75. Participates in reciprocity program. Tram $1.50, Miniature Train Ride $1.75. Elephant and camel rides: adults $3, 61+ and 3-11 $2.*

Directions: *Located on the southside of Louisville. From I-264 (Watterson Expressway), take Exit 14 (Poplar Level Road) North. Follow signs north to Trevilian Way, turn right and zoo is quickly on the right. Direct bus service is provided by the TARC transit system.*
Don't Miss: *HerpAquarium, MetaZoo Education Center, African Veldt Panorama, Australian Walkabout, Miniature Train Ride, Polar Bear Exhibit, Siberian Tiger Exhibit, American Wild Cat Exhibit.*
Touring Tips: *A narrated Tram ride is available. For inexpensive and familiar fast food, the LakeSide Cafe offers a combined menu of entrees from Pizza Hut, Taco Bell, and Kentucky Fried Chicken. The seating area is under African thatched huts situated beside a pretty fountain lake.*
Entertainment: *Movies are shown in the MetaZoo classroom and in the ZooVision building. Seal and sea lion training sessions are presented daily at the Seal Pool. Occasional shows are given at the large amphitheater MetaZoo Stage.*

One of the major attractions of Kentucky's largest city, the 133-acre Louisville Zoo is less than 30 years old. Its youth is an advantage because when it opened in 1968, a new exhibit philosophy was being developed in the zoo world. Most of its animals have benefitted with open, barless enclosures. Its higher elevations offer sweeping views of the lower level exhibits found at the foot of long grassy slopes.

This zoo is playing a major role in saving from extinction North America's most endangered mammal—the black-footed ferret. This very successful and highly publicized program occurs primarily behind the scenes, but a new exhibit of these extremely rare animals opened in late 1993.

FEATURED EXHIBITS

The **HerpAquarium** is the zoo's top exhibit and its only major indoor exhibit. Over 500 amphibians, reptiles, and fish are included in four habitat "biomes" that use the best of modern naturalistic exhibitry. A beautiful coral reef tank, with deadly lionfish, is the centerpiece of the *Water Biome*. Cuban crocodiles and colorful tropical birds enjoy scheduled rain showers in a simulated tropical rain forest. The *Forest Biome* also exhibits deadly Gaboon vipers and slow-moving Parson's chameleons. Local venomous snakes are a part of the *Kentucky Temperate Forests* display. The *Savanna Biome* features iguanas, bearded dragons, and Sinai desert cobras. Desert lizards live in the *Underground Desert* display, which features a cutaway view into their burrows. The popular *Nocturnal Desert* displays rattlesnakes and gila monsters that seemingly live only inches from a kangaroo rat.

The **Australian Walkabout** looks like a small city park in Central Australia. Official flags fly in front of the entry building, while a haunting outback "howl" is heard from hidden speakers. A short boardwalk stroll around a central pool provides close-up views of emus, wallabies, Cape Barren geese, black swans, and kookaburas, and a series of aviaries holds beautiful Aussie birds.

The unusual **American Wild Cat Exhibit** features realistic high cliff habitats with cascading waterfalls and natural plants that allow pumas and lynx to be seen as they would be in the wild. A pair of flightless bald eagles are seen from a raised platform with no visual barriers.

At the newly-renovated **Polar Bear Exhibit**, a pair of polar bears can be observed in their deep blue pool. A shaded seating area is provided in front of a 30-foot wall of glass. Another glass wall at a higher level overlooks the white bears' spacious enclosure.

The **Siberian Tiger Exhibit** offers similar viewing choices. An ascending ramp leads to an overview of the tigers' attractive hillside home. Wide windows allow closer views of the tigers, which can frequently be seen swimming.

The **African Veldt Panorama** area is most notable for its impressive diversity of African animals, many of them rare or endangered. Antlers of many shapes can be compared on the gemsboks, aoudads, blesboks, bongos, addax, sable antelope, and kudus. Giraffes, gazelles, and ostriches are seen in the savanna with lions in the background. Other cats include cheetahs in a large hillside yard and servals in the **Giraffe & Serval House**, a building that also has an interesting exhibit of giant spiders of the world. Other animals include striking gelada baboons, ugly wart hogs, white rhinos, ground hornbills, camels, and mountain zebras.

OTHER EXHIBITS

The **South American Panorama** has an especially wide variety of pampas animals. Guanacos, rheas, and macaws live on a grassy plain that shares a pond with the **Flamingo Yard**. The continent's top carnivores—jaguars and maned wolves—are across the path. Nearby, snow leopards from Asia live in a temporary exhibit.

Children particularly enjoy the **Aquatic Area** with sea lions, gray seals, and a sea gull aviary. Stairs lead down to a wonderful underwater viewing area of river otters.

This zoo is famous for its breeding group of South American woolly monkeys. The large group can be seen on an island, inside bad-weather quarters, or hanging from the bridge that connects the two. Not far away are both African and Asian elephants. A herd of endangered Pere David's deer lives in the spacious **Asian Plains.**

FOR THE KIDS

An elephant skull and ostrich skeleton are mounted behind glass in the main gallery of the **MetaZoo Education Center**, and children line up for the chance to look through the eyes of a giant insect. Many other interactive exhibits are available in this unique building. The *Woodland Pond* room, which is inhabited by local turtles and fish, has easy-to-use microscopes for examining specimens. The *Young Discovery Room* has snakes and other reptiles on display, as well as skulls and eggs for little hands to touch. Some endangered animals, including golden lion tamarins, also live in the MetaZoo.

Children can pet sheep, pygmy goats, and a donkey in the **Small Animal Area**. A barn has stalls holding African zebu cattle, and a variety of attractive birds—

including Hawaiian geese—are exhibited in small enclosures. Cute cottontop tamarins can also be seen.

The **Miniature Train Ride** is one of the better zoo trains. It circles the entire zoo, but kids enjoy most the long tunnels it passes through. Elephant and camel rides are also available.

NEW AT THE ZOO

An ambitious master plan for the future—"Next Generation Zoo"—includes **The Islands Exhibit**. A glass-enclosed atrium will lead to a Kentucky-themed orientation plaza and an outdoor penguin exhibit. In the distant future, new exhibits will feature nearly every continent.

Memphis Zoological Garden and Aquarium

2000 Galloway Avenue
Memphis, Tennessee 38112
(901) 276-WILD

Hours: *9-5 daily, April-September; 9-4:30, October-March. Closed Thanksgiving Day and December 24 and 25.*
Admission Fees: *Adults $5, 60+ and 2-11 $3. Participates in reciprocity program. Amusement park rides 50¢ each. Parking $1 (refundable).*
Directions: *Centrally located in Overton Park. From downtown, take Poplar Avenue east approximately 5 miles to Overton Park. Turn left into park at corner of Poplar and Kenilworth and follow signs to zoo entrance.*
Don't Miss: *Cat Country, Primate Canyon, Tropical Bird House, bear grottoes, penguins, African Veldt.*
Touring Tips: *Beginning in summer 1994, a Zoo Tram will run along the main path, allowing visitors to get on and off at designated spots. The Carnivora Restaurant also opens in 1994 in the old Cats building. It will feature the Tot-Lot children's play area and provide a good view of the lemurs.*
Entertainment: *Special programs are presented in the new **Education Center**. Animal feedings include big cats, sea lions, and reptiles.*

Opened in 1906, the Memphis Zoo has been showing its age. A master plan has been designed to give the citizens of Memphis "a world-class zoo in our time." With the many new exhibits opening in 1993 and 1994, it should meet this goal.

Memphis is named after a city in Egypt. The zoo commemorates the city's Egyptian connection with its dazzling new Egyptian entrance area. Arriving visitors pass the Avenue of Animals, which features animal sculptures on both sides, and then enter through a massive gate decorated with ancient hieroglyphics. Inside the gate, an orientation court features a 40-foot obelisk with a reflecting pool, a full-size replica of the Rosetta Stone, and a stylized Nile River with seven cataracts (little waterfalls) and a pyramid-shaped fountain.

FEATURED EXHIBITS

Though they are old, the **bear grottoes** are still very attractive, with trickling waterfalls and swimming pools. Polar, grizzly, spectacled, and sun bears are the inhabitants of the five concrete grottoes. A real treat, for both humans and bears, is the rare opportunity to feed the bears. Cups of fruit are sold from a stand, and coin-operated dispensers sell other bear food.

Black-footed **penguins** from Africa live in another rocky habitat. Underwater observation windows allow very close views of them as they swim and dive.

In the **Tropical Bird House**, two long hallways of exotic bird exhibits feature fruit doves, finches, parrots, toucanets, and other jewel-colored birds. The colorful exhibits have hand-painted murals as background walls. Two walk-through aviaries filled with free-flying birds resemble lush rain forests.

The **African Veldt** exhibit displays dama gazelles, crowned cranes, white storks, and the nation's largest herd of Nile lechwe in a sprawling, shaded, grassy yard with watering holes and termite mounds.

OTHER EXHIBITS

Near the Veldt, the **African Hoofstock** area includes zebras, scimitar-horned oryxes, greater kudus, and sable antelope. A large herd of giraffes occupy another open yard nearby. Across the zoo, the **Round Barn** has more African hoofed animals in wedge-shaped yards. A path around the barn passes bonteboks, duikers, ground hornbills, and endangered Nilgiri tahrs. The **Asian Hoofstock** area features some extremely endangered animals, including Mongolian wild horses, Pere David's deer, gaurs, hog deer, and the largest group of lowland anoas (dwarf water buffalo) in the U.S.

The **Aquarium** has over 30 small tanks with both freshwater and saltwater exhibits. Among the best are the living coral reef, the Hawaiian Islands reef, an Amazon River tank with giant pacus, and a group of seahorses.

Reptile-lovers should not miss the **Herpetarium**. Rows and rows of terrariums appear to be embedded in the rock walls. The smaller exhibits are grouped into four geographical regions and include king cobras, death adders, albino California kingsnakes, and a wide variety of frogs. Also, three rare species from the crocodile family are exhibited in attractive jungle grottoes.

Other notable exhibits include the **World of Waterfowl**, where flamingos and ducks are viewed from a boardwalk and from a shaded gazebo; bald eagles in a large flight cage; the **Swan and Sea Lion pools**; the largest group of chamois in the U.S. on **Goat Mountain**; the **Pachyderms area**, with indoor pens and outdoor yards for African elephants, white rhinos, and Malayan tapirs; and the **Nile hippos exhibit**. (This zoo is sometimes referred to as the hippo capital of the world because there have been more hippos born here than at any other zoo.)

FOR THE KIDS

The remodeled **Children's Village** is scheduled to reopen in the fall of 1994 with an American Farm theme. Zebu cattle, pigs, sheep, llamas, and goats will be available to pet. There will also be a *Marsh Exhibit*, a *Discovery Center*, a nature trail, a prairie dog town, and a miniature train ride that will circle the area.

A small **Amusement Park**, with a carousel and five other kiddie rides, is adjacent to the Children's Village.

NEW AT THE ZOO

This zoo took a giant step toward increasing its status with the April 1993 opening of **The Commercial Appeal Cat Country**. This 4-acre exhibit features wild cats from three continents in settings that replicate their natural homes. Visitors start the tour by entering an Egyptian temple. In the Asian area, fishing cats, spotted leopards, and clouded leopards are viewed through thin high-tension wire. Across a water moat, Sumatran tigers prowl by the ruins of an ancient Asian city and a crashing waterfall. Down the trail, snow leopards live within view of their natural prey—muntjac deer and red pandas. Latin American jaguars and smaller jaguarundis are displayed near their prey—capybaras (the world's largest rodents). In Africa, a small exhibit of caracal lynx is followed by wide open savanna exhibits for cheetahs and lions. Their natural prey—klipspringer antelope, rock hyraxes, and meerkats—inhabit rock outcroppings known as kopjes.

Primate Canyon is scheduled to open in spring of 1994. It will be a set of natural habitats for the gorillas, orangutans, colobus monkeys, spot-nosed monkeys, and many others. Siamangs and Japanese snow monkeys will inhabit their own islands. The *Madagascar Exhibit* will display ruffed and ring-tailed lemurs within sight of the Carnivora Restaurant diners. The old Primate House will be converted into the **World of Darkness** and feature vampire bats and rarely exhibited kiwi birds.

The Forest, another new exhibit opening in 1994, will take visitors down a pathway to see plants and animals of the woods.

Miami Metrozoo

12400 S.W. 152nd Street
Miami, Florida 33177
(305) 251-0400

Hours: *9:30-5:30 daily. Last admission at 4.*
Admission Fees: *Adults $8.25, 56+ $7.42, 3-12 $4.25. Reduced rates for Florida residents, 9:30-11 Monday-Saturday (non-holidays). Participates in reciprocity program.*
Directions: *Located on Miami's far southwest side. From the Florida Turnpike Extension, take the 152nd Street Exit and follow 1/4 mile west to zoo. From U.S. Highway 1, take the*

152nd Street Exit and follow 3 miles west to zoo. Miami's Zoobus offers express service from the Dadeland North Metrorail station in downtown Miami.

Don't Miss: Zoofari Monorail, Wings of Asia (when reopened), Koala Exhibit, African exhibits, Asian River Life, Asian exhibits, Tiger Temple.

Touring Tips: The air-conditioned Zoofari Monorail is included in the admission price. It provides a narrated tour and offers excellent views of most of the animals. Four elevated monorail stations are well-spaced for convenient, step-saving touring. To adjust for Miami's hot weather, water fountains, soda machines, and concession stands are located throughout the grounds. Personalized tram tours are also available upon request; check at the front entrance for information.

Entertainment: In the large, central **Amphitheatre**, snakes, free-flying birds of prey, and other animals not on display are featured in the **Wildlife Show** three times each day. Within PAWS (the children's zoo), **Elephant Shows** and **Ecology Theatre** shows are presented three times a day. Informal Animal Information sessions are scheduled regularly at various exhibits around the zoo. Animal feedings include bears and tortoises.

Located in Crandon Park, Miami's old zoo was becoming too small for this growing metropolis and worldwide tourist destination. Ironically, its Key Biscayne location was also considered too vulnerable to the area's frequent hurricanes. To alleviate both problems, the new Miami Metrozoo opened in 1981 on 740 inland acres. From the beginning, it has been one of the world's leading zoos.

With 290 of its immense 740 acres developed, it is one of the nation's largest zoos. All of this space provides large exhibit areas for its residents and the ability to display many large animals. It is the top zoo at which to see the large pachyderms. (In fact, it has more pachyderms—elephants, rhinos, hippos, and tapirs—than any other U.S. zoo, as well as one of the most diverse collections of hoofed animals.)

One of the country's newest zoos, it was built from the ground up using the latest exhibit technology. It is called a "cageless" zoo because nearly all of its animals live in spacious, natural habitats separated from visitors by hidden moats.

Because southern Florida's mild, tropical weather allows for year-round outdoor exhibits, it is primarily an outdoor zoo. The weather is also ideal for its lush tropical foliage, which includes plenty of palm trees.

On August 24, 1992 one of the worst natural disasters in U.S. history, Hurricane Andrew, hit the Miami Metrozoo with the full force of its 187-m.p.h. winds. Due to the staff's dedicated preparations, animal losses were remarkably light, but the structures and landscaping sustained over $15 million worth of damage. The zoo was closed for over 4 months to clean up and rebuild. Generous donations from individuals and corporations across the country have allowed a near-total recovery from this tragedy, and the zoo shows strong signs of quickly regaining its former status.

FEATURED EXHIBITS

Most of the fabulous exhibits here are distributed along geographical loops that originate at the central Amphitheatre. Sixteen **African exhibits** are found on the only unfinished loop. Chimpanzees, gorillas, and a large troop of black and white colobus monkeys are inhabitants of large, sloping, grassy yards with artificial climbing devices. The country's largest herd of African elephants, and one of the country's largest black rhino herds, live next to each other in spacious, grassy areas with large watering holes. At the start of this trail, the pygmy hippo exhibit is dominated by a pool of deep water. The multi-species *African Plains* has giraffes, zebras, gazelles, and ostriches in an expansive, open grassland. The unparalleled variety of African antelope seen along this path includes kudus, bongos, waterbucks, nyalas, Nile lechwe, and tiny dik-diks. Most interesting are the skinny gerenuks, who stand up on their two hind legs to nibble leaves from trees high above them. Mixed among the antelope exhibits is a near complete collection of African land birds that include ground hornbills, secretary birds, kori bustards, storks, and cranes.

Asian exhibits are found along another winding loop. The Asian elephant exhibit makes this one of the few zoos with two elephant displays. Indian rhinos and Malayan tapirs are nearby in spacious yards, and three bear species (sun bears, sloth bears, and Himalayan black bears) enjoy deep pools for cooling off. The orangutans can be seen in a wide yard equipped with climbing poles and ropes, but the closest views are through a glass panel in a viewing cave. Two types of wild cattle (bantengs and gaurs), onagers (wild donkeys), camels, endangered Siamese crocodiles, and a wide variety of Asian deer and antelope live in natural habitats on this loop. From Africa, the lions, servals, and Cape hunting dogs are found in grassy yards strewn with rocks. The lions can be watched up close through another viewing cave. Additional African hoofstock, including rare scimitar-horned oryxes and forest buffalo, are also found in this Asian area.

One of the highlights on the Asian loop is the new bi-level **Asian River Life** exhibit. Passing an ornamental sign and a wide waterfall, visitors enter a rocky cave for close looks at blood pythons and clouded leopards. A higher observation level overlooks a muddy riverbank with muntjacs (small deer), large water monitors, and a family of playful small-clawed otters. The otters and monitor lizards are most enjoyable when they can be observed underwater through wide viewing windows.

Australia is represented at the **Koala Exhibit**. (This was the first U.S. zoo outside of California to exhibit these popular marsupials.) A concrete ramp leads up to the glass-fronted habitat, which appears deeper than it is due to a forest mural in the background. The cuddly koalas are sometimes displayed in an outdoor yard surrounded by red kangaroos, wallabies, and geese.

The most photographed exhibit is the **Naomi Browning Tiger Temple**, named in memory of a young zoo volunteer killed by Hurricane Andrew. In front of a convincing replica of an ancient Cambodian temple, a group of tigers prowl an open grassy field. The pair of rare white Bengal tigers here receive the most attention.

Before the hurricane, the premier exhibit was the magnificent **Wings of Asia**.

This 1-acre walk-through aviary was the most severely damaged structure and will be the last to reopen. It will be a 65-foot-high, mesh-covered simulation of a Southeast Asian rain forest. A maze of pathways will take people past rushing waterfalls and over a suspension bridge to a resting area across from a crowded water bird pond. Hundreds of free-flight Asian birds of over 75 species—most notably Great Indian hornbills, fairy bluebirds, green magpies, and Victoria crowned pigeons—will be represented.

OTHER EXHIBITS

The beautiful tropical lagoon filled with a large flock of Caribbean flamingos is not listed as a "Don't Miss" only because its location near the front entrance means it *can't* be missed. Across from the lagoon, a long yard is filled with both live and artificial banyan trees that provide a suitable home for vocal siamangs and gibbons.

A small loop near the Amphitheatre has five exhibits that display two species of duikers (miniature African antelope), pygmy zebus, and rarely-exhibited Baird's tapirs. The **Giant Land Tortoise Exhibit** is dotted with both Galapagos and Aldabra tortoises.

Four more exhibits, near the front entrance, display red ruffed lemurs in artificial banyan trees, endangered addax, and more African hoofed animals.

FOR THE KIDS

To enter **PAWS**, the children's zoo, young and old visitors alike must pass through a colorful arch made of giant Lego building blocks. Inside, this multi-purpose area offers a snack bar, gift shop, two show areas, a play area, and a small petting zoo with pygmy goats and spotted Axis deer.

Another small playground is located across from the African elephant exhibit.

NEW AT THE ZOO

Because of extensive hurricane damage, much of the infra-structure and landscaping here is new. The next exhibit to open will be the reopening of Wings of Asia. In the distant future there are plans for new **South American exhibits** that will complete the African loop, a huge **Batchelor Foundation Rainforest and Education Center**, and a **Cuban Parrot's Plaza** with parrots, macaws, and other colorful birds.

North Carolina Zoological Park

Route 4, Box 83
Asheboro, North Carolina 27203
(919) 879-7000

Hours: *9-5 weekdays, 10-6 weekends and holidays, April-October; 9-4 daily, rest of year.*
Admission Fees: *Adults $5, 63+ and 2-12 $3. Participates in reciprocity program. Tram $1.*

Directions: *From I-85 westbound, take Exit 122 (U.S. Highway 220) South. Follow Highway 220 for 27 miles to Asheboro. From I-85 eastbound, take Exit 96 (U.S. Highway 64) East. Follow Highway 64 for 23 miles to Asheboro. In Asheboro, follow signs to N.C. Highway 159 (Zoo Parkway), then go south 6 miles to zoo entrance.*

Don't Miss: *African Pavilion, R.J. Reynolds Forest Aviary, African Plains, Desert Pavilion, Forest Glade (gorillas), Forest Edge, Chimpanzee Habitat. It is tempting to list the entire zoo in this category.*

Touring Tips: *The total distance on foot to all of the African exhibits is 2 miles. A tram provides easy transportation around the entire zoo, arriving at six convenient stops every 20 minutes. Riders may get on and off all day at no extra charge. Picnic areas are available, as are lockers to store lunch while touring the zoo. Food selection is limited at the far end of the zoo. Binoculars are useful for viewing distant animals. Kids love the carnivorous Venus fly traps that are for sale in one of the gift shops.*

Entertainment: *Special shows and programs are presented in the large outdoor Amphitheater.*

The world's largest "pure" zoo, the 1,448-acre North Carolina Zoo is found in rural Randolph County—far from any major city. As the first state-owned zoo, it was placed in this central location in 1971 so as to be within reach of the state's three largest metropolitan areas. Most animals thrive in large natural habitats, but not all of its expansive acreage is currently in use. In fact, the current African area occupies only 300 acres, but this area alone makes it one of the country's largest zoos.

In addition to its immense size, it is famous for attention to detail in creating an authentic African atmosphere. A paved footpath leads through a mature Piedmont forest. Along this main path are side trails to the animal habitats, which are not visible from the main path or within view of each other, making each of these exhibits an exciting adventure.

This zoo has gone to extremes in putting together a complete collection of African animals. It is awesome to consider that this effort is only the beginning. A Master Plan projects six new exhibit areas, all comparable to the African area, including North America, South America, Australia, Europe, Asia, and the World of Seas. If these new areas approach the excellence of the African area, the North Carolina Zoo will be the 21st century's best zoo.

FEATURED EXHIBITS

The **Forest Edge** is the first exhibit many visitors see. This hillside habitat features giraffes, zebras, ostriches, and African crowned cranes that roam in and out of view of the four different viewing points. The 3-acres of tall grass, boulders, and termite mounds look extremely realistic.

Of the three different exhibits of gorillas, the **Forest Glade** habitat is best. Resembling an open forest clearing, the habitat provides its residents with volcanic boulders to play on, a stream to drink from, and many edible plants to dine on. Kwanza was born in 1989. He is the zoo's first gorilla baby and lives with his par-

ents and another adult female. The
gorillas often come close to the shel-
tered viewing windows.

Another chance to watch great
apes is available at the **Chimpanzee
Habitat**. Termite mounds and fallen
trees are scattered throughout the tall
grass, making the troop of ten chimpanzees feel at home. When they desire privacy, the chimps can disappear over a hill, out of view of the
large, shaded overlook.

The **African Pavilion** is the
zoo's main feature. From the outside,
this 96-foot-high building looks like
a giant tent, but inside small habitats
resembling swamps, jungles, and
grassland savannas are home to 25
animal species. The towering enclosure for the colobus monkeys is visible immediately. A winding downhill path passes colorful mandrill
baboons, slender gerenuk antelope,
and rare wattled cranes. A spot-

Gorillas

necked otter is seen swimming in a glass-fronted pool or playing in a cascading
stream. Brilliant blue and orange cichlids (fish), whistling ducks, Demoiselle cranes,
and dwarf crocodiles are also a part of the aquatic swamp area. Meerkats, colorful
African birds, crested porcupines, bat-eared foxes, caracals, patas monkeys, servals,
and huge ball pythons are all displayed with easy viewing access. The animals
here live among over 2,500 African trees and plants. Outside, the building is surrounded with yards for gorillas, gerenuks, a pair of African leopards, and a pack of
Cape hunting dogs.

In the back of the pavilion is an overlook for the expansive 37-acre **African
Plains**—the zoo's most amazing exhibit. It alone is as large as many entire zoos.
The panoramic view covers the horizon and, with the exhibit's grassy slopes and
watering holes, it could easily be mistaken for the real African veldt. Using mounted binoculars, 12 different kinds of antelope can be identified, including endangered red lechwe. The four species of land birds are easier to find, especially the
gorgeous saddle-billed storks.

Before the opening of the North American exhibits, the only non-African animals were found in the **R.J. Reynolds Forest Aviary**. Serious bird-watchers and
casual observers all react with similar disbelief at the beauty found inside this trans-
parent-domed giant greenhouse. A colorful folder is provided to help identify the

more than 150 birds of over 50 species that fly and hide among the palm, banana, fig, and screw pine trees. Some visitors walk slowly along the winding pathway through the dense indoor rain forest. Others relax on a bench while trying to spot the colorful birds. Finding some of the prettiest birds requires extra patience. Some gems to look for include Lady Ross touracos, grey-headed kingfishers, and endangered Palawan peacock pheasants. In the spring, nests can be seen.

OTHER EXHIBITS

The **Elephant Habitat** and the **Southern White Rhinoceros Habitat** appear to be attached to the African Plains. Though they have a lot of room to roam, elephants and rhinos are kept near the visitors by the pools placed strategically near the over-

Elephant Habitat

looks. When covered with bright red southern clay, they are popular with photographers.

At the **Lion Habitat,** a pride of five lions can be seen through a viewing window at lion-level or from a high vantage point overlooking their entire rocky grotto. The stars of the **Hamadryas Baboon Habitat** scamper all over the bare tree limbs and rocky ledges of their island home. The newest African exhibit is the **Wart Hog Habitat**, found in the forest along the main footpath.

FOR THE KIDS

Portable yellow and white Smart Carts are stationed throughout the zoo to let children experience animals by touching such items as ostrich eggs and snake skins. Zoo volunteers are available to answer questions.

The **Touch and Learn Center** will be one of eight areas in the new North American region. In the barnyard children will be able to pet calves, goats, donkeys, and a variety of other domestic animals.

NEW AT THE ZOO

The North American region is scheduled to open in the fall of 1994. It will occupy over 200 acres, nearly doubling the zoo's present size, and will display 95 species of animals in 40 new exhibits that promise to be as naturalistic as those in the African region.

The **Cypress Swamp** will feature alligators and cougars, while the nearby **Marsh** will be home to golden eagles and native snakes. The **Streamside** will be an indoor/outdoor habitat for bobcats, raccoons, and otters, and it will also feature a game fish aquarium. A tundra world will be re-created in the **Rocky Coast** with polar bears, seals, arctic foxes, and puffins. The **Great Plains** habitat will have bison, deer, elk, and prairie dogs within its 10 acres. Black bears, grizzly bears, and gray wolves will be in the **North Woods** habitat.

North America's **Sonoran Desert Exhibit** opened in late 1993. The Sonoran Desert of the Southwest is replicated under an 85-foot-diameter glass dome. The more than 30 animal species here include various desert reptiles, roadrunners, occlots, and jaguarundis displayed among cacti and sand. Cacomistles and vampire bats reside in nocturnal caves.

Riverbanks Zoological Park

500 Wildlife Parkway
Columbia, South Carolina 29202
(803) 779-8730 or 779-8717

Hours: *9-4 weekdays, 9-5 weekends, April-October; 9-4 daily, rest of year. Closed Thanksgiving Day and Christmas Day.*
Admission Fees: *Adults $4, 63+ $2.50, 3-12 $1.75. Participates in reciprocity program.*
Directions: *On I-77 Southbound or I-20, take Exit 64 onto I-26 South. From I-26 or I-77 Northbound, take Exit 108 (I-126 East). Follow I-126 to Greystone Boulevard Exit. Follow signs to zoo.*
Don't Miss: *ARC (Aquarium Reptile Complex), Birdhouse, African Plains, polar bear and sea lion exhibits, Siamang Island.*
Touring Tips: *The Kenya Cafe is one of the better zoo restaurants. It offers a good selection of fast food and a chance to dine while observing the African Plains animals.*
Entertainment: *Tropical rainstorms occur three to five times daily in the Birdhouse. A milking demonstration is given in the morning in the Riverbanks Farm's barn. Fish feeding and diving demonstrations are presented twice daily in the ARC's coral reef exhibit. Other animal feedings include sea lions and penguins. Check guidemap for schedule.*

Columbia, South Carolina's capital city, seems an unlikely place for one of the nation's great zoos. However, though Columbia has a population of under a half-million, the Riverbanks Zoo pulls in 900,000 annual visitors, making it, per capita, one of the most visited zoos in the country.

Having opened in 1974, it is also one of the nation's newer zoos and was designed using modern exhibit technology. Nearly all of the animals are separated from visitors by non-visible barriers such as moats, water, or light.

FEATURED EXHIBITS

The main attraction is undoubtedly the new **Aquarium Reptile Complex**, known as the **ARC**. Through five distinct galleries, visitors are taken on a trip that starts close to home and progresses farther and farther away. The *South Carolina Gallery* features rattlesnakes from the pine flatwoods, water snakes from the cypress swamps, and long gars from Lake Murray. In the *Desert Gallery*, a room-sized diorama of sand and cacti is inhabited by various Sonoran Desert lizards, including gila monsters. Across the hall, sandfish (lizards from Africa) are seen "swimming" in the sand. The *Tropical Habitat* offers a walk through a lush glass-domed rain forest. Giant anaconda snakes, electric eels, piranhas, Malayan water monitors, and false gavial crocodiles swim in eye-level aquariums. Some of the world's most beautiful and most poisonous snakes are on display in the *Tropical Gallery*: eyelash vipers, green mambas, and king cobras. The *Ocean Gallery* is the ARC's climax. Crystal-clear, non-reflecting glass panels allow floor-to-ceiling views of sharks, moray eels, and more than 400 colorful reef fish in a spectacular 55,000-gallon coral reef tank. A small, walk-in chamber with special curved glass allows viewers the unique experience of seeing jewel-colored fish all around them. Other exhibits include a wolf eel tank and a cylinder-shaped aquarium with loggerhead sea turtles.

Until recently, the **Birdhouse** was the zoo's focal point. All around the inside wall of the circular building, habitats are strikingly re-created for birds from the seashore, desert, and other natural areas. The rain forest aviary is noted for its scheduled thunderstorms. In the rotunda, black-footed penguins and diving ducks can be watched underwater. Wire mesh enclosures surround the outside of the building with an impressive collection of birds—from exotic emerald toucanets and sun conures to rarely-seen birds of prey that include milky eagle owls, ornate hawk eagles, and white-bellied sea eagles.

The **African Plains** exhibit was renovated in 1991. The 4-acre simulated savanna is inhabited by black rhinos, zebras, giraffes, and ostriches.

Seeing the polar bears dive into their deep blue pool is especially inviting on a hot summer day. Featuring a towering waterfall flowing from a rocky cliff background, this is one of the world's larger polar bear enclosures. An underground tunnel takes visitors to underwater viewing panels. Across the path, an equally attractive sea lion pool allows the graceful mammals to swim under and in front of rocky ledges. Harbor seals enjoy their own pool nearby.

A deep water moat encircles rocky, tree-studded **Siamang Island**, home to the zoo's only apes. The siamangs' bellowing calls can be heard all over the zoo.

OTHER EXHIBITS

The first exhibit most visitors see is the long **African elephant yard**. Next to it is a fenced yard with a pool for the Nile hippo. Two **South American yards** feature rheas, a lively pair of capybaras, and one of the few U.S. displays of Baird's tapirs.

The **Small Mammals** exhibits are found in long, open tunnels, where the main path has been completely covered. A wide variety of small monkeys, rare cats, exotic birds, and other animals are displayed in glass-fronted habitats that allow close-up viewing. Notable occupants include lion-tailed macaques, various tamarins, ruffed lemurs, clouded leopards, Chinese alligators, meerkats, and the world's largest group of black howler monkeys.

Four stone grottoes display animals from four regions of the world. Middle Eastern Hamadryas baboons and Nubian ibexes live together. South America is repre-sented by spectacled bears in a grassy habitat with black-handed spider monkeys living on a ledge behind them. A similar configura-tion displays African lions in front of brilliant mandrill baboons. Siberian tigers occupy the fourth grotto by themselves.

The pretty **flamingo pond** and the **waterfowl pond** are among the zoo's best photo spots.

Flamingo and Chick

FOR THE KIDS

The **Riverbanks Farm** was a part of the zoo's recent expansion. Corrals hold goats, sheep, dairy and beef cattle, and Belgian horses for through-the-fence pet-ting. Inside the large barn are more animal pens and a milking parlor where daily demonstrations are held. A special exhibit, *The Backyard Garden*, shows some of the food products grown in local South Carolina gardens.

NEW AT THE ZOO

In 1994, the 70-acre **Riverbanks Botanical Garden** will open across the Saluda River from the current zoo. A tram will shuttle interested visitors across a bridge to the *Visitors Center*. Situated on a Civil War skirmish site, this attraction will dis-play formal gardens in such areas as the *Native Woodland Garden*, the *Bog and Stream Garden*, and the *Native Azalea Bank*.

As fine an exhibit as it is, the current Birdhouse is showing serious signs of age. Recent plans call for its destruction and replacement with a beautiful walk-through **Bird Garden** and a new indoor **Bird Center** featuring an expanded penguin exhibit.

Zoo Atlanta

800 Cherokee Avenue S.E.
Atlanta, Georgia 30315
(404) 624-5678

Hours: *10-5 Monday-Friday, 10-6 Saturday-Sunday, during Daylight Savings Time; 10-5 daily, rest of year. Ticket office closes 30 minutes before listed closing time. Closed on New Year's Day, Martin Luther King Day, Thanksgiving Day, and Christmas Day.*
Admission Fees: *Adults $7.50, 61+ $6.50, 3-11 $5. Participates in reciprocity program. Zoo Atlanta Train $1.*
Directions: *Located in Grant Park. From downtown, take I-20 East to Exit 26 (Boulevard). Follow south 1/2 mile to zoo, on the right. By MARTA, take buses 31, 32, 97, or the Zoo Trolley from the Five Points rail station.*
Don't Miss: *Ford African Rain Forest, Masai Mara, Mzima Springs, Ketambe, Monkeys of Makokou, Harimau Hutan Tiger Forest, World of Reptiles.*
Touring Tips: *Down-home Southern cooking, including fried chicken, and plenty of Dixie atmosphere are on hand at the Okefenokee Cafe. Outside the front gate, the Visitor's Center features the Flamingo Gift Shop and the indoor Safari Cafe. Civil War buffs should visit the Atlanta Cyclorama located just outside the main entrance.*
Entertainment: *The **African Elephant Demonstration** is presented three times daily, year-round, in the **Elephant Demo Yard**. The **Wildlife Show** is held in the outdoor **Kroger Wildlife Theatre** many times daily during summer. Snakes, birds, and small mammals are featured in demonstrations at the small **Elder's Tree Theatre** at the entrance to the Ford African Rain Forest. Animal feedings include gorillas.*

Atlanta, now the capital of the New South, has a history of rising from the ashes. Its zoo has a similar history. First opened in 1889, the former Atlanta Zoo is the South's oldest zoo. Unfortunately, in 1984 it was rated by the Humane Society as one of the nation's ten worst zoos. In response, the city hired new management which immediately began a multi-million dollar facelift of the grounds. The focus of this renovation was to move the animals, including the famous gorilla Willie B, out of bar-and-concrete cages into natural habitats. To disassociate itself from its infamous past image, its name was changed to Zoo Atlanta. Over half of the planned new habitats are open, and the public has responded favorably. Annual attendance has steadily increased, and membership has multiplied ten-fold. In 1996 Atlanta will be focused on by the world as it hosts the Summer Olympics. By then, its zoo might be listed on most Top Ten lists.

FEATURED EXHIBITS

Willie B, a 450-pound silverback gorilla, has been the symbol of this zoo ever since he arrived in 1961. He also has become a symbol of its rebirth. For 27 years, he lived alone in a tile and concrete cage with only a TV set for company. When the

Ford African Rain Forest opened in 1988, TV cameras were on the spot to see Willie B join three other gorilla families in their spectacular new home. Four habitats on 1 1/2 acres are separated by hidden moats. The exhibit, designed to resemble a clearing in the Cameroon rain forest, is built on a sloping, grassy hillside with over 3,500 shrubs and bushes planted around existing tall trees. Banana trees and bamboo plants enhance the tropical effect. The apes can be observed from many excellent vantage points as they forage for food, challenge each other across unseen moats, and care for their babies. Two of these observation points are the *Takemenda Research Camp* overlook platform and the *Gorillas of Cameroon* interpretive building, which has both a seating area behind a wide window for close-up views and a continuous video presentation about gorillas.

The **Monkeys of Makokou** is another lush habitat for black-faced drill baboons and mona monkeys. The monkeys can be viewed from both an outdoor viewing platform and a viewing window in the interpretive building for the *Sanaga Overlook*—a walk-through aviary of brightly-colored African birds.

Another part of Africa is re-created in **Masai Mara**, named for a savanna game reserve in Kenya. The panoramic view of the open African plains—with honey locust trees, tall grasses, and termite mounds—has a uniquely Georgia look because of the bright red clay soil the state is famous for. As a result, the giraffes, zebras, impala, gazelles, and ostriches are all tinted orange. Only a stream-filled moat separates visitors from the endangered black rhinos in their adjacent savanna yard.

Mzima Springs, an extension of Masai Mara, features "red" elephants. The African elephants, which are contained in a large yard with a muddy pool, are usually covered with the red clay. In addition to the Demonstration Yard, there is also *Nyumba Ya Tembo* (House of Elephants)—an interpretive building with informative graphics. The lions, which often bask on kopje rock outcrops, are best seen from a covered glass viewing station.

Just up the path from the gorillas is a large group of Sumatran orangutans living in **Ketambe**, a simulated Indonesian rain forest. They have an assortment of objects to play with and climb on, including ropes and tall trees. An orangutan can often be seen at the top of a 55-foot-tall tree. Like the gorillas, the orangutans have been very prolific, so there are often babies to watch. In a nearby small marsh exhibit, elegant Sarus cranes are displayed.

The **Harimau Hutan Tiger Forest** is another habitat for Indonesian animals. The indoor visitor area offers seating and a wide viewing window to observe the rare Sumatran tigers up on their lush, grassy hillside yard. Featuring bamboo groves, rocky crevices, and waterfalls, the yard is designed to look like an Indonesian forest glade.

The exhibits in the **World of Reptiles** building are quite ordinary, but the extensive collection of reptiles and amphibians living in those exhibits is anything but. The variety of rattlesnakes, cobras, vipers, and mambas are part of one of the most extensive collections of venomous snakes anywhere. Lesser known deadly serpents include bushmasters, death adders, urutus, and taipans from Australia.

Many other interesting and unusual animals live in this building, including gharials, giant salamanders, anacondas, Mexican beaded lizards, bog turtles, alligator snapping turtles, and poison dart frogs.

OTHER EXHIBITS

Flamingo Plaza, part of the new entry area, was the first of the new exhibits. A flock of Chilean flamingos wade here in a pretty pool in front of a lush, green background of marsh plants. The visitor services building is modeled after an African hut and features a 30-foot-high thatched roof.

Remnants of the old zoo still survive in the moated stone grottoes for bald eagles, Kodiak bears; and Asiatic black bears. The adjacent sea lion pool, with its large seating area and snack bar, is a great place to rest. A small exhibit building is the new home of the giant Indian fruit bats, also known as flying foxes.

FOR THE KIDS

The **Children's Zoo** offers a wide array of animals and activities. The *OK-To-Touch Corral* has potbellied pigs, llamas, goats, and a Sicilian donkey available for little hands. At the center of this zoo is a fenced yard with many giant Aldabra tortoises. Many exotic birds and small primates, including hornbills and lemurs, are found here in separate cages. Another nearby yard exhibits emus (tall Australian land birds).

At the train station, the **Zoo Atlanta Train** can be caught for a ride through an underground tunnel and around the exhibit's perimeter. New in 1993, the *Egleston Ark Smart Playground for Younger Children* is a highlight of the Children's Zoo. In addition to 12 rocking animals, the playground features a colorful ark with steering wheels, binoculars, climbing nets, and a slide.

NEW AT THE ZOO

The zoo's renovation, though already very impressive, is far from complete. The next new exhibits, as specified by a new plan, will include the **Okefenokee Swamp**, a **Coastal Lagoon**, a **Koala Station**, and a **Conservation Village**. Also in the future, the Children's Zoo will be remade into the **International Farms**.

BEST OF THE REST

Birmingham Zoo
2630 Cahaba Road
Birmingham, Alabama 35223
(205) 879-0408

This zoo claims to be the first to arrange its animals by life-style themes. In the Social Animals building, creatures whose survival depends on social behavior are exhibited, including red wolves, orangutans, mandrills, baboons, leaf-cutter ants, and piranhas. The other themed building, The Predators, houses animals that eat other animals and includes everything from insects to big cats. Monkey Island, with its playful spider monkeys, is one of the zoo's most popular places. The Birds & Reptiles building is populated with rattlesnakes, cobras, tortoises, lizards, and an assortment of colorful birds. Other exhibits include bear grottoes with three varieties, a Marine Mammals complex with sea lions, a Pachyderms Building (with Asian elephants, rhinos, and hippos), a Small Mammals area, two hoofstock areas, cheetahs, and a full collection of ratites—ostriches, emus, rheas, and cassowaries. The Magic City Express train circles through most of the zoo grounds.

Central Florida Zoological Park
3755 N. US 17/92
Lake Monroe, Florida 32747
(407) 323-4450

Located 22 miles north of Orlando, this is the major zoo closest to Disney World. Under a covering of towering palm, cypress, and Spanish moss-draped oak trees, most of this beautiful zoo is seen from raised, winding boardwalks. The new Florida Trek boardwalk trail gives tourists a good sampling of the Sunshine State's native wildlife. The renowned cat collection includes Bengal tigers, black leopards, cougars, and a new exhibit of clouded leopards. The collection of small cats is highlighted by rarely-exhibited jaguarundis. The Herpetarium features rare crocodiles and a wide variety of venomous snakes, including spitting cobras. Also noteworthy are the mandrill baboons, the rhinoceros hornbills, and the Children's Zoo and elephant rides.

Jackson Zoological Park
2918 West Capitol Street
Jackson, Mississippi 39209
(601) 352-2585

This rapidly improving zoo is in the heart of Mississippi's capital city. Its premier exhibit, the 15-acre African Rain Forest, is seen from a boardwalk. This boardwalk trail leads past pygmy hippos, servals, monkeys, and a jungle-style island populated with chimpanzees. The adjoining African Plains features cheetahs and white rhinos. In the new Discovery Zoo, children can pet animals in the contact area or pretend to be a prairie dog, spider, turtle, or baby bird in a larger-than-life nature playground. A full complement of big cats, African elephants, Cape buffalo, orangutans, and sea lions are also displayed, and there is an exhibit of native Mississippi wildlife.

Jacksonville Zoological Park
8605 Zoo Road
Jacksonville, Florida 32218
(904) 757-4463

Despite its strong African theme, this zoo is most famous for breeding black jaguars. The Okavango Trail, named for the Okavango River in southern Africa, leads past crocodiles, porcupines, and other animals native to that region. The trail ends at the Okavango Village Petting Zoo, which is populated with African domestic animals. In Chimpanorama, playful chimpanzees entertain on their own island. The 11-acre Plains of Serengeti is the home of white rhinos, Cape buffalo, and other savanna animals. Within view of the savanna antelope, the new Mahali Pa Simba lion habitat is the first stage of an ambitious Master Plan designed to make this a first-class zoo. The Florida Wetlands has a winding boardwalk that passes plants and animals native to the Sunshine State. A free-flight Aviary with rare Pondicherry vultures, a scenic train ride, and an Elephant Encounters show are also a part of this attractive zoo.

Lowry Park Zoological Garden
7530 North Boulevard
Tampa, Florida 33604
(813) 935-8552

With its focus on Asian and Floridian animals, this zoo is a perfect complement to the sensational African exhibits of Busch Gardens (also in Tampa). This is the only public zoo where the much-loved and endangered manatees can be seen. They are the main attraction of the new Manatee and Aquatic Center, which includes spectacular underwater viewing opportunities. The modern center also includes the Manatee Hospital, where speedboat-injured manatees can recover from their wounds. Other endangered Florida animals can be seen along a winding boardwalk in the Florida Wildlife Center. Most notable are the bison (extinct in Florida), black bears, red wolves, and a Florida panther—one of the state's most threatened animals. The Asian Domain features a set of natural habitats that exhibit

Manatee

some of the continent's largest and rarest animals, including Asian elephants, Indian rhinos, Malayan tapirs, Persian leopards, Sumatran tigers, sloth bears, Arabian oryxes, and Bactrian camels. The more than 14 species in Primate World include chimpanzees, mandrills, orangutans, woolly monkeys, and tiny marmosets. There is also a petting zoo in the Children's Village and a Free Flight Aviary filled with over 60 types of colorful tropical birds.

Montgomery Zoo
321 Vandiver Boulevard
Montgomery, Alabama 36110
(205) 240-4900

Located on the north side of Alabama's capital city, this zoo expanded from 6 to 40 acres in 1991. In its center, the Overlook features a restaurant and a train station and offers an impressive view in all directions of the cageless habitats that are neatly divided into four continents. In the African Realm, the new African Primate Exhibit has large natural habitats for chimpanzees and colobus monkeys. In a spacious savanna yard, zebras and antelope roam in full view of lions and cheetahs—their natural predators. A similar predator/prey set-up is in the North American Realm where mountain lions can watch pronghorns and bison. There is also an Australian Realm, an Asian Realm with an impressive new tiger habitat, and a new state-of-the-art reptile exhibit.

Virginia Zoological Park
3500 Granby Street
Norfolk, Virginia 23504
(804) 441-2706

Norfolk is home to the state's only major zoo. A complete assembly of pachyderms—African elephants, white rhinos, Nile hippos, and Central American tapirs—are found in the Large Mammals Building. A cute pair of Siberian tiger cubs recently joined the clouded leopards in the Cat Exhibit. In addition to bison and sea lions, the zoo also features an interesting collection of primates, reptiles, and birds. Many beautiful flowers are found around the grounds, which also includes a Botanical Conservatory.

MORE ZOOS

Alligatorland Safari Zoo *(Kissimmee, Florida)*
Discovery Island Zoological Park *(Lake Buena Vista, Florida)*
Dreher Park Zoo *(West Palm Beach, Florida)*
Greenville Zoo *(Greenville, South Carolina)*
Hollywild Animal Park *(Inman, South Carolina)*

Jungle Larry's Zoological Park at Caribbean Gardens *(Naples, Florida)*
Mill Mountain Zoological Park *(Roanoke, Virginia)*
Nashville Zoo *(Nashville, Tennessee)*
Pine Mountain Wild Animal Park *(Pine Mountain, Georgia)*
Santa Fe Teaching Zoo *(Gainesville, Florida)*
The Zoo *(Gulf Breeze, Florida)*
Tote-Em-In Zoo *(Wilmington, North Carolina)*
Waccatee Zoo *(Myrtle Beach, South Carolina)*

South Central Zoos

Audubon Park & Zoological Garden

6500 Magazine Street
New Orleans, Louisiana 70118
(504) 861-2537

Hours: *9:30-4:30 daily. Closed Mardi Gras Day and Christmas Day.*
Admission Fees: *Adults $7.50, 66+ and 2-12 $3.50. Participates in reciprocity program. Mombasa Railroad $1. Camel rides: adults $2, 66+ and 2-12 $1.50.*
Directions: *From I-10, take Exit 232 (S.Carrollton) and follow signs to zoo. From the French Quarter, ride the St. Charles Avenue streetcar to Audubon Park, where a free shuttle bus to zoo is provided. Also, the* **John James Audubon** *riverboat cruises the Mississippi River to and from the zoo.*
Don't Miss: *Louisiana Swamp, Whitney Asian Domain, World of Primates, Reptile Encounter, Pathways to the Past, Tropical Bird House, sea lion show, Wisner Children's Village, Australian Outback, South American Pampas.*
Touring Tips: *The Cypress Knee Cafe, located within the Louisiana Swamp exhibit, offers Cajun specialties such as gumbo, meat pies, and jambalaya. A shaded outdoor picnic area provides views of swamp creatures. A guided tram-tour of the zoo's perimeter is available on the Mombasa Railroad.*
Entertainment: *Excellent sea lion shows are presented one to three times daily, Wednesday-Sunday, in the rocky cove known as* **Sea Lion Theater***. Also very good are the elephant shows in the Asian Domain, presented twice daily Wednesday-Sunday.* **Sun Bear Activity** *shows are given once every morning. Live animal presentations take place regularly in* **Wendy's Wildlife Theatre***. Check the insert given with the Visitor's Guide for show times. Animal feedings include sea lions.*

Less than 20 years ago the Audubon Zoo was called an "animal ghetto" and was threatened with closure by the government. Since then, extensive renovations have made it possibly the best zoo between San Diego and New York. It was one of the first to exhibit its animals with geo-graphical themes and, in fact, has large exhibit areas dedicated to five different continents.

Within its 58 acres, this zoo has a problem most zoos would love to have—too much plant growth. The tropical exhibits are nearly overgrown with lush vegetation, including banana palms, while the open areas have towering oak trees covered with hanging Spanish moss. This makes for a beautiful setting.

FEATURED EXHIBITS

Few zoos offer their visitors a chance to experience the wildlife and culture of the local region as well as this one does. With its award-winning **Louisiana Swamp** exhibit, 5 acres were allowed to revert to their original state as an authentic cypress swamp. An elevated boardwalk

White Alligator

winds past natural exhibits featuring the diverse wildlife found in the Louisiana bayous—black bears, cougars, raccoons, armadillos, nutrias, otters, red foxes, and,

Sumatran Tigers

of course, alligators. Signs of the bayou's human presence are seen in the abandoned shrimp boats and houseboats floating in the swamp, and Cajun shacks are built along the swamp's edge. An open building, *Le Cypriere*, displays some of the poisonous snakes and other reptiles and amphibians from the bayou. Local insects and fish, including toothy alligator gars, are also displayed. The zoo's most famous residents, the white alligators, are also here. (These beautiful blue-eyed gators were found in a local marsh. Due to their diminished hunting ability, they would not survive in the wild. They and their siblings at the downtown Aquarium are the world's only known white alligators.)

A solemn Indian Temple with two elephant statue fountains marks the entrance to the **Asian Domain**, which is one of the more complete displays of Asian wildlife. From a raised wooden walkway visitors can view sun bears, Asian lions, leopards, sacred ibises, and elephants. Some are in natural habitats complete with plunging waterfalls. The large variety of Asian hoofstock include Axis deer, hog deer, swamp deer, and blackbuck antelope. The star of the Asian Domain is Suri, a rare white Bengal tiger. Just off the main trail is an attractive exhibit of brilliant-orange Sumatran tigers.

The center of the **Australian Outback** is a lush walk-through aviary that displays laughing kookaburas. Other animals from Down Under include emus, wallabies, and a koala.

The **South American Pampas** is one of the better exhibits of that continent. Another elevated boardwalk gives views across a large swampy lake to a flock of Caribbean flamingos, guanacos, Brazilian tapirs, and capybaras. The tapirs and capybaras are often completely submerged in the lake.

A side path off the main trail leads through the **World of Primates**. Some of the most acrobatic monkeys and apes reside here, including black and white ruffed lemurs, spider monkeys, colobus monkeys, siamangs, howler monkeys, red-capped mangabeys, and Diana monkeys. Each of the habitats is landscaped with waterfalls and large boulders and equipped with a maze of ropes, sticks, and logs for climbing. Smaller golden lion tamarins, pygmy marmosets (in cages), and a family of gorillas are also exhibited, and the zoo is quite proud of its pair of twin adolescent orangutans.

The newest exhibits are three modern buildings at the front of the zoo. The first to open was **Reptile Encounter** in 1987. Over 200 reptiles and amphibians of more than 100 mostly exotic species are displayed in swamp, desert, or forest habitats. The most noteworthy exhibits include the false gavial crocodiles, the extremely poisonous king cobras and green mambas, a sea turtle aquarium, and an educational rattlesnake area.

John J. Audubon, the zoo's namesake, is remembered with a statue on the grounds. As a painter of birds he would certainly have enjoyed the **Tropical Bird House**, which re-creates a South American rain forest under a glass roof. Many of the over 70 species of jewel-colored birds fly freely, while some are contained behind harp wire. The hornbills and many different kinds of toucans, most notably a rainbow-colored keel-billed toucan, are especially memorable.

Between these two buildings, the characteristics birds and reptiles share with dinosaurs are explored in the hands-on museum, **Pathways to the Past**. A small animated dinosaur greets visitors as they enter. Dinosaur eggs and fossils are among the many topics explored using hi-tech, educational, and fun exhibits.

OTHER EXHIBITS

The South American Pampas is a part of the larger **Grasslands of the World** area. The **North American Prairie** exhibit—with American bison, collared peccaries, tule elk, and wild turkeys—is viewed from the other side of the same boardwalk.

The final part of the Grasslands area is the **African Savanna** exhibit. Ostriches, kori bustards, bongo antelope, and white rhinos share a wide-open savanna, while giraffes, zebras, and cheetahs live in separate enclosures across the path. Nearby, hippos submerge themselves in a pool of crystal-clear water.

The **Odenheimer Complex**, which looks like an ancient Greek coliseum, stands out from a distance. Below its tall pillars is a beautiful rocky sea lion pool with underwater viewing. Highly-endangered red wolves are in a secluded exhibit of their own. The enormous walk-through **Audubon Flight Exhibit**, which features wading birds and waterfowl, is so rich with tropical vegetation that it is sometimes hard to find.

FOR THE KIDS

The **Wisner Children's Village** offers fun-filled diversions. In addition to a large petting yard with goats and sheep, there are two playgrounds and tunnels that kids can climb through to pop up within the prairie dog town. A special area, *Giants of the Past*, emphasizes the tragedy of extinction with giant statues of extinct animals that children can climb on. *Animals of the Night* is a small nocturnal exhibit where owl monkeys, bats, and ringtails can be seen. Other popular animals displayed include ground hornbills, dwarf mongooses, bat-eared foxes, chinchillas, and a flock of brown pelicans—the Louisiana state bird.

Camel rides are available in the Asian Domain.

NEW AT THE ZOO

The zoo's newest star is Leo, a San Francisco-born koala. (In 1992, the Audubon Zoo became only the tenth U.S. zoo to exhibit koalas.)

Plans are underway for an alligator-themed museum that will feature the zoo's famous white alligators.

Caldwell Zoo

2203 Martin Luther King Boulevard
Tyler, Texas 75702
(903) 534-2169

Hours: *9:30-6 daily, April-September; 9:30-4:30, rest of year. Closed New Year's Day, Thanksgiving Day, and Christmas Day.*
Admission Fees: *Free.*
Directions: *From I-20: Eastbound, take Exit 556 South (Highway 69), follow for 8 miles and turn left onto Martin Luther King Boulevard; zoo is immediately on the left. Westbound, take Exit 571A South (Highway 271), follow for 8 miles to Loop Highway 323 West. Follow Loop 323 for 3 miles, turn left onto Highway 69, then a quick left onto Martin Luther King Boulevard and another left into zoo.*

Don't Miss: *East Africa, Native Texas habitats.*
Touring Tips: *A themed visitor center in the middle of the East Africa area offers a spectacular view. Across from the gift shop, a fast-food cafe has covered outdoor tables overlooking the sweeping panorama of elephants, giraffes, antelope, zebras, and lions in their open, natural setting. Large picnic areas are available elsewhere.*
Entertainment: *Milking demonstrations are presented in the Texas Farm.*

Located about an hour east of Dallas, the Caldwell Zoo provides a diversion for families traveling across northern Texas. It is free, compact, and exhibits a wide variety of exotic animals in beautiful natural habitats. The animals are arranged into three continental regions. After entering the zoo, visitors start on one of three different paths that lead to Native Texas, East Africa, or South America.

This zoo exists as a testament to the generosity, vision, and dedication of D. K. Caldwell, who opened the facility in 1954 for the children of the Caldwell Playschool and East Texas. Owned and operated by the Caldwell Schools, Inc., the zoo is designed especially for children and, in accordance with Mr. Caldwell's wishes, is still free of charge.

FEATURED EXHIBITS

The largest and most impressive area is the open savanna of **East Africa**. *Phases I and II* of this natural section opened in 1987 on 6 acres. A central grassland is grazed by three types of antelope, rare Grevy's zebras, and savanna land birds. In front of the antelope yard, African elephants occupy a dusty island and giraffes tramp in front of a tall log fence. Water moats that separate these large animals are essentially concealed. This scenic panorama is seen from a replicated African village where thatched roofs cover the gift shop, cafe, and outdoor terrace. On the other side of an interpretive building, which displays illuminated pictures of the African culture, a pretty plaza displays African flamingos and sacred ibises in a shallow lagoon. Down the hill, a large, fenced aviary holds crowned cranes, secretary birds, and a pack of rock hyraxes. Black rhinos can be watched in a spacious, open yard from an elevated vista. The long, grassy cheetah yard provides its residents with plenty of running space and has viewing windows on both sides. Spirited lemurs inhabit a rocky island in front of three waterfalls.

The award-winning *Phase III* of East Africa opened in 1991. The excited yaps of Cape hunting dogs can be heard from a covered viewing station at the area's entrance. In the *African Reptile/Aquarium* building, a plush, air-conditioned visitor area uses brightly-colored graphics to introduce the Nile crocodiles and African cichlid fish that swim in the long, glass-fronted brook. Behind the brook is a desert habitat for a variety of tortoises, lizards, and snakes—including an African egg-eating snake. Behind the reptiles, glass panels make the outdoor savanna animals a natural backdrop. Lions are also in view, but are better seen from an outdoor viewing station where they appear with their natural prey—zebras and antelope—behind them. The boardwalk leads on through a natural marsh under towering pine trees to a complex where three striking, popular animals are exhibited together in habitats enhanced by tall climbing trees, water holes, rocky cliffs, and waterfalls. The leopards, bongos, and colobus monkeys each have separate viewing ports, but they are always within view of each other.

A boardwalk leads visitors to the animals of **Native Texas**. A series of natural habitats built into the rocks allow very close viewing of coatis, gray foxes, birds, and otters. The rocky otter exhibit, with its waterfalls and underwater viewing, is especially pleasing. On the other side, the boardwalk overhangs a waterfowl pond that counts pelicans among its residents. The expansive *Texas Plains* prairie yard holds wild turkeys, deer, and American bison. The boardwalk continues past birds of prey and cats. In habitats resembling a rocky crag, predatory birds seen through thin harp wire include bald eagles, caracaras, and hawks. Four cat habitats are landscaped with branches, waterfalls, and streams and provide excellent viewing of bobcats, ocelots, mountain lions, and jaguars. The path then opens up and leads around the bison to a natural swamp populated with alligators and turtles.

OTHER EXHIBITS

Smaller animals from the Lone Star state are on display in the **Texas Reptile/ Aquarium**, which is part of the Native Texas area. Catfish, gars, and other fish from local ponds and streams swim in a wide, rocky aquarium. Numerous snakes, lizards, and turtles are displayed in habitat dioramas organized by the region of the state they come from. An assortment of rattlesnakes and other venomous snakes are among the most interesting residents.

The third zoogeographic area, **South America**, is seen along an uphill path shaded by overhanging tree branches. Entering this "Little Amazon," visitors pass flamingos and swans in a pretty waterfall pool, colorful macaws perched in tree branches, and toucans and endangered golden lion tamarins in small enclosures. A large flight cage is filled with tropical wading birds such as rosette spoonbills, scarlet ibises, and purple gallinules. The main exhibit of this area is the long, multi-species habitat that follows a curving path up the hill. Giant anteaters, tapirs, squirrel monkeys, capybaras, seriemas, and king vultures are among the amazing variety of animals that live together in this fenced enclosure. The habitat allows close-up viewing and is landscaped with rocks, trees, waterfalls, and a deep pool for the tapirs.

FOR THE KIDS

Also in the Native Texas area, the *Texas Farm* is the most child-oriented place in the zoo. The contact yard has a friendly flock of goats, sheep, and pigs that seem anxious to be petted. At the yard's entrance is a walk-through aviary with native birds such as quails, pheasants, and little blue herons. The residents of a small cow barn can be seen in an outdoor corral or in their barn stalls.

NEW AT THE ZOO

A small nocturnal building, which includes exhibits of sloths and owl monkeys, opened in 1992 in the South America area. This area is scheduled for a complete renovation in the near future. The renovated South America area will feature natural habitats, a new rain forest exhibit, and a reptile/aquarium building. Other future plans call for an insectovorium and the addition of a fourth continental region—**Asia**.

Dallas Zoo

621 East Clarendon Drive
Dallas, Texas 75203
(214) 946-5154

Hours: *9-5 daily. Closed Christmas Day.*
Admission Fees: *Adults $5, 65+ $4, 3-11 $2.50. Participates in reciprocity program. Monorail $1.50. Parking $2.*
Directions: *Located 3 miles south of downtown. From I-35E, take the Ewing Avenue Exit (southbound Exit 426A, northbound Exit 425C), then follow signs to zoo.*
Don't Miss: *Wilds of Africa (including monorail tour, Nature Trail, and Juke L. Hamon Gorilla Conservation Research Center); Bird, Reptile, & Amphibian Building.*
Touring Tips: *Nothing in the Wilds of Africa should be missed! Ride the monorail first, then walk the Nature Trail. The Ndebele Cafe has African food on its fast-food menu and offers outdoor seating amid colorful African decor.*
Entertainment: *Wildlife encounters are presented frequently in a stage area of the Children's Zoo. On weekends (weather permitting), the zoo hosts birds of prey shows, elephant demonstrations, and Meet the Keeper talks. Animal feedings include chameleons and birds of prey.*

Over 100 years old, the Dallas Zoo recently upgraded its position among Texas and U.S. zoos with the 1990 opening of the Wilds of Africa. It is one of the top zoo exhibits in the world. When completed, the exhibit will more than double the zoo's size. Dallas has the lofty goal of becoming the world's best zoo. This is a possibility if it continues building exhibits of the caliber of the Wilds of Africa.

FEATURED EXHIBITS

The **Wilds of Africa** is, without question, the premier exhibit here. Its attempt to exhibit the major habitats of one entire continent is unique among zoos. The six completed habitats give the remarkable illusion of actually being in Africa.

The first thing most visitors see is the *Wilds of Africa Plaza*, where every building (even the restrooms) is painted with brightly-colored geometric designs from the culture of the Ndebele tribe of southern Africa. Mandrill baboons, also brightly-colored, dwell in a large rocky habitat with a side window for close-up viewing.

The only way to see most of the Wilds of Africa is by monorail. Because all seats face the animals, everyone gets a good view. The *Forest Habitat*, at the start and end of the tour, is highlighted by elusive okapis in a dense forested enclosure. (Okapis are displayed in only seven U.S. zoos, and Dallas has one of the largest and most productive herds.) Bongos, which live in forested yards near suni antelope, are almost as stunning as the okapis. A sudden change in the landscape occurs when the monorail emerges into the *Mountain Habitat*, where vultures and Nubian ibexes are seen on a steep slope close to the riders. The *Woodland Habitat* features Egyptian geese in a splashing stream, with elands and sable antelope dodging in and out of view. In the *Predator-Prey Exhibit*, black leopards (predators) and tiny dik-dik antelope (prey) are very close to the monorail and to each other. Simulating the Nile, the *River Habitat* offers the most spectacular of the monorail views. The tour route parallels a bend in the wide, cascading river that is inhabited by sitatungas and Nile lechwe (aquatic antelope), a variety of waterfowl, and tall wading birds such as Goliath herons and white pelicans. Riders get a Disneyland-style thrill when the monorail passes behind a waterfall. The terrain is noticeably drier at the *Desert Habitat*, which is home to scimitar-horned oryxes, addra gazelles, slender-horned gazelles, and addax—all of which are endangered. Popular animals within the *Bush Habitat* include Grevy's zebras, gerenuks, greater kudus, and ostriches. A huge baobob tree adds to the realism.

The Wilds should also be explored by foot on the *Nature Trail*. Points of interest along the wooded trail include displays of simulated ostrich eggs, birds' nests, elephant bones, and termite mounds. Up the trail, massive boulders make up a kopje, where meerkats, rock hyraxes, and nimble klipspringers dwell. A side path through the kopje boulders is a favorite with children and leads to the best view of the kopje birds display. Also on the trail, the *A.D. Martin Sr. Forest Aviary* is a lushly-planted, walk-through aviary with buffalo weavers, hammerkops, rose-ringed parakeets, and other colorful African birds. The trail also provides closer views of the okapis and bongos. At trail's end is the *Jake L. Hamon Gorilla Conservation Research Center*. In an attempt to keep human contact with the privacy-loving gorillas to a minimum, most of the many viewing areas, including a bunker with one-way glass, are hidden from the gorillas' view. In the thatched-roof building that is the *Field Research Station*, gorilla guides are available to answer questions, and the gorillas can be watched on video screens. The habitat contains tall grass, rocks, and shrubs for the gorillas to hide behind and streams for them to drink from. It replicates as accurately as possible the gorillas' African forest home.

The feature exhibit of the old zoo, **ZooNorth**, is the **Bird, Reptile, and Amphibian Building**. Inside, the lush, walk-through *Neotropical Aviary* features Andean cock-of-the-rocks, blue-crowned hanging parrots, and other colorful birds flying around a trickling waterfall. The most noteworthy residents of the gorgeous bird enclosures are Bali mynahs, thick-billed parrots, and toco toucans. Numerous hands-on exhibits for kids are found in the *Reptile Discovery Center*. Another educational exhibit, *The Other Side*, offers visitors a behind-the-scenes look at a reptile department and displays a reptile egg incubator. The building is particularly well known for its South American snakes. Among the venomous varieties displayed in the reptile gallery are eyelash vipers, death adders, Gaboon vipers, and bushmasters.

OTHER EXHIBITS

Most of the ZooNorth exhibits were built before 1968. They were considered state of the art back then but now badly show their age. Nevertheless, very interesting animals reside in these exhibits. The **Large Mammal Building** is the indoor/outdoor home of African elephants, giraffes, and Nile hippos. **Cat Row** features lions, Siberian tigers, snow leopards, and ocelots in cages near the park-like **Cat Green**. Though they are often hard to see, chimpanzees and an orangutan live in the **Primate Building**. Mona monkeys, ruffed lemurs, dusky leaf monkeys, gibbons, and more are in a nearby row of cages. Red pandas, dwarf mongooses, African crested porcupines, and a desert prairie dog town are in moated yards. The **Hoofed Mammals** area has large gravel yards for black rhinos, llamas, Bactrian camels, and kangaroos, as well as for some new residents that include desert bighorn sheep, peccaries, a wart hog, and dwarf forest buffalo. **Birds of Prey** row features bald eagles, Andean condors, spectacled owls, king vultures, and ground hornbills. A wide pool is filled with flamingos, pelicans, and spoonbills at the front of ZooNorth, and more birds can be seen in **Bird Valley**.

FOR THE KIDS

The hilltop **Children's Zoo** (open April through October) has a goat petting yard and other pettable farm animals. Educational graphics and games are also available.

Children's Zoo

NEW AT THE ZOO

Giant anteaters, fennec foxes, and wallabies are some of the newest residents. The **Butterfly Garden**, which opened in 1992 in Bird Valley, is planted with over 2,300 plants known to attract butterflies.

In the master plan, several major additions to the Wilds of Africa are being considered: a *Savanna Habitat* with elephants, rhinos, giraffes, and lions; a Savanna Overlook Restaurant; and a *Chimpanzee Reserve*. There are also plans to extensively renovate ZooNorth. Among the possible exhibits are a new Texas wildlife area, an insect zoo, and both Central and South American displays.

Fort Worth Zoo

1989 Colonial Parkway
Fort Worth, Texas 76110
(817) 871-7050

Hours: *10-5 weekdays, 10-7 weekends, June-August; 10-5 weekdays, 10-6 weekends, March-May and September-October; 10-5 daily, November-February; noon-5 on New Year's Day, Thanksgiving Day, and Christmas Day.*

Admission Fees: *Adults $5, 65+ and 3-12 $2.50; half-price on Wednesdays. Kiddie train $1. Parking $1 on summer weekends.*

Directions: *From I-30, take Exit 12A (University Drive) South. Follow 1 mile to Forest Park, turn left on Colonial Parkway and follow into zoo parking lot.*

Don't Miss: *World of Primates, Texas!, Asian Falls, (including Asian Rhino Ridge), Herpetarium, Raptor Canyon, Aquarium, African Savannah.*

Touring Tips: *The Small Animal Village and some of the Texas! buildings close early. Within Texas! guests can enjoy authentic Kentucky Fried Chicken at the Yellow Rose Cafe and dessert next door at the Bluebonnet Ice Cream Parlor. Shaded outdoor tables are available. More fast food is available at the Zoo Creek Cafe, where diners can eat either inside at air-conditioned tables or outside with views of black-necked swans. Zootique is one of the more attractive zoo gift shops.*

Entertainment: *The **Birds of Prey Show** is held three times per day (Wednesdays-Sundays, mid-April-Labor Day). This 20-minute educational and entertaining presentation features free-flying raptors. Starting in the spring of 1994 it will be presented in a new 2,000-seat outdoor amphitheater.*

In the Dallas-Fort Worth metropolitan area, it seems that the city of Dallas has always overshadowed Fort Worth. This has not been true, however, when referring to their respective zoos. The Dallas Zoo has made great strides in recent years, but the Fort Worth Zoo seems determined to maintain its status as the area's top zoo and has opened outstanding major exhibits during the late 1980s and early 1990s. Although it has been open since 1909 (making it one of the oldest zoos in either the West or South), most visitors think they are in a much newer zoo.

This zoo is not a leader in Texas only. With more than 5,000 animals of nearly 750 different species, it is surpassed by only two other U.S. zoos in the overall variety of animals.

FEATURED EXHIBITS

Even people who don't enjoy zoos appreciate the unique **Texas!** exhibit. A turn-of-the-century pioneer town is re-created with a brick-paved town square, stone ranch house, operating blacksmith shop, working windmill, one-room schoolhouse, twelve-stall barn, and *Yellow Rose Saloon*. The scene is reminiscent of the way Texas used to be. Jersey cows are in dusty corrals around the barn, and a petting yard is populated with goats, pigs, and sheep. Chicken coops, a brooder, and rabbits are found inside the barn. Some of the small mammals of old Texas— raccoons, nutrias, and prairie dogs—are seen in naturalized grottoes in the town. In open, shaded yards across the river, bison, pronghorns, longhorn cattle, deer, wild turkeys, and javelinas represent the animals that once roamed the open Texas plains. Also in this area is a scaled-down version of the stockyards, with a cattle chute and a high observation tower. Just outside the town, an authentic Native American settlement can be walked through, completing the experience.

With over 600 reptiles and amphibians of more than 160 different varieties, the **Herpetarium** is one of the nation's largest reptile houses. The collection is world-famous, not only for its size and variety, but also for its breeding success with rare and endangered species. Recent attention has been focused on the breeding programs for arboreal boids (tree-dwelling pythons and boas). A special exhibit panel lets visitors push a button to guess whether the exhibited snakes are venomous or harmless. The Herpetarium also has one of the largest collections of rattlesnakes in any zoo and an interesting reptile nursery. Other notable specimens include colorful frogs, turtles, monitor lizards, geckos, cobras, and vipers. A **Gator Swamp** is just down the trail.

The **Aquarium** has more than 2,400 fish of over 300 species (more than any other U.S. zoo aquarium). The majority of fish tanks display interesting freshwater fish, including paddlefish, piranhas, electric eels, Asian stinging catfish, and endangered desert pupfish. Giant fish of the Amazon river can be seen from either above or below water in one of the largest freshwater exhibits in the Southwest. In a separate wing, beautiful saltwater tanks display nurse sharks, seahorses, and other colorful coral reef fish. A side gallery is now the home of the *Insectarium*, which is populated with black widow spiders, tarantulas, water striders, and other native and exotic bugs.

During the construction of Asian Falls, the **African Savannah** was enhanced. Both white and black rhinos are seen in a large, shaded yard. (This is one of only five zoos to display three different rhinoceros species.) Visitors watch from thatched-roof viewing areas and are separated from the animals by a wide, flowing stream lined with reeds and other natural water vegetation. A wooden deck is positioned on the stream to allow viewers a closer look at the giraffes and African land birds. At the trail's end, hippos can be found in a deep pool across from the giraffes.

OTHER EXHIBITS

More animals from the African plains inhabit the **African Diorama**, a pair of unique four-level exhibits. A herd of zebras lives in a long, open yard; wart hogs reside in a similar yard behind them. Further up the hill, a pride of lions are seen in a tall, rocky grotto with aoudads (mountain goats from Africa) on the rocky cliffs above them. A similar set-up has dama gazelles and springbok in the lower yards, another rocky grotto of lions, and curly-horned mouflon sheep above the lions. A trail that bisects these predator/prey exhibits provides a closer view of the upper habitats.

The **Small Animal Village** appears to be a separate community of small mammals, birds, and tortoises on the other side of the river that flows through the zoo. A winding path leads through a tall, mesh walk-through aviary with roadrunners, ibises, ruddy ducks, and other native water birds. A set of four round buildings have wedge-shaped enclosures for African porcupines, lemurs, macaws, rare golden lion tamarins, and others. Wallabies and great gray kangaroos inhabit a shady fenced yard.

The assortment of exhibits found along the central forested pathway include llama, rhea, and giant Aldabra tortoise yards; primate exhibits with squirrel monkeys, spot-nosed guenons, and other small monkeys; and **Bird Row**—a series of small aviaries for macaws, toucans, blue-crowned pigeons, and other multi-colored birds. Flamingos, cranes, and storks are displayed throughout the zoo. (This zoo features the greatest variety of wading birds in the U.S.)

FOR THE KIDS

In the Texas! exhibit, children can enjoy touring *Zoo Creek School*, frolicking on a sandy playground, climbing through a tunnel to pop up in a plastic bubble among the prairie dogs, petting domestic animals, and riding a kiddie train.

Forest Park, which surrounds the zoo, also has a miniature train ride. Covering more than 5 miles of Texas parkland, it is the longest such ride in the nation.

NEW AT THE ZOO

Opened in 1992, the spectacular **World of Primates** is the only place in the U.S. where all four great ape species (gorillas, chimpanzees, bonobos, and orangutans) can be seen. This 2 1/2-acre facility's highlight is an indoor tropical rain forest that is the gorillas' main habitat. Under an expansive glass roof, this lush jungle includes tall palm trees and manmade buttress trees. Two 768-square-foot "living walls" are covered with live moss and tropical plants. The gorilla's rocky, hilly home is separated from visitors by a wide water moat fed by three loud, crashing waterfalls. Over 100 colorful African birds, including fairy bluebirds and various waxbills and wydahs, fly freely throughout the exhibit. From a viewing cave, juvenile apes can be watched playing in the ape nursery, and a colony of colobus monkeys can be seen through thin harp wire along one of the walls. Viewing windows allow the chimps, bonobos (pygmy chimps), and orangutans to be seen at close range in their rocky indoor habitats. Outside, an elevated boardwalk circles the building, passing by grassy island habitats for the great apes, gibbons (lesser apes), and brightly-colored mandrills. These lush islands are separated by waterfalls and cascading streams.

Asian Falls, which also opened in 1992, offers a panoramic stroll past many of Asia's largest animals. An oriental-style gateway is at the start of an uphill board-walk. The tour begins by curving around the fenced yards and deep pools of the 3 1/2-acre Asian elephant complex. The area's newest exhibit, *Asian Rhino Ridge*, is on both sides of the boardwalk. This lush, hillside habitat's pair of greater one-horned Asian rhinos are positioned below an upper yard of Asian cranes, always-spotted Axis deer, and blackbuck antelope. The rhinos can bathe at the foot of a cascading waterfall or wallow in their preferred mud pool. The zoo is working closely with the Kingdom of Nepal to preserve these endangered rhinos. At the top of the hill, a giant 40-foot waterfall is one of many that separate three grassy yards for the Sumatran tigers, Malayan sun bears, and the white tiger named Neela. The tigers enjoy swimming in pools at the bottom of a deep ravine and can be seen face-to-face through a lower viewing window.

Raptor Canyon is a unique new exhibit that displays seven different birds of prey in habitats replicating their native homes. An initial walk-through aviary has small, fruit-eating birds fly-ing freely in and out of the view-ing area and the towering flight cages for Andean condors and king vultures. African pygmy fal-cons, Japanese hawk eagles, and Brazilian spectacled owls are seen in the next viewing area. From a covered walkway, visi-tors can view magnificent bald eagles and rare harpy eagles in flight.

Late in 1993, a wildlife art gallery opened featuring over 40 paintings by Wilhelm Kunhert and other wildlife artists. A koala exhibit will open in 1994.

Bald Eagle

Gladys Porter Zoo

500 Ringgold Street
Brownsville, Texas 78520
(210) 546-2177 or 546-7187

Hours: *9-dusk daily.*
Admission Fees: *Adults $5, 2-13 $2.50. Participates in reciprocity program. Safari Express tour train: adults $1, children 50¢. Parking $1.*
Directions: *From US 77-83 Expressway, take 6th Street Exit. Follow to Ringgold Street, turn right to zoo.*
Don't Miss: *Africa, Indo-Australia, Tropical America, Free-flight Aviary, Herpetarium, Asia, Children's Zoo*, Sea Lion Exhibit, Bear Grottoes.*
Touring Tips: *The extreme beauty of this zoo provides excellent backgrounds for memorable family photographs. Four food concessions offer ample menu choices and shaded seating overlooking the beautiful waterways and exhibits. The Safari Express tour train runs on Sunday afternoons only.*
Entertainment: *This zoo does not present animal acts. Special educational programs are presented in a new 200-seat amphitheater next to the sea lion exhibit.*

Opened in 1971, the Gladys Porter Zoo is one of the country's newest and most spectacular zoos. It is found in a most unlikely place—at the southern tip of Texas, just across the border from Mexico. It was planned, built, stocked, and equipped by the Earl C. Sams Foundation and then given to the city of Brownsville. Mr. Sams was the chairman of the board of the J.C.Penney Company. It was Gladys Porter, his daughter, who oversaw the establishment of the zoo.

From its beginning, the zoo's major goal has been to be a "survival center" for rare and endangered species. This is apparent in its nearly unsurpassed collection of rarely displayed animals. As an example, the world's only Hunter's hartebeests (a rare African antelope) in captivity are found here.

The raw natural beauty of this zoo is a result of its location in the semi-tropical lower Rio Grande Valley. The mild climate is ideal for supporting abundant palm and mesquite trees, bougainvillea vines, hibiscus shrubs, and other tropical plants. The lush botanical collection here is nearly as impressive as the animal collection. The most notable feature of its location are the "resacas," or waterways that were left behind by the Rio Grande River after spring floods. The flowing resacas on the grounds form the moats for most of the exhibits. These natural waterways are spanned by a maze of wooden boardwalks that, along with the splendid use of naturalistic rockwork, create an unsurpassed zoological panorama.

FEATURED EXHIBITS
Most of the large animals are organized into four geographic zones, with their exhibit areas carved out by the resaca waterway system. One of these zones,

Tropical America, displays a variety of South and Central American animals in seven exhibits. The two waterfowl displays, which are across a lagoon from each other, feature endangered Hawaiian geese and three species of flamingos. Both spotted and black jaguars are viewed from inside a rocky cave. An outdoor gallery featuring birds of prey (eagles and king vultures) in tall, natural flight cages is across from a covered visitor area. Other exhibits include Galapagos tortoises and the first of many primate islands in the resaca system. On this grassy island, agile spider monkeys draw plenty of attention when they climb to the top of a towering pole and then slide down again in seconds.

A stone arch is at the beginning of **Indo-Australia**, where two more islands are inhabited by a large family of tree-perching orangutans and acrobatic gibbons. (With five different species, this zoo has the largest and most diverse collection of rare gibbons in the U.S.) The highlight of the Indo-Australia zone is the **Australian Exhibit** building, where kowaris, cuscus, tree kangaroos, bettongs, and sugar gliders are some of the interesting small marsupials found in picturesque glass-fronted habitats. A tawny frogmouth and a colony of bats are exhibited in nocturnal displays. More Australian birds—kookaburas and colorful lorikeets and finches—are found just outside in small aviaries. A nearby side yard has the much larger, but just as beautiful, cassowaries. These land birds from New Guinea are found in very few North American zoos. Saltwater crocodiles—the world's largest reptiles—are seen here in a large pool. (Only two U.S. zoos exhibit them.) The rest of the grassy yards surrounding the Australian building are filled with kangaroos, wallaroos, and wallabies. (This zoo has the largest collection of kangaroos and wallabies in the U.S.)

In the **Asia** zone, the boardwalk bridges provide a great view of three large, open habitats of endangered hoofstock—Bactrian camels, gaurs (Asian wild cattle), and Mongolian wild horses. The pathways also circle around a pair of gibbon islands populated with vocal siamangs.

The largest continental zone of the resaca system is **Africa**, which dominates the southern half of the zoo. Like the other zones, the pathways and boardwalks pass or encircle grassy islands that are excellent habitats for troops of lemurs and a large family of chimpanzees. One of the better photo spots is the gorgeous pygmy hippo exhibit, which features a set of beautiful cascading waterfalls behind its deep pools. African elephants and white rhinos are in nearby dusty yards where rock ledges provide shade. The most attractive of the baboon species—mandrills and gelada baboons—are seen in side-by-side enclosures. Africa's fiercest predators—lions and hunting dogs—can be viewed up close through glass panels, or from a distance, as they overlook the sable antelope yard in a predator/prey display. The zoo's famous collection of African hoofstock also includes large savannas for giraffes, zebras, Arabian oryxes, bongos, and Jentinck's duikers—the world's rarest antelope. At the front of the zoo, the gorilla island is also a part of the African zone. The gorillas, like the other apes here, have been very prolific, producing more than a dozen baby gorillas. Behind the adult gorillas is the *Juvenile Ape Exhibit*, where

King Cobra Hatchling

many viewing windows allow visitors to get very close to the adorable young gorillas that were born here.

The **Herpetarium** is well known in the zoological world. Alligators float below a trickling waterfall in the building's largest habitat. The zoo has received much acclaim for its rare crocodile monitors (extremely large lizards). The impressive collection of venomous reptiles includes king cobras—the world's largest venomous snakes. (Cobras reproducing in zoos is a very rare event, yet in 1992 these cobras produced 13 hatchlings.) Many large snakes, frogs, and dangerous spiders are also on display.

Tucked in the corner of Tropical America is the lush **Free-flight Aviary**. Within this screened-in structure is a dense jungle of trees, ferns, and freely-flying tropical birds. This feathered rainbow includes fairy bluebirds, green jays, and red-billed hornbills. A cool waterfall empties into a pool for exotic waterfowl. Separate aviaries display golden pheasants and toucans.

Near the zoo's entrance are three extravagantly large **Bear Grottoes**. The three most exotic bear species (sun bears, sloth bears, and spectacled bears) inhabit these spectacular grottoes equipped with cooling pools.

OTHER EXHIBITS

The **Aquatic Wing**, an attachment to the Herpetarium, is behind an outdoor koi pond. Notable displays include sea turtles from the nearby Gulf of Mexico, Rio Grande perch from the zoo's resacas, aquatic amphibians, seahorses, and piranhas.

Six species of crocodilians, four of which are endangered in the wild, are displayed in a row of swampy habitats. Cuban, Morelet's and Philippine crocodiles can be seen from above. (This is the only zoo in the world that exhibits or breeds Philippine crocodiles.)

A large yard across from the Herpetarium exhibits a pair of Sumatran tigers that can be seen up close through wide viewing windows. Rare jaguarundis are also behind glass in a nearby enclosure.

The **Texas Aviary** is a row of open-air aviaries that display scarlet ibises, macaws, roadrunners, curassows, endangered thick-billed parrots, and more. Surrounding these aviaries are exhibits of duikers (small antelope), red brocket deer, ground hornbills, cranes, and storks.

FOR THE KIDS

To enter the **Children's Zoo**, visitors must walk through an adobe arch resembling the front of an old Spanish mission. Inside, the *Nursery* has large windows for viewing baby apes, monkeys, and other newborn animals—the smallest of which are often still in incubators. In the contact yard, kids can pet pygmy goats, Barbados sheep, and potbellied pigs. Three types of tiny tamarins are found in a series of open-air mesh enclosures. Other interesting monkeys found here include white-faced sakis and rare douc langurs. An assortment of small mammals includes a large band of meerkats, fennec foxes, a gray fox, a badger, and a chinchilla.

NEW AT THE ZOO

The impressive **Sea Lion Exhibit**, opened in early 1993, has a 117,000-gallon pool and a large rocky beach for the California sea lions to bask on. A new outdoor **Large Lizard Display** features rhinoceros iguanas and other iguana species.

Future plans include renovations of some of the most popular animals' habitats, rebuilt animal buildings in the Children's Zoo, and an expansion of the Aquatic Wing to add four new major exhibits—one of which will be a Gulf of Mexico ecology tank. A new free-flight aviary will house shore and wading birds, and a 4-acre African Veldt exhibit will be developed.

Houston Zoological Gardens

1513 North MacGregor
Houston, Texas 77030
(713) 525-3300

Hours: *10-6 daily.*
Admission Fees: *Adults $2.50, 65+ $2, 3-12 50¢, free on city holidays.*
Directions: *From Downtown, take Nolan Ryan Expressway (US 288) south to North MacGregor Drive Exit. Turn right and follow into Hermann Park, remaining in right lane through two forks in road. Zoo parking lot is on left.*
Don't Miss: *Wortham World of Primates, Tropical Bird House, Cats, Children's Zoo, Gorilla Habitat, Small Mammal World, Kipp Aquarium, Reptile House, McGovern Mammal Marina.*
Touring Tips: *The Tropical Bird House closes early. The Cafeteria and Snack Bar both offer*

a wide variety of fast food, including Mexican items. Both also have shaded outdoor seating. The most scenic dining is along the edge of Waterfowl Lake.

Entertainment: *At the McGovern Mammal Marina,* **Sea Lion Demonstrations** *are given two or three times daily. Exciting Animal Programs and Storytelling are offered to children in the Brown Education Center on weekends. Animal feedings include elephants, vampire bats, alligators, and waterfowl.*

Houston, Texas has quietly become the fourth largest city in the U.S. It is fitting, therefore, that this giant metropolis has a first-class zoo. With over 2,700 animals of more than 650 species, the Houston Zoo has one of the most diverse collections in the country. It ranks in the nation's top ten in variety of mammals, birds, reptiles, and invertebrates. Participating in over 30 Species Survival Plans, it is a leader in saving endangered species.

The title "Zoological Gardens" is appropriate as it is one of the most beautifully landscaped zoos. Somewhat reminiscent of our nation's capital, it has spacious open grassy areas, brightly-colored flowering trees, and a pretty reflecting pool. The towering palm trees and many banana trees are reminders that this is southern Texas.

FEATURED EXHIBITS

The **Gorilla Habitat** is especially impressive when one considers that it first opened back in 1973. This 20-year-old exhibit compares favorably with any of the newer naturalistic gorilla exhibits that have been opening across the nation during the last few years. It is entered through a dark cave where informational graphics light up the walls. Visitors emerge suddenly into a sky-lit opening where they stand face-to-face with M'Kubwa—the only eastern lowland gorilla in the western hemisphere. Tropical vegetation, artificial trees, a trickling waterfall, and a stream that cascades down through five small pools all make this a convincing jungle cave. The gorilla shares his home with Lowe's guenon monkeys and free-flying African birds.

The **Cats** area occupies a large portion of the zoo's center. (Only three other U.S. zoos have a larger and more varied collection of large and small felines.) The largest cats—lions and Siberian tigers—are seen in spacious grassy yards with a rocky backdrop and a wide, deep moat that the tigers like to swim in. A stairway leads down to underground windows for especially close viewing of the lions. In contrast, stairs lead up to a high viewing platform over the tall waterfall of the Bengal tiger exhibit, which includes a white tiger. The large, natural habitats for the snow leopards, cougars, jaguars, and maned wolves include cliffs and rocks to climb on, trees, and pools, and there are wide glass panels along the entire front. Visitors can rest on benches in shaded viewing areas. A row of tall, densely-planted mesh habitats display smaller cats, including clouded leopards, black leopards, servals, caracals, margays, and a rarely-exhibited jaguarundi.

Near the front of the zoo, the **McGovern Mammal Marina** is a wonderful photo spot. Replicating a northwestern wharf scene, it features a wide viewing deck overhanging a 90,000-gallon pool where playful sea lions and harbor seals swim and dive.

With more than 600 reptiles and amphibians of over 170 species, very few U.S. zoos have a larger or more diverse display than that found in the **Reptile House**. Within this remodeled building, the 100 large and small exhibits are divided into four natural biome areas: *Temperate Forest, Desert, Grasslands,* and *Tropical Forest.* The various specimens on display include desert lizards, monitor lizards, tortoises, tree frogs, pythons, vipers, and an egg-eating snake. Numerous rattlesnakes are highlighted in the new *Snakes of Texas* exhibit.

The small, round **Kipp Aquarium** displays over 100 species of fish in beautiful saltwater and freshwater aquatic habitats. Among the best exhibits are the large circular reef tank, the rocky African cichlid tank, and the yellow-bellied sea snake—one of the world's most poisonous snakes. Other notable fish on display include stonefish, seahorses, pipefish, moray eels, and piranhas.

The highlight of the many beautiful bird exhibits is the **Tropical Bird House**. In two circular galleries, a feather rainbow of over 200 exotic birds is found in simulated natural habitats enhanced with attractive background murals. Various kingfishers, finches, and other colorful birds are seen, but the main attraction is the iridescent golden-headed quetzals. (Houston is one of the few zoos to display these stunning birds and the only one to successfully breed them.) Between the two galleries, visitors walk across a wooden suspension bridge leading through a lush jungle room. The most notable birds seen there, flying freely around reproductions of ancient Mayan ruins, are luminous orange cock-of-the-rocks.

OTHER EXHIBITS

Beyond the Tropical Bird House are many other excellent exhibits of multi-colored exotic birds. In a grove of banana trees, the **Fisher Bird Garden** has 17 aviaries and is home to king vultures, great hornbills, and crowned pigeons. The two rows of mesh enclosures in **Pheasant Run** feature pheasants, currasows, and a wide variety of ravishing African touracos. Other bird exhibits include a lush flamingo pool, four tall cages of macaws, and **Waterfowl Lake** with rare Hawaiian geese.

On opposite sides of the zoo are two rows of large, fenced paddocks that exhibit a variety of hoofed animals. Notable grazers in these yards are tapirs (both Brazilian and Malayan), zebras, bison, and over ten species of African antelope, including bongos.

The largest animals—Asian elephants, white rhinos, Nile hippos, and rarely-exhibited Nubian giraffes—are scattered around the zoo in spacious yards. The hippos are usually either completely submerged in their outdoor pool or inside the big, round **Hippo Building**.

Four large stone grottoes are inhabited by three varieties of bears, including spectacled bears. In a much smaller grotto, rare Chinese alligators can be viewed.

FOR THE KIDS

Shaded by the long branches of massive old trees, the **Children's Zoo** has four contact yards. While their parents sit on shaded benches, kids can pet pygmy goats, potbellied pigs, sheep, and African zebu cattle. More cattle, including Texas long-horns, and llamas are in fenced corrals. The nocturnal *Texas Wildlife Building* dis-plays a badger, an armadillo, opossums, and other native animals. One interesting exhibit features flying squirrels leaping from tree to tree. Fennec foxes live outside in a round, glass-enclosed desert habitat, and binturongs and giant tortoises are in nearby exhibits. In a completely enclosed yard, slots in a fence provide glimpses of wallabies, including a rare albino wallaby. In the *Buffalo Bayou Exhibit*, the huge alli-gator snapping turtles are seen underwater, and visitors can walk through a glass "aquatunnel" to observe gars, catfish, and other native Texas fish swimming around them.

In the sparkling, modern **George R. Brown Education Center**, the *Young Discovery Room* is geared to children ages 2 to 6. Besides stuffed animals and touch-able animal artifacts (skins, horns, etc.), the room features an insect display, bio-scanners, and a touch tank with starfish and other marine creatures. It's main lobby displays ever-changing traveling exhibits.

Outside the main gate, across from a life-size elephant sculpture, are a minia-ture train ride and pedal boat rides on a large duck pond.

NEW AT THE ZOO

The Small Mammal House has long been known for its variety of animals. Reopened in 1993 as **Small Mammal World**, this renovated facility displays an unparalleled collection of small Australian marsupials, tiny primates, bats, and rodents. Among the 50-plus species are a large group of sugar gliders, porcupines, pygmy marmosets, slow lorises, mouse lemurs, and meerkats, but vampire bats are the main attraction. At the entrance is a 24-inch glass ecosphere—a completely self-contained ecosystem designed by NASA. On the way out, a high-tech video dis-play near the golden lion tamarins tells of the ongoing success story in saving this beautiful species from extinction.

The newest exhibit is the 2.2-acre **Wortham World of Primates** at the zoo's cen-ter. On an elevated walkway, visitors pass a series of huge mesh enclosures that simulate the rain forests of South America, Asia, and Madagascar. Moated habitats that replicate the African savanna are also seen. From this high level the orang-utans, colobus monkeys, red-capped mangabeys, Diana monkeys, langurs, sia-mangs, gibbons, three types of lemurs, and other primates can be seen at the top of their climbing trees.

Also new, the **Texas Wetlands Exhibit** depicts a cypress swampland. Fish, tur-tles, wading birds, and American alligators can be seen from a shaded boardwalk over the water.

Oklahoma City Zoological Park

2101 N.E. 50th Street
Oklahoma City, Oklahoma 73111
(405) 424-3344

Hours: *9-6 daily, April-September; 9-5, rest of year. Buildings close 15 minutes earlier. Visitors may stay until dusk. Closed New Year's Day and Christmas Day.*

Admission Fees: *Adults $4, 65+ and 3-11 $2. Participates in reciprocity program. Safari Tram $1, Sea Lion/Dolphin Show $2, Sky Safari $1 each way.*

Directions: *From I-35, take Exit 132A (50th Street) West, then follow 1 mile to zoo. From I-44, take Exit 129 (Martin Luther King Avenue), then go 1 mile south to 50th Street. Turn left and follow to zoo.*

Don't Miss: *Noble Aquatic Center: Aquaticus (including Sea Lion/Dolphin Show), Great EscApe, Sky Safari, Canine Exhibits, Giraffe Trail, Island Life Exhibit.*

Touring Tips: *A lot of walking is required to see all of this sprawling zoo. One way to get a good overview is to ride the narrated* **Safari Tram.** *Some of the picnic and eating areas are particularly scenic.*

Entertainment: *The* **Sea Lion/Dolphin Show,** *held many times daily at the Aquaticus, should not be missed. Summer shows are held in an attractive stadium with room for 1,800 spectators, while winter shows are in a more intimate indoor amphitheater. Two sea lions comically demonstrate their balancing, swimming, and flipping skills, and the Atlantic bottle-nosed dolphins are some of the highest jumpers around.*

Bottle-Nosed Dolphin

Established in 1904, the Oklahoma City Zoo is one of the oldest zoos in the Southwest. With more than 2,000 animals from over 500 species spread out over its 110 acres, it is one of the ten most diverse zoos in the nation. The zoo is well known for its exotic hoofstock that live in spacious grassy enclosures. In season, the grounds are colorful with beautiful flower gardens and many wildflowers.

FEATURED EXHIBITS

The **Noble Aquatic Center: Aquaticus** is one of the premier exhibits. The main attraction of this multi-level complex is the Sea Lion/Dolphin Show. At the front of Aquaticus is a large sea lion pool that resembles a rocky California cove. On the lower levels, more than 25 aquatic exhibits feature a variety of marine life. Among the most notable exhibits are a shadowy tank of large sharks, a horde of moray eels in a coral reef, an Amazon tank with long arapaimas, and jawfish that peek out of the sand. At the *Tidepool*, sea stars, urchins, and crabs can be touched. Also, underwater windows provide views of the dolphins and sea lions, and the gift shop has an aquatic emphasis.

For easier touring, the zoo's four major trails are named after the notable animals seen on each trail. The **Giraffe Trail**, with Rothschild's giraffes as a main attraction, is probably the best of the four trails. The giraffes—along with ostriches, ground hornbills, and other birds—live in a tall-grass savanna exhibit. A pair of stunning okapis can be seen nearby. (Okapis are displayed in only six other U.S. zoos). A corner yard holds one of the largest groups of red kangaroos outside of Australia. A large herd of gorals (small wild goats from China), rare sika deer, and Pere David's deer inhabit grassy hillside yards. In this same area, Nubian ibexes, Dall's sheep, and Rocky Mountain goats each have a miniature mountain to climb on.

A long row of **Canine Exhibits** represent the nation's largest and most diverse display of wild dogs. Each of the eight open, grassy yards is landscaped with bushes and trees. Overlooks are strategically placed at watering holes and permit viewing the dogs with no visual barriers. Occupants of these innovative exhibits include the largest packs of maned wolves, bush dogs, and striped hyenas in the U.S. Other exotic dogs exhibited include black-backed jackals, African wild dogs, and Chinese dholes. The last yard is occupied not by canines, but felines—sleek, quick cheetahs.

OTHER EXHIBITS

Historically, this zoo is most famous for its Asian and African hoofstock collection. Hoofed animals found along the **Great Ape** and **Giraffe Trails** include gaurs, zebras, Arabian oryxes, blesboks, bonteboks, waterbucks, sable antelope, and one of the country's largest herds of white-tailed gnus.

The zoo's largest animals are seen in spacious outdoor yards and in the attractive interior of the **Pachyderm Building**. Nile hippos, Indian and black rhinos, and African and Asian elephants are represented here.

The big cats—a jaguar, a black leopard, and several tigers and snow leopards—live in open, red rock grottoes. On the other side of the zoo, spectacled bears, sloth bears, and grizzly bears reside in similar grottoes, while the popular red pandas live in a lush green grotto.

The **Dan Moran Aviary,** which is a small indoor rain forest, displays colorful fairy bluebirds, Lady Ross touracos, and ruddy ducks. Large flight cages scattered through the zoo display exotic eagles, including Eurasian eagle owls, African fish eagles, harpy eagles, and Japanese hawk eagles.

The **Herpetarium** houses a wide variety of snakes, lizards, turtles, and amphibians. (This zoo has received much notoriety for its breeding success with chameleons from Madagascar.) Other notable animals include an egg-eating snake, deadly urutus, and a large variety of frogs. An outdoor alligator exhibit is nearby.

Francois monkeys and Allen's swamp monkeys are seen in the old **Primates building**. An attractive display of kikiyu colobus monkeys is near the zoo's entrance, and a variety of lemurs are also displayed.

FOR THE KIDS

The recently renovated **Children's Zoo & Discovery Area** has gorgeous flower gardens. Familiar ponies, pigs, llamas, goats, and sheep can be petted in corrals. More exotic animals such as Malayan tapirs, tree kangaroos, hog deer, flying foxes, Darwin's rheas, and a babirusa (an Asian wild pig) are also displayed, and small aviaries house hornbills, snowy owls, eagles, and macaws. A desert-landscaped prairie dog town and an educational playground are both particularly popular with children.

A larger playground is available in front of the **Rex Kennedy Rosser Education Center**. Inside the center, the *Discovery Theatre* displays an array of feathers, skulls, and animal skeletons.

The highlight of a visit to this zoo for most kids is a ride on the **Sky Safari**. This chairlift takes riders high above the trees, providing a birds-eye view of the Children's Zoo and other exhibits. (This is one of only four American zoos to offer a sky ride.)

NEW AT THE ZOO

Opened in 1993, the **Great EscApe** is this zoo's most modern and naturalistic exhibit. The habitats for gorillas, chimpanzees, and orangutans cover $3^1/2$ acres and simulate a tropical forest filled with clearings, cliffs, streams, and pools. Visitors feel the sensation of being totally immersed in the apes' forest home. Indoor and outdoor vantage points are strategically located to provide the best possible views of these fascinating great apes. Hands-on educational activities are provided in the exhibit's interpretive building, and an activity trail is available for children.

The former Galapagos Exhibit has been renovated into the new **Island Life Exhibit**. It highlights the diversity of island animals with displays of gigantic Galapagos tortoises and brilliantly colored Caribbean flamingos, plus other wildlife from the Galapagos, Indonesia, Madagascar, and the Caribbean. The former Patagonian Cliffs Exhibit also has been renovated and is now the **South American Aviary**. It continues to feature colorful tropical birds from South America in a lush, free-flight aviary.

Future exhibits in the ambitious master plan include **Big Cat Forest**, **Bear Trek**, and the **Oklahoma Trail**.

San Antonio Zoological Gardens & Aquarium

3903 North St. Mary's Street
San Antonio, Texas 78212
(512) 734-7184

Hours: *9:30-6:30 daily, April-October; 9:30-5, rest of year.*
Admission Fees: *Adults $6, 63+ and 3-11 $4. Participates in reciprocity program. Tropical Tour boat ride $1.25.*
Directions: *From U.S. Highway 281, take the Mulberry Avenue Exit. Turn left onto Mulberry Avenue., then left again onto St. Mary's Street and follow to zoo.*
Don't Miss: *Australian Walkabout, Amazonia Rain Forest, Tropical Tour boat ride, Rift Valley Track, Children's Zoo, Tropical Birdhouse, Cats of the World, Aquarium.*
Touring Tips: *The zoo is in Brackenridge Park. This large municipal park also features a Kiddie Park (with ten rides), horseback riding, a miniature railroad, paddleboats, Oriental gardens, a carousel, and a Skyride. The full-service Riverview Restaurant operates inside the zoo.*
Entertainment: *The **Theater of Birds**, a large outdoor amphitheater, hosts daily bird shows. Sea lion demonstrations are presented at their exhibit several times each day during the summer. Lectures and special events are presented in the Children's Zoo **Animal Arena**. Animal feedings include penguins, fish, and alligators.*

Home to the Alamo, River Walk, Spanish missions, and other historical sites, San Antonio has been a major tourist destination for a long time. In recent years, the openings of Sea World and Fiesta Texas have made the area the top family vacation spot between Florida and California. A little-known fact to most non-Texans is that San Antonio also has one of the country's largest and most beautiful zoos. The San Antonio Zoo has over 3,300 animals of more than 750 species. Only San Diego has a more diverse collection. It is in the top five U.S. zoos in variety of mammals, birds, reptiles, and fish.

Opened in 1914, the zoo occupies an enviable location at the headwaters of the San Antonio River. Built in an abandoned rock quarry that supplied the limestone used to build the Alamo, it features many exhibits backed by spectacular rocky cliffs. The grounds also feature cool waterways, and an abundance of tall oak, pecan, and cypress trees provide shade.

FEATURED EXHIBITS

The **Australian Walkabout** is one of the best overall Australian exhibits in the U.S. The koalas, which arrived in 1989, are seen either up-close perched in trees or behind glass from an elevated wooden walkway. In the *Walk-thru Australian Aviary* visitors are surrounded by colorful birds that include lorikeets, crowned pigeons, fruit doves, and waterfowl; furry wombats are seen on the ground. (This is one of only three U.S. zoos to display wombats.) Two rarely exhibited tree kangaroo species inhabit nearby trees, and red kangaroos, wallaroos, wallabies, emus, and New Guinea singing dogs are exhibited in adjacent arid yards.

The **Rift Valley Track** is, both literally and symbolically, the high point of the fantastic African complex. At the exhibit's peak is an African hut observation tower where visitors can overlook the entire African panorama. A large, open yard has both black and white rhinos on display. (The first U.S.-born white rhino was born here in 1972.) Beyond the rhinos, visitors walk along the *Mount Kenya Forest Trail*. It passes through a huge mesh aviary filled with African forest birds to a cheetah yard featuring manmade termite mounds and a flowing stream. The pathway continues past caracals, dik-dik antelope, flamingos, and African hunting dogs, to another walk-through aviary of touracos, hornbills, and other colorful birds. A towering flight cage nearby holds regal-looking African fish eagles. Other unusual animals in small grottoes include crested porcupines and aardvarks.

South America is another continent that is depicted extremely well here, particularly in the new **Amazonia Rain Forest**. The exhibit's hub is an enormous walk-through enclosure where visitors get close-up looks at a diverse group of animals that includes anteaters, spider monkeys, rodents, sloths, fruit bats, macaws, and scarlet ibises. A waterfall crashes into a pool below, where turtles and dwarf caimans float. In the entrance cave, jaguars can be seen at close range. Armadillos, margay cats, saki monkeys, capuchins, and a variety of little marmosets and tamarins are displayed in a series of smaller exhibits.

Cats of the World takes visitors through an artificial cave populated with more exotic felines, including African wild cats, fishing cats, clouded leopards, and snow leopards. (The zoo is a leader in breeding the endangered snow leopards.) The most popular stop on the cave tour is the red panda habitat. Most people also enjoy viewing the beautiful waterfall splashing into a moat in front of the playful ring-tailed lemurs.

More than 1,100 birds of over 230 species are on display at this zoo. The best of the many bird exhibits is the **F. C. Hixon Tropical Birdhouse**. Inside, a ring of natural habitats backed by colorful murals re-create the bird environments of the world. The desert habitat has roadrunners and burrowing owls living in a cactus garden. Other habitats in the loop depict rain forests, savannas, grasslands, and shorelines. Some of the rare and pretty birds here include Bali mynahs, Guam kingfishers, quetzals, and birds of paradise.

Nearly 200 species of saltwater and freshwater fish are in the **Aquarium** galleries. Notable displays include moray eels, seahorses, electric eels, archerfish, rare Rift Valley cichlids, piranhas, and many other Amazon fish.

OTHER EXHIBITS

Providing a wonderful welcome to the zoo, the newly renovated area just inside the entrance gate features a flamingo exhibit with a cascading waterfall. Aardwolves, hyenas, African hunting dogs, colobus monkeys, and four types of bears (including polar bears) are some of the animals seen here in the **Bear**

Grottoes. The area also includes a gift shop, snack bar, giraffe house, the Aquarium, and the Reptile House.

Unique gharials and a large collection of snakes, lizards, turtles, and frogs are found in the **Reptile House**. Among the many venomous snakes are cottonmouths, vipers, copperheads and various rattlesnakes, including rattleless rattlesnakes and an albino rattlesnake.

The incredible bird collection is distributed in exhibits throughout the zoo. A row of moated grassy yards holds the largest birds, including a double-wattled cassowary, four stork species, and six types of cranes. (Whooping cranes, which are one of North America's most endangered birds, are seen at no other U.S. zoo.) The many aviaries display macaws, parrots, bald eagles, Andean condors, kookaburas, toucans, pheasants, and much more. Two waterfowl ponds provide islands for pelicans and other water birds.

Seal Island, an attractive rocky cove exhibit, is home to harbor seals and sea lions. They can be watched through underwater windows. Other aquatic mammals displayed nearby include Nile hippos, pygmy hippos, and South American tapirs.

This zoo is well known for its hoofed animals. (Only San Diego has a larger and more varied collection.) The largest U.S. herds of topi, Nile lechwe, and lesser kudus are found in a large area of open, arid pens. More unusual and rarer species include bongos, gnus, wart hogs, addax, sand gazelles, dik-diks, waterbucks, and three types of oryxes.

The African panorama mentioned above includes three additional exhibits: the **African Waterhole**—a spacious savanna yard with a viewing outpost for watching zebras, giraffes, and ostriches; the elephant yard, with both African and Asian elephants; **Monkey Island**, which is shared by red-chested gelada baboons and Nubian ibexes.

Other exhibits include lions and tigers in adjacent grottoes, rare gray gibbons, markhors and other hill-climbing animals, and small mammals such as hutias, hedgehogs, and colorful squirrels.

FOR THE KIDS

The **Children's Zoo** is one of the best. Its centerpiece is the **Tropical Tour** boat ride featuring scaled-down versions of the brightly-colored water taxis at San Antonio's River Walk. Visitors are taken on a floating excursion past *Australian Isle* (with wallabies and ibises), *Asian Isle* (small deer and storks), *Monkey Isle* (woolly monkeys and squirrel monkeys), *South American Isle*, and *Lemur Isle*. The boat seems to pass directly through the *Barrier Reef*—an aquarium populated with colorful reef fish, sharks, and sea turtles.

The *Desert Building* displays dwarf mongooses, fennec foxes, reptiles, and other small animals from the world's deserts. The *Anhinga Trail* Everglades exhibit is a walk-through flight cage with alligators and Florida water birds. It also has an indoor penguin exhibit, a playground, and the *Herff Animal Nursery*, where sand cats, echidnas, bushbabies, and baby animals needing special care can be viewed through low windows.

Tropical Tour Boat Ride

Further up the path, **Kids Korner** has a larger playground featuring a fort with swinging bridges and long tube slides. Small cages of birds and a petting yard with sheep and pygmy goats are also found here.

NEW AT THE ZOO

Since the 1991 opening of the Amazonia Rain Forest, most of the changes at the zoo have been minor. The tiger grotto is now inhabited by rarer Sumatran tigers. Spectacled bears occupy the former gorilla grotto, and the mountain goats have left their grotto to the sifakas. (This is only the second U.S. zoo to exhibit the rare and beautiful sifakas.)

A new North American wetlands exhibit will open in 1994.

Tulsa Zoo and Living Museum

5701 E. 36th Street North
Tulsa, Oklahoma 74115
(918) 669-6200

Hours: *10-6 daily, May-August; 10-5, March-April and September-October; 10-4:30, November-February. Closed Christmas Day and the third Friday in June.*
Admission Fees: *Adults $4, 62+ $3, 5-11 $2. Participates in reciprocity program. Train ride $1. Parking $1. Mohawk Park entrance fee: $1/car, April-October.*
Directions: *From I-44, take I-244 through Tulsa, then take Exit 11 (Sheridan Road) North. Follow past airport to Mohawk Park, then follow signs to zoo. From Cherokee Expressway (U.S.75), exit at Highway 11 East. Follow to Sheridan Road, turn left and follow to Mohawk Park and zoo. From Mingo Valley Expressway (U.S.169), exit at 46th Street West, follow to Mohawk Park and zoo.*

Don't Miss: *North American Living Museum, Elephant Center (including Elephant Encounter museum), Chimpanzee Connection, East African Savanna, Zoo Building.*
Touring Tips: *The new Safari Grill offers a varied menu. Some of the many shaded picnic tables are near play areas for children. This zoo is in Mohawk Park, one of the nation's largest municipal parks; other facilities include the Oxley Nature Center, two golf courses, horse rentals, and a boat ramp on Lake Yahola.*
Entertainment: *Live animal presentations are held twice daily at the Children's Zoo's small outdoor amphitheater and in the Southern Lowlands building's indoor amphitheater. Animal feedings include sea lions and alligators.*

As its name implies, the Tulsa Zoo and Living Museum is accredited as both a zoo and a museum. Its premier exhibit, the award-winning North American Living Museum, offers a unique mix of live animals with the cultural exhibits of a natural history museum. Located just a few miles off of I-44, this zoo can be an exciting and educational stop for people traveling between the Midwest and Southwest.

FEATURED EXHIBITS

One of the nation's best new exhibits in 1977, the award-winning **Robert J. LaFortune North American Living Museum** is still one of the country's most unique and educational zoo exhibits. The museum is a four-building complex connected by elevated bridgewalks. Each building represents one of the four major regions of North America, and each building's exterior is covered with tiny colored stones matching the "mood" of the respective environment. The entry area introduces the region with large maps and color photos. In addition to featuring live animals, attractive graphics, and popular interactive exhibits, this museum displays minerals, fossils, mounted insects, and Native American artifacts.

In front of the white *Arctic/Tundra* building, a polar bear exhibit features an underwater viewing window. Near the entrance, the *Time Gallery* exhibit has North American geology displays, among them an earthquake simulator reproducing a 6 on the Richter scale and a 10-foot-tall dinosaur replica known as "Terrible Claw." Arctic foxes and snowy owls in rocky arctic habitats are followed by the *Life in the Arctic Seas* aquarium,

View of Polar Bear from Inside the Arctic/Tundra Building

which displays white starfish and anemones. Outside, a bridgewalk overlooks a large tundra wolf habitat.

Inside the brown *Southwest Desert* building, the *Desert Rainfall Exhibit* is passed on the way to a walk-through desert room landscaped with saguaro and other cacti, plus mesquite bushes, and populated with roadrunners, cactus wrens, and other free-flying desert birds. A gallery of desert reptiles, including gila monsters and rattlesnakes, is seen along the wall. The *Sea of Cortez* marine aquarium has colorful fish from the Gulf of California, and a kit fox and cacomistle are exhibited in rocky nocturnal habitats. Collared peccaries can be viewed at the exit.

On the way to the green *Eastern Forest* building, white-tailed deer and wild turkeys are in view in a marshy exhibit with tall grass. Inside, electronic displays show the seasonal changes of forests, and an 8,000-gallon *Fishes of the Great Lakes* aquarium teems with gars and other freshwater fish. A trickling waterfall marks the beginning of the award-winning *Cave* exhibit. Among the realistic stalactites and stalagmites are exhibits of bats, blind crayfish, and blind salamanders. The novel *Cave Formations* display uses a panel of buttons to light up and point out various geological formations. Animals of the forest—skunks, raccoons, bobcats, and a great horned owl—are featured in nocturnal exhibits. Tall harp wire aviaries house forest songbirds and an entertaining woodpecker. Forest reptiles and *Water Dwellers*—a pond aquarium with salamanders, fish, and turtles—are also in this area. Outside, a hawk aviary and an enclosure of black bears are seen from the bridgewalk.

A tour of the gray *Southern Lowlands* building begins with displays of carnivorous plants, large swamp snakes, and massive alligator snapping turtles. On the *Great Swamp Walk* visitors follow a meandering boardwalk through a simulated cypress swamp with a large alligator pool to the left and a towering free-flight aviary of herons, ibises, and spoonbills to the right. A large coral reef aquarium displays many colorful Gulf of Mexico fish, most notably the Atlantic spadefish for which the zoo is famous. A larger 20,000-gallon tank displays sharks. Just outside is an exhibit of brown pelicans.

Chimpanzee Connection is an indoor/outdoor habitat for a growing troop of chimps. They are provided with plenty of climbing equipment (which experts site as vital to the overall well-being of chimps). *Chimp Island*, surrounded by a water-filled moat, is enhanced with natural vegetation, fake termite mounds, and tunnels. One tunnel leads to a plush indoor viewing area with tall windows.

With over 3 acres of grassland, the panoramic **East African Savanna** is the best of the outdoor exhibits. Zebras, gazelles, ostriches, and Egyptian geese occupy a sloping central yard. On both sides are large, open paddocks of Cape buffalo (one of the most feared African animals) and white-bearded gnus. (Both are common in Africa but rare in U.S. zoos.) Another open savanna yard for giraffes and marabou storks is across the visitor path.

The multi-purpose **Zoo Building** is the nucleus of the primate, bird, reptile, and fish collections. The building's primates include ruffed lemurs, Diana monkeys, Celebes apes, and a large troop of cute squirrel monkeys. All have both indoor and outdoor enclosures. Also exhibited along the building's outside walls are three types of macaws, red-legged seriemas, and Caribbean flamingos. Eleven more glass-fronted aviaries inside display ariel toucans, violet plaintain-eaters, plush crested jays, and many other brilliantly-colored birds. Highlighted exhibits in the reptile section include the reticulated python, the African bullfrogs, and the venomous beaded lizards. *Secrets of Survival*, a small walk-through area, exhibits a diverse group of animals demonstrating survival techniques found in nature. Most interesting here are the rattlesnake exhibits, the seahorses, the archerfish, the color-changing anoles, and the hedgehogs. Additional fish tanks are centered around the *Amazon River Bank*, which exhibits huge pacu and catfish, piranhas, and a *People of the Amazon* display featuring genuine shrunken heads. Another nearby tank has small sharks and fearsome moray eels.

OTHER EXHIBITS

One of the country's largest families of mandrills live in the large stone **Bear/Mandrill Grottoes**. The grottoes for the spectacled bear and Kodiak bears have pools for their comfort.

The **Great Cats** area has two large, grassy grottoes for African lions and Siberian tigers and a rocky, evergreen habitat for snow leopards.

Visitors enjoy watching the playful California sea lions from overhanging vantage points at the oval-shaped **Sea Lion Pool**.

A set of long, hillside yards displays greater kudus, camels, and crowned cranes. The white rhinos have a much larger and muddier yard. In summer, an island in the **Duck Pond** is inhabited by vocal siamangs.

FOR THE KIDS

The **Children's Zoo** is built around a red barn housing silky chickens. Outdoor barnyard corrals are home to potbellied pigs, llamas, donkeys, and Goldie—Tulsa's famous Clydesdale mare. Notable small exhibits include a prairie dog colony, a wallaby and emu yard, and rare golden lion tamarins. At the *Otter Grotto* kids can watch playful river otters in their pool at the foot of a splashing waterfall, and they can crawl through a simulated mine-shaft tunnel to observe the otters in their den. The *Zoolympics Playground* includes a giant rope spider web.

Biosafari is a hands-on interactive area for kids featuring animal biofacts, push-button quizzes, video presentations, and other interpretive exhibits. A colony of leaf-cutter ants is displayed here in a small terrarium.

A ride on a bright red **miniature train** provides a tour around the perimeter of most of the zoo's 70 acres.

NEW AT THE ZOO

New in the Zoo Building, the *Reptile Nursery* shows how reptile gender can be pre-determined by altering the temperature of eggs. Also, an Aldabra tortoise exhibit opened recently near the giraffes.

The next major exhibit to open will be the **Elephant Center** in 1994. This innovative complex will include a new building, a natural outdoor habitat, and *Elephant Encounter*—an interpretive facility. Inside this innovative museum, the *Elephant Parts* section will have hands-on exhibits demonstrating the uniqueness of an elephant's ears, teeth, and feet, as well as a joystick-controlled trunk. Two exhibits that will illustrate the history of elephants are a life-size diorama depicting a Columbian mammoth hunt scene and an authentic mammoth fossil skull. Large viewing windows will allow visitors to see the zoo's three Asian elephants.

Future plans call for a small animal reserve, a sea lion reserve, a reptile reserve, and a **Tropical American Rain Forest Building**.

BEST OF THE REST

Abilene Zoological Gardens
Loop 322 at Highway 36
Abilene, Texas 79604
(915) 672-9771

This zoo in central Texas focuses on comparing the plants and animals of the American Southwest with similar life forms from Africa. Visitors are encouraged to start their tour with a "habitrek" through the new Discovery Center. This facility includes the Discovery Theatre, Aquatic Adventure, Tropical Highlights aviary, and Terrestrial Trail, which displays ringtails from Texas and lemurs and mongooses from Africa. The comparison continues outside in the Texas Plains exhibit (with bison, pronghorns, jackrabbits, and wild turkeys) and the African Veldt (with giraffes, gnus, zebras, and a variety of African birds). Lions, hyenas, and elephants complete the African collection. Reptiles from both continents are compared in the Herpetarium.

El Paso Zoo
4001 East Paisano Drive
El Paso, Texas 79905
(915) 544-1928

Located less than a mile from the Mexican border, this small 5-acre zoo displays a wide variety of animals. It will soon double in size when a new Asian area opens. Tigers, leopards, orangutans, sun bears, tapirs, gibbons, langur monkeys, and elephants will be displayed in an area enhanced by Oriental-style buildings. Animals from South America are well represented by Spider Monkey Island and exhibits of guanacos, rheas, and jaguars. Also, the indoor South American Pavilion has beautiful natural habitats for margays, tayras, reptiles, golden lion tamarins, and a wide variety of tropical birds and Amazon fish. Children especially enjoy the new Prairie Dog Village, with its pop-up bubbles, and the sea lion pool.

Greater Baton Rouge Zoo
Greenwood Park, Highway 19
Baker, Louisiana 70704
(504) 775-3877

Located just north of Louisiana's capital city, this zoo offers a wide variety of activities for children and adults. The new Children's Zoo has a playground and Petting Zoo. An elephant show is presented on weekends. Visitors can take a ride on an elephant, the Cypress Bayou Railroad, or the narrated Zoo Choo tram tour. On its spacious 145 acres are impressive collections of African hoofed animals (rhinos, giraffes, zebras, and various gazelles—including two types of rare, aquatic lechwe), big and small cats (over ten species including clouded leopards, snow leopards, lions, tigers, and cheetahs), and primates (chimpanzees, colobus monkeys, siamangs, and lemurs). The also-impressive collection of rare animals includes maned wolves, red wolves, pygmy hippos, and cassowaries.

Little Rock Zoological Gardens
#1 Jonesboro Drive
Little Rock, Arkansas 72205
(501) 666-2406

In the capital of the Natural State, natural habitats are springing up throughout the city's well known zoo. The new Great Ape Display features chimpanzees, orangutans, and gorillas living in lush, deep grottoes. Visitors view the display from a high walkway on top of the grotto walls. The zoo specializes in primates and has more than 20 species, including siamangs, lemurs, guenons, and saki monkeys. Predator/prey panoramas include giant anteaters and red brocket deer positioned in front of jaguars from South America, and Asian deer and antelope in front of Bengal tigers. More big cats are displayed in the Lion House. Other carnivores include four types of bears, four wild canines, five different small exotic cats, and coatis. Along with the expected elephants, rhinos, zebras, and giraffes, many more unusual animals are exhibited, including wart hogs, pronghorns, and Australian wombats.

MORE ZOOS

Alexandria Zoological Park *(Alexandria, Louisiana)*
Amarillo Zoo *(Amarillo, Texas)*
Cameron Park Zoo *(Waco, Texas)*
Ellen Trout Zoo *(Lufkin, Texas)*
Louisiana Purchase Gardens and Zoo *(Monroe, Louisiana)*
Swamp Gardens and Wildlife Zoo *(Morgan City, Louisiana)*
Texas Zoo *(Victoria, Texas)*
Zoo of Acadiana *(Broussard, Louisiana)*

Great Lakes Area Zoos

Binder Park Zoo

7400 Division Drive
Battle Creek, Michigan 49017
(616) 979-1351

Hours: *9-5 weekdays, 9-6 Saturdays and holidays, 11-6 Sundays, mid-April to mid-October; 9-8 Wednesdays and Thursdays, June-August; closed rest of the year. Call for hours of special Halloween and Christmas season programs.*

Admission Fees: *Adults $4.50, 66+ $3.50, 3-12 $2.50. Participates in reciprocity program. Z.O.&O. Railroad Ride $1.*

Directions: *From I-94, take Exit 100 South (Beadle Lake Road). Zoo is 3 miles south.*

Don't Miss: *Northern Woods, Children's Zoo*, Cheetah exhibit, Siberian lynx exhibit, Z.O.&O. Railroad Ride.*

Touring Tips: *Mimicking a cozy lodge, Beulah's Restaurant in the Zoo has indoor seating by a fieldstone fireplace. Tables are also available on an outdoor terrace. Among the many menu choices are some of the breakfast cereals for which the area is famous. The 3/4 -mile* **Habitat Trail** *is a woodchip path with scenic views of natural marsh, stream, and forest environments.*

Entertainment: *The large outdoor* **Amphitheater** *and the auditorium in the* **Wildlife Education Center** *have occasional special programs.*

Best known for breakfast cereals, Battle Creek is also home to the Binder Park Zoo. Located about halfway between Chicago and Detroit, this small zoological gem is just 3 miles off Interstate 94. It offers travelers a refreshing diversion.

The zoo's natural beauty is amplified by brick pathways and shaded boardwalks designed to leave the surrounding wilderness undisturbed. Boardwalks through the evergreen forests have holes cut in them to accommodate existing trees.

FEATURED EXHIBITS

The **Northern Woods** displays cold-weather creatures from North America and Asia in a natural conifer forest. Adorable Chinese red pandas are the most popular animals of this area. Formosan sika deer, wild turkeys, and Mexican wolves can be observed from an elevated boardwalk. (Mexican wolves are now extinct in the wild, making zoos their last chance for survival.) At one end of the boardwalk, great horned owls hide among pine needles.

One of the most memorable displays is the **Siberian lynx exhibit**. Visitors enter a log cabin to peer through windows at these small Russian wild cats in their wooded habitat.

The **Cheetah exhibit** has tall grass all around the viewing area, making it so realistic that the slender cats are sometimes hard to find.

OTHER EXHIBITS

A boardwalk from the cheetahs leads through the woods to zebras grazing in a large simulated forest clearing, and bald eagles and gibbons living in spacious mesh enclosures.

Ring-tailed and ruffed lemurs, both endangered primates from Madagascar, are side-by-side in enclosures that resemble a thicket. Aldabra giant tortoises, which are also island creatures, are seen in a small yard in front of **Harper Pond**—habitat of some rare trumpeter swans. The **Australian Yard** features wallabies and emus in a grassy meadow with white cockatoos perching in a nearby tree.

Bulky American bison roam a central prairie yard; prairie dogs and ravens are exhibited nearby.

White-Handed Gibbon

FOR THE KIDS

The highlight of the new **Miller Children's Zoo** is the 5-story-high replica of a brachiosaurus dinosaur. Also in this 2-acre area are 14 exhibits of llamas, potbellied pigs, rabbits, chinchillas, and other domestic animals. Kids can pet and feed both sheep and pygmy goats. Other activities for children include a fossil dig, a giant climb-on spider web, and an attractive playground with a tunnel slide.

The **Z.O.&O. Railroad Ride** loops through the heart of the Children's Zoo, passes through a dark tunnel, and then enters a thick evergreen forest.

NEW AT THE ZOO

The Mexican wolves and red pandas are the newest residents. Many acres are available for future exhibits that will be part of a new master plan.

Chicago Zoological Park
(Brookfield Zoo)

3300 Golf Road
Brookfield, Illinois 60513
(708) 485-0263 or (312) 242-2630

Hours: *9:30-5:30 daily, Memorial Day-Labor Day; 10-4:30, rest of year. All indoor exhibits close 30 minutes before the gates.*

Admission Fees: *Adults $4, 66+ and 3-11 $1.50. Discounted fees on Tuesdays and Thursdays, October-March. Children's Zoo: adults $1, 66+ and 3-11 50¢. Dolphin show: adults $2, 66+ and 3-11 $1.50. Motor Safari tram ride: adults $2, 66+ and 3-11 $1. Parking $4.*

Directions: *Located 14 miles west of the Chicago Loop. From downtown, take I-290 (Eisenhower Expressway) to Exit 20 (Brookfield Zoo/1st Avenue), then follow signs to zoo. From I-294 (Tri-State Tollway), take Brookfield Zoo exit (31st Street) and follow signs. Zoo is accessible from the Burlington/Metra train or RTA bus service.*

Don't Miss: *Tropic World, The Fragile Kingdom, Seven Seas Panorama (including dolphin show), Habitat Africa!, Australia House, Aquatic Bird House/Be A Bird, okapis.*

Touring Tips: *The Motor Safari tram ride offers a 45-minute tour with four convenient stops. In winter, a free heated shuttle service called the Snowball Express transports visitors from building to building. The Safari Stop restaurant serves inexpensive fast food.*

Entertainment: ***Dolphin shows** featuring excellent stunts and a strong conservation message are performed several times daily at the **Dolphinarium** in Seven Seas Panorama. Check at ticket booth or zoo kiosks for schedule. **Animals-in-Action** shows are presented summer afternoons at the **Seabury Arena** in the Children's Zoo. Elephant demonstrations are presented once or twice daily in summer in front of the Pachyderm House. In the **Discovery Center**, a 12-minute slide orientation is shown all day. Animal feedings include bears and penguins.*

Better known as the Brookfield Zoo, the Chicago Zoological Park opened in 1934 as one of the nation's first barless naturalistic zoos. Located 14 miles west of Chicago's skyscrapers, this 215-acre suburban zoo is one of the Midwest's largest and best.

From picturesque **Roosevelt Fountain**, long flower- and tree-lined malls stretch out in four directions. Within this park-like setting are some of the most innovative and interesting animal exhibits to be found anywhere.

Because this is a northern zoo, where the summers are short and the winters are cold, most of the best exhibits are in temperature-constant buildings.

FEATURED EXHIBITS

Tropic World is not only Brookfield's top exhibit, but also one of the best and most acclaimed single exhibits in the entire zoo world. Until 1992 the rectangular building it is in, which is larger than a football field, was the largest indoor exhibit in the world. Tropical rain forests of three continents are displayed with amazing realism. In each, at least ten different species of birds, monkeys, apes, and other mammals live together in a habitat that includes 40- to 50-foot-high artificial trees, thousands of live and realistic fake plants, towering waterfalls, a deep river, and rugged cliffs. Visitors walk along a treetop-level path that gives them the feeling of looking out and down into a jungle valley. A highlight is experiencing one of the sporadic thunderstorms. The animals create a delightful show then, as they scurry for shelter. (Thunderstorms happen at least three times each day.)

As visitors enter Tropic World, they are handed a set of three large plastic-coated identification cards. Using these cards, which display the pictures and names of all animals in each exhibit, children can enjoy a fascinating "animal treasure hunt." The first exhibit, the South American rain forest, features playful squirrel monkeys, endangered golden lion tamarins, and sedentary sloths in the trees; Brazilian tapirs and a giant anteater live on the jungle floor. The Asian rain forest has the loudest residents: siamangs, gibbons, and Bali mynahs. The large orangutans and a family of small-clawed otters also draw much attention. Colorful man-

African Spoonbill

drills and colobus monkeys live in the African rain forest along with a pygmy hippo and trumpeter hornbills. The highlight of the African area, the gorilla family, is seen both from an elevated walkway that climbs up and around their rocky exhibit, and from a bamboo bridge near the exit. Upon leaving Tropic World, many visitors remark that they've just experienced a true adventure.

The new **Fragile Kingdom** is nearly as natural as Tropic World, but concentrates more on displaying small animals and carnivores. Three very distinct habitats are re-created. *The Fragile Desert* is an indoor replication of the arid African deserts and exhibits rarely-seen black-backed jackals, meerkats, and African porcupines. The jackals often dart toward visitors at eye-level, providing a startling welcome. Other animals displayed include sand cats, rock hyraxes, and caracals, but the biggest attention-getter is the exhibit of naked mole-rats. These tiny bald mammals live together in colonies, much like insects, and are displayed in what looks like a giant ant farm. *The Fragile Rain Forest* provides a close-up view of colorful animals of the Asian rain forest, such as fishing cats, clouded leopards, and giant squirrels. Outside the building, *The Fragile Hunters* displays the zoo's big cats. Large, heated rocks encourage some of the large felines—which include lions, Siberian tigers, snow leopards, jaguars, and Amur leopards—to repose very close to their human admirers.

In 1960, this became the first inland zoo to exhibit dolphins. Today, in the new **Seven Seas Panorama**, dolphin shows are a big hit. The 2,000-seat *Dolphinarium* is landscaped with palm trees and other tropical plants to resemble a Caribbean coast. A wide underwater viewing gallery enables 300 people to watch the dolphins during and between shows. *Seascape* is home to sea lions, harbor seals, and two enormous walruses from Russia. (Brookfield is one of only three U.S. zoos to exhibit walruses.) The rocky, outdoor pools resemble the shores of America's Pacific Northwest.

In the **Australia House**, a wide variety of birds and marsupial mammals from down under can be seen. Most unique is the nocturnal *Walkabout* room, where visitors walk through an exhibit of wombats, echidnas, bettongs, tree kangaroos, and free-flying fruit bats. Larger animals, such as kangaroos and beautiful cassowaries, are exhibited in outdoor yards, weather permitting. (Brookfield was the first U.S. zoo to dedicate an entire exhibit to animals from Australia.)

The **Aquatic Bird House** is home to some of the zoo's most popular birds. Humboldt penguins are entertaining to watch as they swim and dive underwater. In a darkened side room, kiwis from New Zealand can be

Humboldt Penguin

seen. (This is one of only five places in this country where these flightless birds are exhibited.) The highlight of this building is the educational *Be A Bird* exhibit. A series of hands-on, entertaining exhibits teach participants about different aspects of birds. A special strength machine tests a person's ability to fly, while kids can Build A Bird on a computer screen.

OTHER EXHIBITS

Four additional exhibit buildings offer very diverse collections of animals. At the **Pachyderm House**, black rhinos, pygmy and Nile hippos, tapirs, and African elephants can be seen inside or outside, depending on the weather. An 8-pound goliath frog is a part of the extensive collection in the **Reptile House.** Coatis, tree shrews, and elephant shrews are among the furry creatures seen in the **Small Mammal House**. The **Perching Birds** building holds a walk-in aviary that includes hummingbirds and an assortment of brilliantly-colored exotic birds.

Among the more popular outdoor exhibits are the **Bear Grottoes**, where four types of bears from three continents live in open rocky exhibits. A group of Dall's sheep live on the rocks above them. Two other mountain exhibits display Siberian ibexes (**Ibex Island**) and Guinea baboons (**Baboon Island**), and light-gray timber wolves live in **Wolf Woods. Indian Lake Trail** provides a nature walk around an undeveloped wild lake.

The hoofed animals are exhibited in a long row of large, open paddocks. Pere David's deer, Mongolian wild horses, wisents (European bison), addax, bantengs, and Bactrian camels are some of the rare hoofstock on display. Other notables include Congo buffalo, collared peccaries, two kinds of zebras, and okapis. (The first okapi birth in North America took place here, and this zoo still has one of the largest collections of these unusual animals.)

FOR THE KIDS

The small **Children's Zoo** is an excellent place for children to interact with domestic animals and to get very close to North American animals. A red fox, a porcupine, bobcats, coyotes, badgers, and owls are some favorites seen in a long row of old-fashioned wire cages. The skunks, raccoons, and woodchucks, which are displayed in a rocky pit, are also very popular. In the *Big Barn*, dairy goats and cows are milked twice daily. Many birds, reptiles, and small mammals—including an armadillo—are kept in the barn's upstairs loft. Goats and calves can be petted in the *Walk-in Farmyard*. The Children's Zoo also features Clydesdale horses, reindeer, llamas, and a baby chick hatchery.

NEW AT THE ZOO

The latest project here is **Habitat Africa!**, which will eventually be a 35-acre simulation of a series of African scenes. The first phase of this new exhibit—a savanna featuring a kopje (pronounced KAH-pee) and water hole—opened in May 1993. (A kopje is an island of rocks found in the African savanna.) This indoor replica is home to tiny klipspringer antelope, milky eagle owls, and free-flying kopje birds. Among the rocks, visitors can look for rock hyraxes, dwarf mongooses, lizards, and pancake tortoises. The mongooses can only be seen by climbing through a small opening in the rocks to a large bubble window. Highly endangered African wild dogs, which are among the zoo's most famous residents, live in the kopje's outdoor yard and can be seen through a wide viewing window in a simulated African tourist lodge.

A naturalistic savanna water hole is the centerpiece of an exhibit featuring giraffes, zebras, ostriches, and topi antelope. Set in a fictitious African national park, complete with a ranger station, the savanna atmosphere seems real. Children are kept busy by a set of interactive displays—a 14-foot-tall *Giraffe's-Eye View Scope* and a participatory path where visitors play the role of a zebra in search of water. An existing exhibit that has been incorporated into this new area is the small, nocturnal aardvark exhibit, where the pig-like aardvarks can be watched both above and below ground.

Cincinnati Zoo and Botanical Garden

3400 Vine Street
Cincinnati, Ohio 45220
(513) 281-4700

Hours: *9-6 daily, Memorial Day-Labor Day; 9-5, rest of year. Children's Zoo: 10-4 daily. Grounds close at dusk.*
Admission Fees: *Adults $6.50, 63+ $4.25, 2-12 $3.50. Children's Zoo 75¢. Participates in reciprocity program. Tram and train rides: adults $1.75, 63+ and 2-12 $1.50. Animal rides $1.50. Parking $4.*
Directions: *From I-71, take Exit 5 (Dana Avenue). From I-75, take Exit 6 (Mitchell Avenue). Follow Zoo Paw Print signs to Dury Avenue and zoo's Main Gate.*
Don't Miss: *Insect World, Jungle Trails, Cat House, Gorilla World, Elephant House, Big Cat Canyon, Komodo Dragon Exhibit, Train ride, animal shows, Spaulding Children's Zoo, Wildlife Canyon.*
Touring Tips: *Touring this moderate-size, hilly zoo can be tiring. For an overall perspective, take a Tram tour. The Safari Restaurant offers a good selection of fast food and provides both indoor seating and shaded outdoor tables with a tropical atmosphere. This zoo closes later than most, allowing pleasant evening tours.*
Entertainment: *Three excellent shows are presented twice daily on alternating days in the* **RC Cola Wildlife Theater.** *The* **World of Birds** *show features talking parrots and free-flying birds of prey.* **Cats, Cats, Cats** *has a snow leopard, ocelot, mountain lion, and cheetah showing off their natural behaviors. In* **Cecil Jackson's Animal Show,** *Mr. Jackson, who is a 40-year veteran animal trainer, stars with three elephants. Personalized animal demonstrations are presented regularly in* **Frisch's Discovery Center.** *In the Children's*

*Zoo, The **Hillshire Farm/Kahn's Children's Theater** presents educational skits in summer, and activities for 3- to 7-year-olds are held every half hour in the **Children's Forest**.*

Not being one of America's largest cities, Cincinnati is an unlikely place to find one of its very best zoos. However, the Cincinnati Zoo has an almost unsurpassed collection of popular, yet rarely-exhibited animals. They include Komodo dragons, pygmy chimpanzees, walruses, white tigers, okapis, and a king cheetah. Overall it displays over 750 different species, ranking it as the fifth largest in diversity in the United States.

The zoo was dubbed by *Newsweek* as the "sexiest" zoo because of its successful breeding record with exotic animals—especially white tigers, black rhinos, and gorillas. In 1991, the **Center for Reproduction of Endangered Wildlife** (CREW) opened on the zoo grounds. Inside CREW, high-tech reproduction methods, such as frozen embryo transfer and artificial insemination, are researched and applied in the effort to save endangered species. CREW has an interactive exhibit area open to the public on weekdays.

Increasing public awareness is another conservation method utilized in the **Passenger Pigeon Memorial**. Built in 1875, this former birdhouse is now a monument to extinct animals—particularly the passenger pigeon and the Carolina parakeet. The very last members of these species died at this zoo in 1914 and 1918, respectively. Mounted specimens of each are exhibited here.

As its name implies, the zoo is also one of the country's finest botanical gardens. Most animal exhibits feature vegetation from the same region of the world as the animals displayed. More than 3,000 plant species are found on the grounds. These include numerous plantings of perennials, ornamental grasses, and bamboo, plus 280,000 bulbs that bloom in the spring.

FEATURED EXHIBITS

The most innovative exhibit here is the award-winning **Insect World**—the largest and best display of live insects in the United States. In a museum-like setting, educational graphics, hands-on activities, and living insects are blended together to teach such topics as *How Insects Feed, Who Eats Insects, Camouflage and Mimicry*, and *Insect Lifestyles*. For example, a special scale reports a visitor's weight in insects. (One 6-year-old girl weighed in at over 8.5 million insects!) Insect World is noted for its exotic insects, such as Southeast Asian walking sticks, Hercules beetles, and inch-long bullet ants (one of the world's most venomous insects). Altogether over 100 species are on display. Special exhibits include naked mole-rats, the *Butterfly Rain Forest* (which includes hummingbirds), and a leaf-cutter ant display in which a miniature video camera mounted in the exhibit magnifies the ants onto a video screen.

Using the theme "The Cat as a Hunter," the **Cat House** is probably the zoo's most highly-acclaimed exhibit. More than half of the world's 37 wild feline species are on exhibit here. Each habitat features natural rockwork and beautiful mural backdrops that realistically mimic the cats' native homes. Jaguars live in what appears to be the ruins of an Inca temple, while pumas seem to be living in the Utah desert. Snow leopards, ocelots, servals, and clouded leopards can also be viewed. (The Pampas cats and rusty spotted cats are the only members of their species displayed in the U.S.) The carpeted viewing area also has educational displays, including an authentic fossil skeleton of a saber-toothed cat.

Gorilla World is one of the better displays of its kind. The large lowland apes are in a grassy habitat in front of a splashing waterfall. Only a 15-foot-deep moat separates them from the shaded viewing area. The exhibit also includes two large mesh enclosures displaying smaller primates and rare aardwolves.

If Cincinnati has a trademark animal, it would have to be its rare white Bengal tigers. Even the city's NFL football team is called the "Bengals." (Over half of the world's living white tigers were bred here.) **Big Cat Canyon** provides a spacious habitat for these tigers, which can be seen unhindered from an elevated bridge encircling the exhibit.

Wildlife Canyon features long open yards containing rare animals. Hairy Sumatran rhinos are the canyon's most endangered animals (under 900 remain in existence). Other unusual animals exhibited here include anoa (dwarf water buffalo), a takin (from the mountains of China), zebra duikers, babirusas (fierce-looking wild pigs from Asia), attractive Mhorr gazelles, and a group of wart hogs.

More familiar animals—African and Asian elephants, an Indian rhino, Malayan tapirs, a Nile hippo, and a Masai giraffe—are seen inside and outside of the old **Elephant House**. The main attraction of this 1902 building, which resembles an Indian mosque, is the rarely-exhibited okapis. (Cincinnati is one of only seven American zoos to display these "forest giraffes.")

The **Komodo Dragon Exhibit** is in a special building that offers excellent viewing of the world's largest and most dangerous lizards. (In 1989, when the President of Indonesia presented a pair of Komodo dragons as a gift to President Bush, Cincinnati became only the second U.S. zoo to display them.) These huge lizards are often seen submerged in their pools, with only their snouts out of the water. In warm weather, they can be found in their outdoor yard.

OTHER EXHIBITS

The centerpiece of the many bird exhibits is a large **Bird House**. Inside, traditional galleries display feathered specimens from around the globe, including penguins, toucanets, kingfishers, hornbills, and the magnificent bird of paradise. An enormous **Walk-through Flight Cage** features spoonbills, scarlet ibises, and Mandarin ducks in a lush mesh enclosure. Two more flight cages hold Andean condors and bald eagles. Colorful exotic birds such as toucans and Waldrapp ibises reside in the hard-to-find **Pheasant Aviary**.

Built in 1875, the gazebo-shaped **Reptile House** is one of the zoo's original structures. Among the numerous reptiles inside this small building are a Chinese alligator, Indian pythons, and many types of rattlesnakes.

Among the notable exhibits in the **Lilly Ackerland Fleischmann Memorial Aquarium** are an Amazon tank with giant pacu fish and the *Pacific Kelp Bed* with spotted horn sharks and barracudas. Other interesting specimens include poison arrow frogs, tentacled snakes, lionfish, moray eels, and portly porcupine fish.

The **Nocturnal House** was the world's first display of active night animals to use light-reversal. Among the notable night creatures are barn owls, binturongs, fennec foxes, and vampire bats. In the largest exhibit, fruit bats flutter about pig-like aardvarks.

The **African Veldt** is this zoo's largest exhibit. An expansive, arid plain provides a naturalistic home for zebras, elands, and crowned cranes. Smaller yards hold bongos, black rhinos, ostriches, and Marabou storks. Across the path, a fenced hillside enclosure displays a large group of cheetahs—including the country's first king cheetah, which sports a striking color variation of dark splotches and stripes.

Interesting island exhibits are found throughout the zoo. The gibbons and siamangs on the **Gibbon Islands** enjoy tall bamboo climbing structures. **Monkey Island**, which features loud waterfalls, has an unlikely trio of species—Japanese snow monkeys, Nubian ibexes, and California sea lions (swimming in the moat). **Markhor Island** has curly-horned markhors living with more snow monkeys. The **Red Panda Exhibit** is one of the best of these cuddly animals.

The **Cat Grottoes** display lions, African wild dogs, and the nation's only Indochinese tigers. The **Bearline** has more grottoes with spectacled, sloth, and polar bears. Most of the zoo's seven species of lemurs (more than any other U.S. zoo) are in a set of outdoor enclosures.

FOR THE KIDS

The stated purpose of the **Joseph H. Spaulding Children's Zoo** is to involve children with animals. Especially designed activities for kids include a rock-hopping path over a pond, a rope playground and slide, and tunnels to pop-up acrylic domes in a turkey vulture exhibit. The *Kids Shop* features low, child-level shelves and low-priced souvenirs that appeal to children. Exotic newborn animals requiring special attention may be seen in a nursery, and pygmy goats and zebu cattle can be petted in the *Farm Yard*. Walruses can be viewed in their *Rocky Coast* habitat from either a wooden deck or an underwater gallery. (Walruses are displayed in only three American zoos.) The *Southwestern Desert* exhibit displays skunks and burros, while the *Eastern Woodlands* exhibit displays raccoons and gray foxes and also features a walk-through forest aviary. Flamingos and black-footed penguins are also exhibited in the Children's Zoo.

Rides on Bactrian camels and elephants are available near the **Whiting Grove** picnic area. The old-fashioned **Train ride** is one of the best. As it circles the zoo, it travels across high trestles overlooking the African Veldt and glides over **Swan Lake** on surface-level tracks offering a panoramic view of the fountains and waterfowl.

NEW AT THE ZOO

Opened during the summer of 1993, **Jungle Trails** is the zoo's most realistic exhibit. This remarkable habitat is the new home for an outstanding collection of rain forest primates from Asia and Africa. Visitors walk a mist-covered trail through tropical foliage that includes banana plants, palms, and ferns. After crossing a swinging rope bridge, they encounter loud gibbons in front of a crashing waterfall. Orangutans live in a dense jungle clearing with tall trees for climbing. Rare, ghostly douc langurs, which were nearly wiped out by the Vietnam War, are displayed. (Only two other U.S. zoos display them.) Shoebill and saddle-billed storks wade in a papyrus swamp in the African rain forest, and rarely-exhibited bonobos (pygmy chimpanzees) can be seen up close on a wooded hillside along a jungle stream or through a large window in a viewing cave. Lemurs and colobus monkeys also enjoy tropical habitats. The Asian and African areas both have nocturnal exhibits of smaller primates, reptiles, and birds in beautiful jungle buildings that also provide winter quarters for the outdoor animals.

Cleveland Metroparks Zoo

3900 Brookside Park Drive
Cleveland, Ohio 44109
(216) 661-7511 or 661-6500

Hours: *10-5 weekdays, 10-7 weekends, Memorial Day-Labor Day; 10-5 daily, rest of year. RainForest open until 9 pm on summer Wednesdays. Closed New Year's Day and Christmas Day.*
Admission Fees: *Zoo and Rainforest: adults $7, 2-11 $4. Zoo only: adults $5, 2-11 $3. Participates in reciprocity program. Train ride $1.*
Directions: *From I-71, take Exit 244 South (Fulton Parkway), then follow signs on Fulton Parkway to Brookside Park Drive and zoo's main entrance.*
Don't Miss: *The RainForest; Birds of the World Building; Primate, Cat, & Aquatics Building; Big Creek Commons.*
Touring Tips: *The RainForest is kept a humid 80 degrees. Coat racks are available, but it is wiser to leave coats and heavy sweaters in your car. (The parking lot is located between the RainForest and the rest of the zoo.) Free ZooTrams are available to the far points of the zoo and are espcially convenient for reaching the Upland Commons. It is advisable to take the winding Deck Walk through the woods going downhill. Enjoyable eating areas are available in front of the lions and in a bazaar-like restaurant in the RainForest.*
Entertainment: *The hillside Amphitheatre sometimes hosts special presentations.*

Opened in 1881, the Cleveland Metroparks Zoo has been at its present location in hilly Brookside Park since 1914. It is the country's seventh oldest zoo.

This zoo is separated into six distinct areas: Zoogate Commons, Big Creek Commons, Birds of the World, Upland Commons, Children's Farm, and The RainForest.

FEATURED EXHIBITS

Among the tall oaks of **Upland Commons**, the main attraction is the **Primate, Cat, & Aquatics Building**. Inside, wide carpeted halls are surrounded by rows of glass-fronted enclosures for a wide variety of animals, including gorillas, chimpanzees, mandrills, baboons, howler monkeys, spider monkeys, and jaguars. What the enclosures lack in naturalism they make up for in excellent viewing. The *Rare and Beautiful Animals of China Exhibit* features red pandas, snow leopards, and clouded leopards in a wing that is decorated in a Chinese motif. These animals can also be viewed in outdoor yards. In the Aquatics section, a wall of aquariums displays seahorses, green sea turtles, and huge pacu fish. Sharks and rays are seen through portholes and from a seating area where a recorded soundtrack sets an eerie mood.

Beezer the Macaw

Big Creek Commons is located at the far end of the zoo grounds. Two separate pools of sea lions and polar bears feature roaring waterfalls splashing into natural rocky habitats. The **Northern Trek** exhibit features Bactrian camels, Siberian reindeer, and Thorald's deer—all from the northern Asian plains. A circular set of stone grottoes exhibits Siberian tigers and three types of bears.

Nearly every possible bird habitat—including the seashore, the desert, a bamboo forest, a Cypress swamp, and Antarctica—is strikingly re-created in the **Birds of the World Building**. Notable birds displayed include great hornbills, toucans, colorful jungle birds, and two penguin species.

OTHER EXHIBITS

The **African Plains** are viewed from secluded lookouts off the main trail. Zebras, waterbucks, giraffes, and vultures can be seen there. The world's only **Rhino/Cheetah exhibit** has these endangered animals living together in peace.

The large **Pachyderm Building** has both indoor pens and outdoor yards for African elephants, wart hogs, pygmy hippos, and a Nile hippo. The **Australia** exhibits display kangaroos, wallabies, tree kangaroos, and cassowaries. Rheas and a guanaco herd live in the **South American yard**.

Waterfowl Lake is filled with ducks and swans, and a pair of **Gibbon Islands** can be viewed from a bridge. Endangered bald eagles and Andean condors can be seen from two levels in their large flight cages. The **Greenhouse** holds everything from jungle plants to cacti.

FOR THE KIDS

The *International Farm* is the main attraction of the **Children's Farm** section. It displays exotic breeds of horses and chickens and also has a cute turkey hatchery, a goat petting yard, and a prairie dog town. The **Outback Railroad** and a playground are also found in this section.

NEW AT THE ZOO

With its November 1992 opening, **The RainForest** established this zoo as one of the nation's best. The domed, copper-colored glass building has 85,000 square feet of exhibit space, making it one of the largest and best indoor exhibits anywhere.

The roar of a 25-foot waterfall overwhelms entering visitors. It is part of the *Wall of Green*, where reconstructed temple ruins are covered with orchids, bromeliads, and other greenery. Habitats for four species of endangered South American monkeys are sunken into the wall and are separated from visitors only by thin harp wire.

The Jungle Pathway under the glass atrium leads to the *Jewels of the Jungle* area, which features free-flying colorful butterflies. A spiral staircase inside a giant kapok tree provides a playful way to get upstairs.

The upper level is entered through *The Scientist's Hut*—a replica Malaysian research outpost that sets the exploration theme. Binturongs are visible from the hut's windows, and a screen door opens to the *Amazon River Basin*—where tapirs, capybaras, and giant anteaters inhabit a mud bank and trees are filled with prehensile-tailed porcupines. Near the steamy jungle aviary children can climb through banyan roots, and a cave leads to ocelots and clouded leopards in the *Jungle Cats* area. An underwater view is provided of the fishing cats, which bat fish out of the water and then devour them. The *Asian Primates* section features vine-covered temple ruins where Prevost's squirrels and tree shrews scamper around Francois langurs. Across the path, orangutans have the freedom to climb a tree to the top of the 39-foot-tall dome. Small-clawed otters frolic in the *Bornean Streamside* along with Asian turtles.

On the lower level, an exhibition hall displays more than 300 amphibians and reptiles, including poison dart frogs, tomato frogs, eyelash vipers, iguanas, pythons, and water dragons. Nearby, fruit bats are seen in a nocturnal display, and a bubble-shaped window lets kids "enter" the *African Pond* populated with goliath frogs and lungfish. Rain forest films, shown in the video theater, offer a chance to rest. Six-foot-long water monitors live in a central exhibit that gets drenched every 12 minutes by mock thunderstorms. The *Insectarium*'s most notable display—the leaf-cutter ant farm—is viewed close-up via a joystick-operated video camera. Easy-to-use microscopes provide glimpses of the tiniest microorganisms of the rain forest. The RainForest tour ends at the home of its largest inhabitant—a 12-foot American crocodile that sometimes can be viewed nose-to-nose through glass.

Behind the Primate, Cat, & Aquatics Building, a new outdoor exhibit of gorillas opened in mid-1993. This natural habitat includes live plants, a waterfall, and a pond.

Columbus Zoological Gardens

9990 Riverside Drive
Powell, Ohio 43065
(614) 645-3400

Hours: *9-8 Wednesdays, 9-6 rest of week, Memorial Day-Labor Day; 9-5 daily, rest of year.*
Admission Fees: *Adults $5, 61+ and 2-11 $3. Participates in reciprocity program. North America Train Ride $1.50, Tour Tram Ride $1, camel ride $2. Scioto Belle River Boat: adults $2, 61+ and 2-11 $1. Parking $2.*
Directions: *Located a few miles northwest of Columbus. From I-270 Outerbelt, take Exit 20 (Sawmill Road), then follow signs closely to Riverside Drive and zoo.*
Don't Miss: *North America, Great Apes, Discovery Reef, Australian exhibits (especially koalas), Reptile Building, Aquarium, Cheetah Yard, Pachyderm Building, Tiger Exhibits.*
Touring Tips: *A Wendy's Restaurant provides familiar and inexpensive fast food. Many nice picnic areas are scattered throughout the zoo. The Tour Tram Ride offers a narrated tour of the entire zoo, and the North America Train Ride provides a 15-minute narrated tour of the North American area.*
Entertainment: *Shows are regularly scheduled at the large riverside **Amphitheater**. Various live animal demonstrations are given throughout the zoo.*

Ohio is a state with many great zoos. Located on the northwest side of its capital city, the Columbus Zoo is one of the state's best and is also well-respected nationally. This enormous 404-acre zoo has a long and impressive track record of breeding some of the least reproductive animals. Its animal collection has no weaknesses and includes substantial varieties of mammals, birds, reptiles, amphibians, fish, and even insects.

With all of the above credentials, it may be best known for its famous longtime director, Jack Hanna. When he was hired in 1978, many local people did not even know Columbus had a zoo. Today, after over 14 years of Hanna's leadership, the Columbus Zoo is considered one of the nation's top zoos. Jack Hanna is not just a local celebrity, though. Many appearances on *Good Morning America, Late Night with David Letterman,* and now his own show, *Animal Adventures,* have made Hanna the zoo world's goodwill ambassador. He is today's version of Marlin Perkins.

FEATURED EXHIBITS

This zoo first hit the headlines back in December 1956 with the birth of Colo—the world's first captive-born gorilla. Since then, visitors have consistently been able to see baby gorillas, as there have been more than 20 additional births. Colo, now a grandmother, is part of the nation's third largest group of gorillas. Her group of lowland apes lives in the **Great Apes** area in *Gorilla Country,* which features two large outdoor yards encircled by viewing windows. An attractive new exhibit of bonobos (pygmy chimpanzees) is nearby. (This is one of only five zoos that displays bonobos.)

The zoo has been as successful with endangered cheetahs as with gorillas. More than 80 cubs have been born in Columbus. (One of the world's largest collections of cheetahs resides here.) The unique **Cheetah Yard** has a long, raised walkway extending into the exhibit, providing a chance to "spy" on the world's fastest land animal.

The new **North America** exhibit is one of the best and most complete displays of our continent's animals. After passing endangered Mexican wolves, a wide pathway circles up to the top of a hill to a rolling prairie where bison and pronghorn antelope roam. Nearby, an elevated boardwalk traverses a marshy stream area where sandhill cranes and moose live. (This is one of the few zoos to exhibit Alaskan moose.) Grizzly bears, black bears, and timber wolves live in wooded habitats and are seen through wide viewing windows. The forest is thicker in the exhibits of cougars, bobcats, and bald eagles, and visitors enter a rustic cabin to look through windows at rarely-exhibited wolverines.

With over 1,100 specimens of more than 250 species, this zoo has the nation's largest and most diverse collection of reptiles and amphibians. Two loops through the wheel-shaped **Reptile House** are required to see its vast assortment. The exhibit is well known for its many exotic turtles, but the large black water monitors probably attract the most attention, and the extensive variety of snakes includes cobras.

The **Aquarium** holds one of the most extensive collections of aquatic life found at any zoo. Three distinct sections feature saltwater, freshwater, and Great Lakes creatures. Notable displays include sharks, loggerhead sea turtles, moon jellyfish, and a tide pool, and a complete wing is devoted to frogs, toads, and salamanders.

Inside the massive **Pachyderm House**, a rocky maze-like path through the middle is popular with children. Large outdoor yards resemble African terrain, with tall, rocky cliffs providing a backdrop for Asian and African elephants, black and white rhinos, tapirs, wart hogs, and capybaras.

The newly remodeled **Australian Walkabout** area features close-up encounters with kangaroos, Bennett's wallabies, and emus. The stars of this exhibit are two koalas exhibited behind glass. (Columbus is one of only ten U.S. zoos to display koalas.)

OTHER EXHIBITS

Near the pachyderms, the **Herbivore/Carnivore** yards are traditional predator/prey habitats, with big cats looming behind animals they would kill in the wild. Lions and leopards live on ledges behind zebras, giraffes, secretary birds, bongos, and slender gerenuk antelope. Likewise, jaguars overlook South American animals, including a white rhea, and a white tiger keeps an eye on Axis deer and other Asian hoofed animals. Snow leopards can also be viewed nearby.

Animal exhibits spread throughout the zoo's westside include polar bear grottoes, a gibbon island, an Andean condor flight cage, a penguin pool, and an alligator pond.

In the **Arthropods/Rainforest** building, visitors walk through a small rain forest room. Hummingbirds and ladybugs fly freely in the lush surroundings, while large turtles bask in a pool. Next is a gallery of fascinating invertebrates, with scorpions, walking sticks, and assassin bugs among the most interesting displays.

A beautiful display of rare golden lion tamarins is seemingly hidden in the **Education Building**.

FOR THE KIDS

In the **Children's Zoo**, *Paw Prints Park* is an inviting playground with many structures to climb on, scoot through, and swing on. A *Petting Barn* houses llamas, reindeer, and other domesticated animals that love to have their noses stroked. A large petting yard with small goats lets kids get even closer. A pony ride and exhibits of baby animals and woolly monkeys are also found here.

The new **Paw Prints Park II**, found in the North America area, contains a *Dino Dig Playground*.

Other diversions include a camel ride and a 20-minute cruise on the **Scioto Belle River Boat Ride**. Also, Wyandot Lake Water Park is within walking distance of the zoo.

NEW AT THE ZOO

The **Tiger Exhibit** has been fully remodeled and now has two natural habitats. An elevated walkway provides excellent views of both the Sumatran and Bengal tigers.

Discovery Reef, a new aquarium complex, features a 100,000-gallon coral reef exhibit filled with unusual sharks, stingrays, and hundreds of colorful reef fish.

Brand new in the North America area is *Ohio's Disappearing Wetlands*—a walk-through exhibit with a series of habitats. In addition to underwater viewing of river otters, the exhibit includes a Lake Erie marsh, a stream and pools exhibit, and an interpretive learning center.

Detroit Zoological Park

8450 West 10 Mile Road
Royal Oak, Michigan 48068
(313) 398-0900

Hours: *10-5 daily, May-October (10-6 on Sundays and holidays and 10-8 on Wednesdays, during summer); 10-4, rest of year. Closed New Year's Day, Thanksgiving Day, and Christmas Day.*
Admission Fees: *Adults $6, 62+ $4, 2-12 $3. Participates in reciprocity program. Parking $3.*
Directions: *Located north of Detroit in the suburban city of Royal Oak. From I-696, take*

Exit 16 (Zoo Exit) and follow signs into zoo parking garage or lot.

Don't Miss: *Chimps of Harambee, Penguinarium, Free-flight Aviary, Miniature Railroad, Bear Dens, Museum of Living Reptiles and Amphibians.*

Touring Tips: *This 125-acre zoo is laid out in a long, narrow rectangular shape, making a round-trip walk through the entire zoo an imposing task. Consider riding the free Detroit Zoo Miniature Railroad for the 1¼ miles from the Main Train Station to the African Train Station at the far end of the zoo, then walk back through the zoo (or vice versa). The maze of pathways can be confusing, so keep your Zoo Map handy. Many picnic tables are available.*

Entertainment: *Sea lion feeding/demonstrations are given twice daily in summer at the Marine Mammal Exhibit. There are also elephant care demonstrations. Other animal feedings include penguins and polar bears.*

Opened in 1928, the Detroit Zoo was the first U.S. zoo to emphasize barless moated exhibits rather than cages. Today, many visitors' first impression is that they have entered a theme park. With a four-level parking garage and a landscaped entrance court that includes a train station, fountains, and a gift shop, it could easily be mistaken for one.

The attractive grounds include wild waterfowl lakes, spacious grassy knolls, and huge stone grottoes. The famous **Rackham Memorial Fountain**, with its bronze bear sculptures, is a favorite photo spot in the center of the park. At the front entrance, a 150-foot-tall water tower is another landmark. Painted with colorful animal graphics, it is visible for miles around.

FEATURED EXHIBITS

Unlike many zoos, this one showcases chimpanzees and not gorillas. The largest troop of chimpanzees in any U.S. zoo is found in the natural **Chimps of Harambee** habitat, which is the biggest and best chimp exhibit anywhere. Visitors can watch from eight overlooks as the chimps wander their 4-acre turf representing three different settings: forest clearing, meadow, and rocky outcropping. The intelligent chimps will sometimes send drum messages to their human observers via a specially-placed log. Their grassy slopes are further enhanced with heated rocks, artificial kapok trees, and manmade termite mounds. Inside the *Chimpanzee Reflections* building, skulls and handprints illustrate the differences and similarities between the different apes and humans. A large, one-way glass viewing panel permits visitors to observe the chimpanzees in their roomy indoor quarters.

The triangular **Penguinarium** is also one of the best exhibits of its kind. Four different penguin species (including the only blue penguins in a U.S. zoo) are displayed in three different rocky coastal habitats, each with underwater viewing. Graphics and educational displays present information about all of the world's penguins.

Birds of another kind are seen in the **Matilda R. Wilson Aviary Wing** free-flight aviary. This horseshoe-shaped building houses a lush, tropical jungle with a winding pathway. Spoonbills, ibises, exotic ducks, and other tropical birds are seen among the streams, waterfalls, pools, and palm trees. Imposing endangered Andean condors can be seen in an outdoor courtyard.

Centrally located behind **Island Lake**, the **Holden Museum of Living Reptiles and Amphibians** is one of the zoo's most popular sites. Many large and small terrariums exhibit a host of frogs, newts, turtles, lizards, and snakes. Notable displays include Siamese crocodiles, alligator snapping turtles, pythons, and rattlesnakes that slither right up to the viewing glass.

Polar and grizzly bears live in rocky grottoes with large pools in the **Bear Dens**. Their backdrop, made of large slabs of rock on which the bears can climb, resembles a castle. (Detroit is well known for its success in breeding polar bears and currently has one of the largest polar bear populations in the country.)

OTHER EXHIBITS

Lions can be seen in a rocky outdoor habitat, similar to the Bear Dens, or up close through indoor viewing windows. Nearby, Siberian tigers are visible in a grassy yard or in their den.

The recently-renovated **Elephant and Rhinoceros House** is lush with tropical greenery. In the public area, African birds fly freely above visitors. Black rhinos and Asian elephants can be seen either in large indoor stalls or in spacious outside yards. Behind the Bear Dens, the **Hippo and Tapir House** has a similar setup of grassy yards, deep pools, and grotto-like indoor stalls for the South American tapirs, Nile hippos, and giant tortoises.

The forested pathways lead to habitats that mix compatible animals: the **African Swamp**, with antelope, flamingos, and other African birds; another African pasture of kudus and a large herd of zebras; giraffes and ostriches in front of an Egyptian-decorated wall; and the **South American Exhibit** with guanacos, capybaras, rheas, and other South American animals.

Other hoofed animals in large yards include elk, reindeer, scimitar-horned oryxes, and Bactrian camels.

More popular exhibits include the **Marine Mammal Exhibit** with sea lions swimming in an Olympic-size pool; snow monkeys on a moated, rocky hill; gibbons in a round, mesh-covered habitat; and spider monkeys on the namesake island of **Island Lake**. Other interesting small animals—wolverines, striped hyenas, arctic foxes, bald eagles, prairie dogs, tree kangaroos, and alligators—are found along the maze of pathways.

FOR THE KIDS

The small **Farmyard** has fenced pastures for pigs, sheep, goats, and a cow. Pens for each of the farm animals and a barn owl exhibit are found inside the barn. The **Log Cabin Learning Center**, located inside an authentic cabin with a totem pole in front, offers many hands-on exhibits.

NEW AT THE ZOO

Opened in late 1991, **Backyards for Wildlife** is a small exhibit that demonstrates how wildlife viewing can be increased in urban, rural, and suburban backyards.

The Aviary Wing and the interior of the tiger exhibit are currently undergoing major renovations.

Indianapolis Zoo

1200 West Washington Street
Indianapolis, Indiana 46222
(317) 630-2001

Hours: *9-5 daily, June 1-Labor Day; 9-4 weekdays, 9-5 weekends, rest of year.*
Admission Fees: *Adults $8.50, 63+ $6, 3-12 $5; first Tuesday of the month, 9-noon, everyone $2. Elephant and camel rides $2; train, pony, and carousel rides $1. Parking $2.*
Directions: *From the north or east, take I-65 to Exit 114 (West Street). Follow south to Washington Street, then west 1 mile to zoo. From the south or west, take I-70 to Exit 79A (West Street). Follow north on West Street to Washington Street, then west 1 mile.*
Don't Miss: *Worlds of Waters, Whale and Dolphin Demonstration, Living Deserts of the World, African Plains, Australian Plains.*
Touring Tips: *Though the grounds are easy to get around, a ride on the **horse-drawn trolley** is fun, restful, and free. The many good dining choices include Cafe on the Commons, with outdoor views of playful primates, and the Pizza Stand in the gallery of the Whale and Dolphin Pavilion. On hot days, children should bring swimwear so they can frolic in Clowes Fountain.*
Entertainment: *Daily **Whale and Dolphin Demonstrations** are free year-round in the performance pool of the 1,500-seat Whale and Dolphin Pavilion—the world's largest enclosed structure of its kind. The demonstrations are one of the zoo's highlights. The 600-seat **Performance Arena** presents animal shows featuring birds of prey, horses, or dogs. Special children's shows that are presented in the nearby **Amphitheatre** include the **Bird Show** (featuring parrots) and **Kabaret for Kids**. During feeding times, the sea lions and their keepers often give informal demonstrations.*

The Indianapolis Zoo opened in 1988. It is the nation's newest zoo. An advantage of being so new is that the entire zoo was built using the latest exhibit technology. Indianapolis is one of the best when it comes to displaying animals at close range in naturalistic habitats.

This zoo is the nation's first to arrange its animals into "biomes," or specific environmental areas that animals from around the globe live in. Nearly all of the world's creatures live in one of the biomes represented here: Waters, Forests, Deserts, and Plains.

FEATURED EXHIBITS

This zoo's crown jewel is the semi-circular **World of Waters** complex. Much more than just a fish aquarium, it also exhibits mammals, birds, reptiles, and amphibians that spend much of their lives in water. A rocky pool at the front of the building replicates the northern California coastline and is populated with California sea lions. Visitors entering the building are greeted by an indoor rain tunnel and an overwhelming 26-foot-wide shark exhibit. The *Coral Reef* exhibit, with hundreds of colorful fish, features an inverted bubble window that kids can climb into for a closer look. Six smaller tanks display cuttlefish, a giant Pacific octopus, and other interesting species. After passing the *Living Coral Reef* and the lean-into *Indiana Pond* exhibit, the air gets hot and humid in the *Amazon Exhibit*. Along a looping path that descends from the river's surface to its depths, caimans (alligator relatives), anacondas (the world's largest snakes), piranhas, macaws, and giant Amazon fish are encountered in a lush jungle setting. Another Amazon creature, the electric eel, is seen nearby, as are African cichlids and a *Mangrove Mudflat* exhibit with stingrays and scarlet ibises. Puffins and other northern seabirds rest on rocky cliffs or "fly" underwater in the surf created by the exhibit's wave machine. The same sea lions seen outside are even more amusing when observed from the underwater viewing window. In the *Penguin Exhibit*, the floor of the visitor walkway is 4 feet below the water's surface, so the two penguin species can dive deep, swim under the path, and pop up on the other side. Polar bears are seen above and below water from a split-level viewing panel. When they dive at the spectators behind the window, the area becomes the most crowded place in the zoo. The polar bears' rocky winter habitat is also seen outside.

The **Living Deserts of the World** building is covered by an 80-foot transparent dome, which creates a warm, dry climate. Desert gravel from Arizona lines the winding path through rock formations, canyons, and 210 plant species that include desert palms and giant cacti. Small finches, hummingbirds, and lizards roam freely. An observant visitor can count up to 30 animal species, including large iguanas, endangered tortoises, and attractive quails.

From the initial **African Plains** observation point, zebras, lions, elephants, and giraffes all appear to share a grassland habitat. In reality, the zebras live in the central veldt exhibit with antelope, ostriches, and other African birds.

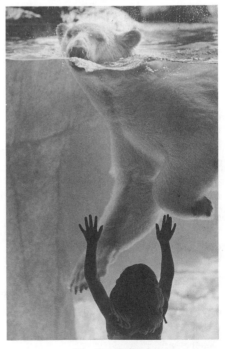

Polar Bear Swimming

The lions, kept away from their natural prey by a hidden moat, can be can seen at incredibly close range through thin harp wire. Another open plains enclosure has giraffes sharing space with gazelles and European storks. A rustic boardwalk takes visitors to within a few feet of the African elephants' 10-foot-deep swimming pool. Large manmade boulders are used to simulate kopjes in the lion and elephant exhibits. A troop of over 25 Guinea baboons, which are especially amusing when they groom or chase each other, lives in another kopje habitat. Aldabra giant tortoises are seen in a small yard nearby.

The smaller **Australian Plains** features kangaroos, wallaroos, emus, and black swans in a hillside exhibit. Sometimes cute little wallabies accidentally hop onto the visitor path, causing a flurry of excitement. Beautiful birds from Australia are seen in a small walk-through aviary.

OTHER EXHIBITS

The **Forests** exhibits are among the zoo's finest. The highlight of the *Eastern Forests* area is the Siberian Tiger exhibit, which features natural vegetation, waterfalls, and a long stream. Thin harp wire barriers provide visitors with close up views of four young tigers. An adjacent small yard displays potential tiger prey— muntjacs (little Asian deer) and a red panda. Snow leopards are often seen asleep on the rocky ledges of their habitat. The most active residents are Japanese snow monkeys, which live in a mesh enclosure with two pools and a simulated hot spring. The *Western Forests* area features intimidating Kodiak bears, which can be viewed from across a moat or up close through a viewing window. Nearby, a towering flight cage displays bald eagles.

Between shows, the dolphins and the only false killer whale in the U.S. can be observed in the **Whale and Dolphin Pavilion** performance pool. A gallery in the lower level offers underwater viewing. Just outside of the pavilion is a rocky cove habitat of harbor seals. An underwater viewing gallery lets visitors watch the plump seals swimming upside down.

In the **Commons Plaza**, two islands on either side of the restaurant are inhabited by flamingos, gibbons, and a large group of endangered ring-tailed lemurs.

FOR THE KIDS

In the **Encounters** area, a central set of corrals feature domesticated animals from around the world, including reindeer, llamas, potbellied pigs, and a yak. American domestics—such as donkeys, sheep, horses, and a cow—can be seen in other pens and inside the *Interpretive Center*. Also inside are domestic pets, a hatchery, and an active beehive, as well as activities for children and volunteers to answer questions. The outside contact yard has a large flock of African pygmy goats for petting.

This zoo has a wide variety of entertaining rides: a train ride that takes visitors on an elevated tour of the Plains areas; a restored antique carousel; elephant, camel, and pony rides.

On hot days, kids can play in the cascading and squirting waters of the **Clowes Fountain**. A playground in front of the Cafe on the Commons is also popular.

NEW AT THE ZOO

Opened in 1993 in the World of Waters complex, *Toads, Frogs, and Polywogs* displays amphibians from around the world. Eighteen glass-fronted natural habitats represent the five climatic zones that frogs and toads live in. Highlights include Surinam toads, African bullfrogs, and a lush display of multi-colored dart poison frogs. Enjoyable hands-on activities are available for children near the bullfrog feeding station.

Two galleries in the perimeter of the Deserts building will open soon with exhibits of both nocturnal and small desert animals. Future plans call for the **North American Plains** to be added to the Plains Biome, and possibly a tropical rain forest building will be added to the Forest Biome.

Lincoln Park Zoological Gardens

2200 North Cannon Drive
Chicago, Illinois 60614
(312) 294-4660

Hours: *9-5 daily.*
Admission Fees: *Free. Parking $3, summer and winter weekends; limited free parking along Stockton Drive.*
Directions: *Located just north of downtown Chicago. From Lake Shore Drive, take Fullerton Avenue Exit, then turn left into zoo parking lot. Zoo is accessible from either the CTA bus or RTA commuter train system.*
Don't Miss: *Great Ape House, Primate House, Bird House, Lion House, Farm-in-the-Zoo, Children's Zoo, Bear and Wolf Habitat, Koala Plaza, Penguin & Seabird House, Large Mammal Area, Sea Lion Pool.*
Touring Tips: *This compact zoo is easy to get around in and excellent for casual walks. Cafe Brauer is composed of a cafeteria and Ice Cream Shoppe and provides outdoor seating along the south lagoon. The zoo's guidebook is an illustrated animal book, and at only 75¢ it makes a bargain souvenir or gift.*
Entertainment: *During warmer months, live animal presentations are offered in the amphitheater of the Children's Zoo. Demonstrations are sometimes given at the Sea Lion Pool. Events are scheduled in an auditorium in the lower level of the Crown/Field Center. Animal feedings take place in various exhibits.*

Boasting a view of Lake Michigan and the Chicago skyline, the cozy 35-acre Lincoln Park Zoo is the country's most visited zoo. It is estimated that 4 million people visit each year. Though the zoo has a fine animal collection and excellent exhibits, its location in the nation's third largest city and its free admission policy are probably the main reasons for such high attendance.

The zoo opened in 1868, making it the second oldest zoo in the U.S. Many charming Victorian buildings still stand, but interiors have been remodeled to provide animals with modern natural habitats.

FEATURED EXHIBITS

In zoo circles, Lincoln Park is sometimes called Gorilla Town, U.S.A. because of the 36 baby gorillas it has produced. The zoo currently has 23 gorillas (the country's largest collection) residing in the **Lester E. Fisher Great Ape House**, which is easily the most popular attraction in the zoo. Other inhabitants of the building include 12 chimpanzees (also one of the country's largest collections) and four orangutans. The three ape species live in six 3-story-high enclosures, each with a hay-covered floor and a maze of ropes and climbing bars. The visitor walkway corkscrews its way around the enclosures so that the apes may be viewed at extremely close range from many levels. The gorillas live in three separate troops, each with a dominant silverback male. In warm weather, one of the troops can usually be seen in the outdoor hillside yard. The Great Ape House is sometimes scorned for its lack of natural habitats, but its unparalleled breeding success and super ape/visitor interactions make such criticism seem absurd.

The **Kovler Lion House**, built in 1912, was the first of the historic buildings to get an overhaul. Both sides of the building's original Great Hall are lined with attractive indoor enclosures. Indian lions, Bengal tigers, snow leopards, pumas, servals, Afghanistan leopards, cheetahs, and Siberian tigers can be seen through thin harp wire in habitats decorated with realistic rockwork and gorgeous background murals that accurately depict the scenery of each cat's homeland. The felines also have outdoor enclosures, and the lions and tigers are in large grottoes. The cheetahs have been very productive lately, bearing many cute cubs.

Originally built in 1904, the **McCormick Bird House** reopened in 1991 after an impressive renovation. Exotic birds from around the world are found in ten unique habitats from the *Seashore* to the *Deep Forest*. Each is enhanced with lush plantings and murals. Feathered gems include paradise wydahs in the *Savanna*, toco toucans in the *Mountain Clearing*, and highly endangered Guam rails in the *Riverbank* habitat. The *Tropical River* has a walk-through aviary with a waterfall cascading into the river and free-flying colorful birds such as rare Bali mynahs and Nicobar pigeons.

The most criticized exhibit is *Koala Plaza*, on the upper level of the **Crown-Field Center**. Critics feel that displaying these popular animals in a round glass enclosure in the middle of a gift shop is tacky, but many visitors enjoy viewing the cuddly koalas while they are souvenir shopping.

Like the Great Ape House, the **Penguin & Seabird House** is built into a man-made hill. Inside, four types of penguins, including king penguins, stand on simulated icy cliffs. A wide glass panel allows underwater viewing of the Antarctic birds swimming through tunnels under the artificial ice flow. The *Seabird Exhibit* has similar underwater viewing of puffins and other birds from the North Atlantic.

The **Joseph Regenstein Large Mammal Area** includes both an indoor exhibit building and outdoor yards with cooling pools for rare Baringo giraffes, Asian and African elephants, black rhinos, pygmy hippos, South American tapirs, and capybaras. The area also includes a wooded habitat for timber wolves that stay outside year-round.

Almost overlapping the Large Mammal Area is the **Robert R. McCormick Bear and Wolf Habitat**. Displays of the nation's largest group of spectacled bears and one of the largest maned wolf packs—both animals from South America—are within long wooded grottoes. The highlight of this habitat is the polar bear grotto—a rocky habitat with a 266,000-gallon pool (the country's largest polar bear pool) and wide, underwater viewing windows.

The most famous site in the zoo is probably the **Sea Lion Pool**. Harbor seals and California sea lions swim and bask in this centrally-located pool, which is a traditional meeting place for many Chicagoans.

OTHER EXHIBITS

In addition to the excellent Bird House, there are three other fine bird exhibits. The **Regenstein Birds of Prey Exhibit** features three towering flight cages filled with bald eagles, owls, various vultures, secretary birds, and Marabou storks. Dense with lush vegetation, the **Waterfowl Lagoon** is the place to watch ducks, swans, and flamingos. In winter they can be seen in the acrylic *Flamingo Dome*. An even better place to see waterfowl may be the **Zoo Rookery**. A trail leads through a forest to a seating area where hundreds of migratory birds swim in a pond adorned with a fountain. It is a bird-watcher's paradise.

The **Antelope/Zebra Area** features pedestrian bridges over large, open yards for the Grevy's zebras, American bison, Arabian oryxes, and Bactrian camels. Side yards display endangered Pere David's deer, reindeer, and sable antelope. During inclement weather, all of these animals can be seen in the **Antelope House**.

Two buildings scheduled for future replacement should not be overlooked while they are still open. The **Small Mammal House**, built in 1889, has African porcupines, armadillos, and meerkats, as well as a *Nocturnal Exhibit* with fruit bats and sugar gliders. Small outdoor yards hold arctic foxes and peccaries. The one-room gallery of the **Reptile House**, which was Chicago's first aquarium, is the home of many of the zoo's oldest citizens. Notable exhibits include king cobras, Cuban boas, alligator snapping turtles, and a basement gallery displaying crocodiles, caimans, iguanas, and other larger reptiles.

FOR THE KIDS

The **Pritzker Children's Zoo** was the nation's first year-round zoo for children. In the main building, glass cases display many small animals, including armadillos, boa constrictors, and woodchucks. All are often brought out for petting. Because of the zoo's breeding successes, the *Nursery* often displays an adorable baby animal that requires some special care. Many hands-on activity stations are available in the new *Conservation Station*. A path through the *Outdoor Gardens* features North American wildlife, including river otters, deer, prairie dogs, porcupines, and raccoons. A small petting zoo with African pygmy goats is also available.

Many urban kids know more about lions and elephants than cows and chickens, which is the reason for the 5-acre **Farm-in-the-Zoo**—a working replica of a Midwestern farm. The many red barns include the *Poultry Barn*, *Horse Barn*, *Livestock Barn*, *Main Barn*, and *Dairy Barn*—where milking and butter-churning demonstrations are given.

NEW AT THE ZOO

The **Helen V. Brach Primate House**, reopened in late 1992, is the final phase of the zoo's renovation of its historic buildings. Like the Lion and Bird Houses, it contains natural habitats lush with living plants, artificial tree trunks, trickling waterfalls, and amazing murals that make the rain forest seem to extend as far as the eye can see. The habitats are 40-feet-high and feature floor-to-ceiling viewing panels. The diminutive pygmy marmosets and emperor tamarins, located just inside the front door, might be the best exhibit. Black howler monkeys, squirrel monkeys, electric-colored mandrill baboons, colobus monkeys, and ruffed lemurs are some of the other endangered inhabitants here. White-cheeked gibbons have the advantage of both indoor and outdoor habitats. The *Historic Cage Exhibit*, once the home of Bushman, the late gorilla celebrity, is found behind the building. Visitors can enter the bare iron bar cage and reflect on how far zoos have come.

Despite opening 16 new or renovated exhibits in 16 years, this zoo is not complete. Its "Heart of the Zoo" project calls for the Reptile House to be converted into a visitors center and for construction of the **Regenstein Small Mammal-Reptile House**. This modern facility will display the current inhabitants of the Reptile House and the Small Mammal House, as well as the koalas, in intimate gallery exhibits. It will have a nocturnal area and a glass-domed natural ecosystem filled with lush greenery, meandering rivers, waterfalls, and a towering canopy of live trees.

Milwaukee County Zoological Gardens

10001 West Bluemound Road
Milwaukee, Wisconsin 53226
(414) 771-3040

Hours: *9-5 Monday-Saturday, 9-6 Sundays and holidays, May-Labor Day; 9-4:30 daily, rest of year.*
Admission Fees: *April-October: adults $6, 60+ $5, 3-12 $4. November-March: adults*

$4.50, 60+ $3, 3-12 $2.50. Milwaukee County residents are admitted at reduced rate on Wednesdays: adults $2, children $1. Participates in reciprocity program. Tourmate $1.50, Oceans of Fun sea lion show $1, elephant and camel rides $2, pony ride $1.50. Zoomobile (April-October) and Zoofari Express Miniature Train: adults $1.50, 60+ and 3-12 $1. Parking $4.

Directions: *From I-94, take Exit 305 (U.S. Highway 45) North. Go 1 mile to Exit 39 (Blue Mound Road) West. Turn left, and zoo entrance is quickly on the left.*

Don't Miss: *Predator/prey exhibits (African Waterhole, African Savanna, South America, Asian and African Panoramas), Aviary, Apes of Africa, Zoofari Express Miniature Train, North America, Stackner Heritage Farm, Australia, Aquarium and Reptile Building, Primates of the World, Monkey Island.*

Touring Tips: *The **Zoomobile** offers a 30-minute guided overview of this large zoo. For a self-guided tour, this zoo is the first to offer Tourmate, an electronic device that transmits interesting information at over 40 animal stations. In winter, the zoo can be viewed on over 2 miles of cross-country ski trails. Skis and equipment can be rented. In addition to the Flamingo Cafe sit-down restaurant, the Woodland Retreat and Lakeview Place offer scenic views and traditional Wisconsin sandwiches of bratwurst or Polish sausage.*

Entertainment: *Four comical sea lions entertain large audiences in the **Oceans of Fun** show, held five times daily during warm weather. The **Raptory Theatre** in the Heritage Farm hosts birds of prey shows featuring eagles, hawks, and owls. Short animal demonstrations, called **Animals-in-Action**, are presented at five locations around the zoo. The multi-media theater in the **Peck Welcome Center** offers slide shows, videos, and "It's Wild"—a multi-media presentation of the zoo. Animal feedings include small mammals, sea lions, and felines.*

With nearly 1 1/2 million annual visitors, the Milwaukee County Zoo is one of the nation's most popular zoos. It is also Wisconsin's top tourist attraction. This may be because its 200 acres represent all of the state's best features—dense forests, an abundance of beautiful lakes, and a variety of native wildlife. With more than 2,500 animals, it is one of the nation's largest and most complete zoos.

Predator/prey exhibits, where predatory big cats and bears are displayed in the same viewing plane as their natural prey, are common in modern zoos. This zoo was a pioneer in this type of exhibit and is still a leader, with predator/prey displays depicting four different continents' animals.

FEATURED EXHIBITS

The effect is stunning at the **African Waterhole,** where zebras, ostriches, waterbucks, and other antelope wander a wide, arid field only yards away from hungry lions or hyenas. Children often ask, "Why don't the lions eat the zebras?" Only a deep, 20-foot moat prevents that. Milwaukee's predator/prey exhibits are extra special because they have such variety. At the **African Savanna**, impala, gazelles, ground hornbills, vultures, and other African birds graze on a sloping grassland, while cheetahs salivate just behind them. The **South America** yard features tapirs, alpacas, rheas, macaws, and other small animals, with both black and spotted jaguars gazing at them as potential prey.

As part of the **Asian Panoramas**, Siberian tigers and Himalayan black bears overlook double-humped Bactrian camels and Malayan tapirs, which are often totally submerged in a deep pool. Indian rhinos and Asian elephants are also here in open, dusty yards. The **African Panoramas** have similar exhibits featuring African elephants, black rhinos, hippos, and elusive bongos.

Among the zoo's most memorable and beautiful sights is **Lake Evinrude**, which attracts trumpeter swans, Canada geese, and other migratory birds to its 6 acres. Most of the impressive **North America** exhibits are near this beautiful lake. One more predator/prey setting has sea lions and harbor seals swimming in a deep pool just in front of a rocky ledge holding polar bears. At a lower level, both can be watched through underwater viewing panels. The huge, marshy *North America Yard* has mule deer, wild turkeys, and moose, which are rare in U.S. zoos. To see the white arctic wolves of the *Wolf Woods* habitat, visitors stand on a raised overlook or stroll on a wooden walkway through a thick evergreen forest. The best known animal here is Blondie—a cinnamon-colored black bear. Grizzly and brown bears are also displayed in rocky, moated grottoes, as are wolverines and badgers— Wisconsin's state animal. Dall's sheep are on a simulated mountain, and reindeer and elk can be seen in yards that replicate a forest clearing.

Animals of Australia represents the zoo's fifth continental grouping. Inside the exhibit's building are the zoo's newest stars—the koalas, which arrived from San Diego in 1992. Tree kangaroos are also displayed behind glass in front of realistic murals. Kangaroos and emus are outside in a large, oval-shaped grassy yard.

Like most of the fine animal houses here, the world-class **Aviary** is found on a wide path that takes visitors through a dense forest. Its 1991 renovation made it one of the country's top birdhouses. More than 200 birds of over 75 species are exhibited in six major habitats. After passing through the colorful *Mercado* (a Central American marketplace) entrance area, visitors enter the *Falkland Islands Rookery*, where penguins are visible from above and below water. Life vests hang from the ceiling, giving viewers the sensation of being on a ship in the South Atlantic. Inca terns, spoonbills, and Waldrapp ibises are seen in the walk-through *Wetlands Hall*, which features a splashing waterfall, running stream, and tall pine and palm trees. In the lush *Rain Forest* habitats of four continents, fairy bluebirds, fruit doves, Bali mynahs, and more are seen through thin harp wire. In the sandy *African Savanna* habitat, plovers and sandgrouses perch on manmade termite mounds. The most photographed habitat may be the *Shoreline*, which features realistic props and a splendid lake mural. The *Oceanic Island* habitats display rare and beautiful birds from three South Pacific islands, including rhinoceros hornbills from Borneo, Micronesian kingfishers from Guam, and tawny frogmouths from Australia. A penguin pool is just outside the exit.

The **Aquarium and Reptile Building** has *Lake Wisconsin* as its centerpiece exhibit. This 65,000-gallon aquarium is stocked with muskies, walleyes, and other

native fish—most of them larger than any fisherman has ever had the good for-
tune to catch. The *Tropical River* is a natural setting for a multitude of small, colorful
fish. Huge pacu fish from the Amazon and brightly-colored saltwater fish can also
be seen here. Reptiles are organized in seven gallery areas and include alligators,
rattlesnakes, cobras, and one of the largest freshwater turtles in the world.

For many years, one of the top attractions has been **Monkey Island**, which is
often completely surrounded by curious visitors. The nation's largest colony of
Japanese macaques (better known as snow monkeys) have little problem with the
cold Milwaukee winters and seem to enjoy entertaining spectators with their antics.

OTHER EXHIBITS

The **Small Mammal Building** should not be overlooked. The main gallery has
tamarins, lemurs, and tayras, plus a large river otter exhibit with underwater viewing. The nocturnal *Animals of the Night* hall displays the nation's largest collection
of bats, as well as hairy armadillos and other rarely seen animals.

The attractive **Taylor Humboldt Penguin Exhibit** is at the very front of the
zoo. This round habitat simulates the rocky Pacific coastline of South America and
has underwater viewing panels all around.

The predators of the predator/prey exhibits have indoor homes in the **Feline
House**, which also exhibits snow leopards, servals, caracals, and the only display
of both spotted and striped hyenas in the U.S. Most of the large mammals of the
African and Asian Panoramas have indoor exhibits in the two-part **Pachyderm
House**. The nearby **Giraffe House** also offers both indoor and outdoor displays.

FOR THE KIDS

In "America's Dairyland" it is fitting that the *Dairy Complex* is the focal point
of the **Stackner Heritage Farm**, formerly known as the Children's Zoo. A big red,
eight-sided barn, originally built in 1896, houses six breeds of dairy cattle, hands-
on learning exhibits about the dairy industry, and the Munchkin Milk Factory—a
dairy-themed play area. Ice cream and other dairy products are available at the
Dairy Store. Kids can also enjoy the *Fantasy Farm* outdoor playground, the *Goat Yard*
petting area, and the *Petting Ring*, where smaller animals like opossums and turtles
can be petted. Other features of this excellent children's area include a pig yard,
hatchery, beehive, and birds of prey exhibit.

The **Zoofari Express Miniature Train** passes through thick woods, over trestles, and around Lake Evinrude on its 2-mile trip. It is so popular that long, but fast-
moving, lines are the norm. Elephant, camel, and pony rides are available around
the zoo, in season.

NEW AT THE ZOO

Apes of Africa, the first part of a two-part primate complex, opened in 1992.
The zoo's most popular animals, gorillas and bonobos (pygmy chimpanzees) live
here in lush replications of the West African rain forests. The bonobos have free

climbing range of their 2-story-high home. (Bonobos are exhibited at only five U.S. zoos.) The wide visitor area seems to be an extension of the two ape habitats, as both are enhanced with manmade trees, root buttresses, and abundant living plants. Only glass separates humans from apes. Visitors can peek at the gorillas through the bushes or study them at the wide viewing area. Realistic jungle murals make the habitats look even larger than they are.

Interconnected to the great apes building, the zoo's old Primate Building received a major overhaul and reopened in mid-1993 as **Primates of the World**. Lush rain forest habitats, similar to the Apes of Africa displays, are the new homes of the orangutans, mandrills, siamangs, colobus monkeys, spider monkeys, Diana monkeys, and three types of marmosets and tamarins. The simulated jungles represent three continents of the world.

The already fine Aquarium and Reptile Building will be renovated during 1994. It will reopen in 1995 with a new 70,000-gallon saltwater kelp exhibit with sharks and stingrays.

The Toledo Zoo

2700 Broadway
Toledo, Ohio 43609
(419) 385-4040

Hours: *10-5 daily, April-September; 10-4, rest of year. Grounds close 45 minutes after closing time. Closed New Year's Day, Thanksgiving Day, and Christmas Day.*
Admission Fees: *Adults $4, senior citizens and 2-11 $2. Participates in reciprocity program. Train ride $1.25, carousel $1. Parking $2.*
Directions: *From north or south, take I-75 to Exit 201A, then follow Anthony Wayne Trail (U.S. 25) south to zoo. From east or west, exit off Ohio Turnpike (I-80/90) at Gate 4, then follow Reynolds Road (U.S. 20) to Glendale Avenue. Turn right and follow to Anthony Wayne Trail (U.S. 25). Turn left and follow north to zoo. In winter, entrance and parking is on Broadway.*
Don't Miss: *African Savanna (with Hippoquarium), The Diversity of Life hall, Kingdom of the Apes, Aquarium, Bird House, Children's Playground*, red pandas.*
Touring Tips: *Situated on only 30 acres, this zoo is easy to tour by following a circular loop. The historic Carnivora Building has been renovated recently and now serves as the Carnivore Cafe, offering fast food, hot lunches, deli sandwiches, and ice cream from Nafziger's Dairy. Its indoor and outdoor seating includes tables behind large steel bars that once caged big cats and other animals.*
Entertainment: *Concerts and presentations are hosted in a 5,000-seat* **Amphitheatre.**

Billed as "the country's most complete zoo," The Toledo Zoo has a wide variety of interesting and innovative exhibits. Opened in 1899, it is famous for its historic Spanish Colonial-style buildings, which were constructed during the Depression as part of FDR's New Deal. Its current fame is due to a unique Hippoquarium that opened in 1986. Attracting over 800,000 visitors each year, this zoo has one of the highest per capita attendance rates in the nation.

Located just 10 minutes off the main highway between Chicago and New York, this zoo is a worthwhile stop for car-weary travelers.

FEATURED EXHIBITS

The **African Savanna** represents a complete range of African scenes. Within this 4-acre area, visitors start at a quiet riverbank, pass through woodlands, and end up at an open savanna. The safari begins at the world-famous *Hippoquarium*— the zoo's premier exhibit. A long glass tunnel allows visitors to watch Nile hippos basking on a natural riverbank, to stare at them eye-to-eye at surface level, and to marvel at the underwater grace of these otherwise clumsy

Hippo Under Water

creatures as they sink 8 feet to the bottom of their 375,000-gallon pool. With its filtered, crystal-clear water and visitor seating area, this exhibit provides the best hippo-viewing outside of Africa. Three underwater births have occurred here. An event never before seen by humans, the births are replayed on a video screen at the exhibit. Visitors continue into the woodlands, where nyalas and kudus (antelope) live in a forest habitat across from their natural predators—black and spotted leopards. These beautiful cats are often seen reclining on a tree limb within their barely-visible mesh dome. Inside the large *Elephant-Giraffe-Aviary Building* is a lush free-flight aviary populated with African water birds, colobus monkeys, and tiny suni antelope. African elephants and giraffes are contained in indoor pens. The elephants are best viewed outside in their lakefront habitat. Continuing along the river, white rhinos, giraffes, and ostriches are seen across the water. As the path snakes through tall kopje boulders, it leads to lookouts for viewing enchanting meerkats and ends at a viewing bay where African lions are seen in a sloping, rocky habitat.

Located in one of the classic buildings, **The Museum of Science** is unusual to find in a zoo. Its halls contain vast displays of mounted fish and insects, minerals, and sea shells, and it includes a *Hall of Man* that displays preserved human fetuses. The most popular area is the award-winning *The Diversity of Life* hands-on exhibit hall, where stereoscopic microscopes are available for young explorers. Live animal exhibits include a hedgehog, fruit bats fluttering behind viewing bubbles, and a glass-encased "living stream" with turtles, crayfish, and other stream life. A new naked mole-rat display allows these ugly-but-cute creatures to be watched as they scurry through simulated underground tunnels and burrows. The stars of this innovative display hall are the Queensland koalas, which are exhibited in their own gallery. During warm weather, these cuddly marsupials enjoy an outdoor yard.

Inside the 1935 **Bird House** are three long halls of glass-fronted bird enclosures that house an interesting and colorful array of feathered species, including yellow-billed hornbills, toucans, mynas, touracos, and various finches. Vocal birds, such as laughing kookaburas, are seen, and heard, behind thin harp wire. This historic building also features two walk-in jungle habitats, a walk-through rain forest room, and outdoor aviaries of macaws, parrots, and snowy owls.

In terms of quantity and diversity, the **Aquarium** is one of the country's largest. It displays over 1,400 fish of more than 140 species. Most of the fish tanks are in separate viewing bays. Notable marine exhibits include moray eels, seahorses, an octopus, sea turtles, and a kelp bed with leopard sharks. The South American area has electric eels, piranhas, giant Amazon fish, and a lush walk-through rain forest room with two-toed sloths and iguanas. Most popular with children is a dark booth where flashlight fish light up.

In 1988 the zoo hosted a visiting pair of giant pandas. The beautiful exhibit built especially for them—a large bamboo clearing with a Chinese motif—is now occupied by an adorable pair of tree-loving **red pandas**.

OTHER EXHIBITS

The first of the Depression-era structures built with Civil Works Administration funds was the **Reptile House**. When it opened in 1934, it was one of only seven reptile houses in the world. Today it houses an impressive assortment of snakes that includes three cobra species, pythons, and pit vipers, as well as crocodiles, lizards, turtles, salamanders, frogs, and toads. (The Toledo Zoo has the largest and most diverse collection of amphibians of any United States zoo.)

Cheetah Valley features the world's fastest land animals in a spacious, open yard. The *Cheetah viewing deck* provides a panoramic view of these handsome cats in their natural habitat.

The **Bear Grottoes** provide attractive rocky habitats for polar bears, black bears, and Bengal tigers. Across from them, a new black-footed penguin exhibit features underwater viewing. Sea lions swim in the round moat of a former monkey island exhibit, and snow leopards and more cheetahs are nearby. A large colony of Sykes' monkeys is displayed behind glass in the Elephant Gift Shop.

The zoo formerly included "Zoological Gardens" in its name, largely because of the **Conservatory**—a long glass greenhouse filled with tropical plants. Outside, a rose garden and formal gardens are additional horticultural delights.

FOR THE KIDS

The well-landscaped **Children's Zoo** features a petting yard with pygmy goats, potbellied pigs, dwarf pigs, and sheep. Reach-through corrals give children access to llamas and miniature horses, and other enclosures display owls and wallabies.

The **Children's Playground** features animal-themed play equipment. Climbing bars shaped like a caterpillar and a butterfly complement a rope spider web. Kids can also climb through a burrow and play in a log fort with a swinging bridge, corkscrew slide, and monkey bars. The area also has a carousel and a train ride that takes visitors on a narrated trek along the edge of the zoo.

NEW AT THE ZOO

The newly renovated **Kingdom of the Apes** displays most of the great apes—gorillas, orangutans, and chimpanzees. Brand new in this outstanding exhibit, the *Interpretive Center* has easy-to-read text, attractive graphics, video displays, and some innovative hands-on activities that allow human visitors to compare and contrast themselves with the different apes. Outside, the chimps and orangs now have naturalistic, mesh-covered grassy habitats that allow them to climb at will. The highlight here is the huge new *Gorilla Meadow*—a replica of the lowland gorillas' African home with living trees and wide viewing windows. The apes' indoor areas provide even closer viewing opportunities.

BEST OF THE REST

Fort Wayne Children's Zoo
3411 Sherman Boulevard
Fort Wayne, Indiana 46808
(219) 482-4610

This zoo may be for children, but the many unique exhibits are enjoyed by adults, too. It is divided into three distinct areas. The 22-acre African Veldt can be seen in two ways. Visitors may either follow an elevated boardwalk leading to the Probstville African Village, or ride in a protected electric safari car for a unique view of giraffes, cheetahs, and other savanna animals. On the other side of the zoo, the Australian Adventure provides one of the country's largest and best displays of Australian animals. A narrated Adventure River Ride takes visitors in log boats around the perimeter of this amazing exhibit. A Walk-Thru Kangaroo enclosure and completely screened Walkabout allow visitors to see Australian marsupials and birds with no barriers. The huge Great Barrier Reef aquarium has hundreds of colorful fish, including sharks. Fruit bats, dingoes, and the nation's only display of Tasmanian devils can also be seen here. The centrally-located Children's Zoo has a contact yard, animal rides, penguins, and other animal exhibits. Starting in 1994, Asia will be represented in the Indonesian Rain Forest. This new exhibit will feature a domed rain forest with free-flying birds and other small animals, as well as an indoor orangutan habitat and outdoor exhibits for Sumatran tigers and other Asian primates.

Henry Vilas Zoo
702 South Randall Avenue
Madison, Wisconsin 53715
(608) 266-4732

In Wisconsin's capital and second-largest city is the state's second-largest zoo. Madison is famous as an educational center, so it is fitting that this free zoo has an excellent learning center in the new Discovery Center/Herpetarium. Children especially enjoy the Touch Tank, Honey Bee Hive, learning stations with magnifiers and microscopes, and live animals arranged to illustrate the diversity of wildlife. The Herpetarium provides underwater views of alligators, anaconda snakes, and Wisconsin fish. The Children's Zoo is on an island in Wingra Lagoon. Among the many hoofed animal exhibits are a 40-foot-high mountain for the Rocky Mountain goats. Endangered species include addax, mountain zebras, and Pere David's deer. Other highlights include four types of bears, a penguin pool, river otters, harbor seals, and big cats in the Feline House, which also has a rain forest display. Near the elephants and rhinos, free camel rides are offered on Sunday mornings.

John Ball Zoological Gardens
1300 West Fulton Street, N.W.
Grand Rapids, Michigan 49504
(616) 776-2590

This old zoo is beginning to look new. One of its featured new exhibits is the South American Panorama, where maned wolves overlook guanacos, spider monkeys, and other potential South American prey. The North American area is equally impressive, with coyotes, bighorn sheep, pumas, prairie dogs, and an otter pool with underwater viewing. The Nocturnal/Herpetarium Building has an

Bighorn Sheep

interesting group of reptiles, monkeys, and small cats. Eberhard Adventure World is a modern children's zoo. Wart hogs, lions, tigers, and snow leopards are also featured, and Monkey Island has a breeding colony of crab-eating macaques (one of only two in the U.S.). A new Living Shores aquarium is being built and will display aquatic animals of Michigan, the Pacific Northwest coast, and South America's Patagonia.

Mesker Park Zoo
2421 Bement Avenue
Evansville, Indiana 47720
(812) 428-0715

Area-wise, this is the largest zoo in Indiana. In the center of its 67 acres is beautiful Swan Lake, on which paddleboats can be ridden. The zoo is famous for its pair of glacier blue bears in the North America area. Two observation decks are available for viewing the African Panorama and its variety of antelope and land birds. Across the lake, the African Rift has giraffes, zebras, and lions. The Asian Plains are inhabited by snow leopards and Bengal tigers overlooking antelope and deer from Asia. The newest exhibits are the Discovery Center-Rainforest Conservation Building, which displays cottontop tamarins and other jungle animals, and the Australian Outback, which displays kangaroos, wallabies, brush turkeys, and emus. Other notable animals seen on the grounds include elephants and a large troop of lion-tailed macaques.

MORE ZOOS

Akron Zoological Park (Akron, Ohio)
Belle Isle Zoo (Detroit, Michigan)
Clinch Park Zoo (Traverse City, Michigan)
Columbian Park Zoo (Lafayette, Indiana)
Glen Oak Park Zoo (Peoria, Illinois)
Henson Robinson Zoo (Springfield, Illinois)
Me's Zoo (Muncie, Indiana)
Miller Park Zoo (Bloomington, Illinois)
Myrick Park Zoo (La Crosse, Wisconsin)
The NEW Zoo (Green Bay, Wisconsin)
Niabi Zoo (Moline, Illinois)
Potawatomi Zoo (South Bend, Indiana)
Potter Park Zoological Gardens (Lansing, Michigan)
Racine Zoological Park (Racine, Wisconsin)
Saginaw Children's Zoo (Saginaw, Michigan)
Scovill Children's Zoo (Decatur, Illinois)
Washington Park Zoo (Michigan City, Indiana)
Wildwood Park & Zoo (Marshfield, Wisconsin)

North Central Zoos

Great Plains Zoo
& Delbridge Museum

805 South Kiwanis Avenue
Sioux Falls, South Dakota 57104
(605) 339-7059

Hours: *9-6 daily, April-October; 10-4 weekends only, November-March.*
Admission Fees: *Adults $4.75, 60+ $3.50, 4-12 $2.50. Participates in reciprocity program.*
Directions: *From I-29, take Exit 79 (12th Street) East, follow for 1/2 mile, then turn right onto Kiwanis Avenue. Zoo is 1/2 mile on the right.*
Don't Miss: *Delbridge Museum of Natural History, North American Plains Exhibit, Penguin Exhibit, Wild Dogs of America, Bird of Prey Island, Grizzly Bear Exhibit.*
Touring Tips: *The zoo's small snack bar has indoor tables by windows overlooking the zebras. The hilltop Shelter has picnic tables with a view of Quartzite Mountain.*
Entertainment: *The Delbridge Museum has a new **Discovery Center** where visitors can handle animal artifacts and ask trained volunteers questions about the museum's collection.*

Located just 5 miles off Interstate 90, the Great Plains Zoo & Delbridge Museum is a convenient stop for vacationers on their way to or from the Black Hills, Yellowstone, or the Northwest. The zoo offers a rare opportunity to get extremely close to exotic and dangerous animals from around the world.

FEATURED EXHIBITS

The **Delbridge Museum of Natural History**, which opened in 1984, is the exhibit that sets this zoo apart from all others. Within full view of the entrance gate, a 16-foot giraffe, an enormous 4-ton elephant, and a white rhino with a long horn combine to provide an imposing scene. They are among the collection of more than 150 mounted animals here (the largest such collection in the world). The front portion of the museum is organized into dioramas displaying animals in natural settings. In the African grassland ecozone, a ferocious lion is seen leaping at a Cape buffalo. This is the closest most zoo-goers will ever get to either of these dangerous animals. One of the highlights of the dioramas is Sioux Chin, a giant panda. The remainder of the museum's collection is arranged in geographical groups. Nearly every large animal from Africa, Asia, Australia, and North America is on display.

Along the banks of the Big Sioux River, which runs through the zoo, the **North American Plains Exhibit** depicts the region for which the zoo is named. Native waterfowl, elk, and both mule and white-tailed deer roam the spacious 6-acre paddock, while American bison live alone on an island in the river. For just 25¢ these prairie animals can be brought closer via mounted binoculars. In front of the open prairie yard, a large grassy mound is populated with chirping prairie dogs.

The **Grizzly Bear Exhibit** is one of the most impressive here. This huge rocky habitat has two waterfalls and a cascading brook. Its lone grizzly can be seen from a high overlook and through a lower viewing window.

Black-footed penguins inhabit the **Penguin Exhibit**. These African penguins enjoy a rocky den, a pebble beach, and a deep pool fed by a waterfall.

OTHER EXHIBITS

Quartzite Mountain—a towering pile consisting of giant slabs of rose quartz— is an attractive habitat for aoudads (rugged mountain goats from Africa) and frisky woodchucks that scurry in and out of view on the rocky ledges.

In the small **Primate Building**, a limited but interesting population includes Diana monkeys, gibbons, black and white ruffed lemurs, and spider monkeys. Smaller primates—mouse lemurs and red-handed tamarins—will soon join this group.

The **African Veldt** display is an open, arid yard that provides ample running room for the zebras. More open paddocks display llamas, bison, camels, and other hoofed animals.

Around the perimeter of an open grassy area, traditional zoo cages hold Siberian tigers and snow leopards for close observation. Nearby, the grassy Australian yard has a red kangaroo and emus.

FOR THE KIDS

A scaled-down log fort from the Daniel Boone era is the setting for the **Children's Zoo**. In the tall log barn and its surrounding corrals, llamas, pygmy goats, donkeys, and sheep can be petted or fed. Coin-operated dispensers provide food. Kids also enjoy climbing through a tunnel to pop up in an acrylic bubble within the prairie dog exhibit. A rustic log cabin provides viewing windows into surrounding habitats of bobcats, lynx, and stocky raccoons. Smaller animals—such as elephant shrews, poison dart frogs, and reptiles—are on display in the center of this cabin.

NEW AT THE ZOO

New in mid-1992, **Wild Dogs of America** provides attractive natural habitats for the zoo's impressive collection of wild canines that includes wolves, foxes, and coyotes.

The **Bird of Prey Island** reopened in 1992 after an extensive renovation. Great horned owls, snowy owls, a large flock of red-tail hawks, and other North American raptors are displayed in a cluster of mesh aviary huts. Golden eagles are nearby in a tall flight cage.

During the summer of 1994, the Asian cats will move into new natural habitats, and in the future an **African Savanna** exhibit will be built.

Minnesota Zoological Garden

13000 Zoo Boulevard
Apple Valley, Minnesota 55124
(612) 431-9200

Hours: *9-6 Monday-Saturday, 9-8 Sunday, in summer; 9-4 daily, rest of year. Closed Christmas Day.*
Admission Fees: *Adults $6, 65+ $4, 3-12 $2.50. Participates in reciprocity program. Skytrail Monorail and camel ride, $2 each.*
Directions: *Located 20 miles south of the Twin Cities in Apple Valley. From I-35E, take Exit 92 (Cedar Avenue) South, then follow signs to Zoo Boulevard and zoo.*
Don't Miss: *Northern Trail, Tropics Trail, Skytrail Monorail, Minnesota Trail, dolphins, Koala Lodge, World of Birds Show.*
Touring Tips: *Children should use the restroom before striking out on the Northern Trail. A pair of binoculars is useful for viewing the Northern Trail animals. In winter, 6 miles of cross-country ski trails and ski rentals are available. The restaurants and snack bars have a wide variety of menu options. The new Zoofari Park Family Picnic Area has a playground and panoramic view of the main lake. On the Skytrail Monorail, front cars provide the best narration.*
Entertainment: *In summer, the excellent **World of Birds Show** is a highlight. It is presented three times daily in the 1,500-seat **Weesner Family Amphitheater**. Among the large variety of birds featured are talking parrots, macaws, toucans, free-flying hawks and owls, vultures, an African fish eagle, and a large Andean condor. **Dolphin training sessions** are held many times daily in the Ocean Trail area; in summer they attract standing room-only crowds. Reindeer and llamas star in the **Domestic Animal Presentations** given in the Children's Zoo. **Live Animal Demos** feature smaller creatures in the intimate **Indoor Theater**.*

In recent years the Minneapolis-St.Paul area has hosted many national sporting events, including the Super Bowl, and it has opened the world's largest shopping center—the Mall of America, which features a branch of the famous Knotts Berry Farm theme park. The Minnesota Zoo is another major Twin Cities attraction for vacationers. Multi-colored flags lining the long entrance driveway, a monorail ride, an attractive restaurant, unique "trail" experiences, and fantastic animal exhibits all combine to make this zoo resemble a theme park without compromising any of its zoological integrity.

In the "Land of 10,000 Lakes," it is fitting that a beautiful lake is in the heart of this state-owned zoo. Around the main lake are 485 acres of hilly grasslands, dense woodlands, natural wetlands, and more lakes. To accommodate the area's well-known harsh winters, the zoo has a renowned trail system that allows most of the animals to be seen from indoors, while the rest can be seen from a heated monorail. Four of the zoo's five trails begin from within the gigantic main building. Also at this center of activity are restaurants, a gift shop, and the monorail station.

FEATURED EXHIBITS

The **Northern Trail** best typifies this zoo's image. Along this 3/4-mile trek, hardy animals of the Northern Hemisphere's colder regions can be seen in vast exhibits rivaled only by their natural habitats. The animals are equipped for the coldest, snowiest days and are exhibited year round. Perhaps the biggest surprise on the tour is the Asian lion exhibit. An elevated boardwalk protrudes into their immense wooded yard for a perfect view of the lions' entire forest. The North American Prairie is represented by bison and elk roaming on spacious, rolling grasslands. Sprawling open fields provide plenty of running room for the prong-horns, which are the world's second-fastest land animal. A prairie waterfowl pond, with snow geese and trumpeter swans, and a prairie dog town complete the prairie panorama. Asia's version of the prairie, the Steppe, is exhibited with massive grass-lands that are inhabited by nearly-extinct Mongolian wild horses and one of America's largest herds of Bactrian camels. The *Wolf Gazebo*, the only indoor facili-ty on the Northern Trail, is a rustic building that has viewing windows overlook-ing the entire forest home of the timber wolves; a video monitor shows the activity inside the wolf den. The numerous muskoxen are often nearly out of sight at the top of their hillside exhibit. A covered viewing area has a high-powered telescope available for a better view of these shaggy arctic animals. Animals of the world's northern evergreen forests include woodland caribou and moose—both seen in natural wetlands habitats. Color-changing arctic foxes are displayed nearby. From the far north regions of Asia, Siberian tigers enjoy a wooded hillside habitat with a babbling brook that empties into a deep pool below the visitor overlook. The return to civilization is over a wooden bridge that crosses a corner of the beautiful main lake.

The Northern Trail is a worthwhile hike but, if either the distance or weather make it prohibitive, the **Skytrail Monorail** passes nearly all of the same animals at a peaceful 4 miles per hour. In fact, the monorail is highly recommended in addi-tion to hiking, because from its 30-foot height some of the animals, most notably the muskoxen, can be better seen. Also, the sweeping view gives a truer perspective of just how big the habitats really are.

The occupants of **Koala Lodge**, found at the beginning of the Northern Trail, have little in common with their outdoor neighbors. Unlike the northern animals, the popular koalas are from the Southern Hemisphere. The dimly lit exhibit encourages these nocturnal animals to be more active. From the carpeted visitor area, the cuddly koalas are seen in a lush eucalyptus forest through a floor-to-ceiling glass wall, and colorful graphics and video monitors provide information.

During the cold winter many Northerners long for the warmth of the tropics. This is one reason the 1 1/2-acre **Tropics Trail** is so popular.

Sun Bear

Inside a domed, 5-story-high building, the rain forests of Asia—from India to Indonesia—are re-created with free-flying birds and more than 15,000 tropical plants. As visitors embark on a journey into the lush jungle, they encounter the sound of crashing waterfalls and the sensation of warm, humid air. After passing habitats of various birds, reptiles, and small deer, the winding path leads to a large mesh enclosure of leopards, including a rare Amur leopard. At the trail's switchback, a viewing area overlooks the sun bears' rocky grotto. As the central *Gibbon Lagoon* comes into view, the spectacular panorama presents pink flamingos in the background and long-armed gibbons in the trees of *Gibbon Island* in the foreground. Next to the trail, small-clawed otters and Malayan tapirs swim in deep pools. After passing large cages of lion-tailed macaques (monkeys) and great hornbills, visitors can look down into the new 82,500-gallon *Coral Reef Sharks* exhibit and maybe spot a shark's dorsal fin rippling the surface. In an underwater viewing area, more than 100 species of colorful reef fish, including six types of sharks, can be seen. The 55-foot-long, floor-to-ceiling windows are so transparent that visitors sometimes get the eerie, but wonderful, sense of being in the water themselves. From the depths of the South Pacific, the trail leads up to a mountain habitat of Nilgiri tahrs before again descending to the dark *Night in the Tropics* gallery. Clouded leopards, Indian flying foxes (bats), and jungle reptiles—including huge water monitors and Burmese pythons—are behind glass in a replicated moonlit bamboo forest.

During the planning of the **Minnesota Trail**, someone must have said, "Let's display *every* animal that has ever been native to Minnesota!" This unique indoor/outdoor exhibit comes very close to meeting that goal in its four distinct areas. The first section has five nocturnal exhibits of flying squirrels, owls, bats, red foxes, and skunks. Around the corner, the daylight section reveals six more glass-fronted, natural exhibits of rattlesnakes, songbirds, and pond turtles. The zoo has received much acclaim for the breeding success of the ermines (weasels) also seen here. The world-famous *Beaver Exhibit* is, by far, the zoo's best single exhibit. The beavers, seen through split-level windows, swim in two pools that are separated by a naturalistic beaver dam. They are enchanting to watch as they gnaw down aspen saplings, repair the dam, or dive and swim underwater. A video monitor enables visitors to see the inside of the beavers' lodge. Walleyes, the state fish, swim in the nearby *Minnesota Lake* exhibit. In the final group of exhibits, the extremely interesting animals—otters, porcupines, gray foxes, fishers, pumas, wolverines, and Canadian lynx—can be seen in their naturalistic outdoor habitats.

OTHER EXHIBITS

The **Ocean Trail** starts at the outdoor dolphin pool. During colder months the pool is covered with an acrylic dome, making it a year-round exhibit. Stairs descend to an underwater viewing area, where dolphins can be seen swimming *over* the visitor path. A gallery of saltwater fish tanks is highlighted by the *California Kelp Bed* exhibit. Bright-orange garibaldis, moray eels, and horn sharks can be seen swimming in a living kelp "forest." Other interesting exhibits include anemones, cuttlefish, rockfish, and another *Coral Reef*.

FOR THE KIDS

The first animals seen by most visitors are the snow monkeys (Japanese macaques). These entertaining monkeys live in an open, grassy yard attached to the main building. This inside-outside exhibit is a part of the loosely-defined **Discovery Trail**.

The **Children's Zoo**, also part of this trail, features a contact yard with pygmy goats, a camel ride, and a *World Barn* where international flags hang over stalls of domesticated animals from abroad—Vietnamese potbellied pigs, reindeer, llamas, exotic ducks and geese, and three different goat breeds. Other exhibits include the *Discovery Center*—a small museum-like learning center—and *Our Backyard*—a demonstration garden for attracting wildlife.

The final link of this trail is **Zoolab**. Located in the main building, it is a great place to get close to the animals. At a touch pool, starfish, anemones, and crabs can be handled. An armadillo is also interesting to touch. Many other small mammals, birds, and reptiles are exhibited, and they are sometimes brought out by a zoo volunteer for a closer look.

NEW AT THE ZOO

The newest exhibits here are the Coral Reef Sharks, the sun bears along the Tropics Trail, the Weesner Family Amphitheater, and Our Backyard. Two dolphin calves were born in the Ocean Trail's dolphin pool in 1992. The newest resident of the Northern Trail is a rare Chinese takin—a relative of the muskox. (Takins are exhibited in only five U.S. zoos.)

Takin

Omaha's Henry Doorly Zoo

3701 South 10th Street
Omaha, Nebraska 68107
(402) 733-8401

Hours: *9:30-5 daily; 9:30-6 on Sundays and holidays in summer. Visitors may stay 2 hours after the gate closes, or until dark. Closed New Year's Day, Thanksgiving Day, and Christmas Day.*

Admission Fees: *Adults $6.25, senior citizens $4.75, 5-11 $3. Participates in reciprocity program. Zoo Train: adults $2.50, 5-11 $1.50. Tram $1.*

Directions: *From I-80, take Exit 454 (13th Street) South. Follow signs to 10th Street and zoo.*

Don't Miss: *Lied Jungle, Free Flight Aviary, Mutual of Omaha's Wild Kingdom Pavilion, Cat Complex, Aksarben Nature Kingdom, Zoo Train, Bear Canyon, Sea Lion Plaza.*

Touring Tips: *To be seen completely, this spread-out zoo requires more than 3 miles of walking. The **Zoo Train** and **Tram** together cover nearly the entire zoo and stop at convenient locations. The delightful train ride features an 1890 steam engine pulling passengers along 2 miles of scenic track. On busy days, tickets with specific times for touring the Lied Jungle (pronounced Leed) are given out at the entrance gate. The cafeteria-style Durham's Treetops Restaurant is one of Omaha's most popular places to dine. The food is good, but the main attraction is the excellent view of the Lied Jungle through a 90-foot-wide window.*

Entertainment: *Presentations, including magic shows, are regularly scheduled in the Wild Kingdom Pavilion's **Wild Kingdom Theater**. Occasionally there are also films or special activities in the Pavilion's **Discovery Theater** and in the **Dairy Theater** in Dairy World.*

With the 1992 opening of the Lied Jungle, Omaha's Henry Doorly Zoo has become the number one tourist attraction between Chicago and Denver. The award-winning Lied Jungle the best single zoo exhibit in the United States. It makes Omaha a prime stopover on Interstate 80—the main highway connecting the Midwest and Northeast with Colorado and the West. This was an excellent zoo even prior to 1992, and many of the exhibits here are the largest of their kind.

FEATURED EXHIBITS

Nowhere is the goal of immersing the human visitor into the animals' environment more successful than in the **Lied Jungle**. While in this immense, 1 1/2-acre re-created rain forest, the zoo-goer is reminded that this is an indoor zoo exhibit and not a real jungle only when spotting the translucent glass roof situated 80 feet above the jungle floor. The roof is supported by massive pillars resembling thick buttress trees. Tall bamboo, palm, and fig trees are planted to blend in with the many man-made trees. More than 2,000 tropical plant species live here. Banana plants, orchids, and bromeliads are just some of the exotic species that can be identified using an available field guide.

After passing through an orientation center, most visitors are overwhelmed by the sheer size of the exhibit. An elevated treetop-level walkway skirts around the perimeter of the building, passing through the jungles of three continents. In the *Asian jungle*, noisy gibbons share an island with great hornbills, while small-clawed otters swim in a water-filled moat. A swaying suspension bridge leads into a cave where fruit bats and other *Jungle Nightlife* creatures, including rare golden cats and clouded leopards, are exhibited. Another Asian island is inhabited by Malayan tapirs and Francois langurs. Africa begins with a cave exhibit of endangered ruffed lemurs. Visitors emerge into the *African jungle* to be confronted by a fat rock python in an overhanging tree branch with a glass barrier. Out in the jungle trees, beautiful colobus monkeys are at eye-level. Directly below, pygmy hippos and goliath herons can be seen wading. The *South American jungle* is entered by ducking under low-hanging vines. Woolly monkeys, squirrel monkeys, and Brazilian tapirs live here on yet another island. Endangered small tamarins, tropical birds, and vampire bats are displayed in a cave filled with stalactites and stalagmites. A cliff-hugging side path leads to *Danger Point*. Located at the crest of a 50-foot waterfall, it is the exhibit's highest overlook. A final island exhibit displays macaws and howler monkeys.

Just when the tour seems to be over, stairs lead down to a walkway on the jungle floor, where it is much darker and more humid. Owl monkeys are displayed at the start of the path. Then most of the animals previously seen from above are seen again, in reverse order, with much closer views. The winding dirt path leads around lily ponds, through a maze of tree roots, and into five underwater viewing areas of hippos, tapirs, otters, African cichlid fish, and false gavial crocodiles. Butterflies, lizards, tree frogs, tamarins, and hummingbirds roam free in the jungle.

With 37,000 square feet of interior space, the **Cat Complex** is the largest feline building in North America. Over 55 big cats—tigers, lions, Chinese leopards, snow leopards, clouded leopards, jaguars, and pumas—can be seen inside through glass, in outdoor cages, and in open grottoes. The zoo is particularly noted for its large tiger collection. (With nearly 30 tigers, it has far more than any other American zoo.) It is also one of the few zoos where Siberian, Sumatran, and Bengal tigers (including five white tigers) can be compared. The most famous member of the collection is the world's first test-tube tiger cub born here in 1990.

Just outside the Cat Complex, visitors can overlook **Bear Canyon** from the top of towering waterfalls that cascade into the impressive bear habitats. In the canyon, polar bears, sun bears, and grizzly bears live in rocky grottoes with trees to climb on and pools to splash in. Special side windows allow close viewing, and the polar bears can be viewed underwater.

The 4-acre **Free Flight Aviary** is one of largest in the world. It is so big that it is difficult to see the opposite end of this massive structure. A boardwalk bridge over a long stream takes visitors through the tropical habitat of over 120 bird species, including golden pheasants, scarlet ibises, flamingos, spoonbills, and storks. Three shaded seating areas are available for relaxed bird-watching.

A giant praying mantis statue greets visitors to **Mutual of Omaha's Wild Kingdom Pavilion**. Inside this sizable learning center, a wide variety of small animals are displayed in glass cases. Poison arrow frogs, saddleback tamarins, bats, hedgehogs, and exotic insects are some of the interesting animals on display. The large collection also includes reptiles such as iguanas, pythons, and gila monsters. In a central atrium area, a circular running stream displays Amazon fish and unique fish of Asia. Included in the *Discovery Room's* large collection of animal biofacts are skins, skulls, eggs, and nests.

Sea Lion Plaza stands out for its relaxing charm. A convenient snack bar and ice cream parlor are nearby, and the plaza has a large seating area for visitors to rest and refuel while watching the California sea lions.

OTHER EXHIBITS

At the top of the zoo, an old baseball field has been converted into **Pachyderm Hill**—the spacious home of African elephants, white rhinos, Bactrian camels, and gaurs (endangered wild cattle from Asia). (The gaur herds represent the largest collection in any zoo in the world.)

In the **Owen Gorilla House** and the **Owen Orangutan House**, gorillas and orangutans are displayed in similar exhibits. These large apes can be seen inside through wide viewing windows or outside in grassy yards. Bushbabies, night monkeys, and other small primates live in side exhibits. In another part of the zoo, colorful mandrill baboons have their own exhibit. The **Lagoon System** has a pedestrian bridge that affords close views of three islands populated with spider monkeys, lemurs, and gibbons. Thousands of koi fish are visible below.

The **African Veldt/Hoofstock Area** occupies a large slice of the zoo. Dama gazelles, ostriches, giraffes, and cranes dwell together in the Veldt exhibit. It displays some of the country's largest herds of Nile lechwe, sable antelope, addax, and scimitar-horned oryxes—all rare or endangered—in separate yards. The center-piece of this area is the **Giraffe Complex**, which features indoor giraffe viewing, an exhibit of ground hornbills, and an especially attractive African bird aviary where only nearly-invisible harp wire confines the superb starlings and other colorful birds. Black-footed penguins inhabit a pool in front of the Veldt.

Seven species of rare cranes can be found throughout the zoo. Other scattered exhibits include South American and Australian animals and an excellent red panda display.

FOR THE KIDS

The **Aksarben Nature Kingdom** has a wide variety of exhibits, mostly designed for children. The highlight is *Dairy World*, where a see-through cow illus-trates the milk-making process and a full-size artificial cow has water-filled rubber udders on which city kids can learn milking skills. Rabbits, barn owls and other small animals are displayed in a big red barn. Outside, the *Petting Zoo*'s contact yard has goats and potbellied pigs, while llamas and ponies are in large corrals. A swampy alligator pool is near the snack bar and picnic area. Many photos are staged on the bridge in front of Aksarben Falls.

Among the many small mammal exhibits up the hill are a prairie dog town with vultures, an otter pool with underwater viewing windows, and a small mam-mals building that features cottontop tamarins, kit foxes, and tamanduas (lesser anteaters)—all animals that are rare in zoos. Primates, including blue monkeys, are displayed in a set of round cages. A large fenced yard holds rare maned wolves, which are viewed from a covered deck extending into the wolves' wooded habitat.

NEW AT THE ZOO

The remarkable new **Aquarium**, scheduled to open in 1995, will probably be one of the country's best. Feature exhibits include an Antarctic penguin habitat and an 800,000-gallon tropical reef tank with sharks, giant rays, and colorful reef fish. A 70-foot-long glass tunnel through the reef tank will give visitors the feeling of walking on the ocean floor. Other exhibits include an Amazon river bank, a man-grove swamp, giant octopuses, moray eels, and jellyfish.

St. Louis Zoological Park

Forest Park
St. Louis, Missouri 63110
(314) 781-0900

Hours: *9-5 daily. Outside area of Children's Zoo open mid-May through September. Closed New Year's Day and Christmas Day.*

Admission Fees: *Free. Children's Zoo: $1 in summer; 50¢ rest of year; free before 10 a.m. Zooline Railroad $2, mid-March through mid-November; sea lion show $2.*

Directions: *From I-64 (Daniel Boone Expressway), take the Hampton Avenue Exit (Museums/Zoo). Follow signs to zoo. From I-44, take Exit 286 (Hampton Avenue), then follow 1 mile north to zoo. From downtown, take BSTA buses—#52 Forest Park or #90 Hampton—to zoo.*

Don't Miss: *The Living World, Jungle of the Apes, sea lion show, Bird House, Zooline Railroad, Charles H. Yalem Children's Zoo*, Big Cat Country, Herpetarium, Land of the Rocky Mountain Bighorn Sheep, Bear Pits.*

Touring Tips: *Pulled by an 1863 replica locomotive, the Zooline Railroad train circles the entire zoo. Riders can get on and off at any of four stations, making this an excellent way to get around the zoo. The 20-minute, 1 1/2 -mile narrated tour passes under a waterfall, through a tunnel, and over a high trestle. To avoid long lines, tour The Living World early in the day. The new octagon-shaped Lakeside Cafe has an 1890s atmosphere and indoor/outdoor seating overlooking the beautiful waterfowl lakes. In The Living World, the Painted Giraffe Cafe offers gourmet entrees.*

Entertainment: *In summer, sea lion shows are presented in the* **Sea Lion Arena.** *The sea lions are as talented as those seen at the famous aquatic theme parks. Show times are listed in the souvenir guide. Some of the finest and most innovative wildlife movies are shown in two theaters in The Living World education center; check for show times. Hourly* **Creature Close-ups** *and storytelling using live animals are presented in the Children's Zoo during summer. Animal feedings include penguins, sea lions, and bears.*

The St. Louis Zoo opened in 1913 in historic Forest Park on the former grounds of the 1904 World's Fair. Today it displays over 3,400 animals of more than 700 species and is one of the nation's largest zoos. Free admission helps make it also one of the most visited: It attracts more than 2.8 million annual visitors.

Many baby-boomers grew up watching the late Marlin Perkins' popular *Wild Kingdom* television show. Perkins was director of the St. Louis Zoo from 1962 to 1970. Today a bust honors him within **Marlin Perkins Plaza.**

FEATURED EXHIBITS

The Living World education center is this zoo's premier exhibit. The building includes two theaters, classrooms, a lecture hall, a restaurant, and a gift shop, but its highlights are two exhibit halls that use an amazing integration of high technology and live animal displays. The halls include 30 computer stations, 52 video screens, 10 interactive video games, 85 short films, and over 150 species of live animals.

An Introduction to Ecology focuses on the environment and man's effect on it. *The Living Stream*, the exhibit hall's centerpiece, is a 65-foot glass-fronted model of an Ozark stream filled with turtles, fish, and crayfish. At *Since You Were Born*, zoo-goers can enter their birth date and receive a computer analysis of how the world has changed since that date. Other displays include a touch pool with local salamanders and a weather station with live satellite reports. The other exhibit hall, *An Introduction to the Animals*, provides a one-room tour of the animal kingdom. The tour begins with *The Invertebrates*—a display of anemones, crabs, insects, and other invertebrates. *A Tour of a Bee* is a fascinating mini-movie made with a scanning electron microscope. *The Vertebrates* features many fish, reptile, amphibian, bird, and mammal oddities such as mudskippers, lungfish, seahorses, poison arrow frogs, anoles, frogmouths, meerkats, and pygmy marmosets. In the hall's inner circle, *The Processes of Life* display uses a leaf-cutter ant exhibit to illustrate the social behavior of animals. Life-size animated figures teach about animal communication and defenses.

In the domed **Jungle of the Apes**, a winding path through a humid imitation rain forest leads to excellent close-up viewing windows of gorillas, chimpanzees, and orangutans. The apes' two-story habitats include rocky outcrops, tall trees, and live plantings. Jungle murals on the back walls enhance the replication of their natural homes. The only group of bachelor male gorillas in the U.S. lives in the exhibit's outdoor yard, which is landscaped with lush grasses, trees, shallow pools, and a 30-foot waterfall and has a viewing cave for visitors.

In **Big Cat Country** visitors use a raised walkway that allows them to overlook lions, Siberian tigers, and jaguars in spacious, grassy yards landscaped with rocks, trees, and cascading waterfalls. Pumas, snow leopards, and rare Amur leopards—all climbing cats—are displayed under unique wire mesh tension structures.

The elevated boardwalk that cuts through the heart of the **Land of the Rocky Mountain Bighorn Sheep** exhibit is a favorite among children. Mountain habitats have been designed for wild goats and sheep of North America and Eurasia. The unusual collection includes Rocky Mountain goats, bighorn sheep, chamois, and a takin from China. (Takins are exhibited at only five U.S. zoos.)

The **Bird House**, built in 1930, has been renovated to be the nation's most beautiful bird building. Inside, lush habitats are enclosed with only fine steel wire, which seems to disappear due to special vertical lighting. This permits some of the world's most beautiful exotic birds—including fairy bluebirds, Bali mynahs, fruit doves, red lories, toco toucans, hornbills, pied avocets, Guam kingfishers, spectacled owls, and bateleur eagles—to be seen with essentially no barriers.

The 1927 Spanish-facade **Herpetarium** displays the nation's second-largest diversity of reptiles and amphibians in updated natural habitats. Missouri hellbenders (big, ugly salamanders), endangered Chinese alligators, New Guinea crocodiles, and a 64-year-old American crocodile are some of the notable residents. (Only two U.S. zoos keep unique tuataras from New Zealand. The five that live here can be seen only by request.)

When the **Bear Pits** opened in 1921, their use of molded concrete to simulate natural rock formations became a model for other zoos. Six different bear species are displayed (the most in any U.S. zoo).

OTHER EXHIBITS

The oldest exhibit, the **1904 Flight Cage**, was built for the World's Fair. Inside the 50-foot-high cage, which is nearly the size of a football field, visitors walk on an elevated wooden platform. Below them, African crowned cranes, golden pheasants, flamingos, and other waterfowl can be seen in the thick bushes and trickling stream. Up in the treetops, scarlet ibises and cattle egrets can be seen flying across the huge aviary.

The **Primate House** is another of the many old buildings that have been renovated into modern facilities. Hamadryas baboons, lion-tailed macaques, colobus monkeys, cottontop tamarins, and various lemurs are some of the interesting primates living in natural habitats behind floor-to-ceiling viewing windows. A loud siamang group occupies a large central cage.

The **Aquatic House** displays fish from around the globe in such exhibits as *African Deep Lakes*, *Giants of the Amazon*, *Mississippi River Community*, *Living Coral Reef*, and two penguin exhibits. Notable fish on display include four-eyed fish, puffers, and desert pupfish.

Asian elephants, Malayan tapirs, black rhinos, and both pygmy and Nile hippos are usually seen in spacious outdoor paddocks that feature pools near the viewing areas. Large pens and a plant-embellished visitor walkway are inside the **Elephant House**.

In a quiet corner of the zoo, 2 acres are set aside for the **Cheetah Survival Center**. Six grassy yards provide the privacy and comfort needed for the cheetahs to produce over 25 cubs since 1974.

The majority of the outdoor exhibits are in the **Hoofed Mammals** area. Endangered or rare animals seen in separate yards include Mhorr gazelles, Arabian oryxes, bantengs, addax, and Grevy's zebras. (The zoo is famous for its work with Spekes' gazelles.) Additional popular animals in this area include gerenuks, bongos, babirusas (Indonesian wild pigs), giraffes, red kangaroos, and Bactrian camels. During the colder months, many of these large animals can be seen in the **Antelope House**.

The **Sea Lion Basin** is an attractive natural pool exhibiting California sea lions. River otters swim in a nearby **Chain of Lakes** yard, and the historic **Small Mammal Pits** display red pandas, prairie dogs, and arctic foxes.

FOR THE KIDS

The **Charles H. Yalem Children's Zoo** offers a wide variety of small animals that can be seen face-to-face, including meerkats, hedgehogs, armadillos, chinchillas, fennec foxes, owls, parrots, snakes, and iguanas. Small hands enjoy comparing the feel of spiny anteaters (echidnas) with the soft fur of guinea pigs and rabbits. Animal babies requiring special attention can be seen in a nursery. In summer, children can explore a 3-acre outside area with pathways, cave-like tunnels, a slide, an extra-large rope spider web, and goats to pet. Among the many North American animals in outdoor displays are raccoons, opossums, and porcupines.

NEW AT THE ZOO

The new star at the zoo is Raja—the Asian elephant calf born here in late December 1992. Raja, who weighed 275 pounds at birth, is a major crowd pleaser in the Elephant House.

Sedgwick County Zoo

5555 Zoo Boulevard
Wichita, Kansas 67212
(316) 942-2212

Hours: *9-5 daily, during Daylight Savings Time; 10-5, rest of year.*
Admission Fees: *Adults $5, 5-11 $2. Participates in reciprocity program. Safari Express $1, Boat Ride $1.50.*
Directions: *Located on Wichita's west side. From I-235, take Exit 10 (Zoo Boulevard), then follow signs to zoo.*
Don't Miss: *Australian Outback/South American Pampas, Jungle, North American Prairie, Boat Ride, Children's Farms, Apes and Man, Herpetarium, African Veldt.*
Touring Tips: *This 212-acre zoo is one of the largest, yet it is easy to get around in. Safari Express, a new trackless train, provides guided tours. Prairie Landing Restaurant, also new, offers western-style meals and excellent views of the boat canal and North American Prairie. The waterfall in the Jungle is turned off in the morning to allow bird songs to be heard more clearly.*
Entertainment: *The R.L. Blakley Education Center holds special programs in its auditorium and amphitheater.*

The Sedgwick County Zoo, which opened in 1971 and sports unique and innovative exhibits, is one of the zoo world's best kept secrets. Because it is in Wichita, a small city that is not a main vacation destination, its attendance is relatively low. Though it is the state's number one tourist attraction and one of the country's best zoo, its fame doesn't reach far beyond the borders of Kansas.

This well-organized zoo is arranged so that planning a tour is an easy task. All nine of the exhibit areas branch out from the **Zoo Centrum**—a park-like central region that provides most of the visitor services. High man-made mounds covered with prairie grass surround the centrum to make each exhibit a separate experience. In addition to having one of the state's largest restored prairies along its perimeter, the zoo has planted and labeled over 600 plant species from around the world.

FEATURED EXHIBITS

When it opened in 1977, the **Jungle** was the best tropical rain forest exhibit in the U.S. Many huge rain forest buildings have opened in recent years, but this 1/2-acre, glass-roofed jungle is still one of the finest. Unlike other zoos' newly planted foliage, the thick tropical vegetation here is mature. This exhibit not only looks and sounds authentic, it even smells and feels like a real jungle. A dirt pathway crosses onto a suspension bridge and then winds downhill past enclosures of little monkeys, sloths, and tricolored squirrels. In the trees above, Indian fruit bats attract the most attention, but more than 100 birds of over 40 exotic species are exhibited uncaged. The path leads down under a jungle lake to a glass tunnel that permits viewing giant Amazon fish and diving ruddy ducks. A jungle cave featuring vampire bats lures visitors off the main path. Endangered Guam rails nest at the top of a crashing waterfall that splashes into a pool with an island habitat of dwarf caimans. A small side stream exhibits piranhas and other fish, and enormous monitor lizards are seen near the exit.

In the **Apes and Man** building, chimpanzees and Sumatran orangutans live in high indoor enclosures with logs to climb on and rocks to relax on. Tall glass panels nearly encircle the apes, giving a viewing opportunity so good that world-famous naturalist Jane Goodall selected the exhibit to be the first training site for her ChimpanZoo project. The apes apparently are happy, as many babies have been born here recently. Animated graphics and hands-on devices allow visitors to compare themselves to apes.

This zoo features the wildlife of five continents in five separate exhibits. Two of the best, South America and Australia, are displayed back-to-back in completely screened yards with visitor paths winding around the pools and streams. (This is one of the largest walk-through exhibits in the world.) At the entrance of the **Australian Outback** section, a moderate-size yard attached to the main exhibit holds stunning double-wattled cassowaries (land birds that are New Guinea's largest animal). Other attached yards hold wallaroos, emus, black swans, nasty Cape Barren geese, and New Guinea singing dogs. Among the most noticeable animals running or flying free are brush turkeys, scrub wallabies, sacred ibises, and noisy silver gulls. A variety of parrot-like birds are displayed in small enclosures, as are tree kangaroos and kookaburas.

The **South American Pampas** section displays what is perhaps North America's most complete and diverse collection of South American animals. Like the outback, the pampas has many beautiful birds flying freely, including spoonbills, multi-colored macaws, Inca terns, and sun conures. Darwin's rheas, collared peccaries, and two different llama relatives are in plain view in attached yards. Among the three small monkey species are squirrel monkeys, which live on an island with black-necked swans swimming around it. Five different meat-eaters—a puma, spectacled bears, weasel-like tayras, king vultures, and spectacled owls—are caged for obvious reasons. The exhibit's most popular animals—coatis and Brazilian tapirs—inhabit moated enclosures.

Another continent is represented in the **African Veldt**. The exhibit that makes this area special is a 40,000-gallon hippo pool with an underwater viewing bay where these heavy mammals can be seen totally submerged. Other large animals roaming in spacious, open yards include African elephants, black rhinos, giraffes, and ostriches. During cold weather, most of these animals can be seen in their indoor holding pens. Lions and Guinea baboons occupy rectangular cages, and fierce Cape hunting dogs are in a moated yard. Some of the endangered species exhibited here include Grevy's zebras, Arabian oryxes, and slender-horned gazelles.

The **Herpetarium,** which has only a modest collection of reptiles and amphibians, is nonetheless special because of its distinctive exhibits. A waterfall and cactus garden beautify the exhibit of Aldabra giant tortoises, which can also be seen inside with no visual barriers. A large, glass-fronted pond displays endangered tropical turtles, and a nocturnal swamp features rare Chinese alligators. In the desert walk-through room, visitors need to be still to find the lizards that hide among the rocks and cacti. Other notable inhabitants include Surinam toads, basilisk lizards, and many venomous snakes.

The guided **Boat Ride** is not just for kids. It is a significant part of this zoo experience. The tour begins with a view of bison and pronghorns in their prairie yards. After drifting under a pedestrian bridge, the boat canal becomes a wild river where careful eyes can find great blue herons, turtles, and water snakes. The ride provides the only way to see the spider monkeys and two types of lemurs on their own islands.

OTHER EXHIBITS

The small **Asian Steppes** exhibit is scheduled for future expansion. Current displays include a tiger enclosure and a walk-through yard of muntjacs (small Asian deer) and tall cranes.

FOR THE KIDS

The **Children's Farms**, the zoo's original exhibit, is reached by crossing a rustic covered bridge. Domestic animals from three continents are displayed in authentic farmyards where different breeds of cattle, swine, and chickens can be compared. Most of the livestock are available for both petting and feeding. The Asian Farm, with bright red and yellow trim on its oriental-style barns, features Karakul sheep, domestic yaks, and water buffalo. The African Farm has a thatched-roof round barn with sandy corrals holding a dromedary camel, Tunis sheep, and giant-horned Watusi cattle. Not to be outdone, the American Farm has a big red barn with white fences and a spacious pasture. Inside the barn, visitors can see cows being milked and eggs hatching, and a broad collection of rare breeds of cattle are displayed.

Kids enjoy climbing to the top of high grassy mounds for a panoramic view of the zoo grounds and the surrounding prairie. Steps are available for adults who wish to join them.

NEW AT THE ZOO

The 11-acre **North American Prairie**, an appropriate exhibit for this Kansas zoo, opened in mid-1993. It is one of the top displays of North American animals in any U.S. zoo and features the nation's first walk-through prairie dog town. The Kansas state song is "Home on the Range," so it also seems appropriate to have unobstructed views of buffalo (bison) "roaming" and deer and antelope (prong-horn) "playing." Other animals in this tall-grass prairie area include elk and sand-hill cranes; eventually bobcats and coyotes will join them. A bridge crosses the boat canal to a more wooded section featuring rare Mexican wolves, river otters, bald and golden eagles in flight cages, and reptiles and other small prairie creatures in an interpretive building. The exhibit's feature animals are grizzly bears in a large naturalistic habitat. Two grizzly cubs can be seen from many vantage points, including a uniquely designed viewing cave that provides close-up views through glass.

Other items on the Master Plan are an **Aquarium Complex**, a **Nocturnal Exhibit**, and an expansion of the Asian Steppes area.

Topeka Zoological Park

635 S.W. Gage Boulevard
Topeka, Kansas 66606
(913) 272-5821

Hours: *Gates open 9-4:30 daily; buildings 9:30-4:30 daily. Closed Christmas Day.*
Admission Fees: *Adults $3, 66+ and 3-12 $1.50. Participates in reciprocity program.*
Directions: *From I-70, take Exit 358B (Gage Boulevard) South. Follow south on Gage Boulevard to zoo.*
Don't Miss: *Tropical Rain Forest, Discovering Apes, Lions Pride, Children's Zoo*.*
Touring Tips: *Picnic tables and shaded benches are available throughout the zoo. Guided tours are offered by advance reservation.*
Entertainment: *Special presentations are sometimes held in the* **Pontoo Plaza** *of the Children's Zoo.*

During the mid-1970s this small city zoo became known as the "World Famous Topeka Zoo." It earned this global acclaim for the first eagle hatched in captivity in 1971, for the opening of the trend-setting Tropical Rain Forest building in 1974, and for its breeding success with extinct-in-the-wild Mongolian wild horses. Located within a park-like setting, today's Topeka Zoo has some exciting major exhibits, as well as some undeveloped enclosures of popular animals.

FEATURED EXHIBITS

In 1974, more than 8 years before most of the spectacular rain forest buildings opened in bigger zoos, the Topeka Zoo opened its **Tropical Rain Forest**. Under a 100-foot-diameter translucent dome, a lush rain forest was re-created with broadleaf plants and trees. Animals that wander freely include scarlet ibises, endangered Bali mynahs, cotton-headed tamarins, green iguanas, and sloths. Up in the trees, Indian fruit bats and black giant squirrels seem to enjoy pestering each other, while scarlet macaws perch on branches and flamingos wade at the foot of a large waterfall. Along the meandering sidewalk, visitors encounter small-clawed otters, beaver-like nutrias, Mexican porcupines, a Burmese python, and rarely displayed gharials (narrow-snouted crocodiles). Children enjoy climbing the stairs for a higher overview of the rain forest, providing an excellent photo opportunity for parents remaining below.

After entering the **Discovering Apes** building, visitors find themselves inside a bamboo tree house with a thatched roof. An artificial tree full of big orange Bornean orangutans is directly ahead. A display gallery, *Apes in the Mind of Man*, illustrates the history of man's relationship with apes. The pathway then enters a rocky cave that turns into the glass tunnel of the *Gorilla Encounter*. Within this innovative tunnel exhibit, gorillas can be seen on both sides as they wander in a tall grass meadow.

Lions Pride is another exhibit that immerses the zoo-goer in an animal habitat. Along a dirt trail leading to the lions, which are seen through thin harp wire, signs welcome visitors on an imaginary safari. (The eight lions comprise the largest pride in any U.S. zoo.) For a closer look, visitors enter a cave built into the lions' rocky exhibit and find a viewing window that puts them only inches away from the tree-climbing lions. At the *Bush Camp View*, visitors view the big cats through windows in a replicated African bush hut.

OTHER EXHIBITS

The zoo's largest animals—Asian and African elephants, giraffes, and Nile hippos—are found inside and adjacent to the **Animals and Man Building**. Gibbons, colobus monkeys, and rock hyraxes are displayed behind glass barriers, while zebras, tiny muntjac deer, and rare Mongolian wild horses are displayed in outdoor yards.

The recently renovated **Hill's Animal Kingdom Building** displays turtles, lizards, frogs, and tarantulas. It also features a display of poisonous snakes native to Kansas. Outside, Aldabra giant tortoises plod through a muddy yard.

At **Waterbird Lagoon** visitors are treated to panoramic views and a chance to feed Hawaiian geese, black swans, and other rare waterfowl. An island in the lagoon is sometimes inhabited by colobus monkeys. The **North Range** has African antelope (elands and sitatungas), white storks, and crowned cranes in open yards, as well as Andean condors and the zoo's famous American golden eagles in large flight cages. The **Cat Line** displays pumas, a Siberian tiger, Canadian lynx, arctic foxes, a binturong, coatimundis, and Japanese macaques. Rare cranes and North American porcupines are found in separate exhibits.

FOR THE KIDS

The **Security Benefit Children's Zoo**, which opened in 1992, is a popular center of activity. In a farm-like setting with a traditional red barn, a petting and feeding yard called the *OK-To-Touch Corral* features pygmy goats, potbellied pigs, sheep, a Dexter cow, llamas, and Sicilian donkeys. Children can reach through rubber flaps to pet rabbits and turtles. The *Animal Antics* play area, with its brightly-colored playground equipment and tunnel maze, lets children simulate animal behaviors. To prevent injuries, the play area is padded with a porous rubber mat through which grass grows. Parents appreciate the tree-shaped *Pontoo Plaza* gazebo. It's a great place to rest and has a fine view of the Waterbird Lagoon and, more importantly, the play area.

Across the street from the zoo, AnimaLand is a much larger playground with animal-shaped playground equipment. A miniature train ride and a restored 1908 carousel are also nearby within Gage Park.

NEW AT THE ZOO

The Children's Zoo is the newest major exhibit. *Fishes of Africa*—a three-aquarium exhibit displaying cichlids and other African fish—recently opened in the Animals and Man building. A new elephant habitat is the next major project.

BEST OF THE REST

Kansas City Zoological Gardens
6700 Zoo Drive
Kansas City, Missouri 64132
(816) 333-7406

Kansas City might soon have one of the nation's best zoos. A $50 million expansion is underway that will more than double the existing zoo's size and add incredible new exhibits. The new 8-acre Australian area displays over 50 species in exhibits that include dingoes, free-roaming kangaroos and emus, two free-flight aviaries, an active sheep station, and camel rides. A dugout canoe ride through crocodile-infested waters, an entry building with an 8-story-tall movie screen, and a jungle path through a naturalistic gorilla habitat are other new features to watch for starting in 1994. For now highlights include a tall Great Apes Building with chimpanzees and orangutans, a Tropical Habitat walk-through aviary, Touchtown children's zoo, a train ride, a newly-renovated African Veldt (with elephants, giraffes, zebras, gnus, and antelope), a Dairy Barn, and a Big Cats area with a winding path that leads through an evergreen forest to four feline habitats. Also notable are the red pandas and maned wolves.

St. Paul's Como Zoo
Midway Parkway & Kaufman Drive
St. Paul, Minnesota 55103
(612) 488-5572

Due to a free admission policy and a collection of exotic animals not found at the much larger Minnesota Zoo, this small urban zoo draws crowds. Seven kinds of primates, including gorillas and orangutans, can be seen in a new Primates building. Wild goats from both North American and European mountains are among the many hoofed animals on display. Harbor seals, sea lions, and pelicans can be fed at Seal Island, and the Sparky the Seal show is a hit in summer. Big cats, polar bears, and Alaskan wolves are also featured. An adjacent Conservatory displays a beautiful collection of palms, orchids, ferns, and other tropical plants.

MORE ZOOS

Blank Park Zoo *(Des Moines, Iowa)*
Bramble Park Zoo *(Watertown, South Dakota)*
Brit Spaugh Park Zoo *(Great Bend, Kansas)*
Chahinkapa Zoo *(Wahpeton, North Dakota)*
Dakota Zoo *(Bismarck, North Dakota)*
Dickerson Park Zoo *(Springfield, Missouri)*
Emporia Zoo *(Emporia, Kansas)*
Folsom Children's Zoo *(Lincoln, Nebraska)*
Grand Isle Heritage Zoo *(Grand Island, Nebraska)*
Lake Superior Zoo *(Duluth, Minnesota)*
Lee Richardson Zoo *(Garden City, Kansas)*
Pine Grove Park & Zoo *(Little Falls, Minnesota)*
Ralph Mitchell Zoo *(Independence, Kansas)*
Riverside Zoo *(Scottsbluff, Nebraska)*
Roosevelt Park Zoo *(Minot, North Dakota)*
Sunset Zoological Park *(Manhattan, Kansas)*
Zoo Montana *(Billings, Montana)*

Southwestern Zoos

Arizona-Sonora Desert Museum

2021 North Kinney Road
Tucson, Arizona 85743
(602) 883-2702

Hours: *8:30-5 daily, October-February; 7:30-6, March-September.*
Admission Fees: *Adults $7.95, 6-12 $1.50.*
Directions: *Located 14 miles west of Tucson via Gates Pass Road. From I-10, take Exit 257 (Speedway Boulevard) West, then follow through Gates Pass to museum. Large motor homes or cars towing trailers should take Exit 99 (Ajo Way) West from I-19, then follow Kinney Road to museum.*
Don't Miss: *Congdon Earth Science Center, Mountain Habitat, Hummingbird Aviary, Riparian Habitat, Canyon Habitats for Small Cats, Life Underground, Walk-In Aviary.*
Touring Tips: *Because the desert here is the real thing, it can get very hot. If visiting between April and October, pack sun hats, sunscreen, and extra cash for liquid refreshments. In summer, take advantage of the unusually early opening time and plan to arrive early, when it is cooler and the animals are more active. Water fountains, concession stands, shaded ramadas, and air-conditioned indoor exhibits are evenly spaced throughout the grounds. If there are long lines at the Orientation and Small Animal Room, bypass it and come back later in the day.*
Entertainment: *Live animal demonstrations are given at various locations. Check the activities board for schedule.*

At first glance, it might seem odd to include a "desert museum" in a zoo guide-book. Though listed by many sources as one of the world's top zoos, the Arizona-Sonora Desert Museum (ASDM) is not a typical zoo. It is actually part zoo, part geology museum, and part botanical garden.

This unique zoo focuses on exhibiting only animals native to the Sonoran Desert of Arizona and Mexico. Far from being a barren wasteland, this desert has a wide variety of wildlife, and the ASDM displays more than 300 types of animals and over 120 plant species.

ASDM is also considered to be one of the most beautiful zoos in the U.S. Situated in a saguaro cactus forest, it is landscaped with desert plants and boasts a backdrop of small mountains. It is said that no zoo takes better advantage of its natural surroundings than this one.

FEATURED EXHIBITS

The tour through the underground **Congdon Earth Science Center** begins with a manmade limestone dry cave, complete with a running stream, large stalactites and stalagmites, and prehistoric fossils. It is so well executed that visitors often refuse to believe it is not real. The cave empties into the *Earth History Room*, where an impressive use of technology interprets the geology of the desert. A dimly-lit room exhibits a collection of over 11,000 minerals from the Sonoran desert, including gold and copper nuggets. A replica 1920s mine tunnel is seen on the way out of the exhibit.

The **Mountain Habitat** is a simulation of the plant and animal communities found on the mountain "islands" that pop up throughout the desert. It is in this rocky habitat, which is forested with oak and pine trees, that some of ASDM's most popular animals are found: mountain lions, thick-billed parrots, and rare Mexican wolves. One of the most photographed spots is the black bear/gray fox habitat.

On hot days, the air-conditioned **Canyon Habitats for Small Cats** exhibit provides cooling relief. Jaguarundis, bobcats, ocelots, and margays can be seen from many angles, though it is sometimes a challenge to find them.

The **Desert Riparian Habitat** surprises many visitors with its beavers and otters. A stairway descends to indoor, underwater views of beavers on one side and otters on the other. The otters are favorites among children, especially when they are swimming and diving. The beavers share their pond with endangered native fish such as Sonora chubs. Visitors can also look into the beavers' lodge, which the beavers enter from underwater. Directly across from the beaver and otter ponds, a herd of desert bighorn

Mountain Lion

sheep climb above and below the visitor viewing level on an artificial mini-mountain.

The enormous **Walk-In Aviary** is impressive from both inside and out. There are many places inside to sit and watch over 110 desert birds of more than 40 species.

Life Underground is aptly named. This dark, 60-foot-long tunnel is an updated version of ASDM's landmark *Tunnel* exhibit. Its purpose is to answer the question, "Where do all the animals go during the heat of the day?" Animals seen behind glass in below-the-surface burrows include kangaroo rats, ringtails, pack rats, snakes, and tarantulas.

The most popular exhibit might be the large **Hummingbirds of the Sonoran Desert Region** aviary. Private seating areas are provided where visitors can relax and admire the grace and beauty of these tiny birds. Eight different hummingbird species fly freely around visitors.

OTHER EXHIBITS

Most visitors start their tour immediately inside the entrance area at the **Orientation and Small Animal Room**. The *Orientation Room* has interesting graphics about the desert, while the *Small Animal Room* features many snakes, lizards, spiders, scorpions, insects, and other small creatures of the desert.

Across the entrance plaza another building houses an indoor/outdoor snack bar, a large gift shop, and the **Aquatic Exhibits**. Frogs, toads, turtles, and fish of Sonoran Desert streams are displayed here, and a unique exhibit features native Apache trout.

Two wedge-shaped cages exhibit a variety of hawks, owls, parrots, and other birds, many of which will soon be moved to new habitats. The desert tortoise and chuckwalla (lizard) enclosures in front of ancient Joshua trees provide another great photo backdrop.

Several interesting and informative exhibits focusing on plants of the Sonoran Desert are found throughout the park. They include the **Saguaro Exhibit, Life Zone Transects**, a **Desert Demonstration Garden** (a local favorite), and a **Cactus/Succulent Garden** with a winding walkway passing 140 species of cacti and other desert plants.

FOR THE KIDS

The cave in the Congdon Earth Science Center is a highlight for children, who delight in exploring and climbing through its maze of narrow passageways.

NEW AT THE ZOO

The Mountain Habitat is the first phase of ASDM's plan to re-create all of the life zones of the Sonoran Desert with natural exhibits. The recently opened **Desert Grasslands Habitats** represents the next phase of this plan. This new area includes a large prairie dog town as well as natural homes for salamanders, toads, and owls.

Planned exhibits include **Arizona Uplands Habitats, Tropical Deciduous Forest Habitats, Lower Colorado Valley Habitats, Baja California Habitats**, and **People in the Desert Exhibits**. Animals exhibited in these new habitats will include kit foxes, coyotes, javelinas, mule deer, coatimundis, badgers, birds of prey, and parrots—all of which are currently on display in traditional caged, fenced, or moated enclosures.

Cheyenne Mountain Zoological Park

4250 Cheyenne Mountain Zoo Road
Colorado Springs, Colorado 80906
(719) 475-9555

Hours: *9-6 daily, Memorial Day-Labor Day; 9-5, rest of year. Last ticket sold 1 hour prior to closing.*
Admission Fees: *Adults $5.75, 66+ $4.75, 3-11 $3. Zoo Tram $1, carousel $1, giraffe food $1/pack.*
Directions: *From I-25, take Exit 138 West (Route 122-Broadmoor). Follow to The Broadmoor hotel, then turn left onto Lake Circle and follow signs to zoo.*
Don't Miss: *Primate World, giraffe feeding, Will Rogers Shrine of the Sun, Giraffe/ Elephant complex.*
Touring Tips: *With its steep hills and high altitude, this zoo can provide difficulties for anyone. In summer use the Zoo Tram, which makes seven stops around the zoo. If you have the energy, don't miss the self-guided nature trail.*
Entertainment: *Elephant demonstrations are held daily at 2:30, in season. Animal feedings include penguins, monkeys, big cats, and birds of prey.*

Literally built on a mountainside, the Cheyenne Mountain Zoo has some very steep hills to climb. Billed as "America's *Only* Mountain Zoo," its altitude at the lowest point is nearly 7,000 feet—making it the nation's highest zoo. One of the few privately-owned zoos, it was started in 1926 by Spencer Penrose, who also established the world-famous Broadmoor hotel situated at the base of the mountain.

This might also be the only zoo that allows cars to drive through. Admission to the zoo includes the toll for the scenic highway leading up to the **Will Rogers Shrine of the Sun**. The panoramic view from the tower memorial, which is positioned at 8,000 feet, rivals the view from atop Pikes Peak. The entire Colorado Springs area is visible on a clear day.

FEATURED EXHIBITS

The **Giraffe/Elephant complex** is home to the country's largest herd of giraffes—the zoo's signature animal. Over 150 giraffes have been born here (more than at any other zoo in the world), so there are almost always baby giraffes on display. At the top of the exhibit, special giraffe crackers can be purchased to feed the long-necked animals, and snapping an extraordinary picture of a friendly giraffe using his long, purple tongue to take a cracker right out of a child's hand is actually quite easy. African elephants enjoy a large yard with a pool, and an elusive and beautiful okapi, a relative of the giraffe, is also seen here. (This zoo is one of only seven in the U.S. to display an okapi.)

The zoo's premier exhibit is the new **Primate World**. The building's carpeted interior features an audiovisual center, interactive graphics, and wide windows for viewing a variety of primates—including a display of endangered golden lion tamarins. Gorillas inhabit a 3/4-acre natural habitat and can be seen from indoor and outdoor viewing points. Orangutans can be seen playing on a variety of climbing structures in their 45-foot-high mesh enclosure, and an indoor viewing area that extends into the habitat allows close-up encounters. (This zoo is famous for its breeding success with orangutans.) Lion-tailed macaques, colobus monkeys, and Sykes' guenons can also be seen inside, as well as in their outdoor enclosure.

OTHER EXHIBITS

Local wildlife is featured at the new **Rocky Cliffs** exhibit. A small herd of Rocky Mountain goats lives here on a mini-mountain made of native Colorado rock. Yellow-bellied marmots can be found in a smaller rocky habitat.

Along one of the steeper hills, a row of paddocks features some of the zoo's most endangered animals, including black rhinos, bongos, addax, Grevy's zebras, chamois, and sable antelope. A rare Szechuan takin from China is also displayed. (Takins are found in only four other U.S. zoos.)

An outdated **Monkey House** displays an impressive collection of primates, including mandrills, siamangs, gibbons, black howler monkeys, and three types of lemurs.

An equally outdated **Feline Building** houses an impressive collection of cats that includes ocelots, Sumatran and Siberian tigers, black leopards, lions, clouded leopards, and pumas. An outdoor **Small Mammal Area** holds snow leopards, bobcats, and arctic foxes. Nearby, the **Tropical Exhibit** is a small-scale rain forest with suni antelope, hornbills, and other tropical birds. Not far away, Kodiak bears live in a large stone grotto.

The **Bird/Reptile Building** exhibits a menagerie of large and small reptiles, beautiful exotic birds, and some small mammals. Huge Malayan water monitors are the most notable residents. Red pandas can be seen outside in a lushly-planted wire mesh enclosure.

The **Aquatics Building** exhibits some of the zoo's most popular animals—Chilean flamingos, Nile hippos, and Asian small-clawed otters—in both indoor and outdoor habitats. Also inside are coral reef aquariums and a pebble beach for a colony of rockhopper penguins.

Located high above the other animal exhibits, the **Birds of Prey Area** requires some effort to reach. The reward is viewing a collection of owls, hawks, eagles, and vultures that is one of the best anywhere. Notable exhibits include white-tailed sea eagles and cinerous vultures in a large flight cage.

FOR THE KIDS

After the giraffe-feeding area, the most popular spot for children is a large, modern playground situated next to a delightful antique carousel. Up the hill, an **Animal Contact Area** has pygmy goats, sheep, and donkeys available for petting. The **Education Center** gives kids the chance to touch feathers, furs, bones, and other animal artifacts. An elephant ride is also offered.

NEW AT THE ZOO

New exhibits opened in 1993 include a bat cave, a hummingird garden, and displays of naked mole-rats, endangered black-footed ferrets, and prairie dogs.

This zoo is in the middle of fulfilling a major master plan. Future exhibits include an **Asian Highlands** with outdoor enclosures of snow monkeys, red pandas, serows, Amur leopards, and other Asian animals. **Las Montanas** will feature animals from the mountains of South America, including mountain tapirs, Andean condors, spectacled bears, and coatis. Highly endangered Mexican wolves will live with their gray wolf cousins in **Wolf Woods**.

Denver Zoological Gardens

City Park
(East 23rd Avenue & Steele Street)
Denver, Colorado 80205
(303) 331-4110

Hours: *9-6 daily, in summer; 10-5, in winter.*
Admission Fees: *Adults $6, 61+ and 4-12 $3. Zooliner: adults $1.50, 61+ and 4-12 $1; Train ride 50¢, under 3 free.*
Directions: *Located in City Park, on Denver's Near Eastside. The main entrance is off 23rd Avenue between York Street and Colorado Boulevard. From I-70, take Exit 276B (Colorado Boulevard) South, then follow to 23rd Avenue, and turn right into zoo. From I-25, take Exit 204 (Colorado Boulevard) North, follow to 23rd Avenue, and turn left to zoo. A Cultural Connection Trolley runs between other city attractions and the zoo.*
Don't Miss: *Tropical Discovery, Northern Shores, Bird World, Feline Building, Bear Mountain, Central Range, Sheep Mountain.*
Touring Tips: *While the zoo's 74 acres are not difficult to get around by foot, the* **Zooliner** *tram provides a guided tour. The best dining atmosphere is at Northern Shores Cafe, which has outdoor terrace seating overlooking Seal Harbor. The Hungry Elephant Restaurant also has pleasant indoor and outdoor seating areas. Both restaurants are cafeteria-style. Snack bars dispense cotton candy and other favorites with kids. (Don't miss getting a cold snack*

at Ice Station Zebra.) Should you have extra time, the impressive Denver Museum of Natural History is within walking distance.

Entertainment: *The sea lion feedings in Northern Shores are accompanied by an informal demonstration of the behaviors these intelligent mammals can do. Other animal feedings include penguins, lions, primates, and felines.*

Opened in 1896, the Denver Zoo is the second-oldest western zoo. Its Bear Mountain is the nation's oldest naturalistic exhibit. Like the state of Colorado, this zoo has many beautiful wide open spaces. Birds, arctic animals, and hoofed species are specialties. With well over 1 million visitors annually, it is the most popular zoo between Chicago and California.

FEATURED EXHIBITS

The zoo's premier exhibit is the 3-acre **Northern Shores**, an area that resembles an aquatic theme park. The centerpiece is *Seal Harbor*, which has a 140-foot-long sea lion pool and a second pool for harbor seals. Sea lions can be seen up close in a habitat that replicates the Pacific coastline, and from underwater viewing windows. A harbor town atmosphere is apparent in an aquatic-themed restaurant and gift shop. The stars of the Northern Shores are the polar bears, which can be observed in their enormous pool through underwater split-level viewing windows. Another fine habitat allows river otters to be observed swimming underwater in a stream. Seen among scattered evergreens, arctic foxes are another cold-climate animal in this exhibit.

Bird World, one of this zoo's top exhibits, is also one of the country's finest birdhouses. It has three lush, walk-through aviaries. The wide array of tropical birds seen in natural habitats embellished with realistic mural backgrounds includes great Indian hornbills, pygmy kingfishers, and golden-headed quetzels. The *Tropical Rain Forest*, entered through a cave, has Nicobar pigeons and fruit bats. The *Aquatic Bird Habitat* features a cascading waterfall and displays ibises. The flight cages and enclosures encircling the Bird World building are also special. At the front entrance, a colony of black-footed penguins can be observed in a pool and on a rocky shoreline. Next to the snowy owls is a tall flight cage with four types of vultures. Across the path, the *Pheasantry* encircles visitors with a set of ten mesh enclosures that display many multi-colored birds, such as vulturine guineafowl. The most famous birds here are the double-wattled cassowaries, which are large land birds with electric blue and red coloring. (Over 90% of all cassowaries in America are descended from this pair.)

The **Felines Building** is actually a set of two newly-renovated structures filled with natural indoor habitats. Among the inhabitants are Bengal and Siberian tigers, Amur and snow leopards, lions, servals, and jaguars. Non-feline residents include meerkats, dwarf mongooses, and striped hyenas. In the central court between the two buildings, visitors can see long-legged maned wolves in a fenced yard. Also outside, the lions and tigers have large, lush grottoes.

Bear Mountain opened in 1918 as the nation's first natural zoo exhibit utilizing artificial rockwork. It has been renovated and is now one of the zoo's prettiest places. In its two tall, moated grottoes, grizzly and Asiatic black bears enjoy pools and waterfalls. Also a part of this historic exhibit, and an excellent photo backdrop, is a small replication of Colorado's Mesa Verde cliff-dwelling ruins that is overrun by a pack of popular coatis.

Another frequently photographed location is the **Sheep Mountain** exhibit. Bighorn and Dall's sheep—both with thick, curly horns—can be seen at different elevations. One of the two "mountains" is a huge pile of boulders, and the other is a towering alpine peak.

This zoo has one of the most diverse and interesting collections of hoofed animals in the U.S. Many of the fascinating hoofstock are seen along an oval-shaped path that surrounds the **Central Range**. The majority of the spacious, tree-lined yards contain African species, many in large herds, including Grevy's zebras, scimitar-horned oryxes, and an exceptional variety of gazelles and antelope. The country's largest herd of dangerous Cape buffalo (seen in only five U.S. zoos) is here. Other animals include ostriches, wart hogs, kangaroos, and rare Mongolian wild horses. The **Giraffe House** is home to the zoo's most recognizable occupant—a pale giraffe known as Bill.

OTHER EXHIBITS

The remainder of the zoo's hoofstock are across the wide visitor path in another row of open yards known as the **South Range**. Many of the interesting animals seen here are from North America, including Rocky Mountain goats, muskoxen, American bison, reindeer, and pronghorn antelope. *Rocky Mountain Predators* is a walk-through loop with plant-filled cages housing Canadian lynx and pumas. At the far end are some endangered Asian species such as Pere David's deer, Bactrian and dromedary camels, and red pandas.

In **Wolf Pack Woods**, a ³/₄-acre pine forest provides a home for a small pack of arctic tundra wolves. The white wolves can be watched or photographed through thin harp wire.

Not all of the zoo's excellent bird collection is in Bird World. Near the West Gate, **Flamingo Plaza** has a lagoon filled with flamingos and other waterbirds. A rushing stream flows through a network of small fenced yards displaying an amazing variety of exotic ducks and geese that includes Falkland Island flightless steamer ducks. Bald eagles and Andean condors share a divided flight cage nearby. Across the zoo, penguins are displayed in a small building.

Asian elephants, black rhinos, Nile hippos, and Malayan tapirs all have large muddy yards around the **Pachyderm Building**. Inside, these massive mammals have rocky grotto-like stalls, some with deep pools. A central enclosure displays rock hyraxes.

The primate collection is distributed in five different locations. The **Primate House** has mandrills, lemurs, macaques, and six different types of marmosets and

Reticulated Giraffe and Calf

tamarins in glass-fronted tile enclosures. The attached **Gorilla Exhibit** offers indoor and outdoor views of the large apes. Attractive **Gibbon Island** has climbing apparatuses to keep the noisy lesser apes busy. Beavers and pelicans utilize the water-filled moat around **Monkey Island**, which is home to playful hooded capuchins. Black howler monkeys and colobus monkeys are in old-fashioned cages across the path.

FOR THE KIDS

A bridge is crossed to enter the wooded **Children's Zoo**. Woodchucks, badgers, swift foxes, and prairie dogs are some of the most popular animals seen here in small grottoes. Three tiny buildings display small mammals, amphibians, and invertebrates. Farm animals—sheep, donkeys, zebu cattle, ponies, and goats—are in large fenced yards. The popular **Pioneer Train** miniature railroad offers rides around the perimeter of the Children's Zoo. It passes through a tunnel and over the surface of a lake. Just outside the Children's Zoo, children can feed rare waterfowl, including Hawaiian geese and black swans.

NEW AT THE ZOO

To overcome its few weaknesses, this zoo is in the midst of a major capital development program. The first project, which opened in late 1993, is the multi-species **Tropical Discovery** complex. This new rain forest building is this zoo's first major exhibit of reptiles, amphibians, fish, and insects. With over 1,000 animals of more than 240 species, Tropical Discovery nearly doubles the zoo's animal collection. Orchids, ferns, and towering palm trees are some of the almost 200 plant species that enrich the ten exhibits inside. The *Mountain Cave* exhibit features a vampire bat cave, and clouded leopards are seen in the *Jungle Pools* area. Under a 45-foot-high pyramid, cobras, vipers, and boas can be seen amid lush greenery in the *Temple Ruins*. The *Jungle Riverbank* has babirusas (wild pigs from Asia) on the ground and leaf monkeys high in the jungle trees. The *Mangrove Swamp* features some of nature's oddities: mudskippers, archerfish, and fiddler crabs. A rainbow of colorful reef fish can be seen in a *Coral Reef* exhibit. The *Cypress Swamp* has many reptiles and colorful amphibians on display, and alligators are seen in the *Tropical Marsh*. Many hands-on exhibits are available in the building's *Discovery Center*.

The next project will be **Primate Panorama**, scheduled to open in 1995. Orangutans will join the gorillas and current Primate House residents in natural indoor and outdoor habitats. This 5-acre walk-through area will feature a central *Forest Aviary* and the *Emerald Forest Building*—an educational interpretive complex. Primate Panorama will be built on the site of the existing Children's Zoo, so a new **Children's Contact Farm** is scheduled. The Pachyderm House, waterfowl ponds, South Range, and main entrance area will all be renovated.

The Phoenix Zoo

455 North Galvin Parkway
Phoenix, Arizona 85008
(602) 273-1341

Hours: *7-4 daily, May 1-Labor Day; 9-5, rest of year.*
Admission Fees: *Adults $6, 60+ $5, 4-12 $3. Safari Train $1.50; camel ride $2, in season.*
Directions: *From I-10, take Exit 152 (Highway 143, Hohokam Expressway) North. Follow north to Van Buren Street. Turn right and follow to Galvin Parkway. Turn left into Papago Park and follow to zoo. The Phoenix Transit System also serves the zoo.*
Don't Miss: *Arizona Trail, Tropical Flights, Safari Train, African Savanna, Children's Zoo, Baboon Kingdom, mountain animals.*
Touring Tips: *The best time to visit is during the winter months of October through April. The sun shines virtually every day then, and the animals are more active due to cooler temperatures. During summer, the early opening time offers an opportunity to visit while the temperature is 20 to 30 degrees cooler than in the afternoon. Do bring along sun hats, sunscreen, and water bottles during summer. Drinking fountains are available throughout the zoo, and snack bars sell ice cream, soda, and other cooling foods. Another heat-beater is the Safari Train—a 30-minute, 2 1/2-mile narrated tram ride through most of the zoo's 125 acres. After this overview, riders can backtrack to their favorite exhibits. Strollers are a must*

for small children and are available to rent, and binoculars can also be very useful. Lakeside picnic areas are available.

Entertainment: *The Children's Zoo **Puppet Theater** sometimes schedules puppet shows.*

Phoenix, Arizona is the second-fastest growing large city in the United States and is also one of the top Sunbelt tourist destinations. The Phoenix Zoo, which is located near the Scottsdale tourist area in lush Papago Park, has benefited from this growing visitor base. It is the largest self-supporting (no tax dollars) zoo in the U.S.

This relatively new zoo opened in 1962 and quickly gained worldwide fame. The many beautiful lakes and palm trees found throughout the grounds make it an attractive desert oasis. In 1963, a last-chance effort was begun to save the Arabian oryx—a desert antelope that was nearly hunted to extinction. Nine of the last oryxes were rounded up and sent here to establish a breeding colony. Thirty years later, more than 215 oryx calves have been born at this zoo. Oryxes are now displayed across the nation, and small herds have been re-introduced into the deserts of Israel and Oman.

FEATURED EXHIBITS

Arizona is famous for its interesting wildlife, so it seems natural that this zoo's premier exhibit is the **Arizona Trail**. Cacti displayed along a wide, level walkway include towering saguaros. Bald eagles and turkey vultures are perched in a large flight cage near the newly renovated natural habitat for coatimundis. Bobcats and mountain lions are seen through thin harp wire in rocky habitats, and three large desert yards with coyotes, peccaries, and pronghorn antelope are viewed from an overlook. A cluster of smaller enclosures include porcupines, gila monsters, roadrunners, and desert tortoises. In one of the few exhibit buildings, the *Nocturnal Exhibit* displays bats, a ringtail, spotted skunks, and a kit fox. Quails and other desert birds can be seen in a walk-through aviary. More than nine types of rattlesnakes are the main attraction of the indoor/outdoor reptile and amphibian area, which also includes alligator lizards, Colorado River toads, and coachwhips. Brush-tailed ground squirrels and jackrabbits roam wild in this exhibit, as they do elsewhere in the zoo.

If this zoo has a specialty, it might be African animals. The 4-acre **African Savanna** displays giraffes, waterbucks, gazelles, ostriches, and other birds from the open plains of Kenya. Tall palm trees and giant boulders are scattered on the grassy slopes of this natural exhibit. The panorama can be enjoyed from convenient benches in front of the habitat. An attached, slightly more arid yard holds rare Grevy's zebras and Marabou storks.

The **Baboon Kingdom,** another natural African habitat, opened in late 1990. The two-part complex displays Hamadryas baboons and beautiful mandrills in grassy yards with high rock backgrounds. Between them, an interpretive area offers information about baboons, plus large viewing windows for close-up monkey encounters.

A gravel detour off the main path leads to an observation point for the future Great Deserts of the World exhibit. Today, two massive buttes on the site provide natural habitats for the **mountain animals**—Arizona's desert bighorn sheep and Africa's Nubian ibexes. They are best viewed through binoculars or through a coin-operated, high-power telescope.

OTHER EXHIBITS

The paved trail surrounding the Savanna yard leads past more African animals, including white rhinos, wart hogs, and cheetahs. An open, grassy pit has an attractive duplex exhibit of lions and rare Sumatran tigers. Black leopards and kangaroos are also found along the trail, as are the famous Arabian oryxes.

Interesting exhibits surround the largest of the many lakes, including the new Tropical Flights, flamingos in a palm grove, river otters splashing in a pool, and orangutans under a netted dome. Ocelots and colobus monkeys are in smaller cages, and the lake's three primate islands are inhabited by lemurs, spider monkeys, and capuchins.

Other significant animal displays include an Everglades-like alligator pond and a large elephant yard, plus rare Mexican wolves, giant tortoises, and iguanas.

Mexican Wolf

FOR THE KIDS

Reached by crossing one of two bridges over a lagoon, the 7-acre **Children's Zoo** was renovated in 1987 and is now a highlight. The contact area features pygmy goats, Shetland ponies, sheep, and a Sicilian donkey in a farmyard setting. An exotic *Poultry Exhibit* displays royal palm turkeys and silky bantams. From inside a viewing cave, raccoons can be seen sleeping in a burrow behind their streamside habitat. Other animals displayed in intimate settings include small monkeys, toucans, wallabies, mice (in the *Mouse House*), giant anteaters, Brazilian tapirs, and prairie dogs. The *Animal Nursery* and *Brooder House* exhibit baby animals and poultry chicks at different stages of development. The *Playground* is enjoyed by both kids and their parents. Kids can frolic on the spider web, monkey bars, and other animal-themed apparatuses, while adults rest and watch from a picnic area next to the refreshment center.

Wildlife Encounters is a small, interactive exhibit intended for children but enjoyed by all. A large woolly mammoth skull is surrounded by hands-on activities that encourage children to compare themselves to animals. A special scale, when stepped on, tells what animal the person's weight is similar to. (This book's author weighs the same as a wart hog!) The zoo's only animal ride is on camels.

NEW AT THE ZOO

New exhibits have been opening almost annually. **Tropical Flights**, an outdoor rain forest exhibit, opened in 1992. Egyptian fruit bats, spoonbills, ibises, and rhinoceros hornbills are some of the exotic and beautiful animals in six tall aviaries surrounded by lush tropical vegetation. Highly endangered Micronesian kingfishers and Guam rails are also displayed. A winding path passes a cascading waterfall that trickles into the nearby lake.

A new exhibit for 1993 has a unique combination of African animals—playful meerkats, insect-eating aardwolves, and a crested porcupine—living together in an arid, rocky habitat.

The zoo plans to open its first bear exhibit in 1995. Spectacled bears from South America will have a natural habitat with a large waterfall. The Arizona Trail's reptile area will be renovated in 1996 to display its large collection in ten bioclimatic zones.

In 1997 this zoo plans to open what will probably become its trademark exhibit—**Great Deserts of the World**. This sensational indoor/outdoor complex will feature separate exhibits of six different deserts from South America, Australia, Africa, and Asia. Arabian oryxes, naked mole-rats, vampire bats, kangaroos, armadillos, dingoes, gazelles, hyenas, meerkats, and foxes are just a few of the many large and small mammals, birds, reptiles, and insects that will be seen in this amazing exhibit. A walk-through aviary, nocturnal exhibits, a camel ride, and interactive stations will combine to make this unique exhibit one of the best anywhere.

Rio Grande Zoological Park

903 Tenth Street, S.W.
Albuquerque, New Mexico 87102
(505) 843-7413

Hours: *9-6 daily, Memorial Day-Labor Day; 9-5, rest of year. Closed New Year's Day, Thanksgiving Day, and Christmas Day.*
Admission Fees: *Adults $4.25, 64+ and 3-15 $2.25. Participates in reciprocity program. Camel ride $1.75, in season.*
Directions: *From I-25, take Exit 224 West. Turn onto Lead Avenue and follow west to*

10th Street. Turn left and follow south to zoo. From I-40, take Exit 157A (Rio Grande Boulevard) South. Follow south to a left turn onto Central Avenue. Turn right onto 10th Street and follow south to zoo. City bus service is available.

Don't Miss: *Seals & Sea Lions Exhibit, Ape Country, Twiga Lookout, Raptor Roost, Cat Walk, Cottonwood Cafe, Free-flying Bird Show, New Mexico Prairie, Amphibians and Reptiles of the World.*

Touring Tips: *Don't miss the new Cottonwood Cafe and its New Mexican food. It is decorated with colorful stained glass windows and beautiful hand-carved corbels (wooden sculptures) of New Mexico's native animals.*

Entertainment: *The entertaining **Free-flying Bird Show** is presented on most days (April to September) in the large, outdoor **Nature Theater**. The wide variety of feathered stars includes talking parrots, free-flying birds of prey, intelligent ravens, and unusual birds such as the red-legged seriema. Animal feedings include seals and sea lions.*

The Rio Grande River, which winds through the heart of New Mexico, is lined by a pretty cottonwood forest called the "bosque." The beautiful Rio Grande Zoo is situated within this setting near downtown Albuquerque. In addition to natural surroundings, the zoo is embellished with magnificent rockwork, dazzling waterfalls, Pueblo-style buildings, and elegant sculptures of wild animals. A spectacular lake in its center is surrounded by lookouts, waterfalls, and attractive exhibits.

FEATURED EXHIBITS

Ape Country, one of the premier exhibits, is hidden around the corner from the entrance area. Two groups of gorillas and one of orangutans dwell in habitats that are visibly separate from each other. The middle habitat of cute juvenile gorillas is especially popular. The apes in these semicircular enclosures play on wooden jungle gyms and relax on grassy lawns. Viewers can watch at close range across a dry moat or, for a very close encounter, peer through a glass panel in a viewing cave. Loud siamangs (lesser apes) live nearby in a tall mesh habitat. Their large enclosure is built around a 2-story tree house overlook that is entered by crossing a bouncing suspension bridge.

The **Seals & Sea Lions Exhibit**, the zoo's most spectacular display, is entered through a tall, rocky cave. Along an uphill path inside this cave, glass panels provide underwater and split-level views of the harbor seals and California sea lions swimming through underwater passageways. On the other side of the path, windows overlook the beautiful lake. Coming out of the cave, visitors seem to enter a California coastal town where seals and sea lions splash in the harbor waters of a rocky cove.

The **Cat Walk** is well known for providing close-up views of a diverse group of large and small cats. Asian lions and cheetahs in natural, open yards are on opposite sides of an elevated walkway. Visitors descend to a long, curving row of large enclosures that display a spotted leopard, clouded leopards, snow leopards, mountain lions, jaguars, bobcats, and servals. Non-feline residents include fennec foxes, meerkats, and red pandas. The path ends at the home of the zoo's high-lighted animals—the royal white Bengal tigers, which are exhibited in a large, open grotto with a waterfall, trickling stream, and wading pool.

An African village outpost is re-created at the **Twiga Lookout**. (*Twiga* is Swahili for giraffe.) Giraffes are seen in both arid and grassy yards. Visitors enter realistic African huts to view native utensils, to read giraffe trivia, and to get a closer look at the giraffes from their windows.

At the beginning of the **New Mexico Prairie**, colorful graphics explain that the state was once part of the Great American Prairie. A herd of bison are at home on an open range shared with sandhill cranes. A charming prairie dog town is on one side of the bison. On the other side, pronghorn antelope are seen from an elevated trail that cuts through the rocks.

A bubbling fountain greets visitors outside the **Amphibians and Reptiles of the World** exhibit. The building is noted for displaying some of the world's most endangered reptiles in large natural habitats. Sudan plated lizards, Round Island skinks, and Dumeril's ground boas are among the most exotic residents. Huge crocodile monitor lizards are viewed through windows in a 50-foot-long exhibit, and many venomous snakes and unusual salamanders are also included in the large collection. Aldabra giant tortoises are exhibited outside.

The six large flight cages of the **Raptor Roost** exhibit hold a variety of birds of prey, including Andean condors, Mexican spotted owls, and caracaras. The bald eagles here are famous for their successful breeding history. Some of their offspring are now flying free in Tennessee.

OTHER EXHIBITS

Visitors go under a waterfall to enter the **Jungle Habitat**—a lush indoor rain forest. Inside, fan palms and other tropical plants provide a green, humid home for over 40 feathered species. The Victoria crowned pigeons and paradise wydahs are some of the prettiest of these tropical birds. The outdoor **Elizabeth Glover Jenks Parrot Exhibit** is another walk-through aviary. Vines arch over a screened-in area where lories and lorikeets fly freely. Colorful parrots, macaws, and cockatoos are seen in six separate displays. More rainbow-colored birds, such as Himalayan monals (the "finest of the pheasants"), are displayed in the horseshoe-shaped **Pheasantry**. Three smaller bird exhibits around the zoo feature flamingos, brown pelicans, and roadrunners—New Mexico's state bird.

Mexican gray wolves (lobos) are found near the outdated—and soon to be replaced—**Bear Grottoes**. This zoo has received much acclaim for its breeding of these wolves, which are extinct in the wild. This success may be partly due to the large, naturalistic wolf habitat.

The zoo is also known for its diversity of hoofed animals, including many endangered species. The **African Plains** exhibit has bongos, gazelles, and secretary birds living together. Siberian ibexes and markhors are provided with small man-made mountains that replicate their natural homes. Other hoofstock in the area includes Nile lechwe, sable antelope, and kudus. Red kangaroos and rare white rhinos are also displayed here.

FOR THE KIDS

While the **Children's Zoo** is being renovated, the most popular spot for kids seems to be the moat in front of the **Bandshell**. This is where a coin-operated dispenser sells food to feed the exotic ducks and big-mouthed koi fish. Camel rides are available.

NEW AT THE ZOO

As part of an expensive 20-year improvement plan, sparkling new exhibits are springing up all over the grounds. The elephants and polar bears are some of the most recent animals receiving larger, more natural habitats. Also new in the elephant exhibit is adorable Rosie—one of two Asian elephants born in the U.S. in 1992.

A major extension of Ape Country opens as this book goes to press. A pathway appearing to enter a cave leads into a new building that displays small and nocturnal primates such as tree shrews, bushbabies, and colobus monkeys. Just outside of this exciting new display hall, the path follows the edge of the beautiful central lake past rocky exhibits of ruffed lemurs.

A new **River Otter Exhibit** that simulates a Rocky Mountain stream will open soon next to the Seals & Sea Lions Exhibit. Future plans call for an exhibit of rarely displayed sea otters.

In coming years, this zoo hopes to add a new **China Exhibit**, featuring red pandas and other interesting Chinese animals, and an **Australian Exhibit**.

BEST OF THE REST

Utah's Hogle Zoo
2600 Sunnyside Avenue
Salt Lake City, Utah 84108
(801) 582-1631

Featuring a beautiful mountain backdrop, this complete zoo displays a diverse collection of primates—including gorillas and chimpanzees—in the Great Apes building. Just as extensive is the variety of cats in the Felines building. There are also many types of North American and African hoofed animals, as well as rhinos, elephants, and sea lions. The premier exhibit is the new Discovery Land. This children's area is divided into five regions: Small Wonders, Forest, Woodland Edge, The Marsh, and Desert Canyon. Within this exhibit are plants and animals appropriate to each specific region, educational displays, a towering geyser fountain, a train ride, Noah's Park playground, a contact zoo, and many nature-themed activities.

Wildlife World Zoo
16501 West Northern Avenue
Litchfield Park, Arizona 85340
(602) 935-9453

Located on Phoenix's west side, this zoo was set up as a private breeding facility to supply rare and endangered animals to other zoos. It opened to the public in 1984. Over 20 half-acre paddocks hold an extensive collection of endangered species, including all of the world's ostrich and oryx varieties, many other antelope species, a variety of Australian animals, and Arizona's only white tiger. Interesting indoor exhibits include the Waters of the World aquarium, the Tropics of the World reptile display, and the new It's a Small World exhibit of monkeys, bats, squirrels, and rodents. Probably the highlight is the Lory Feeding exhibit. Seeking an apple slice, these multi-colored Australian parrots land on visitors' arms, shoulders, and sometimes even their heads.

Black and White Ruffed Lemur in It's a Small World

Zoo Boise
355 North Julia Davis Drive
Boise, Idaho 83702
(208) 384-4125

Located near Idaho's capitol building, this small zoo features animals native to the Rocky Mountain region. One of the newer exhibits, the North American Rivers Exhibit, has beavers and otters. An impressive collection of cats includes Bengal tigers, clouded leopards, snow leopards, mountain lions, ocelots, and bobcats. Birds of Prey aviaries include over 16 different owls, eagles, hawks, and other predatory birds. This zoo is one of the few in the country to exhibit moose, which are found across a bridge near the bighorn sheep and zebras. Other noteworthy exhibits include a primate building, coatis, bears, foxes, and bison.

MORE ZOOS

Alameda Park and Zoo *(Alamogordo, New Mexico)*
Hillcrest Park Zoo *(Clovis, New Mexico)*
Living Desert State Park *(Carlsbad, New Mexico)*
Navajo Nation Zoological & Botanical Park *(Window Rock, Arizona)*
Out of Africa Wildlife Park *(Fountain Hills, Arizona)*
Payson Zoo *(Payson, Arizona)*
Prescott Animal Park *(Prescott, Arizona)*
Pueblo Zoological Park *(Pueblo, Colorado)*
Reid Park Zoo *(Tucson, Arizona)*
Southern Nevada Zoological Park *(Las Vegas, Nevada)*
Spring River Park and Zoo *(Roswell, New Mexico)*
Tautphaus Park Zoo *(Idaho Falls, Idaho)*

West Coast Zoos

The Living Desert

47-900 Portola Avenue
Palm Desert, California 92260
(619) 346-5694

Hours: *9-5 daily, September 1-June 15. Last admission at 4:30. Closed Christmas Day and during summer.*

Admission Fees: *Adults $7, 63+ $6, 3-12 $3.50. Participates in reciprocity program. Tram $4, Wednesday through Sunday, call for reservations.*

Directions: *Located 15 miles east of Palm Springs. From I-10, take the Monterey Avenue Exit. Follow south 11 miles to Palm Desert. Turn left (east) onto Highway 111 for 1 mile, then right (south) onto Portola Avenue and go 1 1/2 miles to park entrance on left.*

Don't Miss: *Eagle Canyon, African area, Walk Thru Aviary, Bighorn Mountain.*

Touring Tips: *Pack sunscreen and sun hats, wear comfortable shoes, and bring water if planning to hike the nature preserve trails. Free guided walking tours are offered once each day, twice daily on weekends. Narrated tram rides depart hourly, and picnic areas are available.*

Entertainment: *Volunteers regularly offer a **Critter Close-up**, which gives visitors an opportunity to meet and learn about an owl, snake, or some other animal brought out for the program.*

Billboards along Interstate 10, which is one of the main highways connecting Southern California with the rest of the nation, invite travelers to stop and experience The Living Desert. Located in the hot Mohave Desert, this zoo might be the only one that closes in summer. A visit to this 1,200-acre park confirms that, despite the heat, the world's deserts are indeed alive with bountiful wildlife.

The Living Desert is like Tucson's Arizona-Sonora Desert Museum in that it exhibits only desert wildlife, but different because it displays and preserves plants and animals native to all of the world's deserts. The 200 acres used for the zoo will,

Grevy's Zebras

over time, be developed to interpret the deserts of North America, South America, Africa, and Australia. Currently, most of the animals on display are from the deserts of North America and Africa.

FEATURED EXHIBITS

The **African area** has animals from AA (aardwolves) to Z (zebras). Many people are surprised to see Grevy's zebras, which are one of the park's most popular animals. These endangered animals from Africa's eastern deserts look spectacular in their large, arid yard. Other endangered animals in this area include slender-horned gazelles, Mhorr gazelles, Arabian sand gazelles, and Arabian oryxes. (This is one of only seven U.S. zoos to exhibit hyena-like, termite-eating aardwolves.) Smaller enclosures exhibit colorful African birds, meerkats, Arabian wildcats, sand cats, and black-footed cats.

Bighorn Mountain, which is a *real* mountain, is home to a herd of desert bighorn sheep. The herd's dominant ram is often seen posing on top of the mountain.

Just off the paved main path, a large **Walk Thru Aviary** features some of the birds found in the local desert, including turkey vultures.

OTHER EXHIBITS

Most visitors enjoy the coyotes, which seem to howl all day. The coatimundis are also entertaining in their new habitat. Other animals spaced along the main path include tortoises, owls, hawks, kestrels, and thick-billed parrots. The **Sonoran Pond** is a natural home for desert waterfowl and endangered desert pupfish.

This facility is as much a botanical garden as it is a zoo. Ten separate gardens replicate the ten major North American desert regions. Some of the beautiful desert plants seen within these well-marked gardens include smoke trees, palo verdes, Joshua trees, more than 50 different palm trees, and various cacti, including saguaros. The **Indian Ethno-Botanic Garden** illustrates how Indians used plants in their daily lives and includes an authentic kish (dwelling house).

Visitors can experience the creatures of the desert night in the cool **Nocturnal Animal Exhibit**, where a variety of reptiles and other small animals—including bats, deer mice, kangaroo rats, and rattlesnakes—are displayed behind glass.

Over 6 miles of hiking trails wind through the 1,000 acres that have been designated as a permanent nature preserve. The trails, which wander into canyons and up Eisenhower Mountain, are interpreted with 60 exhibit stations.

FOR THE KIDS

The *Discovery Room*, in the **Hoover Education Center**, is geared to children. Open only on weekends, it offers many hands-on activities, puzzles, games, and exhibits.

NEW AT THE ZOO

The new **Eagle Canyon**, which opened in 1993, is the premier exhibit. Through the power of modern exhibit design, visitors are made to feel as if they have entered the natural habitats of the animals around them. Along a winding covered pathway, more than 30 animal species can be seen with the real desert as a backdrop. In some places, similar animals from Africa and North America are displayed for comparison. They include caracals and bobcats, fennec foxes and kit foxes, and springhaas and jackrabbits. Large desert predators that can be seen close-up include mountain lions, Mexican wolves, badgers, and a golden eagle. Another interesting exhibit is the walk-through streamside aviary; ringtails, javelinas, and naked mole-rats are also displayed.

Los Angeles Zoo

5333 Zoo Drive
Los Angeles, California 90027
(213) 666-4090

Hours: *10-6 daily, in summer; 10-5, rest of year. Closed Christmas Day.*
Admission Fees: *Adults $8, 66+ $5, 2-12 $3. Participates in reciprocity program. Safari Shuttle: adults $3, 66+ and 2-12 $1.*
Directions: *Located in gigantic Griffith Park, at the junction of the Ventura (Highway*

134) *and Golden State (I-5) Freeways. From the Golden State Freeway, take the Zoo Drive Exit and follow signs to zoo. From the Ventura Freeway, take the Victory Boulevard Exit and follow signs to zoo.*

Don't Miss: *Adventure Island, Australia (especially the Koala House), Africa, South America, Monkey Island, Aviary, Eurasia, North America, World of Birds Show.*

Touring Tips: *If planning to tour all or most of this large, hilly zoo, make use of the Safari Shuttle. This tram stops at convenient locations around the perimeter of the zoo. Food stands are found throughout the zoo, with Mexican food available in Adventure Island and pizza in the South America section. A super picnic spot is provided at Treetops Terrace on a rise overlooking most of the zoo. The area is shaded by 10-story-high African-style roofs.*

Entertainment: *A great selection of excellent shows is available. The* **World of Birds** *show in the* **Wildlife Theater** *features talking birds, such as macaws, and various raptors, including a large Andean condor. In Adventure Island's 250-seat* **Pepsi Zoorific Theater***, a raccoon, coyote, opossum, and some other animals that live within the city limits star in the* **Wild in the City** *show. Aimed at children,* **Animals and You** *provides close-up comparisons of small animals in the intimate* **Pepsi Zoopendous Center***. A show schedule is provided at the entrance gate. Animal feedings include sea lions.*

The Los Angeles Zoo opened in 1966 as the world's fifth largest zoo. It is the only zoo ever to begin its existence as a major zoo. During the late 1960s, a collection of rare animals was gathered so quickly that even Noah would have been impressed. Its lush tropical foliage, including tall palm trees and many flowering trees and bushes, make it also one of the most beautiful U.S. zoos. Still, it has remained in the shadow of the San Diego Zoo, which is located 125 miles south, and the many other entertainment attractions of Southern California.

The zoo is basically divided into five continental habitat regions and a sixth Aquatics section. Each of the six sections has a winding trail that loops through it; some connect with the outer perimeter pathway. It is easy to get lost here! Within each of these six sections, many landscaped and shaded exhibit yards are inter-mingled with half-circle wire-mesh enclosures, where visitors can see animals all around them. (The arrangement of animals here should not be used to teach geography, as there are many geographic violations, such as Arabian oryxes found in the North America section and giant anteaters found in the Africa section.)

The zoo has received much acclaim for its efforts

Condor Chick Hatching

and successes with endangered species, especially for its role in saving the California condor from extinction. An innovative display explains the plight of the condors and what the zoo is doing to help. Because of their critical situation, no condors can be displayed.

FEATURED EXHIBITS

One of the first exhibits seen in the main part of the zoo is **Monkey Island**—a beautiful habitat for the attractive woolly monkeys. Across the path, ever-popular meerkats stand up on their hind legs and stare at visitors directly overhead. Among the nicest spots in the entire zoo is the African flamingo exhibit—a lush tropical garden with a cascading waterfall.

One of the premier exhibits is the **Ahmanson Koala House**. Unlike other koala exhibits, this one is nocturnal, which makes L.A.'s koalas more active than most. The dark eucalyptus grove is also inhabited by echidnas (egg-laying spiny anteaters) and fast-hopping bettongs. Different than the koalas found in most U.S. zoos, these are of the Victoria subspecies—the largest and longest-haired variety. Another nocturnal house in the **Australia** section displays tawny frogmouths and rarely seen kiwi birds from New Zealand. Kangaroos and wallabies are also displayed, as is a rarely seen double-wattled cassowary (a tall land bird with beautiful coloring).

Two gorilla troops in naturalistic grottoes are highlights of the **Africa** section. (This zoo has 30 different types of primates. This represents the third largest display in variety of primates in the U.S.) Nearly half of the assorted lemurs, monkeys, and apes are in this section, including drill baboons (the most endangered primate), red-crowned guenons, chimpanzees, and sifakas (a strange type of lemur seen at only one other U.S. zoo). Another animal type exhibited in great variety is the diminutive duiker; Jentinck's duikers (the world's most endangered antelope) are among them. Other interesting hoofstock include sable antelope, bongos, Grevy's zebras, Masai giraffes, and the nation's largest herd of gerenuks (slender antelope that stand on their hind legs to feed on acacia shoots). Two open yards exhibit both African and Asian elephants, and a Nile hippo pool is nearby. Black rhinos are found in this section, as are hairy Sumatran rhinos from Indonesia that are nearly extinct. (This zoo has more rhinos than any other U.S. zoo.)

In the **North America** section, a lone bison lives with a large herd of pronghorn antelope. Dog-like carnivores include endangered red wolves, a coyote, red foxes, and wolverines. Thick-billed parrots (the only parrots still native to the United States) are seen here, and three species of wild pigs (all non-American) are displayed (including red river hogs that are seen in only two U.S. zoos). Bactrian camels and Arabian oryxes round out the section's foreign residents.

The **Eurasia** section features the popular Indian rhinos, which occupy a large chunk of the area. Sloth bears, orangutans, and siamangs also draw crowds. Island hornbills, which have rainbow-colored bills, might be the most beautiful animals at the zoo. (They are seen at only two other American zoos.) African animals found in this section include caracal lynx, African fish eagles, and handsome gelada baboons.

No other U.S. zoo can match the collection of New World monkeys in the **South America** section. Notables include spider monkeys, howler monkeys, sakis, and the nation's only bald-headed red uakaris. Also seen in few other zoos are Central American and hairy mountain tapirs. Impressive birds seen here include Andean condors, king vultures, and toco toucans. More animals include pudus (the world's smallest deer), Galapagos tortoises (the world's largest turtles), maned wolves, spectacled bears, and a jaguar.

This zoo exhibits more than 250 types of birds. (It is the third largest diversity in the country.) Over a fifth of these feathered species can be found in the walk-through tropical **Aviary**. A jungle path ascends to the top of a crashing waterfall, where the entire screened exhibit can be viewed with many of its gorgeous birds in flight.

OTHER EXHIBITS

The **Aquatics** section's Magellanic penguins, gray seals, California sea lions, and polar bears are some of the most popular animals in the zoo. Other creatures seen swimming in large concrete pools include American alligators, pelicans, and capybaras (the world's largest rodents).

The least visited section is the row of **Hillside Animals** exhibits. Bighorn sheep, Rocky Mountain goats, and the only Japanese serows in a U.S. zoo are some of the animals seen from the bottom of the hill.

An interesting variety of reptiles can be observed through low viewing windows surrounding the **Reptile House**. Notable inhabitants include Egyptian cobras, American crocodiles, gila monsters, and an amazing two-headed snake.

The indoor/outdoor **China Pavilion** habitat, which was built for visiting pandas, now houses snow leopards.

FOR THE KIDS

The zoo's main attraction is **Adventure Island**, a new 2-acre children's zoo. Just below the colorful entrance sign, sea lions shower in a splashing waterfall. In habitats with virtually invisible barriers, animals from the American Southwest

Rocky Mountain Goats

are exhibited in five California environments: Cave, Desert, Mountain, Meadow, and Shoreline. Participatory exhibits lure children into learning more about the displayed animals. Behind the waterfall, the *Cave* has vampire bats fluttering around stalactites, ringtails living in a mine shaft, and a miniature hologram human inside the spotted skunk exhibit. The *Desert* features burrowing owls and roadrunners, while the *Meadow* has a prairie dog town with tunnels leading to acrylic domes where kids can pop up and imitate the burrowing rodents. Nearby, kids line up to see what the world looks like through the eyes of the oversized heads of a mountain lion, prairie dog, and bee. Not far away, mounted microscopes aimed at a pond give a close look at pond life, and the bronze footprints of a bear and mountain lion trigger growls when stepped upon. Adventure Island also has a *Nursery* with low viewing windows offering views of newborn animals. Exotic cattle, goats, and Navajo sheep can be petted through split-rail fencing in a Spanish-style petting yard called the *Hacienda*.

The **Play Park** playground in the main zoo is surrounded by a spacious picnic area.

Rides available within Griffith Park include ponies, a miniature stagecoach, several miniature trains, and the SR-2 Simulator thrill ride.

NEW AT THE ZOO

Tiger Falls, which opened in 1993, is a beautiful natural habitat renovation of the tiger exhibit. Found in the Eurasia section, the exhibit features new pools and waterfalls.

Metro Washington Park Zoo

4001 S.W. Canyon Road
Portland, Oregon 97221
(503) 226-1561

Hours: *Opens at 9:30 daily; closing time varies with season.*
Admission Fees: *Adults $5, 66+ $3.50, 3-11 $3. Participates in reciprocity program. Washington Park & Zoo Railway: adults $2.50, 66+ and 3-11 $1.75.*
Directions: *From I-5 northbound, take Exit 300A (I-405). From I-5 southbound, take Exit 302B (I-405). Follow I-405 north or south to Exit 1D (U.S. Highway 26) West. Follow signs on Highway 26 to zoo.*
Don't Miss: *Africa!, Africa Rain Forest, Washington Park & Zoo Railway, Alaska Tundra, Elephant Museum, Elephant Complex, Cascade Exhibit, Penguinarium, polar bear exhibit.*
Touring Tips: *AfriCafe is one of nation's best zoo restaurants. Inside, diners have views of the African Aviary; outside, they have great seats for the bird show.*
Entertainment: *An excellent **Birds of Prey Show**—featuring a king vulture, owls, and an Andean condor—is presented on the **Main Stage** in summer.*

Portland, Oregon is known as the "City of Roses." It has also been called the "City of Elephants." The inspiration for both of these titles can be found within beautiful Washington Park, which holds both a rose garden and a zoo.

Over the last decade the Metro Washington Park Zoo has become one of the most improved zoos. All animals are displayed in ten clearly defined exhibit areas. Seven of these exhibits either opened or were renovated during the 1980s and 1990s.

FEATURED EXHIBITS

The most important date in the zoo's history is probably April 14, 1962, when Packy was born. He was the first elephant born in North America in 44 years. Since then, with 24 additional births, this zoo has become world famous for its success in breeding Asian elephants. The ten elephants here represent the largest breeding herd outside of Asia, and so the likelihood of seeing a baby elephant is quite high. (No other U.S. zoo has more than six elephants.)

Today, Packy still lives in the **Elephant Complex**. This 1 1/2-acre exhibit includes two separate yards—one with an 80,000-gallon pool. The many elephants are sometimes seen in the holding barn behind a wide, floor-to-ceiling glass wall. A path follows the length of the larger yard and then climbs up a hill to Elephant Overlook.

Everything you've ever wanted to know about elephants can be learned at the **Lilah Callen Holden Elephant Museum**. A giant mastodon skeleton is the center-piece of this round building with Thai decor, and a variety of exhibits explain the history of elephants.

The most spectacular exhibits are the two new African areas. **Africa!** is an incredible 4-acre replication of the dry East African plains. A path descends inside a simulated dry riverbed to viewing points where visitors can see endangered black rhinos, Nile hippos, giraffes, impalas, land birds, and rarely exhibited Hartmann's mountain zebras. From the *Treetops*, an elevated deck gives excellent overviews of some of the natural savannas. DeBrazza's monkeys, weaver birds, savanna reptiles, and rarely-seen cusimanses are displayed inside. The domed walk-through *Howard Vollum Aviary* is inhabited by red-crested touracos, African jacanas, hammerkops, and 17 additional bird species.

Vegetation becomes denser as the path leads into the new **Africa Rain Forest**. Excellent exhibits abound in this replication of the West African tropics. Some of the most popular include a colony of banded mongooses, numerous fruit bats under a rocky overhang, and Cape clawless otters and L'Hoests monkeys in a for-est stream habitat. The authentic-looking *Kongo Ranger Station* exposes the horrors of poaching with a display of animal hides, elephant tusks, and other confiscated articles. A walk through the *African Swamp Aviary*, with its wading birds and water-fowl, leads to the main attraction—the *Bamba du Jon Swamp* building. In a humid jungle setting, slender-snouted crocodiles inhabit a crystal-clear aquarium that per-mits close-up encounters. Other creatures in nearby exhibits include an African lungfish, leeches, Nile monitor lizards, beautiful cichlid fish, and free-flying birds.

Sometimes the building darkens for a thunderstorm, which includes lightning and a torrential downpour on the crocodiles.

An entirely different climate is represented in the unique **Alaska Tundra** exhibit. Visitors enter through a path cut into the "permafrost" and are immediately confronted by the eerie vision of a herd of caribou standing in the dim light of a winter sun. A room filled with hi-tech interpretive activities provides a short course in tundra life. Mouse-like brown lemmings, which are the lifeblood of the tundra's food chain, are displayed. A covered walkway leads past the rest of the exhibit's animals in large natural habitats, including muskoxen, short-eared owls, snowy owls, and waterfowl of the marshy tundra. The wolves and grizzly bears can be seen on a grassy hill and inside their dens. Before leaving, visitors can experience the tundra summer through a nine-projector slide show.

Wildlife from the local region, specifically Oregon's Cascade Range, is featured in the award-winning **Cascade Exhibit**. A 1/4-mile nature trail leads past a great horned owl and a golden eagle to the *Stream and Pond Building*. A rushing waterfall flows down a hill and appears to enter the building. Inside, assorted aquariums and terrariums display the fish, frogs, and insects of the region. At the beaver pond, which includes an authentic beaver dam, the beavers can be seen above and below water along with great blue herons and diving ducks. River otters are displayed in a similar manner across the hall. More aquatic birds of the region, such as ruddy ducks and the Northwest's famous dippers, are exhibited outside.

At the entrance to the **Penguinarium** a sign reads "Welcome to Peru." Inside, the rocky coastal waters of Peru are replicated. A large colony of warm-weather Humboldt penguins and a flock of Inca terns can be seen from three outstanding viewing areas. The naturalistic habitat even includes artificial waves and underwater currents for penguins to swim through.

OTHER EXHIBITS

This zoo exhibits seven different kinds of bears (more than any other U.S. zoo). Most are in large concrete grottoes. The **polar bear exhibit** features an underground simulated ice cave for "under the polar ice" viewing.

Chimpanzees, the stars of the zoo's **Primates** exhibit, can be seen indoors or out on their 1-acre "chimp island." Mandrills, siamangs, gibbons, and lemurs also enjoy excellent large habitats. Other

Baby Francois Leaf Monkey

primates found here include orangutans and Francois leaf monkeys.

The cages and moated enclosures around the **Feline building** are inhabited by lions, tigers, jaguars, snow leopards, cougars, and red pandas. The **Insect Zoo** (one of only five in the country) displays giant walking sticks and other creepy crawly curiosities in small terrariums.

FOR THE KIDS

In the *Masai Goat Kraal*, located in the Africa! exhibit, children can pet, and sometimes feed, African pygmy goats. The nation's best zoo train ride is the **Washington Park & Zoo Railway**. Three different trains carry passengers on a 4-mile course that passes by many animals, then through a beautiful thick forest, and on to a depot near the International Rose Test Gardens. Summer passengers can ask for a stopover pass and get off the train for a tour of the magnificent rose gardens. From the gardens, the panoramic view of Portland and snow-capped mountains on the horizon is spectacular.

NEW AT THE ZOO

Most of the exhibits here are relatively new. The zoo is currently building the **Center for Species Survival**—a facility that will focus on breeding and researching many of the world's most endangered animals.

Point Defiance Zoo & Aquarium

5400 North Pearl Street
Tacoma, Washington 98407
(206) 591-5335

Hours: *10-7 daily, Memorial Day-Labor Day; 10-4, rest of year. Closed Thanksgiving Day and Christmas Day.*
Admission Fees: *Adults $6.25, 63+ $5.75, 5-17 $4.50, 3-4 $2.25. Participates in reciprocity program. Elephant ride $1.75, summer only.*
Directions: *From I-5, take Exit 132 (Highway 16). Follow Highway 16 east to the 6th Avenue Exit. Turn left onto 6th Avenue, then right onto Pearl Street. Go north on Pearl Street into Point Defiance Park, and follow signs to zoo.*
Don't Miss: *Discovery Reef Aquarium, Rocky Shores, North Pacific Aquarium, World of Adaptations, Polar Bear Complex, Sharks: the Survivors.*
Touring Tips: *Because of its late closing time, this zoo is especially enjoyable during summer evenings. The Farm Cafe offers indoor seating overlooking The Farm and shaded outdoor seating on a deck with a panoramic view of Puget Sound. Point Defiance Park has many other interesting attractions.*
Entertainment: *In summer,* **Bird Shows** *are held twice daily (except Mondays and Tuesdays).* **Marine mammal talks** *take place regularly at the Rocky Shores. On scheduled*

evenings, concerts are held at the **Centerstage**. *Animal feedings include the marine mammals.*

The Point Defiance Zoo & Aquarium is known as the Pacific Rim Zoo because most of its animals are native to the volcanic nations bordering the Pacific Ocean. Although it originally opened in 1905, this newly-renovated zoo was rededicated in 1983.

With its beautiful natural habitats and ultra-close viewing points, this zoo is a pacesetter. It is undeniably one of the nation's most unique zoos, and some consider it one of the best.

FEATURED EXHIBITS

Since its 1982 opening, **Rocky Shores** has been the premier exhibit. It is said to be an exact replica of a rocky cove on the Washington coast. White beluga whales are enchanting to watch, especially from underwater, and Pacific walruses, which live and play with California sea lions and harbor seals, are nearly as popular and almost as big. Playful sea otters are often seen doing the backstroke or diving for clams, and puffins, whether building nests up on the cliffs or "flying underwater," attract a lot of visitor attention in their rocky cliff habitat. All of the Rocky Shores animals can be seen underwater from a delightful common viewing area. Like the whales, the walruses seem to enjoy getting as close as possible to visitors who peer at them through wide glass panels. (This is the only U.S. zoo to display beluga whales and sea otters, and one of only three zoos exhibiting walruses.)

No ordinary aquarium, the **Discovery Reef Aquarium** is a complete South Pacific experience. After following a winding tropical path, visitors pick up a printed nature guide containing an identification key and checklist for the creatures on display. A short, interesting walk through a realistic research hut leads to a pretty lagoon exhibit called *The Island*. At the seashore, where the only barrier is a fallen palm tree, small fish and stingrays swim in shallow water. Bird sounds, gentle warm trade winds, and an ocean horizon mural all combine to fool the senses and make it hard to remember that this is an indoor exhibit. Down a few stairs in the *Inner Reef*, colorful fish and small sharks become visible behind a 5-foot-high glass wall. A few more steps down takes visitors into the *Blue Hole*, where sunlight appears to stream in from the surface, visible far above. Larger sharks and menacing zebra moray eels are seen here. When visitors reach the *Outer Reef*, they are nearly surrounded by a crystal-clear, open ocean tank holding more than 40 large sharks.

The older **North Pacific Aquarium** features a round, 160,000-gallon community tank inhabited by marine life from the cold waters of the Pacific Northwest and Puget Sound. Large sharks can be seen swimming past viewing windows encircling the tank, and live kelp plants and giant starfish are seen at its bottom. Around the tank's perimeter, 34 exciting exhibits include a Pacific octopus, wolf eels, and some scallops. The highlight is a display of moon jellyfish, which are rarely seen by

Sand Tiger Shark

humans. Special purple lighting and an eerie soundtrack make watching these saucer-shaped blobs a mesmerizing "other world" experience. A side room contains the interactive *Simpson Marine Discovery Lab*. Outside, a new *Tidepool* exhibit has sea anemones living in mechanically-generated waves.

The **World of Adaptations** building exhibits a wide variety of interesting small animals in naturalistic habitats. Among the residents that stray from the zoo's Pacific Rim theme are golden lion tamarins from Brazil and black lemurs from Madagascar. Mammals include aardvarks, North American porcupines, coatis, and hundreds of fruit bats in a nocturnal cave. Pythons, rattlesnakes, gila monsters, and poison arrow frogs are some of the many reptiles and amphibians also seen here. Birds are abundant as well, including various owls, hornbills, and colorful finches.

The award-winning **Polar Bear Complex** has received much acclaim. This unique exhibit depicts the Alaskan coast and features a stream of "melted snow" flowing down a gravel beach. When not on the beach, the 12-foot-tall bears are often seen diving for live mackerel in their 11-foot-deep, glass-fronted pool. Color-changing arctic foxes reside nearby in a grassy yard. A special window keeps them in view even when they are asleep in their den.

OTHER EXHIBITS

The Polar Bear Complex is one part of the **Arctic Tundra** exhibit area, which also includes a herd of rarely-exhibited muskoxen and an enclosed walk-through tundra marsh with Alaskan waterfowl. Elusive **red wolves** live in their own enclosed forest. (This zoo is the breeding center for these endangered wolves.)

In a new, bright-red elephant barn, Asian and African elephants are the main attraction of the **Southeast Asia** complex. Tall wire-mesh enclosures hold spectacled langurs and vocal siamangs, both from Asian jungles.

Penguin Point simulates the South American coastline for a Magellanic penguin colony, and reindeer and llamas graze nearby in open hillside yards.

FOR THE KIDS

The Farm is probably the most popular exhibit for children. Goats, sheep, llamas, pigs, and sometimes even a baby muskox are usually close enough in their fenced corrals for little hands to pet. Goat food can be purchased from coin-operated dispensers. Chickens, turkeys, chinchillas, and rabbits are found in a barn.

Elephant rides are available.

NEW AT THE ZOO

Sharks: the Survivors could easily be renamed "Everything You've Always Wanted To Know About Sharks." This innovative new exhibit combines graphics, videos, artifacts, and live sharks to provide an entertaining short course on sharks. Their blood-thirsty image, built up by the media, is examined and refuted. Most amazing is a display of live egg-casings that are illuminated to reveal the wiggly fetal sharks inside.

San Diego Zoo

Zoo Place & Park Boulevard
San Diego, California 92103
(619) 234-3153 or 231-1515

Hours: *9-5 daily, mid-June-Labor Day; 9-4, rest of year; grounds close later.*
Admission Fees: *Adults $12, 3-15 $4, under 3 and military in uniform free. Bus tour: adults $3, 3-15 $2.50.*
Directions: *Located in Balboa Park. From San Diego Freeway (I-5), take Pershing Drive exit, then follow signs to zoo. Bus Route 7 stops 2 blocks from zoo.*
Don't Miss: *Tiger River, Gorilla Tropics (including Treehouse), giant pandas, koalas, Skyfari, bus tour, Pygmy Chimps at Bonobo Road, African Rock Kopje, Reptile House and Mesa, Children's Zoo, animal shows, Sun Bear Forest, Elephant Mesa, Wings of Australasia, okapi/meerkat exhibits.*
Touring Tips: *It is advisable to purchase Deluxe Tour tickets, which include the bus tour. Located within 100-acre Balboa Park, this zoo has miles of trails winding in and out of steep canyons. Therefore, it is a good idea to start the day by boarding one of the double-decker buses for a guided tour. The 40-minute tour, which covers over 3 miles and nearly 80 percent of the animal exhibits, provides a good orientation, and drivers share interesting information and entertaining stories about the animals. After the tour, visitors are better*

*equipped to take a closer look at the animals. The zoo's restaurants and gift shops are, like everything else, superb. The new **Treehouse**, located adjacent to Gorilla Tropics, is a 4-story replica of an African plantation house on stilts. It consists of a gift shop and two restaurants with outdoor eating areas that provide sweeping views of the zoo.*

Entertainment: *The outstanding, free animal shows recently have been updated. For the **Wegeforth National Park** show, the **Wegeforth Bowl** stage is set up like a national park ranger station. The show features sea lions, harbor seals, wolves, owls, hawks, and Andean condors. These animals demonstrate their natural behaviors and present a conservation message. Additional shows using a variety of North American and exotic animals will probably be held in **Hunte Amphitheater**.*

The San Diego Zoo is one of the world's best. In the United States, only New York's Bronx Zoo is in the same league. Over 4,000 animals of 820 species are exhibited (a greater diversity than any zoo in the U.S.). Many of the most rare and popular animals can be viewed in some of the best reproductions of natural habitats anywhere.

Many of the tourists who visit Disneyland and Sea World will also spend a day of their vacation at this zoo. This popularity means crowds, especially in summer. But San Diego's near perfect climate makes a visit here pleasant any time of the year.

The plant collection is so superb that the zoo has been accredited as a botanical garden and also as a museum. Orchids, coral trees, ferns, banana trees, palm trees, cacti, and redwood trees are just some of the interesting species that contribute to this beautiful botanical diversity.

For visitors who want to see even more, the San Diego Wild Animal Park (see "More Places To See Animals" chapter) is just 32 miles away. This vast animal reserve is run by the same zoological society as, and shares animals with, the San Diego Zoo.

FEATURED EXHIBITS

Among zoos outside Australia, this one is known as the world's "koala capital." Over 20 of these immensely popular marsupials are in its collection. A wooden walkway makes a semi-circle around a small yard shared by a few koalas and wallabies. The majority of the koalas are behind glass on the opposite side of the walkway. Another yard displays tree kangaroos. Because the koalas here have been very fruitful, it is not unusual to see babies.

Near the zoo's entrance, a colorful sign marks the start of **Tiger River**—an award-winning replica of an Asian rain forest. With the sweet smell of jasmine and ginger plants hanging in the misty air, the exhibit has not only the look, sound, and feel of a real jungle, but also the fragrance. Along a winding path, visitors encounter 10 exhibits featuring over 100 animals. Gharials (crocodiles with pointed noses) can be viewed through glass from above and below water. Tropical birds, a Burmese python, web-footed fishing cats, and Malayan tapirs are also seen. The 3-acre exhibit climaxes with the hillside habitat of deep-orange Sumatran tigers. Blanca, a female white Bengal tiger, is also exhibited here for a few hours each day.

Another Asian jungle is simulated nearby in the **Sun Bear Forest**. In a habitat with giant trees, pools, and waterfalls, sun bears (the world's smallest bears) and lion-tailed macaques (endangered monkeys) are amusing to watch from many different viewpoints in their separate enclosures. The *Forest Aviary*, filled with brilliantly colored birds from Asia, is also a part of this forest.

Another award-winning habitat is seen at the **African Rock Kopje**. Klipspringers (small agile antelope) are at home on the giant boulders, while pancake tortoises often hide between the rocks, and dwarf mongooses and rock hyraxes scurry in and out of view. Kopje birds displayed include black eagles.

The world-renowned **Reptile House**, a Spanish-style structure, is unusual in that visitors do not go inside; they "window shop" around it. Its extensive collection includes rattlesnakes, pythons, cobras, lizards, turtles, and frogs. Thelma & Louise (a two-headed corn snake) and a newly-acquired 8-foot-long Komodo dragon draw the most attention. (In 1993, San Diego became only the third U.S. zoo to display these largest of all lizards.) Behind the main building is **Reptile Mesa**, with four smaller reptile buildings (one displays highly-poisonous sea snakes) and large outdoor enclosures for Galapagos and other tortoises as well as alligators and related

Thelma & Louise, the Two-Headed Corn Snake

species. (It is the best reptile exhibit in the nation.)

Up on **Elephant Mesa**, African and Asian elephants live in a large area with their own pool. Around them, corrals hold two species of rhino, one of which is the shaggy, nearly extinct Sumatran rhino. Other animals in this area include giant anteaters, fennec foxes, and margay cats. Short, flightless kiwi birds—the national symbol of New Zealand—are kept in a small nocturnal building that is one of the zoo's few indoor exhibits. Not far away, flying foxes (bats) hang upside down at the front of their cage.

Rare and beautiful okapis are displayed near the other African animals. Not far away, a band of meerkats has constructed an intricate burrow system. These are two of the most popular animals from the African continent.

OTHER EXHIBITS

The **Hummingbird Aviary** is a very popular spot. These tiny multicolored birds hover and dart just inches from visitors in a compact walk-through jungle.

The zoo's collection of parrot-like birds includes over 130 species. (It is the largest such collection in the world.) Most of these feathered gems reside on **Bird and Primate Mesa**. Other enclosures and aviaries housing birds of all sizes and colors are found throughout the zoo. The **Rain Forest Aviary** has a steep, winding path from which to view its beautiful tropical birds. Two large waterfowl ponds host pelicans, cranes, and other wading birds. A raised walkway offers high-level views of various eagles—bald, martial, and harpy—and Andean condors in spacious flight cages. Not far away, ostriches, Manchurian storks, and other tall birds are seen in open yards. Perhaps the most beautiful birds here are the rarely exhibited birds of paradise.

Bird and Primate Mesa is also the site of the **Whittier Southeast Asian Exhibits**—a collection of extremely rare primates. One, the ghost-faced douc langur monkey, was nearly wiped out by the Vietnam War. (It is seen in only three U.S. zoos.) The orangutans and siamangs each have their own playgrounds.

Most of the carnivores reside in two canyons on either side of Elephant Mesa. **Bear Canyon** has five species of bears (including polar and Manchurian), a small pride of African lions, and a pool full of sea lions. Other wild cats, including jaguars and leopards, are found in **Dog and Cat Canyon** along with an impressive collection of wild dogs, including Chinese dholes, jackals, and dog-like hyenas and aardwolves.

Much of this zoo's amazing variety of hoofed animals can be found along the trail on the ridge of **Horn and Hoof Mesa**. The difference between bison and buffalo can be observed here in the endangered European wisents and the Asian water buffalo. Antelope, gazelles, and other hoofstock of many colors and sizes are on display. Most notable are the bongos, the rare takins from China, the Arabian oryxes, and the Mongolian wild horses. An African area features Baringo giraffes, zebras, and wart hogs, and pygmy hippos and tapirs are often found submerged in their pools near Tiger River.

FOR THE KIDS

The **Children's Zoo** here is one of the nation's largest. A petting paddock allows children to pet goats, sheep, and potbellied pigs. Smaller animals, such as an echidna (a spiny anteater) and newly hatched chicks, are also within reach of small hands. Popular small mammals on exhibit include red pandas, pygmy marmosets, spider monkeys, naked mole-rats, and Asian small-clawed otters. A hairy large mammal, the rare mountain tapir, also lives here. Scaled to a 4-year-old's level, two baby animal nurseries are a highlight for most children. Through viewing windows, human "moms" can sometimes be seen caring for diapered baby apes, and sometimes leopard or tiger cubs can be seen playing with stuffed animals.

The rides and shows available at this zoo are the best any has to offer. The colorful gondolas of the **Skyfari** aerial tramway carry riders on a $1/3$-mile-long cable across the zoo at a height of 170 feet. At its peak riders get a superb panoramic view of the zoo, downtown San Diego, and the Pacific Ocean. The moving sidewalks that transport weary walkers from the deepest canyons to higher elevations are not really "rides," but most small children think they are.

NEW AT THE ZOO

An ambitious plan is underway to reshape the zoo into ten bioclimatic regions in which plants and animals native to the same environment are displayed together. The first three habitats established under this plan (Tiger River, Sun Bear Forest, and the African Rock Kopje) seen so authentic that at times visitors feel as if they have actually left California.

The fourth habitat is a lush African rain forest, re-created in the new **Gorilla Tropics**. The path to the gorillas crosses a bridge over a beautiful cascading waterfall. A troop of six lowland gorillas can be viewed from many angles in their natural habitat, which is planted with bamboo, banana, and fig trees. (This exhibit has more African plants than anywhere outside of Africa.) One of the world's largest walk-through flight cages, **Scripps Aviary**, has the top of its mesh shell painted sky blue, which has the effect of making it seem to disappear from sight. Inside, a tree-top-level walkway provides good views of the jewel-colored African birds—among them Lady Ross touracos and blue-breasted kingfishers—while a ground-level path provides a closer look at jungle vegetation.

Pygmy Chimps at Bonobo Road, which opened in 1993, is another African rain forest exhibit featuring great apes. The agile and acrobatic bonobos (also known as pygmy chimpanzees) live on a grassy hillside habitat that is enhanced with waterfalls, pools, and a natural playground formed by curved and twisted palm trees. (This zoo is well-known for its breeding successes with bonobos.) Colobus monkeys, crowned eagles, rock pythons, and chameleons are also displayed in attractive habitats.

The **Wings of Australasia** complex, which also opened in 1993, has a set of 23 lushly-planted aviaries exhibiting a rainbow of over 90 tropical birds from Australia, Southeast Asia, and the Pacific islands situated between them. Notable feathered specimens include Guam kingfishers, various rare lories, Blythe's tragopans, blue-crowned hanging parrots, beautiful fruit doves, and double-wattled cassowaries from New Guinea.

The zoo hopes to receive soon a pair of **giant pandas** from China on a 3-year breeding loan. Certain to draw large crowds, these most popular of all zoo animals will be exhibited in a new canyon exhibit.

San Francisco Zoological Gardens

1 Zoo Road
San Francisco, California 94132
(415) 753-7080

Hours: *10-5 daily.*
Admission Fees: *Adults $6.50, 65+ and 12-15 $3, 6-11 $1; free on first Wednesday of each month. Participates in reciprocity program. Children's Zoo $1, under 3 free. Zebra Train: adults $2.50, 65+ and under 16 $1.50. Carousel $1.*
Directions: *Located 2 miles south of Golden Gate Park, just off the Great Highway. From I-280, take the Junipero Serra Boulevard Exit (Highway 1). Follow north and stay to left onto 19th Avenue for 2.2 miles, then turn left onto Sloat Boulevard. Continue toward the ocean for 1.7 miles. Zoo is on left. Zoo is also accessible from MUNI/BART metro system.*
Don't Miss: *Primate Discovery Center, Insect Zoo, Koala Crossing, Gorilla World.*
Touring Tips: *A 30-minute orientation tour is available on the Zebra Train tram ride. A free walking tour is offered at 1 p.m. on weekends. Four outdoor cafes offer an unusual variety of food that includes Polish sausage, baked potatoes, and chimichangas. Because the zoo is located just a few hundred yards from the Pacific Ocean, be prepared for the city's famous fog to roll in at any time: Bring jackets.*
Entertainment: *In the Insect Zoo, the **Incredible Insects in Action** macro video is shown daily. During summer a **Livestock Presentation** occurs in the Children's Zoo's Barnyard, a **Parrot Program** occurs in the **Nature Theater**, and **Wildlife Theater Presentations** are scheduled twice daily. The big cats are fed at 2 p.m. in the Lion House (except on Mondays, when they fast). The echoing loud roars of these ferocious cats is unforgettable. Other animal feedings include penguins.*

In a city that features the Golden Gate Bridge, cable cars, Fisherman's Wharf, and Chinatown among its attractions, the zoo might be overlooked. However, it obviously isn't, as more than a million people visit the 65-acre San Francisco Zoo each year.

FEATURED EXHIBITS

With the addition of the exhibits that opened during the 1980s, this zoo has made its mark as one of the premier zoos in the country for primate-watching. In tall outdoor atrium cages and in lush meadows, the **Thelma and Henry Doegler Primate Discovery Center** displays 15 species of rare and endangered primates, including colobus monkeys, fast-running patas monkeys, stunning mandrills, emperor tamarins, Francois monkeys, owl-faced monkeys, and lion-tailed macaques. The adjoining *Kresge Nocturnal Gallery* holds tree shrews, mouse lemurs, bushbabies, and other primates of the night. The *Phoebe Hearst Discovery Hall* offers 23 interactive and educational exhibits and a monkey-themed gift shop.

Gorilla World, a circular outdoor habitat, is one of the world's largest gorilla displays. It is lush with waterfalls, trees, rocky outcroppings, and even authentic kikiyu grass from Africa. This natural habitat can be viewed from above or from a wall of viewing windows.

Koala Crossing displays five of these cuddly marsupials in an outdoor eucalyptus grove. In inclement weather, they are moved inside behind a viewing window. An adjacent video provides information.

OTHER EXHIBITS

Musk Ox Meadow is the 2.6-acre home of a herd of rare white-fronted musk oxen from the Alaskan tundra. (In 1972, when China sent pandas to the United States, two musk oxen from this zoo were sent to China in return.)

Penguin Island is a 200-foot-long pool with the country's largest colony of Magellanic penguins from Chile (over 50). More than 100 penguin chicks have hatched here.

The colorful inhabitants of the **Tropical Aviary** include herons, egrets, ibises, and spoonbills.

The big cats are seen in outdoor grottoes surrounding the **Lion House**. They include lions, rare Sumatran tigers, and Bengal tigers—among them a white tiger named Prince Charles. Many other cats—including leopards, jaguars, pumas, lynx, jungle cats, and a prolific group of snow leopards—are displayed in nearby cages. The **Greater One-Horned Rhinoceros** exhibit features a pair of rare rhinos from Nepal. They have a large wading pool available for cooling and wallowing.

Other notable animals found throughout the zoo include African and Asian elephants, black rhinos, pygmy and Nile hippos, giraffes, tapirs, Rocky Mountain goats, water buffalo, four types of bears, five different kangaroo species, more great apes (chimpanzees and orangutans), and a pool full of seals and sea lions.

FOR THE KIDS

The **Children's Zoo** is one of the most attractive areas. It includes the *Barnyard* petting area, the *Animal Nursery*, and exhibits of small animals such as coatis, squirrel monkeys, and prairie dogs. On the educational *Nature Trail*, volunteers provide close-up views of various uncaged animals.

The popular and unusual *Insect Zoo* consists of glass terrariums housing more than 60 species of interesting and exotic arthropods (insects and their relatives). Scorpions, tarantulas, walking sticks, a leaf-cutter ant colony, a 10 1/2-inch gigantic centipede, and a rare flower mantid from Malaysia are among the featured specimens. (This is the second-best exhibit of insects in the country.)

When kids tire of animals and bugs, they can ride on an antique 1921 Dentzel carousel situated just outside the Children's Zoo.

NEW AT THE ZOO

The new **African Wild Dogs** exhibit features rare and colorful hunting dogs from southern Africa. These powerful predators hunt in large packs like wolves.

Woodland Park Zoological Gardens

5500 Phinney Avenue North
Seattle, Washington 98103
(206) 684-4800 or 684-4026

Hours: *9:30-6 daily, mid-March to mid-October; 9:30-4, rest of year.*
Admission Fees: *Adults $6, seniors and handicapped $4.50, 6-17 $3.50, 3-5 $1.50. Participates in reciprocity program. Pony ride $1.50, in season. Parking: $2/up to 4 hours, $4/over 4 hours, in summer; half-price in winter.*
Directions: *From I-5, take Exit 169 (50th Street) West, then follow 50th Street west to zoo.*
Don't Miss: *Elephant Forest, Lowland Gorilla Exhibit, Tropical Rain Forest, African Savanna, Nocturnal and Tropical House, Northern Trail, Feline House.*
Touring Tips: *The spacious North Meadow is a great place to picnic.*
Entertainment: *Educational elephant demonstrations, which include a chance to pet the huge beasts, are given at scheduled times in the Elephant Forest's Thai logging village. A* **Raptor Demonstration**, *which includes a bald eagle and a very rare gyrfalcon, is presented at scheduled times at the* **Raptor Barn**. *Other animal talks are held in the* **Open Air Theater**, *and free films are shown in the* **Education Center's Discovery Room**.

In recent years, the Seattle area has become a relocation mecca for many families looking for a better lifestyle. The area also has benefited from an increasing number of people choosing the "Emerald City" as their vacation destination. To keep up with this growing visitor base, the Woodland Park Zoo is making major strides to upgrade. In 1979, it opened a definitive outdoor gorilla exhibit. Since then, zoos from around the world have followed the lead of this very natural ape habitat. The zoo has followed up on this success with three more equally impressive natural habitat exhibits. By 1997, the zoo's capital plan will have three-fourths of the zoo converted into a series of eight "bioclimatic zones" (Tropical Rain Forest, African Savanna, etc.).

FEATURED EXHIBITS

When this zoo opened the **Lowland Gorilla Exhibit**, it was one of the first to move its gorillas out of cages and into a natural outdoor habitat. Today, most zoo experts still recognize this exhibit as the best—for both gorillas and visitors. Four different viewing areas allow close-up views of the gorillas. The concept of "landscape immersion" is nearly perfect here, with the same lush foliage that makes the forest clearing habitat appear so real extending into the visitor areas. While heated rocks and forageable food encourage the apes to stay in view, they are still able to find privacy by climbing over a man-made hill.

The **Elephant Forest** was recognized as the country's best new zoo exhibit of 1990. This excellent natural habitat for Asian (and one African) elephants is this zoo's most unique exhibit. It duplicates both the landscape and culture of northern Thailand. Within the exhibit's 4.6 acres, the herd of elephants can roam in a long, 1-acre wooded yard with an 11-foot-deep swimming pool. Human visitors can observe the elephants from many vantage points positioned along a winding pathway through a thick bamboo forest. Asian waterfowl, including cranes, can be seen in a marsh that is fed by a pretty waterfall. In cold weather, the elephants are behind the viewing windows in the *Kong Chang* (Thai for "House of Elephants")— a large elephant barn designed to look like a Buddhist temple. Five more authentic Thai buildings are clustered together in the *Thai logging village*, where the elephants demonstrate their power and logging skills.

The central **African Savanna**, also an award-winner, looks much bigger than it is. One of the best features of this exhibit is that the savanna is never visible from the main path, thus making it seem more removed from civilization. Giraffes, zebras, topi, and a large herd of springboks graze on grassy slopes, and fast-running patas monkeys are seen on rocky outcrops. One overlook is directly over a large hippo pool, and the shaded *Savanna Lion Overlook* offers close views of a pride of lions. A mesh-enclosed aviary of savanna birds includes cattle egrets and bright-yellow masked weaver birds.

The **Nocturnal and Tropical House** has long been a favorite here. A large variety of snakes, lizards, turtles, frogs, and insects are seen in desert and tropical settings. Two large, lean-into swamp habitats display water monitors and dwarf crocodiles. At the entrance to the nocturnal section, graphics set the mood. A long hallway with glass walls on both sides gives visitors a chance to search for the many small creatures of the night: fruit bats, African hedgehogs, springhaas, owl monkeys, and a rare tamandua (a unique type of anteater).

The **Feline House** is sometimes criticized for its age, but nevertheless has a fascinating collection of mostly small cats in modest enclosures. These animals include African civets (seen in only one other U.S. zoo), servals, clouded leopards, and meerkats. Outside cages exhibit Pallas' cats, jaguars, and cougars, while the Sumatran tigers reside in a green, rocky grotto.

OTHER EXHIBITS

The natural *Marsh and Swamp*, a re-creation of a New England wetlands habitat, is the highlight of the current **Temperate Forest** zone. An interpretive building uses graphics to explain what wetlands are and their importance. Visitors exit into a towering mesh aviary with water birds (such as bitterns and herons), a cascading waterfall, marsh reeds, and flowering water plants. The *World of Pheasants* walk-through aviary has many colorful pheasants, touracos, and other exotic birds from northern Asia. Fenced yards within this thick coniferous forest display red pandas and Asian deer. The *Family Farm* is also a part of this zone.

The small **Australasia** zone includes a billabong (pond) with black swans, indoor views of tree kangaroos and kookaburas, and an open yard of wallaroos.

Snow leopards hide among evergreen trees in their rocky habitat, and a row of rocky grottoes displays hyenas, sun bears, and Kodiak bears. Llamas, tapirs, rheas, and other South American animals roam a grassy yard, while rare maned wolves are found in a distant cage. Other notable exhibits include a prairie dog town, a round Humboldt penguin pool, and a flamingo yard.

FOR THE KIDS

Located within the Temperate Forest zone, the **Family Farm** is the closest thing here to a children's zoo. Unlike most zoo farmyards, which tend to be set in an open and dusty pasture, this one is found in the clearing of a thick evergreen forest. Corrals for horses, donkeys, cattle, sheep, and potbellied pigs are found both inside and outside of the non-traditional farm buildings. Also on hand are a baby animal nursery with low viewing windows, a chicken hatchery, a raccoon exhibit, a home gardening display, and a small aviary for a spotted owl—the unfortunate symbol of the current "jobs versus wildlife" controversy.

Pony rides are available for children at the **Pony Ring** near the North Meadow.

NEW AT THE ZOO

The new centerpiece here is the indoor/outdoor **Tropical Rain Forest**, which was recently honored as the best new exhibit of 1992. The rain forests of Asia, Africa, and Central and South America are represented with more than 60 animal species at three different levels of forest growth. The path to the glass-domed building is lined with visibly impenetrable vegetation. Once inside, visitors encounter food-bearing plants such as banana trees, pineapple plants, and fig trees, which illustrate the rain forest's farming value. The tour begins on the dark, damp *Forest Floor*, where endangered ocelots are seen among lush greenery, massive buttress tree trunks, and shallow pools. Realistic murals behind live plants exaggerate the habitat's depth. Leaf-cutter ants, poison dart frogs, and dangerous bushmasters and anacondas are seen up close in similar glass-fronted habitats. Sunbitterns and other jungle birds are visible through harp wire. A few stairs ascend to a wooden boardwalk where animals of the forest's *Understory* are found. Brilliantly-colored birds such as red-billed toucans are exhibited among equally beautiful orchid

Pygmy Marmosets in Tropical Rain Forest

plants, but tiny pygmy marmosets may be the most memorable animals here. Just past an exhibit of hornbills, visitors ascend to a *Canopy* overlook above the treetops where over 15 species of free-flying birds, including Bali mynahs, can be spotted. After passing through the *Conservation Station*, where rain forest ecology is taught using interactive devices, visitors follow an outdoor pathway to natural island habitats for lemurs, Debrazza's monkeys, and bushy-tailed colobus monkeys. Along the pathway, animal tracks, seeds, fruit, and other biofacts further enhance the rain forest experience. Over a bridge, the pathway concludes at the Lowland Gorilla exhibit, which is now a part of the Tropical Rain Forest exhibit.

Scheduled to open in the fall of 1994, the **Northern Trail** will replicate the cold, harsh environments of the world's northern regions. The *Montane* section will display Rocky Mountain goats and hoary marmots in a rugged, rocky habitat. Inside the *Alaska Taiga interpretive center* will be underwater viewing of brown bears and river otters. Gray wolves, red foxes, and bald eagles will live in a dense coniferous forest with a cascading waterfall, and elk and snowy owls will be featured in the *Tundra* zone.

Several additions to the Temperate Forest zone are also opening in 1994. They include a Northwest forest exhibit and, at the Family Farm, the *Imagination Trail—* an animal-themed playground with a giant spider web, an otter slide, and a crawl-through beaver burrow.

The Elephant Forest is the first phase of the **Tropical Asia** zone. Phase two, scheduled to open in 1995, will take visitors to an Indian jungle, a Sumatran rocky outcrop, and a Bornean boardwalk. A tree-top observation platform will provide a view of orangutans, siamangs, macaques, snakes, and muntjacs frolicking among waterfalls, bamboo trees, and vines.

Other plans include new **Desert** and **Steppe** zones and extensive renovations to the Australasia and Family Farm exhibits. All should be completed by 1997.

BEST OF THE REST

Alaska Zoo
4731 O'Malley Road
Anchorage, Alaska 99516
(907) 346-2133

One of the easiest ways to get acquainted with native Alaskan wildlife is to visit this zoo located just south of Anchorage. It is ironic that its best known resident is one of its few exotic animals—an Asian elephant named Annabelle that is famous for her painting skill. Most of the more than 50 species displayed here are found in the Alaskan wilderness. Moose, reindeer, and muskoxen are some of the large hoofed animals exhibited. Fierce predators include polar and grizzly bears, wolves, mountain lions, and wolverines. An extensive collection of predatory birds includes eagles, hawks, owls, and a rare gyrfalcon. Arctic foxes, arctic marmots, snowy owls, glacier blue bears, seals, and river otters are also displayed.

Chaffee Zoological Gardens of Fresno
894 West Belmont Avenue
Fresno, California 93728
(209) 488-1111

This zoo is probably best known for its South American Tropical Rain Forest—a lush jungle situated under a 70-foot-high mesh screen. This natural habitat has free-flying tropical birds, small monkeys, and giant anteaters. The zoo claims to have the world's first computerized Reptile House, where exact climate-control has led to many breeding successes. Asian elephants enjoy a 1/2-acre exhibit with a waterfall and a deep cooling pool. The thorough collection of large animals includes rhinos, hippos, giraffes, bison, tigers, lions, chimpanzees, and orangutans. The first stage of a new Australian Exhibit—a walk-through aviary filled with parakeets, cockatoos, and lories—opened recently.

Honolulu Zoo
151 Kapahulu Avenue
Honolulu, Hawaii 96815
(808) 971-7171

This zoo is one of the main attractions of the Waikiki Beach area. It is famous for its collection of tropical birds, which includes Hawaiian geese and rarely exhibited birds of paradise. The reptiles are highlighted by a huge Burmese python and unusual-looking gharial crocodiles. Asian elephants are showcased in daily demonstrations. The spectacular new African Savanna is toured from a winding path that passes through 30 natural habitats. Giraffes, lions, hippos, rhinos, cheetahs, hyenas, and antelope—as well as fascinating birds and small mammals—are all seen with Diamond Head Crater as a dramatic backdrop. A huge outdoor Tropical Forest exhibit will open in the future and feature elephants, gibbons, reptiles, and birds.

The Oakland Zoo
9777 Golf Links Road
Oakland, California 94605
(510) 632-9523

Once considered one of the nation's worst, this zoo has recently made radical changes and gained national respect. New exhibits that feature African elephants, chimpanzees, lions, and gibbons have given these animals spacious natural homes. Other entertaining primates include red-chested gelada baboons and vocal siamangs. (This is one of the few zoos in the U.S. that displays the unusual raccoon dog.) The Children's Zoo offers a chance to pet and feed domestic animals from around the world. A 15-minute chairlift ride travels high above the bison and elk pasture and also provides a great view of San Francisco Bay. (This is one of only four U.S. zoos to offer a sky ride.) A Streamliner miniature train, a carousel, and other kiddie rides are also available.

Sacramento Zoo
3930 West Land Park Drive
Sacramento, California 95822
(916) 449-5885

Located on the south side of California's capital city, this small zoo features a new Rare Feline Center with jaguars, margays, and Geoffroy's cats in a rain forest setting. Chimpanzees and orangutans are in new natural habitats with plenty of trees and ropes to climb on. The Kenneth Johnson Reptile House is also noteworthy, as are the cheetahs, hippos, lions, and tigers, and the large desert antelope yards holding addra gazelles and Arabian oryxes. Just across the street is Fairytale Town—a children's theme park.

Santa Barbara Zoological Gardens
500 Niños Drive
Santa Barbara, California 93103
(805) 962-5339

With the San Ynez Mountains in the background and a sweeping view of the Pacific Ocean in the foreground, this zoo has one of the most beautiful and dramatic settings in the country. The grounds consist of sloping lawns framed by towering palm trees and gorgeous flower beds. Many parrot-like birds can be seen in a walk-through Tropical Aviary, and unusual small primates and reptiles are displayed in an adjoining Nocturnal House. California sea lions have a newly renovated natural pool. Other animals with their own pools include small-clawed otters, Chilean flamingos, and capybaras. South America is further represented by Baird's tapirs, giant anteaters, and coatimundis. The elephants star in daily training demonstrations. Other notable animals seen here include red pandas, lions, rare Nubian giraffes, and a large collection of endangered California desert tortoises. For children, the Discovery Area has a petting yard, a carousel, and a train ride.

MORE ZOOS

Applegate Park Zoo (*Merced, California*)
Charles Paddock Zoo (*Atascadero, California*)
Folsom City Park Zoo (*Folsom, California*)
Happy Hollow Park and Zoo (*San Jose, California*)
Micke Grove Zoo (*Lodi, California*)
Molokai Ranch Wildlife Safari (*Maunaloa, Hawaii*)
Noah's Ark Petting Zoo (*Cave Junction, Oregon*)
Santa Ana Zoo (*Santa Ana, California*)
Sequoia Park Zoo (*Eureka, California*)
Walk in the Wild (*Spokane, Washington*)
Washington Zoological Park (*Issaquah, Washington*)

More Places To See Animals

Zoos, of course, are not the only places to see animals. The United States is filled with many fine aquariums, wildlife parks, and other animal-exhibiting facilities. All of these places could technically be considered zoos. The primary differences between the "pure zoos" of the preceding pages and the places listed below are the variety of animals displayed and the admission price: Zoos usually display a wider variety of animals and are generally much less expensive. On the other hand, these other places often provide entertainment options not available at most zoos.

WILDLIFE PARKS

Brookgreen Gardens
Murrells Inlet, South Carolina
(803) 237-4218

The lush gardens are the main attraction here, followed by the art and sculpture collection. A 100-acre natural wildlife area displays only native animals from the American Southeast. Highlights include an otter pond, two aviaries, and an alligator swamp.

Buena Vista's Exotic Animal Paradise
Springfield, Missouri
(417) 468-2159

The nation's largest drive-through wild animal park is located 12 miles east of Springfield. Over 3,000 animals from around the world are seen from a winding 9-mile road. Llamas, zebras, bison, Watusi cattle, elk, and a wide variety of antelope and deer frequently surround each car, begging for food that visitors can purchase at the front gate. At the halfway point, the Safari Land Center has a petting area, small animal exhibits, and major exhibits of monkeys, bears, and various big cats.

Catskill Game Farm
Cairo, New York
(518) 678-9595

Located in the heart of eastern New York's Catskill Mountains, this small park boasts animals from around the world. Giraffes, rhinos, and many endangered hoofed animals are among the over 2,000 creatures on display. A Recreational and Amusement Center features kiddie rides, a playground, and picnic areas. Three different animal shows are offered, and children can feed deer and other animals.

Fossil Rim Wildlife Center
Glen Rose, Texas
(817) 897-2960

This little bit of Africa is located deep in the heart of Texas, just an hour south of Fort Worth. Zebras, giraffes, ostriches, antelope, and deer roam freely on over 3,000 acres that resemble African terrain. White rhinos and cheetahs are among the center's phenomenal breeding successes. Most guests see the animals from their car. The park also offers a Petting Pasture, personalized tours, horseback riding, and luxurious overnight accommodations at The Lodge. The more adventurous can stay at the Foothills Safari Camp for a 4-day safari.

Grassmere Wildlife Park
Nashville, Tennessee
(615) 833-1534

Located on the south side of Tennessee's capital city, this wildlife park specializes in animals that are, or were, indigenous to the Volunteer State. Most of the animals (wolves, bears, cougars, otters, bison, and more) are seen outside in natural habitats, including a new golden eagle habitat. The indoor Croft Center has a native bird aviary, and The Cumberland River exhibit features fish, reptiles, and other aquatic life.

Natural Bridge Wildlife Ranch
San Antonio, Texas
(512) 438-7400

Located 17 miles northeast of San Antonio, this drive-through safari park is adjacent to Natural Bridge Caverns. Each car entering the park is given a guide map and a cup of food to feed the antelope, zebras, and ostriches that wander up to the cars. Of the more than 60 animal species, the most noteworthy include cougars, kangaroos, and Cape buffalo. A petting zoo and cages with small animals are at the Visitor Center.

Northwest Trek Wildlife Park
Eatonville, Washington
(206) 832-6116

Located about 35 miles south of Tacoma, this natural park is a refuge for animals native to the United States. A 50-minute tram tour provides close encounters with herds of bison, pronghorns, elk, bighorn sheep, and more. In the Core Area, where many smaller animals can be seen in natural habitats, the main attraction is the beaver pond. Bears, cougars, eagles, owls, and other predators can also be found here. Cheney Discovery Center has small exhibits for children.

Olympic Game Farm
Sequim, Washington
(206) 683-4295

Located near beautiful Olympic National Park in northwest Washington, this facility features animals that have been on television or in the movies. Over the years, Walt Disney Studios has worked closely with the farm. Seeing movie sets, a studio-barn, and a trained bear show are included in the admission price. Along the driving portion of the tour, animals seen just outside car windows include rhinos, zebras, bison, llamas, and bears. An enjoyable prairie dog town is also part of this tour.

San Diego Wild Animal Park
Escondido, California
(619) 747-8702

A sister facility of the San Diego Zoo, this enormous refuge is located 32 miles north. Many San Diegans actually prefer it to the zoo. Currently using a massive 700 acres, the park has many herds of endangered animals and unrivaled breeding successes. The rhinos, tigers, and a large variety of Asian and African hoofed animals are best viewed from a 5-mile, 50-minute monorail ride, but most can also be seen by hiking the Kilimanjaro Trail. The central visitor area, Nairobi Village, has a Petting Kraal, superb animal shows, tall walk-through aviaries, and numerous animal exhibits—including koalas, gorillas, and okapis. The newest exhibit, which opened in 1993, is the walk-through Hidden Jungle with over 2,000 exotic butter-flies and other interesting insects.

Southwick's Wild Animal Farm
Mendon, Massachusetts
(508) 883-9182

With more than 600 animals, this park in southern Massachusetts is New England's largest animal display. Because it is a supplier for the nation's zoos, many rare and endangered species are seen here. Notable animals include giraffes, rhinos, monkeys, big cats, and fallow deer. Daily circus shows feature dogs, llamas, horses, and elephants. Children can ride on an elephant, a pony, and an assortment of kiddie rides.

Wildlife Prairie Park
Peoria, Illinois
(309) 676-0998

Located in the center of the state, 10 miles west of Peoria, this park displays only animals that are, or were, native to Illinois. Visitors view a 15-minute slide show before embarking on any of nine walking trails. Bison, wolves, foxes, otters, bears, and skunks are among the many animals that can be seen. Features include the Prairie Railroad train ride and the Pioneer Area, where farm animals can be petted.

Wildlife Safari
Winston, Oregon
(503) 679-6761

In this super drive-through reserve in southwestern Oregon, a wide variety of antelope, deer, and other hoofed animals, as well as rhinos, ostriches, bears, chee-tahs, and even lions can be seen up close from the comfort of an automobile. Nearly 100 types of animals are grouped according to their continental homes. Also avail-able are a miniature train ride, elephant rides, a petting zoo, and animal programs that sometimes feature rare white tigers.

SPECIALIZED ZOOS

Black Hills Reptile Gardens
Rapid City, South Dakota
(605) 342-5873

The nation's largest collection of reptiles is found in the heart of the Black Hills. A highlight is the Sky Dome—a walk-through terrarium with free-roaming birds, lizards, and harmless snakes in simulated desert and rain forest habitats. On the building's other levels are displays of crocodiles, bats, and many venomous snakes. A new Death Row exhibit displays the world's deadliest snakes. (This is the largest such exhibit in the U.S.) Galapagos tortoises and miniature horses can be ridden among the colorful flower gardens on the grounds, and animal shows include a Snake Program, an Alligator Show, a Birds of Prey Show, and the Bewitched Village—where animals perform amazing tricks. This park offers many unique opportunities to touch the various reptiles.

Clyde Peeling's Reptileland
Allenwood, Pennsylvania
(717) 538-1869

In this central Pennsylvania attraction, over 60 varieties of snakes, lizards, alligators, crocodiles, and turtles are displayed in tropical garden settings. Demonstrations featuring live reptiles are held four times daily, and visitors can, if they care to, touch some of the large snakes.

Gatorland
Kissimmee, Florida
(407) 855-5496

Just a few miles from Walt Disney World hundreds of alligators and crocodiles can be seen from a boardwalk built over a swamp. Other features include a train tour, a cypress swamp walk, Gator Jumparoo and Gator Wrestling shows, and exhibits of other animals.

International Crane Foundation
Baraboo, Wisconsin
(608) 356-9462

Located in the popular Wisconsin Dells tourist area, this preserve displays and breeds all 15 of the world's crane species—including the endangered whooping cranes and Siberian white cranes. The adorable crane chicks are most engaging. Both guided tours and self-guiding nature trails are available.

Monkey Jungle
Miami, Florida
(305) 235-1611

Roles are reversed here: Hundreds of monkeys roam free in jungle settings, while human visitors are caged in wire mesh walkways. Ape Encounter, which features chimpanzees, is one of three entertaining shows. A second show has crab-eating macaques diving for food in their own pool, while a third show features chattering monkeys in the Amazonian Rainforest. Other highlights include the orangutans, the golden lion tamarins, and the rarely-exhibited bald uakaris.

Parrot Jungle and Gardens
Miami, Florida
(305) 666-7834

Over 100 feathered species can be found in this preserve on Miami's south side. Multi-colored parrots, cockatoos, and macaws live in lush tropical gardens that feature orchids, bromeliads, and an array of flowering trees and shrubs. The Parrot Bowl Theater is where talking, bike-riding, and counting parrots put on a show, while the Native Habitat Show includes alligators and other reptiles and mammals of Florida. Other features include Flamingo Lake, a playground and petting zoo, and a chance to hand-feed and hold some of the colorful birds.

Pittsburgh Aviary
Pittsburgh, Pennsylvania
(412) 323-7235

With over 500 birds of more than 200 different species, this unique "bird zoo" has one of the country's most diverse feathered collections. Especially noteworthy are the hummingbirds, rare cranes, parrots, Andean condors, king vultures, and snowy owls. The Marsh Room is a walk-through, free-flight aviary featuring wading birds and waterfowl.

St. Augustine Alligator Farm
St. Augustine, Florida
(904) 824-3337

One of Florida's oldest tourist attractions, this alligator farm is located in the country's oldest city. Thousands of alligators and their crocodilian relatives can be seen from elevated boardwalks over the swamps. In the new Land of Crocodiles exhibit, all 22 of the world's crocodilian species are displayed in large, natural habitats that are arranged geographically. In the hourly Florida Wildlife Show, trainers demonstrate the behaviors of alligators and rattlesnakes. Bobcats, raccoons, and other animals and birds can also be seen on the grounds.

Tracy Aviary
Salt Lake City, Utah
(801) 596-5035

Over 800 birds of more than 200 species make this one of the largest displays of birds in the country. Rare and exotic specimens from around the world are exhibited in both indoor and outdoor natural habitats. Trained bird shows are presented on weekends.

AQUARIUMS

Aquarium of the Americas
New Orleans, Louisiana
(504) 861-2537

Located on the riverfront, this aquarium is the French Quarter's newest major attraction. The five exhibit sections include a transparent underwater tunnel providing up-close looks at sharks and other creatures of the Caribbean Reef; a lush Amazon Rainforest under a glass roof; a Living in Water gallery with interesting aquatic animals such as penguins and an octopus; paddlefish and white alligators in the swampy Mississippi River; and sharks, barracudas, and other giants of the open ocean swimming under an oil rig replica in the half-million-gallon Gulf of Mexico tank. New in 1993, Sharks! features an amazing variety of large and small sharks, plus a touch tank with nurse shark pups.

Dallas Aquarium
Dallas, Texas
(214) 670-8453

This aquarium in central Dallas is under the same management as the Dallas Zoo. Notable displays include sharks, alligators, a giant snapping turtle, and fish from Africa, Mexico, the Caribbean, and Texas.

John G. Shedd Aquarium
Chicago, Illinois
(312) 939-2426

America's most visited aquarium is built along the Windy City's lakeshore. More than 7,000 saltwater and freshwater creatures are found in over 200 exhibit tanks in six long galleries. Silent Witness is a new interactive exhibit that lets kids help catch poachers. The main focus, however, is the new Oceanarium—a convincing replica of the Pacific Northwest, with lifelike evergreen trees lining the indoor rocky coves. Beluga whales and Pacific white-sided dolphins offer demonstrations in their amazing 2-million-gallon pool. Sea otters, harbor seals, and penguins are also seen in this award-winning exhibit.

Monterey Bay Aquarium
Monterey, California
(408) 648-4800

Located on Monterey's famous Cannery Row, this ultra-modern facility is in a former sardine cannery. It displays the wide variety of wildlife found just outside in the open bay waters. The centerpiece is a 28-foot-high Kelp Forest aquarium. (It is

Sea Otter

the world's tallest aquarium.) Leopard sharks and other giant fish are seen swimming through the tall kelp (giant seaweed). Other features include a sea otter tank, the Monterey Bay Habitats (a re-creation of five bay habitats in gigantic tanks), the Sandy Shore aviary, hands-on tide pool exhibits, Octopus and Kin, pettable bat rays, and a moon jellyfish exhibit. A new wing will include a 1-million-gallon tank displaying fish of the open ocean and deep sea, including 7-foot ocean sunfish, blue sharks, tuna, and more jellyfish.

Mystic Marinelife Aquarium
Mystic, Connecticut
(203) 536-9631

Located in Connecticut's historic seaport, this aquarium puts an emphasis on education. Sea lion and dolphin demonstrations are held in the Marine Theater. Of the over 50 exhibits, the huge tank of belukha whales and dolphins is the highlight. Seal Island, which has four different seal species, and the African penguins of the new Penguin Pavilion are also particularly popular.

Belukha Whale

National Aquarium
Washington, D.C.
(202) 377-2825

The country's oldest public aquarium is found on the ground floor of the Commerce building. The enjoyable collection includes alligators, sharks, piranhas, flying fish, and sea turtles, and a touch tank pleases children.

National Aquarium in Baltimore
Baltimore, Maryland
(410) 576-3823

The variety of exhibits in this innovative aquarium is staggering. A prime attraction of Baltimore's scenic Inner Harbor, it features a lush South American Rain Forest under a glass roof. The new Marine Mammal Pavilion has a 1,300-seat amphitheater where beluga whale and dolphin shows are presented, and the new Wings Under Water displays over 50 large rays. Like the whales and dolphins, the rays can be seen above and below water. A walkway spirals up through the center of two gigantic cylindrical tanks—the Atlantic Coral Reef and The Open Ocean—that display sharks and sawfish. Other features include a large Children's Cove, lean-into Maryland habitats, and an outdoor seal pool, plus puffins and poison dart frogs.

New England Aquarium
Boston, Massachusetts
(617) 973-5220

Located at Central Wharf on the city's historic waterfront, this Boston landmark is most famous for its spiraling Giant Ocean Tank, where hammerhead sharks and sea turtles can be seen. Nearly 10,000 animals, including penguins, are on display here in over 70 exhibits. Sea lion and dolphin shows are given on the *Discovery*, an old ship that now serves as the marine mammal pavilion. Whale-watching cruises can be boarded at a dock next to the aquarium.

New Jersey State Aquarium at Camden
Camden, New Jersey
(609) 365-3300

One of the nation's newest aquariums is just across the river from Philadelphia. A 760,000-gallon Open Ocean tank contains sharks, rays, and other North Atlantic fish, as well as a submerged shipwreck. This enormous tank is best viewed at the Edge of the Abyss, which features a 432-square-foot viewing panel. Other highlights include a large Seal Shores exhibit, a touch pool where rays and small sharks can be petted, some sea turtles, and a variety of interactive and educational exhibits. The new interactive exhibit What About Whales? has no live whales, but does feature a life-size model.

New York Aquarium
Brooklyn, New York
(718) 265-3400

More than 8,000 animals live at this facility in the famous Coney Island amusement district. The aquarium is renowned for its Oceanic Tank holding beluga whales. Walruses, sea otters, sea lions, and seals are in the Sea Cliffs habitats, while African penguins have their very own Rookery. The new Discovery Cove has innovative animal exhibits, hands-on activities, and touch tanks for children. Sharks, sea turtles, moray eels, and more are in unique re-creations of the world's aquatic habitats—from the Bermuda Triangle to the Red Sea.

North Carolina Aquariums
Fort Fisher, North Carolina
(919) 458-8259
Atlantic Beach, North Carolina
(919) 247-4004
Roanoke Island, North Carolina
(919) 473-3494

North Carolina has not just one, but three official state aquariums spread along its Atlantic coast. All have exhibits of alligators, sharks, and sea turtles. The largest, the North Carolina Aquarium on Pine Knoll Shores, is centrally located near Morehead City and features a scenic nature walk and a 700-gallon touch tank. Near the Nags Head tourist area, the North Carolina Aquarium on Roanoke Island has a new Carolina Gators exhibit. Down south, the North Carolina Aquarium at Fort Fisher has river otters, a shark tank with an aquascanner, and interpretive exhibits about humpback whales.

Seattle Aquarium
Seattle, Washington
(206) 386-4300

Over 20,000 sea creatures are displayed here on Seattle's famous Pier 59. The Underwater Dome has more than 100 acrylic windows for viewing the interesting marine life of Puget Sound. A fascinating salmon hatchery and salmon ladder are seen from a boardwalk. Featured animals include sea otters, sharks, seals, and spiny dogfish.

Steinhart Aquarium
San Francisco, California
(415) 750-7145

A part of the excellent California Academy of Sciences, this facility houses penguins, alligators, sea turtles, and nearly 14,000 fish in one of the world's most diverse collections. Highlights include a seal and dolphin tank, a tide pool, and a circular Fish Roundabout in which the fish swim in a tank surrounding the viewers.

Stephen Birch Aquarium-Museum
La Jolla, California
(619) 534-6933

Formerly using the name "Scripps," this educational facility is on San Diego's panoramic north shore. The view from pretty Tidepool Plaza is spectacular. The aquarium has 33 display tanks with species from California and Mexico, plus a Kelp Forest exhibit. The museum, which is the largest oceanographic exhibit in the country, has displays about weather, waves, and related topics.

Tennessee Aquarium
Chattanooga, Tennessee
(800) 262-0695

This new aquarium, which opened in 1992, is dedicated to the wildlife of the world's freshwater lakes, swamps, rivers, and streams. Inside this sparkling 4-story, glass-roofed structure is the Nickajack Lake exhibit with paddlefish, alligator gars, and more. It is the largest freshwater exhibit tank in the world. Other highlights include river otters; two living forests; alligators and venomous snakes in a Mississippi Delta exhibit; bonnethead sharks, barracuda, and other reef fish in a Gulf of Mexico exhibit; and a Rivers of the World area with six special re-creations of major rivers in Canada, Asia, South America, and Africa.

Texas State Aquarium
Corpus Christi, Texas
(512) 880-5858

Opened on the beach in 1990, this aquarium focuses on animals of the Gulf of Mexico. A 35-foot-tall Islands of Steel tank allows visitors to use a remote-controlled video camera to get a closer look at sharks, rays, barracudas, and other giant fish living under an artificial oil rig. Other features in the Gulf of Mexico Building include a beautiful Gardens in the Gulf coral reef tank and a Sea Star Discovery Pool touch tank. River otters, shorebirds, and endangered sea turtles are displayed in large outdoor habitats.

Virginia Marine Science Museum
Virginia Beach, Virginia
(804) 425-3474

Both hands-on exhibits and live animals help interpret the local marine environment here. Highlights include a 50,000-gallon aquarium with sharks and sea turtles, a touch tank, a 90-year-old giant lobster, and an outdoor boardwalk from which marsh animals can be viewed.

Waikiki Aquarium
Honolulu, Hawaii
(808) 923-9741

Located just yards away from the famous beach, this is one of the nation's oldest aquariums. The main attractions are rare and unusual animals from the Hawaiian Islands, which include giant clams, sharks, and Hawaiian monk seals. In the SeaVisions Theater, a video on jellyfish is shown next to fascinating exhibits of the real thing. The Mahimahi Hatchery is interesting, as is the Reef Machine that allows a living coral reef to thrive.

AQUATIC PARKS

Marine World/Africa USA
Vallejo, California
(707) 644-4000

A unique combination of aquatic park and zoo, this is one of the top attractions in the San Francisco Bay Area. At least eight different shows are presented daily featuring killer whales, dolphins, sea lions, elephants, tigers, chimpanzees, exotic birds, and human water-skiers. Close-up experiences with the animals include riding on an elephant or camel, feeding giraffes, and walking through Butterfly World, the Lorikeet Aviary, and Shark Experience (via an underwater acrylic tunnel). For children there is a life-size blue whale-themed play area, a prairie dog town with pop-up viewing bubbles, a playground, and a petting zoo.

Marineland of Florida
Marineland, Florida
(904) 471-1111

Among the unique entertainment offerings at this Atlantic Coast park is Sea Dream—an exciting 3-D movie shown in the Aquarius Theatre. Shows featuring both porpoises and electric eels are offered daily, and visitors can watch divers feed barracudas, sharks, stingrays, and sea turtles. Wonders of the Spring is a re-creation of a Florida freshwater spring. Penguins, otters, sea lions, flamingos, and other aquatic birds are also featured.

Miami Seaquarium
Miami, Florida
(305) 361-5705

Completely refurbished after Hurricane Andrew, this Miami coastal attraction features the famous TV dolphin that starred in the Flipper Show. Other shows feature killer whales, sea lions, more dolphins, and a scuba diver who emerges from a submarine to feed hungry sharks and moray eels. Monorail and boat rides are popular, as are exhibits of manatees, tropical birds, marine life, stingrays, and Everglades wildlife.

Sea Life Park
Waimanalo, Hawaii
(808) 259-7933

Located on Oahu's leeward (east) coast, this oceanarium takes a full day to experience and is a must on any Hawaiian vacation. During the entertaining history-based shows, visitors have a view of the open ocean behind the performing dolphins and sea lions. Endangered seals can be seen at the Hawaiian Monk Seal Care Center, but the rarest animal here is the world's only wolphin—a whale-dolphin hybrid. Other highlights include a large Hawaiian Reef Tank, a Penguin Habitat, a tidepool exhibit, a touch pool, sea lion feeding, and the Pacific Whaling Museum.

Sea World of California
San Diego, California
(619) 222-6363

All four Sea World parks feature killer whale shows in Shamu Stadium, funny shows in the Sea Lion & Otter Stadium, a superb Penguin Encounter exhibit, Shamu's Happy Harbor playground, a World of the Sea Aquarium, a seal feeding pool, a nighttime laser-light and fireworks show, and an atmosphere rivaled only by the Disney parks.

The California park, which in 1964 was the first of these wonderful parks to open, also includes a Bayside Skyride, a 265-high Skytower Ride, moray eels and bat ray feeding at the Forbidden Reef, a 1-acre walk-upon map of the United States at Places of Learning, presentations featuring the world's smallest dolphins in the Underwater Theater, a Water Fantasy Show, the new Rocky Point Preserve with dolphins and sea otters, and special exhibits of sharks, walruses, and more.

Adelies Penguins

Sea World of Florida
Orlando, Florida
(407) 351-3600

A day here can easily be included in a Disney World vacation. In addition to the core Sea World attractions, this park also has a 400-foot Sky Tower, stingray feeding, and Terrors of the Deep—a walk-through glass tunnel that permits up-close viewing of moray eels, barracudas, sharks, and venomous fish. The Mission: Bermuda Triangle sea adventure thrill ride uses aircraft simulator technology, and Manatees: The Last Generation? is an enormous new habitat for endangered manatees, alligators, and other Florida wildlife.

Sea World of Ohio
Aurora, Ohio
(216) 562-8101

Centrally-located and within easy reach of Cleveland, Akron, Pittsburgh, and most of the Midwest and East Coast, this is the smallest Sea World and is open only from May to September. Beyond the core attractions, this park features water ski shows on Geauga Lake, a high-dive show, and a Trout Pond. New in 1993, Shark Encounter features an acrylic underwater tube that takes visitors below a school of sharks and a sawfish. Also new, Birds of the World features 20 exotic species.

Sea World of Texas
San Antonio, Texas
(512) 523-3000

This newest and largest of the Sea World parks has all of the core attractions plus a Rio Loco raging river raft ride, a Texas Splashdown log flume ride, a Lost Lagoon waterpark with a walk-through tropical bird aviary, Shamu's Happy Harbor waterpark for kids, Cypress Gardens West botanical gardens, and a Places of Learning giant United States map. There is also a humorous show featuring white beluga whales and some of the few hammerhead sharks on display in the U.S.

THEME PARKS

Busch Gardens
Tampa, Florida
(813) 987-5250

Sub-titled "The Dark Continent," this full-scale theme park combines animal exhibits, shows, shopping bazaars, restaurants, and over 20 thrill rides to create a believable African atmosphere. Many experts consider this park to be one of the nation's top four zoos. Lions, elephants, hippos, rhinos, chimpanzees, giraffes, zebras, Cape buffalo, and other antelope can be seen via Skyride, Monorail, or Trans-Veldt Railroad in the Serengeti Plains—the park's premier animal attraction. Koalas, eagles, and other birds are exhibited in the Bird Gardens area, which also offers a Brewery Tour. Visitors can also see a Snake Charmer show in Morocco, a Dolphins of the Deep show, Nocturnal Mountain exhibits, white tigers on Claw Island, and the new award-winning Myombe Reserve—The Great Ape Domain. Soon a pair of giant pandas from China will arrive on a 10-year breeding loan.

Cedar Point
Sandusky, Ohio
(419) 626-0830

Jungle Larry's Safari is one of the incredible attractions offered at this giant Midwestern theme park. It has animal shows featuring white tigers, Asian leopards, and wolves. Exotic birds, primates, and reptiles can also be seen. In the park's Oceana section, dolphin and sea lion shows are performed many times daily.

Florida's Silver Springs
Ocala, Florida
(904) 236-2121

Located an hour north of Orlando, this park presents opportunities to see animals in unique ways. Glass Bottom Boats give an excellent view of the natural springs and the fish that thrive in them. In the narrated Jungle Cruise boat tour, visitors go up river to see exotic animals from six continents. On the Jeep Safari, a four-wheel-drive jeep takes riders close to tapirs, alligators,

Sobek, the World's Largest Captive American Crocodile

Raccoons

and deer. Other highlights include the Amazing Pets and Reptiles of the World shows, Doolittle's Petting Zoo, and the Lost River Voyage—a trip back to early Florida.

Hersheypark
Hershey, Pennsylvania
(717) 534-3862

The 11-acre ZOOAMERICA North American Wildlife Park is part of this chocolate-oriented amusement park. It can also be entered separately for a lower admission price. Bison, prairie dogs, wolves, bears, alligators, otters, and owls are some of the many North American animals seen here in five different natural regions. Dolphin and sea lion shows are presented inside the main amusement park.

Foreign Zoos

All of the world's best zoos are not, of course, within the borders of the United States. Excellent zoos are found throughout the world, with particularly noteworthy ones in western Europe, Australia, Singapore, South Africa, Canada, and Mexico. Though most of the zoos in Asia and South America are neither spectacular nor modern, they do offer unique opportunities to see some native animals that are displayed in few, if any, U.S. zoos.

Touring any foreign zoo is an excellent way to mingle with the local population and to learn a great deal about their culture. Here, then, are 66 of the world's best, most famous, and most popular zoos.

NORTH AMERICA

CANADA

Calgary Zoo, Botanical Garden, and Prehistoric Park
Calgary, Alberta
(403) 232-9300

Calgary is well-known for the Stampede, the Olympics, and its many nearby National Parks. It is also home to western Canada's finest zoo. The zoo is located on St. Georges Island in the middle of the Bow River, which runs through the heart of Calgary. Highlights include the Polar Bear Complex (with polar bears, seals, beavers, and otters), the Tropical Aviary with its many colorful birds, and the Canadian Wilds with its many native animals and impressive birds of prey collection. The most unique feature is a 6-acre Prehistoric Park that displays over 20 life-size dinosaurs. Other displays include Eurasia (with red pandas, snow leopards, and snow monkeys), Nocturnal World, the Primate Complex, the Children's Zoo, the Conservatory, and exhibit areas for Large Mammals, Cats, Australia, and Reptiles.

Granby Zoo
Granby, Quebec
(514) 372-9113)

Located less than an hour east of Montreal, this zoo has a very complete collection of exotic animals. From Africa, the gorillas, elephants, rhinos, hippos, zebras, and giraffes are most noteworthy. The impressive array of cats includes Asian lions, Siberian tigers, jaguars, and ocelots. The Serpentarium, with its numerous snakes, is the zoo's feature exhibit. Gray seals, red pandas, penguins, and polar bears are also displayed. Visitors can ride an elephant, a train, and a skyway monorail.

St-Félicien Zoological Park
St-Félicien, Quebec
(418) 679-0543

Located in northern Quebec in the lakefront town of St. Félicien, this zoo is one of Canada's largest, best, and most natural. An international collection of more than 2,400 animals is exhibited in large natural settings. The North American Habitat includes many native Canadian animals. The park also has a children's zoo, a train ride, and a nature trail, as well as re-creations of an Indian village, a lumberjack camp, a trading post, and an old farmhouse.

Metropolitan Toronto Zoo
Toronto, Ontario
(416) 392-5901

This zoo is often listed as one of the top ten zoos in the world. Situated on an immense 710 acres, its more than 4,000 animals of over 800 species make it one of North America's largest zoos. In addition to displaying most of the common zoo animals, it also features a ghost tiger, rare wood bison, Barbary apes, Mongolian wild horses, Tasmanian devils, wombats, wisents (European bison), hyenas, dwarf forest buffalo, mandrills, beavers, muskoxen, red pandas, moose, and much more. Four color-coded trails (including a Round the World Trail) cover the zoo's six geographic regions—Indo-Malaya, Africa, the Americas, Canada, Australasia, and Eurasia. Most of the animals can be seen year-round, thanks to the "Indoor Zoo" design that spaces eight

Agnes, the Orangutan

tropical indoor pavilions within close proximity of one another. This massive zoo can also be seen by Zoomobile and Monorail tours.

MEXICO

Chapultepec Park Zoo
Mexico City, D.F.
553-62-29

Any city with over 20 million people should have an excellent zoo, and Mexico City does. With five zoo-born giant pandas, this zoo has the largest collection outside of China. It caters to families with a train ride, pony rides, elephant shows, and a funny Seal Show. Its large collection of animals includes bison, hippos, polar bears, giraffes, zebras, and much more. Among the featured animals here are Andean condors in a vast flight cage and ash-colored volcano rabbits, which are found only in Mexico.

Up on the northeast side of Mexico City, the **San Juan de Aragon Zoological Park** is much smaller but also draws large crowds.

Guadalajara Zoo
Guadalajara, Jalisco
36-38-43-07

Located just off the central Pacific coast, Mexico's second largest city also has one of the country's largest zoos. The many primates here include gorillas, chimpanzees, and orangutans. Nearly the full spectrum of African animals are displayed—including elephants, rhinos, hippos, lions, zebras, and giraffes. More unusual are the rare crocodiles and dwarf forest buffalo. A children's zoo is also available, and dolphin shows are presented.

ZOOMAT
Tuxtla Gutierrez, Chiapas
98-961-29943

ZOOMAT is located in the tropical southern state of Chiapas, which is near Guatemala. Named for the man (Miguel Alvarez del Tore) who gave this special zoo to the people of Mexico, it displays only animals native to southern Mexico. The diverse collection includes jaguars, ocelots, coatis, javelinas, caimans, snakes, harpy eagles, king vultures, Baird's tapirs (Mexico's most endangered animal), and a large spider monkey troop. Some animals, such as the loud howler monkeys, roam free, while others are seen in large natural enclosures.

SOUTH AMERICA

ARGENTINA

Buenos Aires Zoological Park
Buenos Aires

Recently reopened after an extensive renovation, this historic and architecturally beautiful zoo has South America's highest attendance rate. A worldwide collection of animals is displayed surrounding a towering flight cage of endangered Andean condors. The wild dog exhibits are also notable.

BRAZIL

Rio de Janeiro Zoological Park
Rio de Janeiro

More than 2 million visitors come here annually to see the lions, tigers, gorillas, hippos, giraffes, and kangaroos, as well as the large collection of Brazilian animals. Jaguars, caimans, macaws, and monkeys are among the fascinating native animals from the Amazon River region.

Sao Paulo Zoological Park
Sao Paulo

South America's largest city holds the continent's finest zoo. Among the wide variety of species displayed in natural settings are tapirs, anteaters, and sloths. Many tropical birds and an abundance of predatory birds are also displayed. Indeed, a visit here is a decent substitute for a trip up the Amazon. Just behind the zoo, the drive-through Simba Safari park is filled with lions, cheetahs, and other African animals.

PERU

Park of the Legends Zoo
Lima

This small, but popular, zoo excellently reflects the contrasts found within Peru. Animals native to the Andes mountains, to the Amazon tropical jungles, and to the desert coastline are displayed in three distinct sections. Notable species include a herd of rare vicuñas, jewel-colored Amazon birds, and imposing Andean condors. The lions and elephants, which are the only non-Peruvian animals, are favorites of the local population.

EUROPE

AUSTRIA

Schönbrunn Zoo
Wien (Vienna)

Dating back to 1752, this zoo is considered by many to be the world's oldest. Situated in a park-like setting next to the famous Schönbrunn Palace, it is divided into two distinct sections. The historic section includes traditional enclosures for the many large mammals, big cats, wolves, and great apes. A variety of birds are spread among the Bird House, Pheasantry, and birds of prey aviaries. The new section is highlighted by rocky bear grottoes, a European bison pen, and a set of mountain habitats for ibexes, chamois, and other mountain sheep and goats. Other features include a small Children's Zoo and an Aquarium.

BELGIUM

Antwerp Zoo
Antwerpen

Open since 1843, this small zoo near the Belgian coast is one of the best in the world. In the past it has benefitted from Belgium's former colony—the Congo (now Zaire). During the early 1900s two amazing animals were discovered in the Belgian Congo—the strange okapi and the beautiful Congo peafowl. Both were displayed here first, and the zoo still has more than ten okapis. Built in 1914, the renovated Aquarium and Reptile House is now one of the best and most modern anywhere. Other outstanding exhibits include the Dolphinarium, Insect House, Nocturama, Winter Garden (for tropical birds), and a new Children's Zoo. The Great Ape House displays a complete collection: gorillas, orangutans, chimpanzees, and bonobos. Among the zoo's more than 700 species are elephant seals, kiwis, and extensive varieties of hoofed animals and birds of prey. The zoo grounds also hold a Planetarium, a concert hall, and a Museum of Natural History.

CZECH REPUBLIC

Prague Zoo
Prague

Despite showing signs of the country's recent economic problems, this remains one of the leading zoos in Eastern Europe. Its large site on a wooded hillside is just a few miles from the city center. It has very few animal buildings and features a definite park-like atmosphere. The animal it is most famous for is the Mongolian (Przewalski's) wild horse. A large herd of about 40 of these handsome horses, which are extinct in the wild, is seen in one of the many open paddocks. By coordinating the international breeding of these wild horses, this zoo has played a major role in keeping them from extinction. Many other rare hoofstock are displayed nearby, including addax, oryxes, rare deer, and European bison. The zoo also has a large herd of giraffes and complete collections of great apes and pachyderms. A highlight for children is a chairlift ride that takes visitors over an aviary to the top of the hill.

DENMARK

Copenhagen Zoo
Copenhagen

Founded in 1859, this is one of Europe's oldest zoos. Within its historic older section, Arctic World displays muskoxen from Greenland, polar bears, seals, and reindeer. The new Ape Jungle is the home of chimpanzees and gorillas. A tunnel leads to Søndermarken — a new area with spacious, open enclosures for large African animals (including rare okapis) and a Children's Zoo with a Biological Playground. The entire zoo can be viewed from atop a 144-foot-tall steel tower at the entrance gate.

FRANCE

Jardin Des Plantes Menagerie
and
Paris Zoological Park
Paris

While the small Jardin des Plantes Menagerie situated on the Left Bank of the Seine River generally is not considered among the world's great zoos, no other has a richer history than this one. It was begun in 1792 using the survivors of the personal menagerie of King Louis XIV. During its 200 years, many distinguished zoologists have worked closely with the Jardin. One of its highlights is a Vivarium with insects, reptiles, amphibians, and small mammals. Other features include the Grand Rotunda, built to honor Napoleon, which now houses under its central dome camels, other mammals, and tropical birds. It also has large collections of both birds of prey and medium-size monkeys from Africa (guenons and mangabeys).

A few miles away is a slightly larger sister institution—the **Paris Zoo**. When it opened in 1934, most of its exhibits were barless and moated. Its most notable display is the **Grand Rocher**—a 240-foot-high artificial rock with elevator rides to the top for a spectacular view of Paris. Penguin pools surround this giant rock, and mountain sheep and goats live on its slopes. The zoo is also noted for its rare okapis and a wide variety of bear species, which includes a single giant panda.

GERMANY

Berlin Tierpark
(East) Berlin

When Germany was divided after World War II, the people in and around East Berlin lost their access to the magnificent Berlin Zoo. Within 10 years, however, the new communist government provided this enormous animal park. Covering over 320 acres, it is the largest urban zoo in the world. Built from scratch on the grounds of a 1695 Baroque mansion, it uses the modern approach of hidden barriers to display its large collection of more than 7,000 animals of nearly 1,000 species. With so much space, large herds of interesting hoofstock can be featured—including European bison, Russian saiga antelope, okapis, and many deer species. The mini zoo inside the massive Alfred Brehm House, which covers $1^1/2$ acres, features a diverse group of large and small cats, a Tropical Hall of free-flying birds, and exhibits of small mammals, reptiles, fish, and insects. Just outside the house, the Great Aviary is one of the world's largest exhibits of birds of prey.

Berlin Zoological Gardens
(West) Berlin

Founded in 1841, this zoo has the world's largest animal collection. Located in the famous Tiergarten, it has more than 15,000 animals of nearly 1,700 species (the largest variety in the world). Its most famous citizen is Bao-Bao, the giant panda. Its grand Aquarium might be the world's finest. On its ground floor, tanks feature colorful reef fish, sea turtles, various sharks, sawfish, and even jellyfish. In the center of the first-floor Terrarium, which houses Komodo dragons and tuataras, is the renowned walk-through Crocodile Hall with over ten crocodilian species. An

Insect and Amphibian section is found on the top floor. The gigantic Bird House, which is the world's finest, displays more than 700 species (including kiwis). The impressive Carnivore House, which holds both large and small cats, is on top of the underground Nocturnal House and its wide variety of small mammals. Other features of this amazing zoo include its spacious, natural Bear Rocks exhibits, many varieties of deer and antelope, and herds of wild cattle and rhinos.

Carl Hagenbeck's Tierpark
Hamburg

Called "the father of modern zoos," Carl Hagenbeck (1844-1913) patented his ideas for making zoos into barless, natural places with hidden barriers. He originated concepts such as artificial rock backgrounds, predator/prey exhibits, ethnic architecture, and the use of moats rather than fences. This privately-owned zoo, located just north of Germany's second-largest city, has been directed by the Hagenbeck family since 1902. It was "modern" when it opened, and it remains so today. Highlights include beautifully landscaped grounds, a towering rocky mountain with a special window at the top for visitors to look down at Barbary sheep, and a set of coastal pools for seals, polar bears and walruses. Special animals include a large colony of coatimundis on an island and giant otters from Brazil. Visitors have the opportunity to feed the many elephants, and special shows are presented in the Dolphinarium.

Duisburg Zoo
Duisburg

Located near the Rhine River, this underrated zoo has an amazing variety of marine mammals. Along with a pair of white beluga whales, the Whale and Dolphin Area also has three types of dolphins (including diminutive Commerson's dolphins and freshwater Amazon dolphins). Other aquatic animals on display include a variety of both seals and penguins, an aquarium full of fish, and endangered giant otters. The complete collection of land animals includes African hunting dogs in a new innovative exhibit, a large and productive group of orangutans, red pandas in the China Garden, rare fossas, the only breeding group of red river hogs, and a major population of birds.

Frankfurt Zoological Gardens
Frankfurt

One of Germany's oldest zoos, this facility was almost totally destroyed during World War II. After the war it was completely rebuilt to its former grandeur under the direction of Bernhard Grzimek, an internationally famous wildlife author. Its feature attraction, the Grzimek House for Small Mammals, is named for this great man. A wide range of animals that includes kiwis, bats, aardvarks, aardwolves, bush dogs, howler monkeys, and wide-eyed tarsiers—the zoo's mascot animal—is displayed in the nocturnal and daylight sections of this massive building. The Exotarium, which is one of the largest aquariums in Europe, displays penguins and a variety of reptiles and insects in simulated natural habitats. A growing family of gorillas lives in a large, round outdoor yard surrounded by thick glass. (This was the world's first zoo to breed all four types of great apes.) Other notable exhibits include the Carnivore House, the Bears' Castle, the African Veldt, and some okapis.

Hellabrunn Münchener Tierpark
München (Munich)

This "geographical zoo" arranges animals according to their continental origins. An emphasis on natural habitats is typified in the beautiful Polarium that displays four types of penguins, four types of seals, and polar bears in spacious, pseudo-Arctic pools. The zoo is also noted for its large children's area, vast aviary, and major collections of big cats, pachyderms (elephants, rhinos, and hippos), and large hoofed animals (muskoxen, bison, moose, wild cattle, giraffes, wild horses, and mountain goats).

Köln Zoological Gardens
Köln (Cologne)

This might be the world's top primate zoo. Incredible exhibits include the Lemur House, which displays more than 100 lemurs of five species; the South American Primate House, which displays rare uakaris and many other small monkeys; and the Tropical House for Great Apes, which features gorillas, pygmy chimps, and orangutans. Douc langurs and proboscis monkeys—two of the most stunning and rare monkey species—are also seen here. The Aquarium is also noteworthy with its reptile Terrarium, Insectarium, and more than 200 fish species. Outside displays include bears, muskoxen, a variety of wild horses, and Russian saiga antelope.

Leipzig Zoological Gardens
Leipzig

One of the best in old East Germany, this zoo receives more than 1.5 million visitors each year. It is internationally famous for its breeding successes with big cats, especially Siberian tigers. Over 5,000 animals can be seen, many of them in a large aquarium building. Bonobos (pygmy chimpanzees), gorillas, and orangutans are found in the Great Ape House.

Wilhelma Zoo
Stuttgart

Originally created as a Moorish garden for King Wilhelm I, this outstanding zoo is still famous for its botanical collection. Special buildings feature palms, orchids, cacti, and other exotic plants. The centerpiece of the impressive animal collection is the Aquarium and Reptile House. This long, massive structure includes a crocodile hall, a renowned display of multi-colored coral reef fish, and a sea lion and elephant seal pool. The zoo displays all four of the world's great ape species, as well as endangered drill baboons and proboscis monkeys. Among the numerous other excellent exhibits are the Kiwi Nighthouse, the Insectarium, and the spacious, highly-rated South American area.

GREAT BRITAIN

Bristol Zoo
Clifton, England

This small zoo in western England features a very comprehensive set of animals displayed among beautiful landscaped gardens. Notable residents include a troop of crab-eating macaques in the Monkey Temple, Antarctic penguins, a variety of exotic pigeons, and unusual okapis.

Chester Zoo
Chester, England

Located just south of Liverpool, this moderate-size zoo is well-known for its innovative use of plants indigenous to the lands of its exhibited animals. For example, the palm-filled Tropical House displays reptiles, insects, free-flying birds, gorillas, and chimpanzees. The Elephant House is also lush with greenery. A Waterbus takes visitors for close-up looks at the waterbirds. The renowned collection here includes many lemurs, coatis, and pheasants, plus large herds of African antelope and rare Asian deer.

Edinburgh Zoo
Edinburgh, Scotland

Scotland's National Zoo is considered by many to be one of Europe's best. Its fame began in 1914 when it became the world's first zoo to exhibit penguins. Today penguins are still the specialty, with over 200 members of 4 different species. On summer afternoons, a majestic Penguin Parade is presented. Primates are also featured, most notably chimpanzees, Diana monkeys, gorillas, and Barbary apes. This park is also known for its "open zoo" design in which open enclosures are filled with both exotic wildlife and native Scottish animals such as Highland cattle and Soay sheep.

Jersey Wildlife Preservation Trust
Trinity, Channel Islands

Located out on the Channel Island of Jersey, just off the French coast, this small zoo is unique in its complete focus on saving and breeding the world's endangered animals. Nearly all exhibited species are listed as endangered. Well-known animals include snow leopards, gorillas, orangutans, and spectacled bears. Lesser known animals include many types of tiny marmosets and tamarins, volcano rabbits from Mexico, and rare reptiles and birds from the Indian Ocean island of Mauritius. The conservation theme extends even to the restaurant, the Dodo Cafe, which is named for the extinct bird.

London Zoo
London, England

Perhaps no zoo is more famous worldwide than this one. Located in Regent's Park, its fame is due to a number of things: an early start in 1826, an excellence in pioneering many new exhibit ideas, and a massive animal collection of more than 900 species. It is also where author A.A. Milne found the name for Winnie-the-Pooh (from a bear cub named Winnipeg that lived here long ago). Presently the best known exhibit is Moonlight World—an excellent nocturnal gallery on the ground floor of the large Charles Clore Pavilion. This building's display of small mammals is one of the largest anywhere and includes Tasmanian devils, yellow mongooses, bats, and tiny monkeys. The Snowdon Aviary—a giant walk-through flight cage designed by the husband of Princess Margaret—holds a variety of bird habitats. A spectacular coral reef aquarium and a new Arctic Wilderness exhibit with polar bears, arctic foxes, and various birds are both found in the old Mappin Terraces area. Other fine exhibits include a castle-shaped Elephant and Rhino Pavilion, a variety of cats in the Lion Terraces, beautiful birds in the Small Bird House and Tropical House, the Children's Zoo and Farm, the Sobell Pavilion for Apes and Monkeys, the Insect House, and okapis in the Giraffe House. The zoo's most famous resident is Chia-Chia, a giant panda.

Marwell Zoological Park
Winchester, England

The best known residents at this highly respected zoo in southern England are a breeding pair of elusive okapis. Many tiny monkeys from South America are displayed, and the outdoor exhibits hold numerous herds of exotic deer, African antelope, and oryxes, plus one of the world's largest herds of endangered Mongolian wild horses. More than 20 tigers compose one of the largest collections in Europe.

Whipsnade Zoological Park
Dunstable, England

Located 30 miles north of London, this is the London Zoo's country cousin. Built on a former 500-acre farm, this zoo can be toured in three distinct ways—by foot, car, or train. Visitors who walk can enjoy the company of hundreds of free-roaming wallabies, wild turkeys, marmots, Chinese water deer, and peafowl. Visitors who drive can tour the perimeter. Those who opt for the Whipsnade & Umfolozi Railway are pulled by an historic steam engine that takes them into the sprawling pastures of rhinos, zebras, ostriches, and antelope. Because this zoo has so much space, the deer, Asian antelope, and wild horses roam in gigantic breeding herds. Other highlights include a chimpanzee island, a prolific group of cheetahs, an assortment of rare cranes, and ever-popular dolphin shows.

HUNGARY

Budapest Zoological and Botanical Garden
Budapest

Dating back to 1866, this zoo is filled with many stately old buildings that have been deemed "historic monuments." The Elephant's House, Great Cats building, House of Rodents, and a large aquarium are among these historic structures. An interesting bird collection is spread out in exhibits such as the Aviary, Pheasantry, and Owlery. The modern Ape House is one of the few new buildings.

THE NETHERLANDS

Artis Zoo and Planetarium
Amsterdam

Located in the heart of Holland's largest city, this small urban zoo, which originally opened in 1838, is not small in either reputation or animal collection. (It is now one of only two zoos in the world with over 1,000 different species on display.) The Aquarium (the second largest in Europe) holds over 400 types of fish and a famous coral reef collection. Many of the large animal houses here are protected as historic monuments. Though featuring old architecture on the outside, they are thoroughly modern inside. Among them are a Monkey House, a Bird House, and a Reptile House that features a large crocodile pool. The stars of the newer Hippopotamus-Tapir-Manatee Building are, of course, the rarely displayed manatees from the Caribbean. Other notable buildings include the Nocturnal Animals House, the Small Mammal Building, and a Planetarium. The new Bear Terraces are found in an outdoor setting, as are the extensive feline collection, the African hunting dogs, the chimpanzees, some large herds of deer, an impressive colony of endangered penguins, and a large herd of rare European bison.

Blijdorp Zoo
Rotterdam

Opened in downtown Rotterdam in 1857, this zoo moved to its present suburban site in 1940 and actually thrived during the city's occupation by the Nazis. Since then it has evolved into one of the world's finest. Its centerpiece is the Riviera Hall complex—a massive all-weather facility that features rare tropical plants, aquariums, reptiles, spectacular birds of paradise and other jungle birds, the Crocodile House, the Amazon Hall, and indoor quarters for elephants, rhinos, hippos, and apes. Nearby is a large cat complex where more than 500 tigers have been born. The Monkey and Nocturnal House holds a large collection of marmosets, small Australian marsupials, and other small mammals. The new outdoor Asia exhibit features Mongolian wild horses and red pandas in an oriental-themed area. Other notable animals include okapis, Tasmanian devils, and an assortment of African antelope.

Burgers Zoo and Safari Park
Arnhem

This is an interesting combination of zoo and drive-through safari park. The zoo is highlighted by Gorilla Island, a large Chimpanzee Colony, Wolf Woods, and a large collection of hoofed animals in beautiful stone enclosures. The impressive bird collection includes both large and small birds of prey, penguins, and colorful hornbills. The new jungle building, Burgers' Bush, provides a lush habitat for tapirs and crocodiles, as well as a pool for some plump, lovable manatees. The Safari Park can be toured by automobile or safari train ride. Lions, leopards, and cheetahs are seen in the Lion Park section, while giraffes and rhinos are in the Savannah section.

Noorder Dierenpark Zoo
Emmen

The most visited of the excellent Dutch zoos is not found in a big city. Located up in the northern tip of Holland, this small town zoo started in 1935 in the backyard of its founder. It now draws visitors from all over Europe. An emphasis on education is typified in its four museums. The Biochron museum displays fossils, dinosaurs, and other ancient creatures—including the only frozen woolly mammoth in the Western world. The African Savannah is one of the largest of the many natural habitats that are organized geographically. It displays rhinos, giraffes, zebras, and ostriches. The Butterfly Garden is a lush simulated jungle where over 40 types of butterflies can be seen in all stages of life. In the Children's Zoo, visitors can tour the Breeding Center to see eggs, incubators, and baby animals. In the upscale De Dromme Daar restaurant, diners are sometimes joined by an elephant.

RUSSIA

Moscow Zoo
Moscow

Despite an extremely cold climate and recent economic and political crises, Moscow maintains one of the world's major zoos. In a forested park on the northwest side of the Russian capital, cold weather animals are featured. Among them are snow leopards, muskoxen, polar bears, and a herd of Mongolian wild horses. Animals from warmer regions (Africa, tropical Asia, South America, and Australia) are also well represented. Most notable among them are cheetahs, wart hogs, orangutans, elephants, and a large collection of small and medium-size monkeys. Other animals found in great abundance include rare cranes, birds of prey, reptiles, and over 240 fish species in the Aquarium.

SPAIN

Barcelona Zoo
Barcelona

The world's most famous zoo animal is probably Snowflake—the world's only known albino gorilla. He and his offspring are part of this highly-rated zoo's impressive Anthropoid Pavilion, which also includes chimpanzees, orangutans, and mandrills. Many other primates are displayed throughout this long, narrow zoo. The second must-see here is Aquarama, a complex that includes seal pools, a 2-story Aquarium, and the Dolphinarium—where dolphins and a killer whale entertain huge crowds. For a close-up view of the mouflons and rare Spanish ibexes, visitors can hike up into the Montserrat Mountains habitat. Other features include a Terrarium with a large array of crocodilians, an indoor Aviary of jungle birds, the open-air Doñana Aviary of Spanish birds, and many open, moated habitats for the wide variety of bears, big cats, pachyderms, deer, antelope, and bison.

Casa de Campo Zoo
Madrid

In Spain's largest city is a zoo that offers a chance to see some of the world's rarest creatures: a pair of giant pandas, a Komodo dragon, some Atlas lions, and some Spanish ibexes. The largest crowds congregate at the new Dolphinarium for the dolphin and sea lion show. The boat ride is also popular. The zoo is noted for its large collections of apes, bears, antelope, and birds of prey, and for its sizeable herds of peccaries and rare Barbary sheep.

SWEDEN

Borås Djurpark Zoo
Borås

Located in the rural outskirts of Göteborg, this large zoo displays some of Sweden's rarest native animals. They include Swedish moose, a pack of Scandinavian wolves, and wild reindeer. The natural settings include sprawling grassy pastures, green rocky grottoes, and thick conifer forests. The zoo may be most famous for its pride of dark-maned lions, which shares a new complex with tigers. African animals are well represented with elephants, rhinos, cheetahs, African buffalo, and chimpanzees. A Boat Safari operates on a large lake that is populated with sea lions.

Kolmården Safari Park
Norköping

Not just a zoo or safari park, this 600-acre facility on Sweden's Baltic coast is a complete animal-themed adventure. There is even an attached hotel. Situated in a tall primeval forest on the site of a former monastery, this drive-through wildlife park allows herds of Asian and African hoofed animals to be viewed at close range. On foot visitors can view chimpanzees and a host of other exotic animals, including Bengal tigers in the world's largest tiger enclosure, and one of Europe's longest gondola rides also permits seeing this beautiful park from above. A Dolphinarium draws large crowds for its spectacular shows.

SWITZERLAND

Basel Zoological Gardens
Basel

In the middle of this beautiful city—where Switzerland, Germany, and France join—is this spectacular zoo the Swiss call their "Zolli." Natural habitats abound in this small, but lush, park. The collection emphasizes large mammals, most notably pygmy hippos and Indian rhinos. Also special are the okapis in the Antelope House, a large family of gorillas in the Monkey House, the extensive collection in the Cats' House, and a herd of Somali wild asses. The feature exhibit is the Vivarium, where spectacular marine habitats are seen behind large glass panels. Sharks, sea turtles, moon jellyfish, and a large selection of reptiles and amphibians are highlights. Popular shows demonstrate the intelligence of both the elephants and sea lions.

Zürich Zoological Gardens
Zürich

This small zoo in Switzerland's largest city features a pair of nearly extinct Indian lions in a lush new Feline House. The Ape House is home to large groups of chimpanzees, gorillas, and orangutans, and the Elephant House holds above average-sized herds of hippos, black rhinos, and Asian elephants. An aquarium and open-air aviary are also noteworthy.

THE MIDDLE EAST

ISRAEL

Jerusalem Biblical Zoological Garden
Jerusalem

Animal-loving pilgrims to the Holy Land will enjoy visiting this unique zoo. All of the mammals, birds, and reptiles mentioned in the Bible are displayed here, with the appropriate passages quoted alongside the enclosures. A recent expansion has added a children's train and some non-Biblical species such as chimpanzees, cheetahs, and American bison.

UNITED ARAB EMIRATES

Al Ain Zoo and Aquarium
Abu Dhabi

Located in the oasis town of Al Ain, this massive desert zoo is the most comprehensive in the Middle East. Highlights include a Large Cat and Crocodile House, a Monkey House, and an Ape House. In addition to a large bird collection that features rare Houbara bustards, there are amazing herds of over 100 Arabian gazelles, blackbucks, Nubian ibexes, and Arabian oryxes.

ASIA

CHINA

Beijing Zoological Gardens
Beijing

Located in China's capital city, this zoo is one of only two worldwide to receive more than 10 million visitors each year. Most head straight to the Panda House, which is part of a new panda complex located near the main gate. (The first captive giant panda birth occurred here.) The big cats and bears in the Carnivore Enclosure are nearly as popular. Some of the most unusual animals, which include Chinese river dolphins and giant sea turtles, are found in the Aquatic Animals House. Beautiful multi-colored goldfish are seen in rows of barrel-like enclosures. Other important exhibits include some endangered varieties of deer, Yangzi alligators, takins, rare monkeys, and a splendid outdoor bird sanctuary featuring many rare pheasants and cranes.

Chengdu Zoological Gardens
Chengdu

Chengdu is located in the central Chinese province of Sichuan, which is the natural home of the giant panda. It is thus natural that this city's zoo has over ten pandas (the world's largest collection). Rare golden monkeys are also featured here.

Guangzhou Zoological Gardens
Guangzhou (Canton)

Located in southern China not far from Hong Kong, this excellent zoo attracts well over 4 million visitors each year. In addition to the animals that are traditional Chinese favorites—giant pandas and golden monkeys—the tigers, African animals, and aviary exhibits are also noteworthy.

Shanghai Zoological Gardens
Shanghai

This 185-acre zoo is best known for its bird collection, which includes many rare Chinese birds, and for its display of a wide range of Chinese wildlife. Elephants and leopards from the south, tigers from the north, alligators from the nearby Yangzi River, and giant pandas are among the major attractions. Africa is also well represented with lions, giraffes, hippos, rhinos, and chimpanzees. Popular novelties include a skating rink and a pedal-powered monorail.

Taipei Zoo
Taipei, Taiwan

Situated on over 400 acres, this new zoo is one of Asia's largest. The star here is Lin Wang—a 70-year-old bull elephant who served in Burma for the military during World War II. Other features include a large nocturnal house and a children's zoo. Among the endangered animals from Taiwan that are highlighted is a large troop of Formosan macaques. (Formosan macaques are not seen in any U.S. zoo.)

INDIA

Calcutta Zoological Garden
Calcutta

India's most popular zoo attracts over 2 million visitors each year. Its grounds are enhanced by attractive flower gardens and pools. Though the beautiful white tigers are the main attraction, it also features African animals, exotic birds, a Small Carnivore House, and an unusual reptile facility displaying native gharial crocodiles and venomous snakes.

National Zoological Park
New Delhi

The official zoo of India, this modern facility features many of the country's most interesting and endangered animals, including Indian rhinos, Thamin deer, white tigers, and a free-roaming troop of lion-tailed macaques. A harmonica-playing elephant is among the zoo's stars.

Nehru Zoological Park
Hyderabad

One of Asia's largest and nicest zoos is located just outside of Hyderabad in tropical central India. Many big cats, rhinos, elephants, hoofed animals, monkeys, and large birds can be seen in open, natural habitats. A train ride circles around the perimeter of the vast grounds. The main feature is Lion Safari Park, where visitors ride a minibus for close-up views of Asian lions.

INDONESIA

Ragunan Zoo
Jakarta

This enormous zoo, which covers almost 500 acres, is found approximately 6 miles south of the city center. The diverse jungle wildlife of Indonesia is featured—

including orangutans, Komodo dragons, and a major bird collection—and the New World Monkey House displays tiny monkeys from South America.

Surabaya Zoo
Surabaya

Indonesia's second-largest city is home to one of Asia's top zoos. Its aquarium has over 140 species and is one of the main features here. Other noteworthy exhibits include a nocturnal house, some playful otters, and Komodo dragons (which can be found in their natural home only a few hundred miles away). The collection of exotic birds includes beautiful birds of paradise, and animals of the African savanna and large herds of deer can also be seen.

JAPAN

Tama Zoological Park
Tokyo

Overcrowding of both animals and people at the Ueno Zoo forced Tokyo to open this larger satellite zoo in 1958. The spacious park allows the animals to enjoy open, moated enclosures. The Lions Park area offers visitors a minibus ride among the free-roaming lions. The most unique exhibit here is the spectacular Insect Ecological Land. It features a nocturnal animals gallery and massive walk-through enclosures of butterflies, grasshoppers, and fireflies. The biggest crowd-pleasers are the Japanese macaques, which live on an island, and the koalas.

Ueno Zoological Gardens
Tokyo

This small zoo in urban Tokyo is the most popular of Japan's many well-attended zoos. A pair of giant pandas and their offspring are the stars. One of the main attractions is the Aquarium, which has a massive saltwater tank and displays a wide variety of reptiles, amphibians, and fish. Other features include a large and varied penguin population, three types of great apes, a tropical walk-through aviary, a modern Children's Zoo, and the African Plains with hippos, giraffes, and oryxes. A monorail tour is also available.

KOREA

Seoul Grand Park Zoo
Seoul

This zoo is located within a gigantic new park that opened on the city's southside just in time for the 1988 Olympics. (A botanical garden and Seoul Land—Korea's version of Disneyland—are also part of the park.) The zoo's population is among the world's largest. Features include an African safari exhibit, many endangered cranes, kokiri (electric car) rides around the zoo, and immensely popular dolphin shows.

MALAYSIA

Zoo Negara
Kuala Lumpur

Literally a zoo in a jungle, this zoo's emphasis is on the rich diversity of animals native to Malaysia. Examples include seladang cattle, Malayan tapirs, sun bears, tigers, tropical birds, orangutans, gibbons, and an impressive variety of macaque monkeys. Australian, African, and even South American wildlife are also displayed, and sea lion shows are presented three times daily in a large pool near the Aquarium.

SINGAPORE

Singapore Zoological Gardens
Singapore

Asia's top zoo is also one of the world's best. It is known as "the open zoo" because it has perfected the art of displaying its amazing animal collection in open, moated enclosures. The re-created habitats here are as good as, and sometimes better than, any in the U.S. Primate Kingdom displays some of the over 30 primate species at the zoo, and a pair of tropical islands are home to a large troop of chimpanzees and the world's largest orangutan troop. A highlight here is having Breakfast or High Tea with an Orangutan; reservations are required. Cat Country and Wild Africa are also impressive exhibits with wide varieties of interesting creatures. Among the many rare and endangered animals are a variety of civets, African hunting dogs, Sumatran tigers, Malayan tapirs, bearded pigs, and Komodo dragons. The many exciting shows feature chimps, orangutans, elephants, sea lions, polar bears, and crocodiles.

The bird collection here is thin. This is probably explained by the fact that the city/state of Singapore is also home to the **Jurong Birdpark**, which is likely the world's most comprehensive, most entertaining, and best facility devoted to birds.

AFRICA

Giza Zoological Gardens
Cairo, Egypt

This zoo, which is one of the world's oldest, once boasted the largest collection of African wildlife in the world. It still exhibits an extensive variety that includes many hoofed animals, a large chimpanzee troop, and Nile hippos from the nearby Nile Valley. An international array of animals is spread out among an interesting network of gravel paths.

National Zoological Gardens of South Africa
Pretoria, South Africa

The official zoo of a nation long committed to wildlife conservation, this sprawling facility compares well with any zoo in the world. It has a comprehensive collection of animals from all over the world, and its collection of African hoofstock, which is displayed in open paddocks, is unsurpassed. The rhinos, hippos, and other large animals enjoy spacious, natural homes. Rarer species—aardwolves, hyenas, African hunting dogs, cheetahs, and Cape fur seals—are also noteworthy. The bird population is equally impressive and includes rare hornbills in a Large Flight Aviary, a penguin exhibit, and a top-rated collection of birds of prey. The inhabitants of the Aquarium and Reptile Park are equally diverse and imposing. A sky ride provides a panoramic view of the entire zoo, as well as of the surrounding city.

AUSTRALIA

Perth Zoological Gardens
South Perth

Located in an isolated city in western Australia, this zoo concentrates on the wildlife of Australia, Southeast Asia, and Africa. Most notable of the native animals are koalas, Tasmanian devils, numbats (not seen in any U.S. zoo), and many different types of kangaroos and wallabies. A new African Savannah exhibit provides a natural home for giraffes, rhinos, zebras, hyenas, and antelope. Brown bears and sun bears are also displayed in beautiful new habitats. Children particularly enjoy the large collection of primates and a carousel.

Royal Melbourne Zoological Gardens
Parkville

This zoo, which is the world's third-oldest, is one of the best places to get an overview of Australian wildlife. Duck-billed platypuses and bandicoots are some of the native animals that can be seen here (neither are seen in the U.S.). Koalas, wombats, and many kangaroo species are also displayed. An excellent primate collection is highlighted by a new Gorilla Rainforest exhibit. Other features include a diverse cat collection, a lion park, a reptile house, and a tropical Butterfly House.

Sydney's Taronga Zoo
Mosman

Located on spectacular Sydney Harbor, this zoo is one of the world's best and is reputed to have the most beautiful setting of any zoo. An excellent new seal pool is situated right in the harbor waters and is home to six different seal species, including some enormous elephant seals. A large group of koalas is part of its top-rated Australian marsupial collection. A nocturnal house displays more native animals, among them egg-laying echidnas and duck-billed platypuses (seen only in Australia), as well as a variety of Australian bats. An Aquarium features colorful fish from the nearby Great Barrier Reef, and the reptile house displays many venomous snakes, endangered saltwater crocodiles, and a Komodo dragon. Other highlights include a walk-through aviary, kiwis from New Zealand, and a large troop of chimpanzees.

Appendixes

I
The Top Ten U.S. Zoos Lists

We live in a competitive society that always wants to know what's best. There are "Top 10" lists for everything from city populations to college sports teams. In this book zoos are not ranked from best to worst, nor are they given an overall numeric score. Ranking zoos is a subjective matter. Some visitors want to see lots of birds. Others aren't interested in birds and want to see reptiles or bears. So rating a zoo is dependent on the particular interests of the individual visitor.

To account for the varying interests of visitors, the 53 zoos that have been fully reviewed are evaluated here in 16 specific categories. These categories represent the major geographic regions and habitats of the earth, the various types of zoo animals, the Children's Zoos, and the extra features that zoos offer. For each of these categories, the ten highest rated zoos are listed.

My choice as the best zoo in each category is labeled "#1," while the runner-ups are listed in alphabetical order as "#2." The remaining zoos in each top ten are listed next, also in alphabetical order.

Africa
(Animals and Exhibits)

#1
Dallas Zoo
#2
Brookfield Zoo
North Carolina Zoo
San Diego Zoo
&
Bronx Zoo
Caldwell Zoo
Gladys Porter Zoo
Metro Washington Park Zoo
Milwaukee County Zoo
San Antonio Zoo

Asia
(Animals and Exhibits)

#1
Bronx Zoo
#2
San Diego Zoo
&
Audubon Zoo
Brookfield Zoo
Cincinnati Zoo
Fort Worth Zoo
Miami Metrozoo
Minnesota Zoo
National Zoo
Woodland Park Zoo

North America
(Animals and Exhibits)

#1
Minnesota Zoo
#2
Columbus Zoo
North Carolina Zoo
Sedgwick County Zoo
Tulsa Zoo
&
Arizona-Sonora Desert Museum
Audubon Zoo
Denver Zoo
Metro Washington Park Zoo
Milwaukee County Zoo

South America
(Animals and Exhibits)

#1
Sedgwick County Zoo
#2
National Zoo
San Antonio Zoo
&
Brookfield Zoo
Caldwell Zoo
Cleveland Zoo
Lincoln Park Zoo
Los Angeles Zoo
Omaha's Henry Doorly Zoo
Woodland Park Zoo

Australia
(Animals and Exhibits)

#1
San Diego Zoo
#2
Los Angeles Zoo
San Antonio Zoo
&
Brookfield Zoo
Gladys Porter Zoo
Indianapolis Zoo
Louisville Zoo
Oklahoma City Zoo
San Francisco Zoo
Sedgwick County Zoo

Birds
(Collection and Exhibits)

#1
Bronx Zoo
#2
San Diego Zoo
&
Audubon Zoo
Cleveland Zoo
Denver Zoo
National Zoo
Philadelphia Zoo
Rio Grande Zoo
San Antonio Zoo
St. Louis Zoo

Reptiles & Amphibians
(Collection and Exhibits)

#1
San Diego Zoo
#2
Bronx Zoo
&
Audubon Zoo
Columbus Zoo
Fort Worth Zoo
Houston Zoo
National Zoo
Philadelphia Zoo
St. Louis Zoo
Zoo Atlanta

Small Mammals
(Collection and Exhibits)

#1
National Zoo
#2
Bronx Zoo
Philadelphia Zoo
&
Brookfield Zoo
Cincinnati Zoo
Houston Zoo
Los Angeles Zoo
Milwaukee County Zoo
San Diego Zoo
Woodland Park Zoo

Primates
(Apes, Monkeys, Lemurs)

#1
San Diego Zoo
#2
Brookfield Zoo
Fort Worth Zoo
San Francisco Zoo
&
Cincinnati Zoo
Gladys Porter Zoo
Lincoln Park Zoo
Los Angeles Zoo
Milwaukee County Zoo
St. Louis Zoo

Carnivores
(Cats, Bears, Wild Dogs)

#1
Omaha's Henry Doorly Zoo
#2
San Diego Zoo
&
Brookfield Zoo
Cincinnati Zoo
Denver Zoo
Knoxville Zoo
Lincoln Park Zoo
Memphis Zoo
Philadelphia Zoo
St. Louis Zoo

Pachyderms
(Elephants, Rhinos, Hippos, and Tapirs)

#1
Miami Metrozoo
#2
Bronx Zoo
Fort Worth Zoo
Los Angeles Zoo
&
Baltimore Zoo
Columbus Zoo
Metro Washington Park Zoo
Milwaukee County Zoo
San Diego Zoo
Toledo Zoo

Hoofed Animals
(Collection and Exhibits)

#1
San Diego Zoo
#2
Denver Zoo
&
Bronx Zoo
Brookfield Zoo
Cincinnati Zoo
Dallas Zoo
Los Angeles Zoo
Miami Metrozoo
Oklahoma City Zoo
San Antonio Zoo

Aquatic Animals
(Aquariums, Seals, etc.)

#1
Point Defiance Zoo
#2
Indianapolis Zoo
&
Brookfield Zoo
Columbus Zoo
Milwaukee County Zoo
Minnesota Zoo
Oklahoma City Zoo
Omaha's Henry Doorly Zoo
Pittsburgh Zoo
Riverbanks Zoo

Insects
(Animals and Exhibits)

#1
Cincinnati Zoo
#2
San Francisco Zoo
&
Arizona-Sonora Desert Museum
Cleveland Zoo
Columbus Zoo
Fort Worth Zoo
Metro Washington Park Zoo
National Zoo
Philadelphia Zoo
Pittsburgh Zoo

Tropical Rain Forest
(Realism and Animals)

#1
Omaha's Henry Doorly Zoo
#2
Bronx Zoo
Brookfield Zoo
Cleveland Zoo
&
Franklin Park Zoo
Minnesota Zoo
National Zoo
North Carolina Zoo
San Diego Zoo
Sedgwick County Zoo

Children's Zoos
(Size and Quality)

#1
Baltimore Zoo
#2
Bronx Zoo
Los Angeles Zoo
&
Houston Zoo
Lincoln Park Zoo
Oglebay's Good Children's Zoo
Phoenix Zoo
San Antonio Zoo
San Diego Zoo
San Francisco Zoo

Extras
(Rides, Shows, Restaurants, and Special Exhibits)

#1
San Diego Zoo
#2
Bronx Zoo
Cincinnati Zoo
&
Dallas Zoo
Fort Worth Zoo
Indianapolis Zoo
Milwaukee County Zoo
Minnesota Zoo
Philadelphia Zoo
San Francisco Zoo

World's Top 10 Animal Collections
(#Species and Population)

#1
Berlin Zoo (Germany)
#2
Berlin Tierpark (Germany)
Bronx Zoo (New York)
San Diego Zoo (California)
&
Artis Zoo (Netherlands)
Frankfurt Zoo (Germany)
London Zoo (England)
National Zoo (South Africa)
San Antonio Zoo (Texas)
Wilhelma Zoo (Germany)

II

The Top 25 U.S. Zoo Exhibits

All of the zoos reviewed in this book have some outstanding exhibits. Each Zoo Review includes a "Don't Miss" section that mentions its best and most unique exhibits. Here is my rating of the country's 25 best exhibits. The exhibits are rated according to their scope, realism, and size, as well as the variety, popularity, and number of animals included. This list includes only exhibits that opened before mid-1993.

#1   **Lied Jungle** (Omaha)
#2   **Wilds of Africa** (Dallas)
#3   **Tropic World** (Brookfield)
#4   **Northern Trail** (Minnesota)
#5   **Louisiana Swamp** (Audubon)
#6   **Tropics Trail** (Minnesota)
#7   **The RainForest** (Cleveland)
#8   **Children's Zoo** (Baltimore)
#9   **JungleWorld** (Bronx)
#10   **North American Living Museum** (Tulsa)
#11   **Fragile Kingdom** (Brookfield)
#12   **World of Primates** (Fort Worth)
#13   **Discovery Reef Aquarium** (Point Defiance)
#14   **Insect World** (Cincinnati)
#15   **Tiger River** (San Diego)
#16   **African Pavilion** (North Carolina)
#17   **Outback/Pampas** (Sedgwick County)
#18   **African Tropical Forest** (Franklin Park)
#19   **World of Waters** (Indianapolis)
#20   **R.J.Reynolds Forest Aviary** (North Carolina)
#21   **Texas!** (Fort Worth)
#22   **Jungle Trails** (Cincinnati)
#23   **East Africa** (Caldwell)
#24   **Wild Asia** (Bronx)
#25   **Gorilla Tropics** (San Diego)

III

More Zoo Books

American Zoos by Steve Dale (Mallard Press, 1992). This beautiful, fully-illustrated coffee table book tours 18 of America's best zoos.

Beastly Behaviors by Janine M. Benyus (Addison-Wesley, 1992). This is the perfect book to read before and after a zoo visit for detailed information about the various animals.

A Guide To American Zoos & Aquariums by Darcy & Robert Folzenlogen (Willow Press, 1993). This guide provides brief overviews of 173 zoos and aquariums in the United States.

Keepers and Creatures at the National Zoo by Peggy Thomson (Harper Collins Publishers, 1988). Here is an in-depth look at the keepers, animals, and exhibits at the National Zoo in Washington, D.C.

Lions and Tigers and Bears by Jefferson G. Ulmer and Susan Gower (Garland Publishing Inc., 1985). This reference book contains facts and figures about zoological parks in the United States and Canada.

Monkeys on the Interstate by Jack Hanna with John Stravinsky (Doubleday, 1989). This is an entertaining and interesting autobiography of America's favorite zookeeper, Jack Hanna—Director of the Columbus Zoo.

My Wild World by Joan Embery with Denise Demong (Delacorte Press, 1980). The focus of this autobiography of the San Diego Zoo's wild animal ambassador, Joan Embery, who was a frequent guest on the *Johnny Carson Show*, is on her experiences at the San Diego Zoo.

A View From the Zoo by Gary Richmond (Word Books, 1987). The experiences of a former zookeeper at the Los Angeles Zoo are told from a very unique perspective.

Where the Animals Are by Tim O'Brien (The Globe Pequot Press, 1992). This guide provides brief descriptions of over 250 wildlife attractions in the United States and Canada.

Zoo: A Behind-the-Scenes Look at the Animals and the People Who Care for Them by Don Gold (Contemporary Books, Inc., 1988). This book contains real-life stories of keepers, curators, directors, and other employees of zoos across the nation.

Zoo Animals by Donald F. Hoffmeister (Golden Press, 1967). Despite its age, this is still the best little guidebook to take along to the zoo for capsulized information about the animals.

Zoo, The Modern Ark by Jake Page (Key Porter Books Ltd., 1990). This coffee table book has large, color photographs and provides a comprehensive overview of zoos and zoo animals from around the world.

Zoos Without Cages by Judith E. Rinard (National Geographic Society, 1981). Many beautiful color photographs illustrate the animals, exhibits, research, and conservation efforts of the modern American zoo.

ESPECIALLY FOR CHILDREN

Animals and The New Zoos by Patricia Curtis (Lodestar Books, 1991). This detailed look at modern zoos, and some of the featured and unusual animals in them, is illustrated with color photographs.

Dear Bronx Zoo by Joyce Altman & Sue Goldberg (Macmillan Publishing Company, 1990). Some of the best questions that children have asked about the Bronx Zoo are answered, and lots of fascinating zoo trivia is included.

I'm in the Zoo, Too by Brent Ashabranner (Cobblehill Books, 1989). Using beautiful watercolor illustrations, a child's first visit to the zoo is re-created through the eyes of Burl the squirrel.

Let's Go to the Petting Zoo with Jungle Jack by Jack Hanna (Doubleday, 1992). Very young children are encouraged to experience the "feel" of the animals—both in the book and at the zoo.

New Zoos by Madelyn Klein Anderson (Franklin Watts, 1987). This is an educational look at the history of zoos and at how today's zoos have changed.

A Visit to the Zoo by Sylvia Root Tester (Childrens Press, 1987). Full-color pictures and easy reading text provide an entertaining overview of a zoo.

What Do You Do at a Petting Zoo? by Hana Machotka (Morrow Junior Books, 1990). Information is provided for young readers about seven common petting zoo animals.

Windows on Wildlife by Ginny Johnston and Judy Cutchins (Morrow Junior Books, 1990). This book provides an interesting look at six of the most innovative new exhibits in zoos and aquariums (including Toledo's Hippoquarium and the Bronx Zoo's JungleWorld).

Zoo by Gail Gibbons (Thomas Y. Crowell, 1987). For early readers, this is a colorfully illustrated look at an entire zoo.

Zoo Clues: Making the Most of Your Visit to the Zoo by Sheldon L. Gerstenfeld (Viking Penguin, 1991). This book full of facts, figures, and cartoon illustrations teaches children about zoo animals.

Zoo Day by John Brennan and Leonie Keaney (Carolrhoda Books, Inc., 1989). This large-text book is illustrated with color photographs and presents an hour-by-hour account of a typical day at a zoo.

Zoos by Daniel and Susan Cohen (Delacorte Press, 1992). This introduction to the modern zoo is aimed at young readers and uses large, color photographs of many rare animals.

Zoos by Miriam Moss (The Bookwright Press, 1987). This easy-reading book with color photographs covers zoo history, animal care, exhibits, and conservation.

Indexes

Reviewed Zoos, Wildlife Parks, Specialized Zoos, Aquariums, Aquatic Parks, and Theme Parks

Listed by State and Nation

General Information

Some animals are listed here under their species grouping. For example, "cobra" is listed under "snake." Photos, definitions, and pronounications are referenced at the end of each listing.

More Great Books From Carousel Press

MILES OF SMILES:
101 Great Car Games & Activities

Anyone who has ever been trapped in a hot car with bored kids is well aware that the world needs a sure-fire way of easing the resulting tensions. This clever book fills that need. In fact, according to one enthusiastic user it just "may be the ultimate solution for back seat squabbling." The book is filled with games and activities that have travel-related themes. Ninety-seven require just your minds and mouths to play, and the other four need only simple props: a penny, a pencil, and some crayons. A helpful index categorizes each game and activity according to age-appropriateness, and humorous illustrations that kids can color add to everyone's enjoyment. *128 pages. $8.95.*

THE FAMILY TRAVEL GUIDE:
An Inspiring Collection of Family-Friendly Vacations

This anthology of articles chronicles unexpected destinations for family travel. Excursions include out-of-the-way spots such as Tom Sawyer country in Hannibal, Missouri and Tunisia in Africa. Jamaica with kids is no problem, mon! You can even trek with the kids in Nepal. A section of Helpful How-Tos provides the nitty-gritty on dealing with children in restaurants, on selecting souvenirs, and on traveling with teens. An extensive resource section lists businesses that specialize in helping families plan trips, plus books that are useful in planning family vacations. *320 pages. $14.95.*

SAN FRANCISCO FAMILY FUN

With the help of this book, parents can easily plan a daytrip or a week-long vacation. In fact, there is enough information included to keep a family busy throughout an entire childhood! Information about the family-friendliness of lodgings and restaurants is detailed, and all the best attractions are described. In addition to San Francisco, the book covers the East, South, and North Bay areas. Helpful indexes guide you to the best spots for brunch, for the big splurge—even where to go with teens! *296 pages. $12.95.*

WEEKEND ADVENTURES FOR CITY-WEARY PEOPLE:
Overnight Trips in Northern California

The vacation riches of northern California outside the San Francisco Bay Area are detailed—including the Gold Rush country, ski resorts, and family camps. This guide covers where to stay, where to eat, and what to do and also provides appropriate information for families—such as the availability of highchairs, booster seats, and cribs. Don't leave home without it! *320 pages. $13.95.*

God's
Beautiful
Daughter

Other books in the growing Faithgirlz!™ library

Bibles

The Faithgirlz! Bible

NIV Faithgirlz! Backpack Bible

Faithgirlz! Bible Studies

Secret Power of Love

Secret Power of Joy

Secret Power of Goodness

Secret Power of Grace

Fiction

From Sadie's Sketchbook

Shades of Truth (Book One)

Flickering Hope (Book Two)

Waves of Light (Book Three)

Brilliant Hues (Book Four)

Sophie's World Series

Sophie's World

Sophie's Secret

Sophie Under Pressure

Sophie Steps Up

Sophie's First Dance

Sophie's Stormy Summer

Sophie's Friendship Fiasco

Sophie and the New Girl

Sophie Flakes Out

Sophie Loves Jimmy

Sophie's Drama

Sophie Gets Real

The Girls of Harbor View

Girl Power (Book One)

Take Charge (Book Two)

Raising Faith (Book Three)

Secret Admirer (Book Four)

The Lucy Series

Lucy Doesn't Wear Pink (Book One)

Lucy Out of Bounds (Book Two)

Lucy's Perfect Summer (Book Three)

Lucy Finds Her Way (Book Four)

Boarding School Mysteries

Vanished (Book One)

Betrayed (Book Two)

Burned (Book Three)

Poisoned (Book Four)

Nonfiction

Faithgirlz! Journal

The Faithgirlz! Handbook

The Faithgirlz! Cookbook

No Boys Allowed

What's a Girl to Do?

Girlz Rock

Chick Chat

Real Girls of the Bible

Faithgirlz! Whatever

God's Beautiful Daughter

The Skin You're In

Girl Talk

*Everybody Tells Me to Be Myself
but I Don't Know Who I Am*

Girl Politics

Check out www.Faithgirlz.com

faiThGirLz!
the beauty of believing

God's
Beautiful
Daughter
Discover the Love
of your heavenly father

TASHA K. DOUGLAS

ZONDERkidz

ZONDERKIDZ

God's Beautiful Daughter
Copyright © 2012 by Tasha K. Douglas

This title is also available as a Zondervan ebook.
Visit www.zondervan.com/ebooks

Requests for information should be addressed to:
Zonderkidz, 3900 *Sparks Dr. SE, Grand Rapids, Michigan* 49546

This edition: ISBN 978-0-310-74594-5

This title formerly published as *My Beautiful Daughter*

Library of Congress Cataloging-in-Publication Data
Douglas, Tasha, 1974-
        My beautiful daughter : what it means to be loved by God / by Tasha
Douglas.
          p. cm. — (Faithgirlz)
        ISBN 978-0-310-72643-2 (softcover)
        1. Girls — Religious life — Juvenile literature. 2. Preteens — Religious
life — Juvenile literature. 3. God (Christianity) — Love — Juvenile literature.
4. God (Christianity) — Fatherhood — Juvenile literature. I. Title.
BV4551.3.D68 2012
248.8'2—dc23   2011043730

Cover design: *Kris Nelson*
Interior design and composition: *Greg Johnson, Textbook Perfect*

Printed in the United States of America

15 16 17 18 19 20 21 /DCI/ 19 18 17 16 15 14 13 12 11 10 9 8 7 6 5 4 3 2 1

To my beautiful daughters,

Téa Carise and Tori Nicole

Contents

CHAPTER 1

Recognizing Your Father's Face

I got it!" Briana Robinson leaped from her bed and sprinted to the telephone. Not much longer and she'd have her own cell phone. It was the call she'd anticipated all morning long. In sixteen more hours, she would begin her first day as a seventh-grader at Live Oak Junior High School. It was the biggest day of her life so far. After years of watching her older sister, Ashley, do cool stuff like hosting sleepovers, Briana figured the time had finally come for her to have some fun too.

The consummate fashionista, Briana's idea of fun meant facing life's monumental moments in style. She considered the matter of what to wear on the first day of school a major decision. The incoming call from her best friend, Jessica Moore, would help her make a good one. Briana grabbed the telephone, catching her breath before speaking.

"Hey Jess! What are you wearing tomorrow?"

"I don't know yet. How 'bout you?"

"I'm not sure either."

"Nothing we can't solve with a trip to the mall, right? Do you think your mom would take us?"

"Maybe. She doesn't get home 'til four thirty, though."

"Call her and ask her."

"No, I'm only supposed to call for something serious. She'll call to check on me. Then I'll ask."

"Cool. What are you gonna get?"

"Ashley has a cute pair of jeans that I like. And I know the perfect hoodie to go with 'em."

"Why don't you just borrow Ashley's jeans then?"

"Please. They are so big on me I can't even walk. I'd rather have some skinny jeans anyway. Besides, Mom doesn't let us share clothes."

Briana and Jessica desired to look good. They were glad their school permitted them to wear their own clothing instead of uniforms. In the sixth grade, Briana earned the best-dressed award and her picture in the yearbook. She was determined to keep that status in junior high too. The telephone beeping with another call interrupted her goal-setting daydream.

"Jess, let me get that. It's probably my mom."

"Okay. Call me back when you get done."

"I will." Briana switched calls. "Hey, Mom."

"Hello, Bree. Is that the proper way to answer the telephone?"

"No. But I knew it was you. We do have caller ID, remember?"

"Don't get sassy, Briana Robinson. You still need to answer the phone correctly. You doin' alright?"

"Kinda. Well actually, no. Not really ... Mom?"

"Mmm hmm."

Briana zipped her question out as fast as she could. "Do you think you can take me and Jess to the mall when you get home? I really want to get a hoodie like Ashley's to wear to school tomorrow ... please." She grimaced as she waited for her mother's response.

"Oh, sweetheart, I'm sorry. I have to work late. That's what I was calling to tell you. I'm really sorry, Briana. I promise I'll make it up to you. Anyway, what about all the stuff your grandmother sent you?"

"It's nice. But I want to wear something slammin' on the first day."

"Slamming?"

"You know what I mean, Mom. Something cool. All that stuff Granny got is too babyish."

"I understand. Well, try to find something in your closet just for tomorrow. We're not going to the mall tonight. I won't make it home until six thirty."

With that, Briana's hope of becoming the most popular girl in school began evaporating. Her mother seemed not to care. "Where's Ashley?" she asked.

"She's in her room."

"Let me talk to her please."

"I'll get her."

Briana pushed the hold button and then placed the telephone back on the cradle. She also hung her head, disappointed that her pursuit of popularity was now on hold, and Mom wouldn't take her to the mall. She considered begging, but it was useless. Briana envisioned her mom planting her hands on her hips, with that look on her face. You know the one. It means, I said no. Now no more whining, and do not ask me again.

In moments like that, Briana thought about her father.

She gently tapped on Ashley's closed bedroom door. "Mom's on the phone."

Ashley opened the door, noticing the tears slowly filling Briana's brown eyes. "What's wrong?"

Briana shrugged. "Nothin', I'm fine." She turned from her sister, hurrying off to her own bedroom. Closing the bedroom door behind her, she sighed and plopped down at her desk. The huge calendar on top almost completely covered it. It was easy for her to notice the dreaded Saturday date. She had circled it at least a hundred times with a hot pink heart.

Briana had her dress. She had her shoes. And of course, she had her jewelry. There was only one thing she was missing for the Father-Daughter Sweetheart Dance: *her father.* Even though her uncle William would take her as he did every year, the fact that he was not her actual father only made her even sadder.

She understood the importance of being grateful for Uncle William's love and kindness, and she was. Still, knowing all the other girls would be at the dance with their fathers, and that she would not, left Briana feeling empty.

Drumming her fingers on the desk, Briana resolved to make the best of her situation. She thought, oh well, he's not going to magically appear 'cause I'm sitting here tapping this desk. She got up and slowly opened the closet door, as if she were afraid of the clothes inside.

The door creaked, reminding her that everything in her closet was old, and nowhere near good enough to wear on the first day of junior high. She stood there, arms crossed in disappointment, deciding what outfit would have to make do for her debut. "Ugh!" she yelled, slamming the closet door. The wall shelf holding her cheerleading trophies shook. All her awards tumbled to the floor.

The crash alarmed Ashley. She dashed through the door to Briana's room. "What happened?"

"I just closed my closet door too hard. Geez, don't you knock? Calm down."

"If there's something bothering you Briana, you should just say so. What's up?"

Ashley could be a cool big sister at times. When Briana felt like her mother didn't understand, Ashley was willing to listen. "What's up with that," Briana said, "is I'm tired of not having Dad around! Don't you ever wonder why our dad left us and Mom?"

Ashley sat down on Briana's bed and patted the vacant spot beside her with her hand. Briana complied with the request and sat down. "You know, Bree, I used to wonder but not so much anymore. There are times when I miss Dad too. But, I'm learning that adults have a lot of responsibilities.

They have to make choices that we don't even think about yet. Sometimes they make good ones, sometimes they don't. But it doesn't mean they don't love us."

"Yeah. But shouldn't you be with someone if you love them so much?"

Ashley held up her pointer finger, got up from the bed, and walked out of the room. When she came back in, she carried a mustard yellow colored photo album. Sitting down on the bed with Briana, Ashley opened the old album and took out a picture. She showed it to Briana. "Does this look like someone who doesn't love you?"

"Is that baby me?"

"Yes. And that's Dad holding you. Mom told me he had just finished giving you a bath. It was his nightly routine. You would scream when he took off your clothes to get you all cleaned up. But after that, you loved it! He would bathe you, dress you in that goofy looking outfit, and then read you a story before you went to sleep. Every single night."

"How embarrassing!" In the picture, newborn Briana is naked, and her dad is holding her close to his chest, bundled in a white hooded robe with pink rabbit ears and feet. "He looks handsome, don't you think?"

"I guess you could say that. I think he looks proud mostly. Look at that big smile."

"Maybe." She handed the picture back to Ashley. "Guess he wasn't proud enough to stay though."

Before leaving the room, Ashley leaned over and kissed Briana on the forehead. "You keep it."

Making her way back to the closet, Briana stared into the eyes of the man in the picture, a man she hardly knew and had no memory of having seen. She could not recognize her own father's face. In that moment, at first, everything felt unacceptable. Her clothes felt unacceptable. Her life felt unacceptable. She felt utterly unacceptable. Yet, the picture seemed to nag Briana, begging her to stare. The longer she looked, the more she thought that maybe Ashley's story was true. Maybe this man had loved her, cared for her, and wanted her more than she ever knew. "Where are you," she whispered. "Don't you understand how much I need you?"

Thinking her whispers were only unheard words falling to the ground, Briana sank to the floor of her closet. Her heart was sunken too. She started pounding her fists on the floor, angry with Mom for not taking her to the mall, her dad for leaving her, and herself for crying like a baby. Maybe angry with God too, wherever he was.

She took one last jab at the floor, but this time it felt like the floor punched her back! "Ouch!" Briana said. "What was that?" She looked down to see that she had hit her hand on the buckle of a glittery pink belt. Mmm. That's cute, she thought. Briana picked up the belt and studied it, trying to remember the last time she wore it. Then she noticed the price tag dangling from the buckle. Wait a minute, she thought. Have I even worn this belt yet?

That one question led Briana on a style expedition, hunting vigorously through her closet. Just minutes earlier, she'd considered it a wilderness of toxic material destined for a hazardous waste bin. Not anymore. In the middle of her frustration, Briana had discovered first day fashion that would launch her immediately into the Live Oak Junior High hall of fame for fashion! Yes!

Briana's Box

How is a girl supposed to understand what it means to be her father's daughter when he's not even around? It's tough. But understanding what it means to be the much-loved daughter of your father is a huge deal in your life, because it shapes how you think about God, your Father in heaven. What you think of your heavenly Father affects your life more than any other belief you have.

If your dad's not around much, you might feel that Father God is absent when you need him too. That would be totally wrong thinking about God! So, *Faithgirlz!* is here to help you believe that understanding and receiving Father God's love is possible and even more than that — it's actually your future!

The connection you share with Father God matters more than any other relationship you have. The beauty of believing that you are his beautiful daughter means you get to . . .

- Experience a love-filled relationship that lasts forever.
- Expand your family to include all Father God's children.
- Envision the bright future prepared for you by Father God.

Sound good? Then get to it, girl! Start by doing a special Faithgirl assignment called a daughter deed.

Daughter Deed

Do you understand how Briana felt because you miss your father too? Maybe he died when you were too young to remember. Is your father one of the brave people serving our country in the military? Perhaps your mother and father divorced. Does your dad spend so much time working to take care of your family that you two share little time together? Do you, like Briana, whisper, "Where are you," unsure if anyone hears your voice?

Can you do a daughter deed, and share with Briana how you feel about your dad? Take all the time you need, and in the space below write down some of your experiences with your father. If you have any encouraging words for Bree, be sure to write those down too. Let her know what cheers you up when you're feeling down about your dad.

_____

_____

_____

_____

_____

_____

Thanks, Faithgirl. Sometimes it might seem that no one hears you, or even cares about the special thoughts you just shared with Briana. The truth is there is someone who always hears you. He is Father God, and he's been waiting on you. Are you ready to break out of the box and meet him? Then read on! Briana's showing you the beauty of believing and what it means to be loved by God.

Believing with Briana

You can think of Briana's quest for the perfect outfit as a good way of learning how to begin experiencing the love of Father God. Do you remember why Bree ended up staring into her closet in a fashion fog? First, her big sister's jeans were too big for her, and she wanted a narrow, skinny fitting pair. What was the second barricade to Briana earning her best-dressed bragging rights? She had no way of getting to the mall. Right. And the final wake-up call from her fashion fantasy was her mom's injunction against the borrowing of clothing. In the end, whatever Briana was going to wear to school was already in her closet.

In the same way that Briana wanted skinny-fit jeans, you will receive God's love by walking a path that is narrow and focused on him. Also, just as she was unable to depend on anyone else to take her to the mall, you are responsible for your own spiritual journey. Finally, in the same way that Briana submitted to her mom's guideline of no clothes sharing, God's daughters learn to submit to him and obey the guidelines he establishes for your own good. In the end, you too will find everything you need in your closet. You just have to look again and discover what's inside.

The story captured in Briana's photograph with her own dad also pictures the story of Father God's love for you. Just as Briana's dad loved sharing the nightly ritual with his precious daughter, Father God loves doing special things for you. His desire is to love you so well that he irresistibly draws you to loving him right back and trusting him with your life!

Love the Lord your God with all your heart and with all your soul and with all your mind. This is the first and greatest commandment.

— *Matthew 22:37–38*

Like Briana's dad, Father God has a special way of lavishing his love on his daughters. You know that Father God loves you, his beautiful daughter, because he tenderly . . .

- Cleans you
- Clothes you
- Calms you

Has anyone ever told you how a newborn baby looks? It is a grimy sight at first! Before wrapping you in a toasty warm blanket, dressing you in cute infant clothing, and presenting you to your anxiously awaiting family, health care professionals washed off the messy residue caused by your previous life inside your mother's womb. That first bath, though, was only one of many. It started a practice of regular washing that would keep you healthy and clean for the rest of your life.

As a baby, you needed help keeping clean. As you grew older, someone taught you what to do, and you were able to wash yourself off regularly, keeping yourself clean on your own. And even though you know what to do now, sometimes the mess gets so big, you need help getting cleaned up.

In Briana's family, her dad was the one who enjoyed washing his daughter. Father God loves washing his daughters too! Just like that newborn baby, when you're first born into God's family, all the grubbiness of your life before you knew him clings to you. Messy birth was a part of being born into your family. It's also a part of being born into the family of Father God.

> **Surely I was sinful at birth, sinful from the time my mother conceived me.**
>
> — *Psalm 51:5*

Yet, God never intends to leave you icky! Like Bree's father, it pleases him to wash you clean when dirty situations start to pollute your life. When you're not in the best of moods, your parents don't seem to understand, or if your friends start treating you unkindly, your Father in heaven will wash you clean.

As you grow to know him more and more, God will teach you to keep yourself clean. And yes, there will be those times when, although you are all grown up, you still need help getting cleaned!

When you bathe, what do you do after drying off? You put some clothes on! After all, it's chilly, right? Knowing his baby daughter was unable to dress herself, Briana's dad clothed her, keeping her protected from the harsh elements—the heat or the cold—of her surroundings. Ashley thought the outfit Briana's dad chose looked ridiculous. Still, Briana was held close and snuggled by her father, wearing a white rabbit-eared robe as a sign of her father's great love for her.

Father God has great love for you, and he too loves clothing you, knowing you're unable to do it yourself. His desire is to cover and protect you from the harsh experiences that inevitably you will encounter in life. At times, life's pressures make you feel like your heart is being scorched! Other times, situations may seem so cold and dismal that your heart begins to freeze up on you. In those times, remember what it means to be Father God's daughter. No matter how ridiculous it seems to anyone else, it means he's intimately covering you in relationship with him, and you're protected.

Wouldn't you be ready to get some rest after being all toasty in your cute white robe? Well, yeah! Briana's dad knew she was too. That's why the last thing he used to do was softly tell her a story so she could go to bed and rest peacefully. After a long day of drooling, babbling, scooting, eating, and napping—all the tasks of hardworking babies everywhere—he understood that she needed some rest. He lulled Briana into calmness with the sound of his voice, giving her peace and rest from her work.

Father God also softly speaks to you, his daughter, knowing that when you focus on his voice, it calms you, gives you peace, and makes you rest. After all the hard work that you do—studying for school, your responsibilities in your home, serving with your club, and hanging with your friends—God wants you to make time to restore all that energy you've expended!

Praise Prompt

Psalm 23 is a favorite song of many of God's daughters. It shares all the wonderful things Father God does because he loves his children so much. Think about this song, and express your gratitude to Father God however you like. You can dance, sing, clap, or even write your own melody!

Psalm 23

The Lord is my shepherd, I lack nothing.
He makes me lie down in green pastures,
he leads me beside quiet waters,
he refreshes my soul.
He guides me along the right paths
for his name's sake.
Even though I walk
through the darkest valley,
I will fear no evil,
for you are with me;
your rod and your staff,
they comfort me.
You prepare a table before me
in the presence of my enemies.

You anoint my head with oil;
my cup overflows.
Surely your goodness and love will follow me
all the days of my life,
and I will dwell in the house of the Lord
forever.

Don't you just love praising God? He so deserves it! Now, let's take a closer look at how Briana learned the beauty of believing, and you can too. Like brilliant gemstones, Briana's tidbits are principles of great value to help you understand what it means to be God's beautiful daughter. As you grow to recognize your heavenly Father, your journey will include …

- Intentionality
- Intimacy
- Submission
- Seeking
- Seeing

Briana's Tidbit #1: Intentionality

As much as Briana liked her sister Ashley's jeans, she was unable to wear them because they were too big. Bree's preference was for narrow, skinny jeans that complement a girl her size. That's a great choice! The way to finding Father God is a bit like wearing a pair of great fitting skinny jeans. It's narrow. You'll begin to experience God's love as you intentionally focus on him, and then walk in the way he directs you. Make it your single purpose to focus on God, and you will enter into a life of love with him.

Enter through the narrow gate. For wide is
the gate and broad is the road that leads to
destruction, and many enter through it. But small
is the gate and narrow the road that leads to life,
and only a few find it.

— *Matthew 7:13–14*

Briana's Tidbit #2: Intimacy

It bummed Briana out that she had no one to take her and
Jessica to the mall. Unable to drive herself yet, she was
dependent on adults to take her places. Briana learned a
valuable lesson though. She realized she had to limit her
dependence on other people. She could only occasionally
count on others to take her where she wanted to go. The
same is true for you, daughter. You still need other people
to help you grow into your love walk with Father God.
Yet, you won't always depend on other people to take you
where you want to go in your relationship with him. You
will walk with God in the company of other daughters and
sons, and you will definitely need help from your brothers
and sisters along the way. Still, being loved by God means
having your own personal bond with him that carries you
to the special, secret place only the two of you share.

Briana's Tidbit #3: Submission

Sometimes Briana thinks her mom's rules make little
sense. Seriously, what's wrong with borrowing a cute

jacket or sweater from Jessica or Ashley? Despite her own opinion though, she does what her mom tells her to do. Okay. She does what her mom tells her to do most of the time! That's because in her heart Briana believes her mom only wants good things to happen in her life. Even when she disagrees with her mom's plans at first, they always seem to work out for Briana in the end. So she's learned to smile in her heart because her mom's only looking out for her best interests. After smiling on the inside, she follows Mom's directions.

In the same way that Briana yields to her mom's plans for her, being loved by Father God means that you yield to his plans for you. Sometimes God's thoughts are senseless to you. It's because his thoughts are higher than yours! As his daughter, though, you can trust that his plans for you are good.

> **"For I know the plans I have for you," declares the Lord, "plans to prosper you and not to harm you, plans to give you hope and a future."**
>
> —*Jeremiah 29:11*

When you agree to do things God's way because you understand how much he loves you, he works things out so they turn out good for you, just as they did for Briana.

> **And we know that in all things God works for the good of those who love him, who have been called according to his purpose.**
>
> —*Romans 8:28*

Daughter, You Decide

What do you do when you disagree with your parents or other leaders in your life? How do you feel when they ask you to do things and you don't understand why? Do you do exactly what you are directed to do immediately and with a smile inside your heart?

Briana's Tidbit #4: Seeking

After pillaging her closet, Bree learned that often the purpose of a problem is to help you make unlikely discoveries in unlikely places. She didn't know she had amazing outfits yet to be worn stashed right in her very own closet! Fashion success, present the entire time! And to think it all started on her closet floor with one simple question.

That's part of how it starts for you too. When you find your closet, your secret place of talking alone with God, you discover this about what it means to be loved by God: he's given you everything you need to face any challenge in life—and win! That doesn't mean you won't face challenges. You will. It's a fact of life. But you can trust God is with you through everything. What you're looking for is inside of you!

> Then you will call on me and come and pray to me, and I will listen to you. You will seek me and find me when you seek me with all your heart.
>
> —*Jeremiah 29:12–13*

You're really on your way to discovering the hidden treasure Father God has for you when you start asking him questions. Like Briana, you may think he doesn't hear you, but he does. He will answer. Maybe not in exactly the way you want, but God is able to see the big picture, and he will provide for you in the best way he sees fit.

> Ask and it will be given to you; seek and you will find; knock and the door will be opened to you. For everyone who asks receives; the one who seeks finds; and to the one who knocks, the door will be opened.
>
> — Matthew 7:7–8

Briana's Tidbit #5: Seeing

Do you remember Briana returning the photo of her and her father to Ashley? She really didn't want to keep it. Briana had difficulty believing her father loved her or wanted her. She questioned her dad's love because she'd never seen him before. It's hard to trust someone you've never even seen! Yet, as Ashley told her the story of how much her father loved her, her thoughts about her dad started changing. The longer she stared at the picture, the more her way of thinking about her father—and herself—shifted. With each fresh glance, she had a new vision of who her dad really was, and even though she couldn't see him, she believed that he loved her.

As it was with Briana, so it is with you and Father God. Receiving Father God's love is mind-boggling! Trust the love of someone invisible to you? Yeah, right. But that's exactly what faith is all about—the beauty of believing!

Now faith is confidence in what we hope for and assurance about what we do not see.

—Hebrews 11:1

How's that supposed to happen for you? Just like it did for Bree as she heard the story of the picture with her father. You'll experience the beauty of believing as you hear the story of God's love for you, over and over again. The more you hear it, the clearer the image you have of him becomes. With each new glance, you'll look at and think differently about God, and yourself, than you already do, until at last, you've got it! The more you open yourself up to him, trust him with your life and decisions, the more he will reveal himself to you. You're loving and looking toward Father God by faith—to lead you in your life, help you make decisions, and trust that he is with you (and he is). That is faith! Remember, you are God's beautiful daughter!

Aren't you? Maybe reading all of this is causing you to look at your situation differently. Are you ready to love and look toward Father God through faith? Are you ready to hear Father God call you? Then it's time to make that step toward your beginning.

Beginnings with Briana

Oh, wait! There's one detail remaining in Briana's story about her dad. She thought it was totally embarrassing, remember? Ashley said it made Briana scream at the top of her lungs! No one likes being exposed, but before he could bathe her, Briana's dad had to make her a bit uncomfortable and remove her clothing.

You see, before Father God can clean up the messiness of life, he has to remove everything that's covering it up. That means helping you to see what might be hovering over you, around you, like smog. Maybe it's placing too much time into worrying how others think of you, wondering if you are "cool" in their eyes. Are you trying to be a girl that fits into the "world"? As God's daughter, you have an inner beauty, an inner light to show to the world. But sometimes the light has to be cleaned before it can put forth its brilliant shine. Sure, nakedness can be uncomfortable, but the discomfort is temporary. The pleasure of being cleaned, clothed, and calmed in connection with Father God lasts forever and blows those bare-skinned moments to smoke!

So go ahead and scream if you want, but just be honest with God. Let him know exactly how you feel. Seriously, he already knows what's in your heart anyway! By sharing and keeping it real with God, you invite him to become a part of your world, like a friend. The more you talk and share, just like with any friend, the closer you become. Then you'll recognize his voice that's been inviting you to become a part of his all along.

Daughter, Declare Your Prayer!

Father, thank you for your love! Lead me to your banquet hall, where your sign over me is love. For many waters cannot quench love, and rivers cannot sweep it away. You are making me see and think about things the way you do, and I'm glad. I want to love and look to you through faith. Please, show yourself to me.

CHAPTER 2

Respecting Your Father's Favorite

Lunchtime is Briana's favorite hour of the day. When she's with her friends, their stories about the morning's activities fill her up. That, plus the freshly baked banana-nut muffins the cafeteria lady makes every day!

Bree's third period social studies classroom is right around the corner from the cafeteria, and around 11:30 the smell of those muffins made her stomach grumble in expectation. She rushed through the food line, heading straight for the designated lunch table where Jessica and the rest of the cheer squad were waiting. That's when she saw him.

The sight of Austin Thomas suddenly made Briana feel more like hurling than eating.

"What's up, Butterfingers?" he said. "Don't drop your tray like you do the basketball." He made an exaggerated gesture like she was going to cover him with her milk.

"Go away, Austin."

He followed her to their table. "I'm just saying. You seem to have a hard time holding on to stuff."

The girls strategically chose where to sit. From the back of the cafeteria, they could monitor everyone. The rear location was also the only spot that allowed them to peek out the large window to the outside commons area. From there, they could admire the football players sitting under the massive live oak tree planted in the middle of the commons. Every year, new football players carved their name and number into the sturdy, wide trunk. It was their way of connecting with the title-winning champions of the past who played for the Live Oak Lions.

Besides that, the school board had approved the installation of new lighting meant to brighten up the aging space. Until the workers completed the job, their window seat preference was the best-lit and illuminated place in the cafeteria — perfect for "people-peepin'," as Briana called it.

Jessica noticed how irritated Briana was with Austin's unrequested escort. "Well, she has no problem holding on to you though, does she? I'm going to start calling you 'Tag-a-long Thomas' since you can't seem to get enough of my girl. From now on, if you want to talk to her, make sure you go through me first, Tag-a-long." Briana and Jess fist bumped.

People admired Bree and Jessica's relationship. They met when they were seven years old, when their families moved into the neighborhood at the same time. Their neighbor, Mrs. Jenkins, hosted a barbeque in her backyard to welcome them. With an awesome swimming pool in the backyard, she had the best house on the block. It was the perfect spot to endure the sweltering summer heat. The day of the party, the two girls wore the exact same bathing suit! Bree knew that any girl who would pick the same water wear had to be wonderful. Through cheerleading camps, youth group, retreats, big sisters, and baby brothers, they've been besties since day one! Briana and Jessica love each other, and they don't take kindly to insults.

Bree sat down next to Jessica, and Austin bent over to whisper in Briana's ear. "Just a helpful hint. You catch the ball first, then you take off and dribble with it." He stood up and made catch and dribble motions with his hands. All the guys at the other end of the table laughed.

"Catch this!" Bree yelled. She elbowed Austin in his stomach.

The sound of her angry voice drew the attention of Mrs. Gray, one of the seventh grade English teachers. Mrs. Gray walked over to their table, "Is there a problem Miss Robinson?"

"Yes. Allow me to introduce you." Smiling, Briana extended her hand toward Austin. "Mrs. Gray, meet Problem."

Everybody laughed, even Austin.

"What's going on you two?"

"Austin's making fun of me because I messed up in gym class!"

"Is that true?" Mrs. Gray looked at Austin.

"No," he said.

"Okay, but, it was just a joke," Austin confessed.

"So you've got jokes, is that it? How does Coach Sanders feel about all those jokes? Doesn't he like to be notified when his comical basketball players, such as yourself, crack one joke too many?"

He looked at Briana. "My bad." Smiling, he tapped her on the shoulder. "I'm sorry. I was just playing around." He extended his hand for her to shake. "Are we cool?"

Briana shook his hand as briefly as possible. "Whatever." She looked at the teacher. "Thank you, Mrs. G."

"That's why I'm here." She patted Briana on the shoulder. "It's my job to keep you out of trouble." She looked toward Austin. "Now finish your lunch before it's time to go."

Briana sat back down and resumed her conversation with her friends while they finished eating. When only five minutes remained until the start of the next lunch period, the crowded cafeteria quickly thinned. The mass exodus of students leaving the cafeteria collided with the

Daughter, You Decide

What do you do when someone makes jokes about you? How do you feel when they attempt to gain laughs at your expense? Do you return the insult and make jokes about them?

famished group attempting to enter. Can you say, major chaos?

"I never have understood why we're not allowed to use the other door to get in here," Jessica said.

"The problem is not that there's only one way in," said Briana. "The problem is the people who don't get the plan and follow directions."

Jessica surveyed the long line of students trying to exit through the entrance. "You mean people like your boy Austin?"

Briana saw Austin standing in the line, knuckling Nicholas's arm. "First of all, he's not my boy. Second of all, right. People exactly like Austin. They just don't understand what's up."

"I'm sure he wouldn't mind if you showed him the way," Jessica said, winking.

"What's that supposed to mean?" Briana felt her face heating up.

"It's so obvious, Bree. He likes you."

"Yeah, right. The only way I care to show Austin Thomas is back to California where he came from."

"Don't be so hard on him. You know he's cute. And smart too. He's probably still just trying to figure things out, you know what I mean? They've only been here since the summer. It's basically like he's starting a brand new life. You wouldn't know what to do either."

"Maybe. But this is not that serious. And I can't believe you're sticking up for him and not me, by the way!" She pointed to the cafeteria's entrance. "That door is for coming in." She turned and pointed to the cafeteria's exit. "That door is for leaving. Notice the prominent sign that says *exit* in big ... red ... letters. Duh! If he's so smart, why can't he read the signs?"

"Wow. I knew it! You like him too! But I didn't know you liked him that much," Jessica said.

Briana's Box

You've probably been called something other than your name, just like Austin called Briana "Butterfingers." How did that make you feel? If it was a name meant to highlight a weakness or shortcoming of yours, like "Butterfingers" in Bree's case, you were likely hurt and angered by it. Here's why.

Names are special. Father God honored Adam, the first human being, with the responsibility of naming every living creature.

> **Now the Lord God had formed out of the ground all the wild animals and all the birds in the sky. He brought them to the man to see what he would name them; and whatever the man called each living creature, that was its name.**
>
> — *Genesis 2:19*

Names make up our identity. Yet your name goes beyond simple identification of you as a person. To Father God, your name represents *you*. In the Bible, there are many stories of families naming their children based on the experiences the family had in bringing that child into the world.

> **So in the course of time Hannah became pregnant and gave birth to a son. She named him Samuel, saying, "Because I asked the Lord for him."**
>
> — *1 Samuel 1:20*

The name Briana means "noble." Her parents chose that name for her because they envisioned their daughter as a woman of honor and dignity. When others negatively refer to you instead of using your name, it hurts because your name suggests who you are as a young woman.

Daughter Deed

Do you know what your name means? Can you do a daughter deed, and research the meaning of your name? Start by asking your parents. You will learn a lot about yourself, and you'll have fun doing it too! Be sure to write down what you find out in the space below. You'll want to keep your notes forever!

_____

_____

_____

_____

_____

_____

Praise Prompt

Name-calling is just uncool. When people call you names and say bad things about you, it can really stress you out. Instead of stressing, read and think about the words below from Psalm 139. When you're finished, go stand in front of a mirror. Then look at yourself, and say "I am who Father God says I am! He made me marvelously! Thank you, Father!" And, Faithgirl, make sure you say it loud and proud!

Psalm 139:13–18

For you created my inmost being;
you knit me together in my mother's womb.
I praise you because I am fearfully and wonderfully made;
your works are wonderful,
I know that full well.
My frame was not hidden from you
when I was made in the secret place,
when I was woven together in the depths of the earth.
Your eyes saw my unformed body;
all the days ordained for me were written in your book
before one of them came to be.
How precious to me are your thoughts, God!
How vast is the sum of them!
Were I to count them,
they would outnumber the grains of sand—
when I awake, I am still with you.

Believing with Briana

Now that you understand the significance of names to Father God, are you curious about the name of God himself? Well, grab something to take a few notes because there is much to learn! God's nature is so big and full that you cannot understand everything about who God is with just one name. Throughout history, God has shared many different names for himself with the people who love him. For girls like you who want to know what it means to be loved by God, two connected names mean the most.

The first name comes from a conversation between God and a man named Moses. Moses was a great leader who God directed to free Hebrew people from slavery. Like you, Moses was curious about God's name. Moses knew that the purpose of naming exceeds identification, and lets you know the nature of a person or thing. So, Moses asked God his name. The answer God gave Moses will help you learn a lot about who God is and how you can know him for yourself. Listen in on the conversation between God and Moses:

> Moses said to God, "Suppose I go to the Israelites and say to them, 'The God of your fathers has sent me to you,' and they ask me, 'What is his name?' Then what shall I tell them?"

> God said to Moses, "I AM WHO I AM. This is what you are to say to the Israelites: 'I AM has sent me to you.'"

> God also said to Moses, "Say to the Israelites, 'The LORD, the God of your fathers—the God of Abraham, the God of Isaac and the God of Jacob—has sent me to you.' This is my name forever, the name you shall call me from generation to generation."

41

Can you imagine asking someone their name and they answer with "I am"? What would you think of them? Maybe you'd be tapping your foot, waiting for them to finish their sentence thinking, okay, so you were saying ... you are? Thankfully, Jesus Christ came along and clarified the fuzziness of the "I AM" answer! It is his name and character that is the most special and highly regarded name to Father God. That name of Jesus Christ deserves more respect than any other name. Here's why.

Has anyone ever told you that you look and act like one of your parents? Maybe you've heard that you have your father's nose, or you walk and talk like your mother. This is because you inherited your physical attributes from your parents. You have a chemical in your body called deoxyribonucleic acid, or DNA for short. DNA is what determines how you look and behave. The reason you resemble your parents is that you have the same DNA they do.

Spiritually speaking, Jesus Christ looks just like his father too! Just as your parents passed down their DNA to you, Father God passed down his DNA to his unique Son, Jesus Christ. Jesus Christ has the exact nature and character of Father God. In fact, Jesus even told his first followers that

"Anyone who has seen me has seen the Father."
— *John 14:9*

Though God the Father is invisible, Jesus Christ the Son is visible. By looking at this Son, Jesus, you can see exactly what God the Father is like.

42

But, there's a little more to this Jesus looks like his father thing! Not only does Jesus look like the Father, he is actually one with the Father. That's why Jesus could say, if you've seen me, then you've seen the Father. When you wonder what God the Father is like, you can discover him by focusing on Jesus Christ.

> **Then Jesus cried out, "Whoever believes in me does not believe in me only, but in the one who sent me. The one who looks at me is seeing the one who sent me.**
>
> *—John 12:44–45*

Jesus spoke the words "I AM" too. Just as Father God said the words "I AM" when he talked to Moses, Jesus spoke the words "I AM" frequently as he shared his life with and taught his followers his ways. Jesus shared with his followers that whatever he said is just what the Father told him to say.

On seven special occasions, Jesus said "I AM," and his words make it clear that Jesus is the one who leads daughters to Father God. Now, take a close look at Jesus's statements. Remember, these tidbits are principles of great value to help you understand what it means to be loved by God, and exactly how you can find Father God for yourself! Jesus said:

> **I am the bread of life.**
>
> *—John 6:35*

> **I am the light of the world.**
>
> *—John 8:12*

I am the gate.

—John 10:9

I am the good shepherd.

—John 10:14

I am the resurrection and the life.

—John 11:25

I am the way and the truth and the life.

—John 14:6

I am vine; you are the branches.

—John 15:5

Briana's Tidbit #1: I Am the Bread of Life

Do you remember what fills Briana up at lunchtime besides hanging with her friends? That's right! Those freshly baked banana-nut muffins in the cafeteria. Even though her appetite is small, Briana understands the importance of healthy eating habits to give her body the energy it needs to function at its best. Grainy foods, like Briana's favorite muffins, are those made from wheat, rice, oats, cornmeal, barley, or other cereal grains.

Grains are an important part of a healthy diet because they provide many nutrients you need every day such as fiber, vitamins, and minerals. If you're anything like your bread-loving friend Briana, you know this for sure: when you eat bread, a muffin, or a bowl of brown rice, it fills you up for a long time!

It's the fiber in bread that makes you feel full. Fiber also lowers the chance that you'll ever have heart disease, and it helps your body eliminate waste. The vitamins in grains, especially vitamin B, help your body release stored up energy and keep your brain sharp. The minerals found in grains, like iron and magnesium, help your body carry oxygen in the blood and build up your bones.

Now do you see why Jesus said, "I am the bread of life"? God is loaded with the goodness you need to experience a satisfying life, every day! He is the source of the daily spiritual nutrition you need. Just like eating foods loaded with dietary fiber, when you take God in, he keeps the cares of life from contaminating your heart with disease. When you mistakenly make bad choices and even purposely do things you know are wrong, it's a sign that your heart is unhealthy. In those times, remember that your Father is like fiber! If you make a step to reach out to him, he'll reach out for you, too, and keep your heart healthy.

Just like the vitamin B found in foods from the grain group, God gives you energy and helps your mind stay sharp and focused on the work he needs you to do. That's right, Faithgirl! God's daughters have work to do—and that means you! Your relationship with him gives you the strength of body and mind you need to get the job done well. You may have days when you feel tired and sluggish, or you think you're unable to do something you know you're supposed to do—like homework or soccer practice perhaps! Tell yourself, my Father is like fiber! Then get to it!

I became a servant of this gospel by the gift of God's grace given me through the working of his power.

—Ephesians 3:7

For the Spirit God gave us does not make us timid, but gives us power, love and self-discipline.

—2 Timothy 1:7

Lastly, God is just like those minerals found in the grainy breads Briana enjoys so much. The iron from grain group foods is critical in helping oxygen stick to the blood that flows through your body. Think of iron as the glue that holds everything together. It's a really big deal if your body lacks the iron to make the oxygen bind to your blood. Every single system, organ, and cell in your body must have oxygen to function normally—and that means you need your iron, Faithgirl.

You also need God. He's just like that iron too. God is the glue that holds everything together so that you can get out there and take action like his strong daughter! With God, all things are possible.

Speaking of strong, how much strength would you have without a sturdy skeleton? You got it. Not so much. The magnesium in Bree's bread keeps your bones tough enough to support you. Guess what, Faithgirl? Your relationship with Father God does the same thing for you. When you're with God, you can celebrate because he's strong and tough enough to support you no matter what challenges or obstacles you have to stand up to each day.

Now it is God who makes both us and you stand firm in Christ.

— 2 Corinthians 1:21

Are you excited yet? If you're like Briana and you spend little time with your dad, you might feel unsure. That's understandable. After all, the whole father thing hasn't worked out that well for you in the past, right? Well, believe this, Faithgirl. Father God created a special place in your heart that is only for him. He is the only one who can fill you with the love and acceptance your heart wants.

Is it possible that you are trying other things or relationships to fill what only Father God can? If you've begun sexually intimate relationships with others, started using drugs and alcohol with some of your friends, or you treat people around you harshly, it might be because you're missing the Father's love.

Daughter Deed

Can you think of anything in your own life that you are using to fill you up instead of your relationship with Father God? Can you do a daughter deed, and write a list of things that you turn to instead of him?

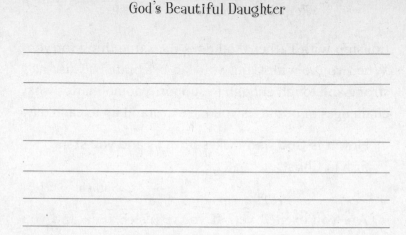

Thanks for being brave. It takes a lot of courage to own up to it when you've been heading in the wrong direction. But you took the first step, which was admitting you've got some changing to do. G-double O-D-J-O-B! Good job, good job! Now, let's get back to Briana's tidbits to learn more about what Father God is all about!

Briana's Tidbit #2: I Am the Light of the World

Do you remember why Bree, Jessica, and the squad chose to sit in the back of the cafeteria?

That's right! They wanted to be able to see what's going on with everybody else! But that wasn't the only reason, right? Remember, the huge window in the back of the cafeteria allows the sunshine in. The sun's radiance illuminates the large room, making it easy for the girls to see what's up in the world of Live Oak — at least among the people who have second lunch like Briana! Also the sunshine helps light the cafeteria itself, which feels dark while new lighting is installed. Lastly, the heat of the sun beaming through the window prevents the frigid cafeteria air from freezing Briana's limbs to icicles!

Jesus said, "I am the light of the world." His words are your reminder that God is like that sunshine bursting through the cafeteria window. As you learned from Briana, the light of the sun helps you see. Light also brightens dark places and it keeps you warm. As his daughter, you can count on Father God to help you see, to displace darkness in the world around you, and to keep you from growing cold.

God enables you to see the way on your path through life. Do you ever feel like your life is a maze? As you're learning, life is full of unexpected twists and turns. Sometimes the decisions you make—which club to join, if you should borrow the money you need for those jeans, if you should go to the dance, or how hard to study for the next test—get overwhelming, and you are unsure of what to do. In those instances, remember that God is light, and he will help you see the best way to walk out of your situation.

God is also the light whose radiance transforms dark places and situations in the world around you. How do you feel when you read about current events or watch the news on television? Do the stories make you sad sometimes? It may be difficult to do at first, but make a decision to focus on the good news, instead of the bad. Here's the good news: even in the middle of the sad and dark circumstances of the world around you, the light of God continues to rise and shine around you because you are his daughter.

Arise, shine, for your light has come, and the glory of the Lord rises upon you. See, darkness covers the earth and thick darkness is over the peoples, but the Lord rises upon you and his glory appears over you. Nations will come to your light, and kings to the brightness of your dawn.

— Isaiah 60:1–3

Besides helping you see and overcome darkness, God's light also helps keep you warm.

Have you ever dissed anyone else? Usually it's because they treated you badly first, right? When Briana was cold toward Austin, it was because he'd called her "Butterfingers", remember? Because he's the light of the world, what God does in situations such as Briana's is warm your heart up so you can forgive the person who hurt you. Instead of reacting with a cold heart, the light of his love inside you will motivate you to let go of hurtful words and actions against you.

Briana's Tidbit #3: I Am the Door

Briana allowed Austin's hurtful words to freeze her heart up toward him. Do you remember the conversation she had about him with Jessica? Harsh, don't you think? Being new to Live Oak, Austin still needed help learning the order of things, like which doors to use in the cafeteria. He was ignorant of which door granted access into the room, and that there was only one door students were permitted to use for entering.

Just as the one door used for entering the cafeteria, Jesus Christ is the only door for entering a loving relationship with Father God. Jesus Christ is the person who gives you access to Father God. Since Jesus is God's special son, as God's daughter you can consider Jesus your awesome big brother who leads you to your Father!

At first, this might be a tough idea for you or other people in your life to understand. But, it's like what Briana told Jessica about understanding the plan and following directions. Bree's school officials established a specific point of access into the cafeteria because they wanted to maintain a peaceful environment during the lunch hour. Teachers like Mrs. Gray on duty, the flow of the food lines, and yes, the door through which students enter were all designed to uphold a unique atmosphere, without confusion, in the cafeteria.

Father God desires a peaceful environment too. Seriously, think about how many times you've heard a grown-up talk about how much they just want some peace and quiet! To be honest, sometimes you want that too. What about after a long day of practice? Think about how you feel after wracking your brain over that last math test. Or what about when you came home from that trip to the fair or amusement park? You were ready to lay it down and rest peacefully, girl!

To keep the peace of his environment, Father God had to establish certain guidelines, just as those in the cafeteria. One major disruption to the peace God so loves occurs when his daughters misunderstand or forget that he wants them to live special lives committed to him. These unfortunate memory lapses lead to God's daughters making bad choices and experiencing unpleasant consequences! You remember from the last chapter that God wants his daughters to learn to stay clean, don't you? But he knows that because you are human, sometimes you're going to make messes.

Still, he wants to enjoy being with you! Wanting to enjoy his peaceful environment and the presence of his children, Father God thought of a plan that would accomplish both at the same time. His Son, Jesus Christ, is at the center of that plan. Jesus is the entry point of knowing Father God. He chose Jesus because he is the one son who is able to exist perfectly—without any misjudgments, mistakes, errors, or sin—just as the Father does himself.

So keep the peace, and hit the door, Faithgirl!

Briana's Tidbit #4: I Am the Good Shepherd

Briana liked junior high much better than fifth grade. She felt the teachers treated the students with more respect, like they weren't babies anymore. For example, some of the cafeteria rules in elementary school were different from those in junior high. At Live Oak, students could sit wherever they chose, rather than in assigned seats. One thing that did not change, though, was the presence of teachers in the cafeteria serving lunch duty.

Teachers like Mrs. Gray were essential to keeping cafeteria confusion to a minimum. Do you remember what other duties Mrs. Gray told Briana were a part of her job during lunchtime? Yep, you got it! Mrs. Gray said she was there to protect Briana and to keep her from involvement in troublesome situations.

School cafeterias can be one crazy place, right? When Jesus said, "I am the good shepherd," he was telling you that he serves you in the same way as Mrs. Gray does on cafeteria duty. Jesus is your source of protection and guidance as you go through potentially dangerous environments. When you find yourself involved in the middle of an unpleasant experience, like Briana's exchange with Austin, remember, God's got your back!

One of the main jobs of a shepherd is to keep the sheep he tends from danger. Wouldn't it be nice if you could see everything and know exactly when some situation was about to harm you? The truth is, that's humanly impossible. It is possible for God though. He can see you no matter where you are. He also sees and understands the things that are headed your way — both good and bad. Like a good shepherd, he works to prevent you from putting yourself in harm's way because you can't see what's coming.

But, what about if it's too late, and harm is encroaching? Well, he's there in that instance too. It's a fact of life that sometimes a girl needs rescuing from unplanned disasters! God, the good shepherd, will be there, just like Mrs. Gray was for Briana, to help you out of your miserable situation.

One of the reasons why sheep stay out of danger is they know and trust the voice of their shepherd. This is very important for you too, Faithgirl. As you grow, you will learn when God is speaking to your heart, just as a sheep knows the voice of its shepherd. It is critical that you learn to recognize and trust his voice. He speaks to give you words of direction that will help you stay out of trouble.

> "His sheep follow him because they know his voice. But they will never follow a stranger; in fact, they will run away from him because they do not recognize a stranger's voice."
>
> —John 10:4–5

Briana's Tidbit #5: I Am the Resurrection and the Life

Because he hurt her feelings, Briana was unhappy with Austin, to say the least! Jessica suggested that Briana consider forgiving him. Do you remember the reason why Jessica thought Austin was unfamiliar with the cafeteria rules? Girl, you're good! Austin and his family were new in town.

If you've ever relocated to a different city or state, you

know how tough it can be packing up and heading out. It takes courage to change communities. You have to adjust to a new climate, new people, and a new way of doing things. As Jessica said, moving from one place to a different one means major change!

Being the new kid on the block is challenging, but it can also be fun. Transition from old experiences to new ones are a part of life, Faithgirl—like Briana graduating from elementary school to junior high. As tough as it might be at first, if you approach a new beginning with the right attitude, it can be rewarding for you.

New life is exactly what Jesus was talking about when he said, "I am the resurrection and the life." With this statement, Jesus was saying that following him leads you to a new way of existing and living. When you recognize that Jesus picked you to become a part of the love between him and Father God, you choose whether to participate. If you say yes, your life as you know it will change drastically, for sure! Yet, new life in the city with Jesus is always better than the life you leave behind!

New life with Jesus means your community of friends will change. You will lose some old friends along the way, but God will replace them with new friends who are also walking with Jesus Christ into the love of Father God. When you are Father God's daughter and a sister of Jesus Christ, your environment changes. Physically, you are still earthbound, of course! Yet, your thinking and your heart are with Jesus Christ.

Since, then, you have been raised with Christ, set your hearts on things above, where Christ is, seated at the right hand of God. Set your minds on things above, not on earthly things. For you died, and your life is now hidden with Christ in God.

— *Colossians 3:1–3*

In your new life with Jesus Christ, you learn to live in a way that is different from your old life. Every town, city, and state has its own unique way of doing things. For example, in some cities you can ride a bus for transportation. Some cities have curfews for youth. While some locations have mayors to help govern, smaller towns have managers. Each location has its own pattern.

God has a pattern for your life too. When you receive new life from Jesus Christ, day by day, he makes your mind new by shaping it to God's pattern, instead of the old one to which you were accustomed. Before too long, he has transformed you, and the life you once knew no longer exists!

You might be thinking, well, what's so wrong with the life I have right now? Perhaps things are going well for you, and there is little you want to change. That's fantastic, Faithgirl. God is good to people who receive the new life of his Son, Jesus Christ, and to those who do not receive him. A life overflowing with God's goodness, though, is an exclusive benefit of those who choose to follow Jesus Christ to Father God. What will you choose? Keep on reading for more tidbits to help you decide.

Briana's Tidbit #6: I Am the Way and the Truth and the Life

The unfolding events of the mild altercation between Briana, Austin, and Mrs. Gray contain great information to help you understand what Jesus meant by saying, "I am the way and the truth and the life." Here's why.

Briana was irritated when she saw Austin following her to their table, wasn't she? In Briana's defense, Jessica had some strong words for Austin. She told Austin that in the future, if he wanted to speak with Briana, he had to come through her first. Now that's what best friends are for! Jessica is determined that no one is going to get to her best friend and upset her.

Jesus Christ had the same idea in mind when he said, "I am the way and the truth and the life."

Just as Jessica decided that she herself would become the only way Austin could get to Briana, Father God decided that his Son, Jesus Christ, is the only way God's daughters get to him.

> Jesus answered, "I am the way and the truth and the life. No one comes to the Father except through me."
>
> —*John 14:6*

Now, Jesus was a bold leader. He said many things that enraged religious leaders. This, however, is one of Jesus' most controversial statements. As you grow in your love for Jesus and the Father, other people will question whether it is true. That's why the next thing Jesus said is that he's the truth! Faithgirl, remember this: following Jesus Christ is the only way you can get to Father God.

If you think about the bond between Briana and Jessica, you can understand why. Do you remember how old Briana and Jess were when they first met? Seven, right! They've shared tons of memories and have grown to love each other deeply. That's how Father God and Jesus Christ are too. The love they share is extraordinary! Like Briana and Jess, they refuse to stand by and watch other people displease their loved one. God loves you no matter what choices you make. Yet, it is still displeasing to him when you are disagreeable and ignore his directions.

Jesus is incapable of ignoring Father God. He loves the Father too much to disregard his ways and hurt God's heart. Consequently, Jesus Christ is the only person who always pleases Father God because he heeds Father God's words without fail. Knowing you—both how much you crave Father God's love and how you can sometimes displease him, Jesus is the awesome big brother who steps in to help you. He simply tells you, "follow me."

Daughter Deed

To help you think the same way Father God does, will you do a daughter deed and focus on your BFF for a few moments? How long have you known him or her? Where did you meet? What would you do if you knew someone was irritating or displeasing your BFF? When you finish, take a few more minutes and write your friend a note of thanks for his or her friendship. Remember to drop it in the mail!

Thanks, Faithgirl! One of the ways you know God loves you is that he gives you good friends!

Do you remember what happened next, when Briana got mad and raised her voice at Austin? Their teacher, Mrs. Gray, approached the table and tried to get the truth. Initially, Austin denied that he'd called Briana "Butterfingers." Briana told Mrs. Gray that Austin was giving a false impression of the way things were.

Unlike Austin's version of the story, the truth is information that accurately expresses the way a matter or situation actually is. When you tell the truth, it means you're sharing knowledge as it is in reality. The truth is different from your opinion, thoughts, or speculation about the way things are. It is permanent, unchanging, and double-checked over time. For example, in Briana's case, she does not really have fingers made of butter. She never has. She never will. Nothing (including the number of times Austin counts her dropping the basketball!) will ever change that. It is the truth and points to what's really going on.

Jesus Christ described himself as the truth because he's what's really going on! Have you ever heard grown-ups say "It's not about you"? Sure seems like it's all about them, right? That is untrue. According to Father God, it's actually all about Jesus Christ. Everything you know as real in life is pointing to him. This is why he could declare he is the truth.

You see, God's plan is that the world you experience with your five senses—what you see, hear, taste, touch, and smell—serves as a foundation to help you comprehend the true, spiritual reality as you grow up. Your physical life comes first to prepare you for the new spiritual life you can experience in Jesus Christ.

You see, the world as you know it is temporary. Things around you are unpredictable and constantly changing. Jesus Christ remains the same. Remember, one of the qualities of the truth is that it never changes.

Jesus Christ is the same yesterday and today and forever.

—Hebrews 13:8

Another quality of the truth is that other people validate it. Austin confessed, and in the end Mrs. Gray orchestrated the extension of justice, requiring Austin to make amends for dishonoring Briana.

Austin's confession did more than enable Mrs. Gray to make a fair decision. When Austin finally told the truth, it relieved Briana. She was free to continue enjoying her lunch with her friends. That's because knowing the truth liberates you from the traps and pitfalls of life that try to get you down. When you're not tangled up or stuck in messy situations, you're free to live a joyful life!

That's why Jesus Christ followed up saying he is the truth by saying he is the life. Knowing God's Son, Jesus Christ, who is the truth, sets you free too! Free from what? you ask. From the temptations and tricks that try to slip you up and keep you from enjoying life. Following Jesus the truth gives you freedom from bondage, enabling you to walk joyfully into new life!

> Jesus said, "If you hold to my teaching, you are really my disciples. Then you will know the truth, and the truth will set you free."
>
> —John 8:31–32

Are you ready to walk? Then keep reading, Faithgirl; you're on your way!

Briana's Tidbit #7: I Am the Vine; You Are the Branches

Do you remember where most of the football team sat during lunch? Yep, you got it! Outside in the big open space called The Commons. They showed their team spirit and honor for the football players of the past by etching their names and player numbers into the tree trunk. It was a tradition that started when Live Oak first opened. To the team, that trunk was the vital connection that motivated them to win games on Friday night.

The trunk of a tree is like a vine on a plant. Just as the trunk of the Live Oak tree does, the vine provides stability for the branches of a plant, holding those branches up. Although the ground usually obscures the root of a plant, you can see the vine extending up through the earth. Vines also serve as a connector, supplying a pathway for the life-giving nutrients and water to flow to the branches. If you sever the branches from the vine for any reason, the branches soon wither and die.

Are you beginning to see why Jesus Christ said, "I am the vine; you are the branches"? He was sharing the reality that he is the strong, stable support you need to hold you up in life. It can get tough at school sometimes, right? Do you ever feel misunderstood by your family? What about boys like Austin Thomas who insist on annoying you? Sure you're strong, Faithgirl! But all of that is a bit much to bear. Instead of bearing those frustrations, trust that Jesus Christ is your true lifeline of support. With him, you'll exchange your frustrated life for one that is filled with good fruit—and makes Father God smile!

This is to my Father's glory, that you bear much fruit, showing yourselves to be my disciples.

—John 15:8

The vine is the extension of the unseen root showing up through the ground. In the same way, Jesus Christ is the extension of God whom you are unable to see. The unseen spirit of God provides life, like an obscured plant root. Nevertheless, it is Jesus Christ, the true vine, who extends that life to you, one of the branches. He is the one through whom all the blessing and riches of God flow.

And my God will meet all your needs according to the riches of his glory in Christ Jesus.

—Philippians 4:19

Aspire to make that flow through Jesus Christ uninterrupted. By saying he is the vine and you are a branch, Jesus stressed the need for you to stay connected to him. Branches are cut off vines for many reasons. Environmental issues like wind and cold, hungry wild animals, and bugs and insects worming their way through all pose threats to branches on a vine. You too face cold situations sometimes. Your circumstances might make you feel like a wild beast is trying to eat you up! Little by little, worries seem to sneak into your heart, like a pesky inchworm. These all threaten to cut you off from Jesus Christ, the vine.

One of the ways branches are protected is by covering or wrapping them. You can cover yourself too! Ban these branch cutters from your life with a covering of prayer, Faithgirl. Continue talking with God each day. Spend time sharing your thoughts with him and listening for his voice to speak to you. You may feel drawn away from God by many different things and situations. Yet to remain attached to Jesus Christ is to remain in the love of Father God. And his love is what you want, right?

Then, look to Jesus Christ because that is where the Father's love is located. Remember, in Father God's heart, Jesus Christ is the name and character who is far above everything and anyone else. Father God chose to invest all of his love in Jesus for one reason. Although Jesus is one with Father God, he diminished himself to the status of an ordinary, common person. Because Jesus willingly humbled himself in this way, Father God designated the character of this unique Son as the highest aspiration of all other sons and daughters.

Faithgirl, your beginning into the love of Father God starts with the humility of Jesus Christ. Humility is making yourself—your ways, your thoughts, what feels right to you—lower than God's ways and thoughts. You acknowledge that you can do nothing by yourself and become entirely dependent on God. And in that place of humility, you will find that Father God gives you the strength to love him back in the way that pleases him the most.

Daughter, Declare Your Prayer!

Father God, thank you for giving grace to the humble! Your special Son, Jesus Christ, is the way, the truth, and the life. May I follow him, my older brother, all the way to you. May I find your love in him and always stay connected. Thank you for choosing me and making me free to experience new life!

Briana's Banana-Nut Muffins Recipe

What You Need

1/3 cup applesauce

1/2 cup honey

1 teaspoon vanilla extract

2 eggs

3 medium bananas, mashed

1 3/4 cups whole wheat flour

2 teaspoon cinnamon

1 teaspoon nutmeg

1/2 teaspoon salt

1 teaspoon baking soda

1/4 cup hot water

Preheat oven to 350 degrees.

In a large bowl, beat oil and honey together with a wire whisk.

Add eggs, one at a time, and mix well after each addition.

Stir in mashed bananas and vanilla extract.

In another bowl, mix flour, salt, cinnamon, and nutmeg together, and add it to the wet ingredients.

Add baking soda to hot water and stir. Add to mixture.

Spread batter into a greased 9x5 inch loaf pan or into greased muffin tins.

Bake for 60 minutes for the loaf pan or 18 minutes for muffins.

Bread is done when browned and a toothpick inserted in the center comes out clean.

CHAPTER 3

Requesting Your Father's Presence

Briana looked forward to Saturday mornings. She was normally an early riser, but having one day a week just to snooze a little longer was nice. She was bothered when blaring music startled her from her sleep. Her sister's favorite song rang up the stairs, and Briana jumped up out of the bed, threw on her bathrobe, and marched down. Ashley was dancing and shaking carpet freshening powder on the living room floor.

"Excuse me!" Briana said, with her hands on her hips. "In case you didn't notice I'm trying to get some sleep around here."

"Oops. My bad. Sorry Bree. Got little people headed over for the day."

"What little people?"

"Madison and Mason."

"Why can't you go to their house like you usually do?"

"Their parents are doing some painting around the house, and they want to give it time to air out ... and keep the twins from putting their cute little handprints all over the place."

"Makes sense. Well, next time you decide to do housework, can you please try to think about those of us who need a little rest?"

"What's wrong, kiddo? Did you do one backflip too many? I was hoping you'd be up to helping me out."

"No way, those rascals are twice as much work—"

"Fun ... you mean fun. Twins are twice as much fun. I'll even give you a share of the money I make."

"Half?"

"Done."

"So, why are you so willing to share with me all of a sudden?"

Ashley shrugged her shoulders. "I need the help. I'm going to have to wash my hair for a dance at school tonight. While I'm doing that, you can keep an eye on the twins for me."

Briana gave her sister the thumbs up sign. "It's a deal. What time are they coming?"

"You still have your freedom for a couple more hours."

Briana went back up to her room and started getting ready for the arrival of the Foster twins. *I can't wait until I'm a teenager,* she thought. She had a list of all the things she was going to do in a couple of years. Her first priority was to take the babysitting class at the community center, just as Ashley had done. That way, she could earn money and save up for the musical horse carousel-figure she wanted to add to her collection of horse figurines. Ashley made a lot of money babysitting. Briana hoped to do the same.

By the time Mr. Foster rang the doorbell, Briana's focus on her money-saving plan had motivated her enough that she felt up to the challenge of helping Ashley care for energetic Madison and Mason. Boy, was she wrong! Ashley opened the door, and both of the three-year-olds were wailing as they flailed and kicked their poor father, demanding to return home with him.

"Maddie ... honey ... it's okay," Mr. Foster said. "Daddy will be back soon. Don't you want to play with Miss Ashley for a little bit while Mommy and Daddy paint your room?"

"No. Me go home with Daddy!" she said.

Mason jumped down from his father's arms, kicked Ashley in the shin, and then held on to his father's leg as if his life depended on it.

"Hey tough guy," Mr. Foster said, "that's not nice. Tell Miss Ashley you're sorry, okay?"

Mason started crying. "I don't want you to go, Daddy."

Ashley laughed. "Maybe I could help you more if I go paint!"

"Seems like it, huh?" said Mr. Foster. He looked at Madison, and then Mason, rubbing his head. "I'll tell you what, why don't we all go in the house together?"

They all came in, and it seemed like an hour to Briana before Mr. Foster was actually able to leave. He promised the twins he would come back and get them soon. He sang their favorite song. He offered to take them to their favorite candy store, if only they would stay with Ashley until he returned.

Finally, Ashley managed to distract the kids by pulling out some watercolors and letting them finger paint. It was a mess, but it worked ... for a little while.

Briana pointed to the objects in Madison's painting. "Who's that?"

Madison smiled. "Daddy!"

"Here's Daddy! Here's Daddy!" said Mason, pointing to the green blob on his painting.

"Good job!" Briana said. "Can I take these and put them over here to dry? We'll show Daddy as soon as he comes back."

The twins had forgotten their dad was gone. But Briana's words reminded them. She and Ashley looked at each other. "Way to go, Bree," Ashley said.

Madison started humming the nursery song "Frére Jacques" and crying.

"You want to sing, Maddie? I know that song," said Briana. "Are you sleeping ... are you sleeping—"

"No! Not that song!" said Madison.

"Then what song?" said Briana.

"Where is Daddy ... where is Daddy ... where is Daddy?" Madison sang repeatedly.

Ashley joined in, "He's right here ... he's right here," and pointed to Mr. Foster in the family photograph that was stashed in the diaper bag.

Ashley realized Madison was actually starting to sing herself to sleep. They all continued singing the song until finally, Madison and Mason were asleep in their high chairs. Briana ran and grabbed the fluffy red comforter from the linen closet upstairs. When she returned, Ashley had unrolled the futon mattress that the girls used for relaxing while they watched TV. Briana spread the comforter on top of the futon. They moved the Foster twins to the temporary bed for their nap.

Ashley held her pointer finger up to her mouth. "Do you think you'll be okay with them while I wash my hair?" she said.

Briana nodded her head up and down and pretended to swipe the sweat off her eyebrow. "Sure. I think I can handle it," said Briana. "After all that, I need a nap too!" As Ashley walked back up the stairs, Briana peeked over at the twins to make sure they were comfortable. That's when she noticed Madison's big brown eyes filled with water, and one single tear rolling down her chubby cheek. Too tired to put up a fight, the little girl just laid there, crying. Briana laid down on the futon beside her. "Madison, what's wrong?" she said.

Madison's bottom lip was perfectly pink and full. Briana thought if she stuck it out any farther, it would hit the floor. "I want Daddy. Go see Daddy ... pwease?" She looked at Briana, waiting for an answer to her tender request to go be with the father she loved more than anyone else in the world.

Briana's Box

Though Madison is only three years old, she does have Briana in a tough situation! Those big brown eyes were piercing Briana's heart. Now that Madison was no longer screaming, but instead softly pleading to be with her dad, Briana was turning to mush! With Ashley upstairs washing her hair, she knew she was supposed to be the mature, responsible one in the situation. Yet, she was confused about what to do.

If she went to get Ashley, she would prove that she was actually unable to handle it herself. If Briana called Mr. Foster, it would interrupt his painting project. If she did nothing, Madison would continue crying, saddened by her father's absence. As far as Briana could determine, she was stuck in a situation without a way to win.

She inched closer to Madison and stroked the little girl's hair. "Madison, I'm sorry you miss your daddy. I know how you feel," Briana said. Wait a minute, she thought to herself. Where did that come from? "I miss my daddy sometimes too."

Madison shook her head up and down.

"It's true," said Briana. "I wish my dad was here with me, just like you do."

"Where is him?" Madison said.

That's a good question, Briana thought. "He's away for a while. But, do you know what I do when I miss my daddy? I read stories that make me feel better. Can I read you a story?"

"No story. Daddy."

Briana could see that Madison was still exhausted. As she continued stroking Madison's hair and talking, it was becoming more difficult for Madison to stay awake. Her eyes kept rolling back in her head, and Briana knew it would be just a few minutes more and Madison would be back to sleep. Since not talking about Mr. Foster failed to appease Madison, Briana decided that if she listened to Madison talk about her dad long enough, the tired tot might fall back to sleep.

"Do you know your daddy's favorite song, Madison?" Briana said.

Madison smiled and shook her head. "Hmm hmm." She sang a tune that Briana was unable to recognize. "Daddy's favorite."

"Wow. That's a really pretty song," Briana said. "What about Daddy's favorite color? Do you know the color he likes most of all?"

Too close to drifting away to sleep, she pointed to the comforter Briana had spread over the futon.

"Red?" Briana said. "Is Daddy's favorite color red?"

Madison nodded one last time. "My daddy be back soon. Daddy said him be back soon." She closed her eyes, comforted only by the thought that her father would return to get her.

"That's right, Madison. Daddy will be back soon." Briana stared at Madison, thankful that she seemed to be at peace.

Believing with Briana

Have you ever spent time with small children like Briana did? If you have, then you know you can learn a lot by observing them. You can also learn about your relationship with Father God from the attitudes and behavior of small children. Sometimes big kids and grown-ups dishonor small children. Father God honors them above all.

On one occasion, people brought their children to Jesus, hoping that he would touch them. Some of Jesus' followers attempted to prevent the children from touching him. These followers completely dissed the little kids! Jesus was mad about it! He said to them,

> "Let the little children come to me, and do not hinder them, for the kingdom of God belongs to such as these. Truly I tell you, anyone who will not receive the kingdom of God like a little child will never enter it." And he took the children in his arms, placed his hands on them and blessed them.
>
> — *Mark 10:14–16*

Daughter Deed

Why do you think Father God values children so much? Can you do a daughter deed, and write what you know about the attitudes of small children? Think about Mason and Madison and their behavior when their father dropped them off at Briana's house. Why do you think they acted that way?

_____

_____

_____

_____

_____

_____

Briana's experience with Madison and Mason shows you how children feel about their father, and why God values what is in the heart of a small child. Remember when Mason kicked Briana's sister in the shin? Children, like the twins, love spending time with their father. They simply want to stay in his presence forever. Just as Mason and Madison kicked and screamed at the thought of Ashley and Briana taking them away from their father, children of Father God resist when people or the circumstances of life attempt to carry them away.

Father God also loves it when his children know what pleases him. Remember when Briana asked Madison about her father's favorite things? Just as Maddie was able to sing her father's favorite song and point out his favorite color, God loves it when his daughters focus on the things that please him.

What was the last thing Madison told Briana before she finally drifted off to sleep? Right! Our little sleepyhead was at peace when she remembered the promise her father had made to return and pick up her and Mason. She was able to rest because of the trust she had in her father's word. The unwavering trust in the heart of a child is something Father God really loves. Just as Madison rested peacefully because she believed her father's promise, you can rest because you believe in the promises God makes to you.

Let's take a closer look at the beauty of believing captured in Briana's babysitting adventure with Madison and Mason. Now that you've found Father God, the following tidbits will help you receive his love — and love him right back! Adoring Father God includes focusing on . . .

- The Father's Presence
- The Father's Pleasure
- The Father's Promise

Briana's Tidbit #1: The Father's Presence

Madison and Mason were adamant about staying with their father, right? Here's why. The twins know that being with their father is fun! Their father picks them up and puts them high on his shoulders where they can see everything. He sets the twins on his knee and bounces them up and down, like he's a horse galloping through an adventure in the woods. He lets them stand on his feet when he walks so they can take bigger steps. And when they are afraid of the dark at bedtime, Daddy comes and kisses them on the forehead, assuring them that he is there, and everything is going to be okay.

Father God's children know that being with him is fun, too! One of the best things about being with Father God is that he lifts you up higher. In the presence of God, you're like a small toddler on the shoulders of her father, seeing things the way he does. Maybe you didn't earn the grade you wanted on that test. Perhaps Mom won't let you watch that movie. Is there an Austin Thomas-type situation on your mind? You are not always able to see the good in every situation, but Father God can. When things try to take you to a low, sad place, remember to resist leaving your Father's presence! Ask your heavenly Father to pick you up and put you on his shoulders so you can see your life the way he does.

Being in Father God's presence is also like a small child bouncing on the knee of her father, as if riding a horse. As her father hums that old familiar, lively, and upbeat horse-riding melody, she closes her eyes and squeals with delight. Though the terrain beneath them is treacherous with bumps and pits, she trusts that she is safe in her father's arms. Likewise, the road of your life is complete with obstacles meant to slow you down or even wipe you out altogether. Yet focus on staying in the presence of Father God, Faithgirl! There in the Father's presence, potentially disastrous experiences become delightful days shared with the one who loves you most.

Praise Prompt

Psalm 16 helps daughters focus on Father God's presence. As you read it, think about all of the ways you benefit by staying with God. Thank him for the blessing of simply being with him!

Psalm 16

Keep me safe, my God,
for in you I take refuge.
I say to the Lord, "You are my Lord;
apart from you I have no good thing."
I say of the holy people who are in the land,
"They are the noble ones in whom is all my delight."
Those who run after other gods will suffer more and more.
I will not pour out libations of blood to such gods
or take up their names on my lips.
Lord, you alone are my portion and my cup;
you make my lot secure.
The boundary lines have fallen for me in pleasant places;
surely I have a delightful inheritance.
I will praise the Lord, who counsels me;
even at night my heart instructs me.
I keep my eyes always on the Lord.
With him at my right hand, I will not be shaken.
Therefore my heart is glad and my tongue rejoices;
my body also will rest secure,
because you will not abandon me to the realm of the dead,
nor will you let your faithful one see decay.
You make known to me the path of life;
you will fill me with joy in your presence,
with eternal pleasures at your right hand.

Madison loved standing on top of her father's feet while he walked. The steps that her father takes are much bigger than her three-year-old strides. His long, strong legs are able to travel farther distances much faster than she could ever hope to! Also, by standing on him and letting him do the work of walking, she can know beyond a doubt that she will get safely to her destination. Lastly, walking with her dad helps her understand how to walk on her own.

Father God loves this about little children! It shows that their hearts understand how to walk. He wants his daughters to love walking with him just as Madison enjoys walking with her father. Just as Madison's dad's legs are stronger and faster than hers are, Father God is stronger and faster than you are. By walking with him, you'll be able to go the distance in life, without quitting or giving up too soon. Also, walking with Father God is the only way to be sure you will arrive to the future he has planned for you, Faithgirl. Finally, walking with Father God initially will teach you how to stand up tall and walk on your own as his daughter. If you learn from Father God first ...

When you walk, your steps will not be hampered; when you run, you will not stumble. Hold on to instruction, do not let it go; guard it well, for it is your life.

— Proverbs 4:12 – 13

Nighttime can be a scary experience for toddlers like Madison and Mason. Admit it, Faithgirl. You even get frightened sometimes at night, don't you? What about after you watched that scary movie? Even though you know it's just a movie, sometimes the images that you've seen spook you just a touch. For small children, the knowledge of their father is assurance enough that everything is fine. They trust him to protect them from darkness and evil.

Father God longs for his daughters to demonstrate the same trust in him, even in times of growing darkness. Watching a movie is one thing. You can always remind yourself that a movie is not real, right? But, what about the reports of wars all around the world? Have you heard the true stories of young girls your age being kidnapped?

Those sad, dark realities could make you fearful. Instead of embracing fear, forbid it to enter your heart. If you feel afraid, act with strength and wisdom that comes from your Father. Use wisdom to stay out of dangerous situations in the first place. But if you do find yourself sensing trouble, shout for help, run to a well-lit place, do what you have to until you're safe. Discernment is a gift from God that helps us detect danger. It gives us an awareness to seek safety both physically and spiritually. Remember, you are a Faithgirl! What it means to be loved by Father God is that in his presence, you are safe from evil.

Daughter, You Decide

Do you know what to do if a stranger approaches you? What should you do if you were walking in the park and someone you did not know called you by name? What can you do to keep yourself safe?

Praise Prompt

Psalm 91 describes the safety experienced by daughters who learn to trust Father God and stay in his presence. As you read it, think about some of the dangerous situations you've heard about young girls like you being involved in recently. Consider some of the situations in your own life when you think God protected you. Thank Father God for keeping you safe!

Psalm 91

Whoever dwells in the shelter of the Most High
will rest in the shadow of the Almighty.
I will say of the Lord, "He is my refuge and my fortress,
my God, in whom I trust."
Surely he will save you
from the fowler's snare
and from the deadly pestilence.
He will cover you with his feathers,
and under his wings you will find refuge;
his faithfulness will be your shield and rampart.
You will not fear the terror of night,
nor the arrow that flies by day,
nor the pestilence that stalks in the darkness,
nor the plague that destroys at midday.
A thousand may fall at your side,
ten thousand at your right hand,
but it will not come near you.
You will only observe with your eyes
and see the punishment of the wicked.
If you say, "The Lord is my refuge,"
and you make the Most High your dwelling,

no harm will overtake you,
no disaster will come near your tent.
For he will command his angels concerning you
to guard you in all your ways;
they will lift you up in their hands,
so that you will not strike your foot against a stone.
You will tread on the lion and the cobra;
you will trample the great lion and the serpent.
"Because he loves me," says the Lord, "I will rescue him;
I will protect him, for he acknowledges my name.
He will call on me, and I will answer him;
I will be with him in trouble,
I will deliver him and honor him.
With long life I will satisfy him
and show him my salvation."

Briana's Tidbit #2: The Father's Pleasure

When you love someone, you know what pleases him or her. Not only do you know it, but you also want to be pleasing to him or her. That's why Madison started singing her father's favorite song when Briana asked her if she knew it. Madison knew the song true enough. Beyond that though, she enjoyed singing it because she knew it made her father happy.

Father God loves that small children know what is pleasing, and they want to do it. He desires that you too, as a daughter, will learn what pleases him, and that you will long to do it with all your heart as an expression of the love you have for him. Like Madison, Father God hopes that you will discover his favorite songs and sing them to him from your heart, even if nobody else understands!

He also wants you to learn his favorite colors. Yes, colors are special to Father God too! Didn't Madison tell Briana her dad's favorite color was red? Well, Father God likes red too, and he wants you to believe in the power of what the color red represents. Here's why.

When Father God sees red, it reminds him of his favorite Son, Jesus Christ. The color red makes Father God think about how willing Jesus was to give his life — his own blood — so that you and God's entire creation could be connected to the Father. Remember, God is fair and just. One of Father God's guidelines to keep things fair is that when you make an agreement with someone, you prove it by giving blood. Jesus Christ and Father God made an agreement in which Jesus chose to give his life, and Father God would forgive us and fill our hearts with love and devotion to him. Thanks to that red blood of Jesus Christ, Father God forgives you and draws you close to him as a daughter!

Briana's Tidbit #3: The Father's Promise

Since you're already thinking about promises sealed with blood, let's think back to what finally got little Miss Madison to drift off to sleep. Do you remember what she said to Briana as she closed her eyes? That's right!

Madison was at peace because she remembered her father said he was coming back to pick her up. In three years time, the toddler had enough experience with her father to know that the words she heard from him were always true. Even though she could not see him at that moment, Madison trusted her father enough to know that if he said it, he was going to do it. Rather than worrying about whether he was coming back, she took the rest that her tired little body so desperately needed.

More than anything else, it's that kind of heart attitude that pleases Father God. Children demonstrate this faith better than anyone else! If pleasing God is your goal, you will only be successful with faith like this. Here's why.

The faith Madison showed was based on who her father was. It wasn't that Madison believed it because it was a small or easy promise. She didn't only believe because he had picked her up from other places in the past. And, if anyone else had said those same words, she might not have believed them. Madison believed because she heard words from her daddy.

In the same way, Father God wants you to trust in him because you understand his character. As you grow in relationship with him, his desire is that you expect him to fulfill every promise he gives you because you understand the nature of your Father who made you the promise.

Among the things you have learned about God's character through his Son, Jesus Christ, focus on this as you think about walking with childlike faith. Father God cannot lie. Lying is inconsistent with God's nature. A person—like only God is—who is compassionate, gracious, slowly angered, fair, and full of love and loyalty for thousands of other people is incapable of lying.

The rest of us, though, are perfectly capable of lying, and unfortunately, we do. Often, we make commitments, vows, and promises to each other and we break them for many different reasons. With so many broken promises between you and other people, you could easily forget that God does not and cannot lie. Yet remember ...

God is not human, that he should lie, not a human being, that he should change his mind.

- -Numbers 23:19

So, when it comes to the words of your heavenly Father, Faithgirl, remember Briana's adventures in babysitting Madison. Get the rest that you need from worrying about your situation. Father God's vows and promises to you are unchangeable!

Daughter, You Decide

Hate is a strong word, don't you think? It's hard to believe that Father God would ever use it, but there are some things he hates. One of the things God despises is a tongue that tells lies. Sometimes we lie because we think telling the truth might hurt someone else's feelings. Now that you know how Father God feels about lying, would you tell a fib to protect someone else's feelings?

Beginning with Briana

You, however, might feel yourself changing as you're reading all of this. That's a good thing! Maybe you're starting to realize you've let the business of school, practices, or church take you out of Father God's presence. Sometimes you can focus so much on pleasing yourself or other people that you forget all about pleasing him. Or maybe you want to believe in Father God's promises to you, but you have never even heard what those promises are!

Daughter Deed

If you feel like that might be you, can you do this daughter deed, Faithgirl? Grab a sheet of paper and some colored pencils, markers, or crayons if you have them. Write the words below on your paper, and decorate it however you like. Then hang it on your mirror in your room or in your bathroom. Every time you look in that mirror, say these words aloud with a smile, because they are Father God's greatest words to you!

(Insert your name here), love the Lord your God with all your heart and with all your soul and with all your mind. This is the first and greatest commandment.

Got it posted up? Good job! Now, think about when you can spend some time alone with Father God each day. Can you wake up a little earlier before you start dressing for school? Do you have a few minutes after school? What about turning off the TV for thirty minutes and talking to Father God instead? On the lines below, write down when you think you can make time to share with him. What time and the length of time are between you and God, but do try to set a goal and stick with it every day!

_____

_____

_____

_____

_____

As you make special time with him your number one priority, everything else—even pleasing him and receiving his promises—will fall into place!

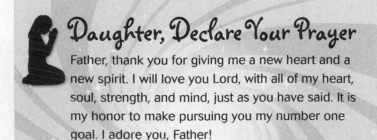

Daughter, Declare Your Prayer

Father, thank you for giving me a new heart and a new spirit. I will love you Lord, with all of my heart, soul, strength, and mind, just as you have said. It is my honor to make pursuing you my number one goal. I adore you, Father!

CHAPTER 4

Receiving Your Father's Children

The collective gasp of the crowd was the last thing Briana heard. After that, the pain in her leg was so intense she could only think one thing. Lord, please send someone to help me! With that simple prayer, Briana closed her eyes and drifted off to sleep.

When she woke up, she was a little confused at first. It didn't take long, though, for her to rub the icky crust caused by her dried up tears from her eyes. That's when she saw her right leg dangling from a leg brace, and understood why she was in Children's Hospital. Briana had broken her leg performing a cheerleading stunt at the half-time show of Friday night's football game. Not cool.

Jessica was the first one to notice Briana was awake. "Hey, Bree!" she said.

"Hey Jess. Please tell me I did not break my leg in front of the entire school at the game."

"Sorry. Don't besties always tell each other the truth? Everyone knows that it wasn't your fault, though. They think you're completely brave."

"Did Austin Thomas see it?"

"Yeah, but who saw you isn't important."

Briana's mom stood up from her chair and walked around to the side of the hospital bed opposite Jessica. "Not so fast, Jessica. Austin—and a lot of other folks—are deeply concerned about you. In fact," she said pointing to the door, "they are all just outside waiting to find out your condition."

Briana dropped her head and put her hands over her eyes, hiding her face. "Are you serious?" Briana said.

"Absolutely," she said. "They even decided to reschedule the game for a later date so your classmates and teachers could come be with you."

"So you mean I totally ruined the game? What a disaster! How can I go back to school now?"

A soft tap on the door interrupted Briana's frustrated inquiry. It was her pediatrician, Dr. Sutton. "Well hello, Briana, Mrs. Robinson," she said. "Looks like you have a nasty fracture there young lady!"

Briana's mom said, "Exactly how bad is it, Dr. Sutton?"

"Mom, chill," said Briana. "It's not that serious. The main thing is that the entire school saw me make a clumsy mistake and ruin a perfectly good football game."

"You know, Briana," Dr. Sutton said, "that's only one way of looking at things. The way I see it, what you call a clumsy mistake was actually a gutsy move that really kept one of your teammates from sustaining an injury much worse than yours."

"She's right, Bree," said Jessica. "Don't you remember at camp how we learned about spotting during a basket toss? If you would have let Isa hit the ground after throwing her up like that, she could've ended up paralyzed."

"That's correct," said Dr. Sutton. "Isa and her family have been right here with you since you got here, and I'll tell you what. They certainly don't think you made a clumsy mistake."

"We practiced that toss a million times. I don't understand what went wrong."

"And all of your practice paid off. You caught Isa exactly as you should have."

Briana's mom sighed. "Does she need surgery, Dr. Sutton?"

"I'm afraid so. The swelling is severe right now, so we're going to have to wait a few days at least. But I think surgery is our best option in her case. Take a look."

Dr. Sutton walked over to the X-ray viewer and put the pictures of Briana's leg to the light for everyone to see. Mrs. Robinson and Jessica gathered around as Dr. Sutton showed them the fracture in Briana's leg and explained why she needed surgery. When she was done, she walked back over to Briana and gave her a rub on the head.

"She'll still be able to cheer though, right?" said Jessica.

Dr. Sutton looked at Briana. "The rest of this year is out. You will have to go through physical therapy for a few months to get your leg strong again. But by summer camp, you should be good to go."

The thought of missing the rest of football season, not to mention all of the spring sports and activities, was devastating to Briana. What kind of captain sits out on the sidelines while her team does all of the hard work? She felt like she was disappointing everybody, including herself.

"You're a good friend to have around when a girl needs a little help. Is it okay with you if I go and share with your friends out there what's going on with your leg?"

"Sure. That's cool," she said.

"And how about visitors? I want to keep you in here this weekend and let the nurses help you get that pain under control. But you've got a lot of people out there who really want to see you now. Do you mind?"

Briana's mom answered. "Yes, Dr. Sutton, let's wait on the visitors—"

"No, Mom. It's fine. I'm okay, really."

"Are you sure, sweetheart? You really need to get some rest—"

"Seriously, Mom. I'm fine."

"Great," said Dr. Sutton. "I'll let your nurse know that it's okay for you to have visitors. Two or three at a time, okay?"

Briana nodded her head and attempted a small smile. "Thank you." Dr. Sutton walked out of the room, and Briana prepared for the onslaught of concerned Live Oak Lions headed her way. "How do I look?" she asked Jessica.

"A mess." Jessica grabbed a brush from Briana's hot pink duffle bag. She pulled Briana's hair up to a high ponytail on top of her head, finishing it off with a white bow. "There. That's better."

Briana tugged at the dingy hospital gown she was wearing. "And what about this?"

"Uh ... that stays on for now. You need to stay comfortable."

"Who says comfortable can't be cute? This is horrible! Can't I at least put a cute tee shirt on top before my friends come in? You did bring me something nicer than this to put on, right Mom?"

Mrs. Robinson shook her head yes. She had packed Briana's bag with everything she would need during her hospital stay. But it was too late for Bree to change clothes.

There was a soft tap on the door and Mrs. Thomas, Austin's mother, poked her head inside. "Knock, knock," she said. Briana's mom signaled that it was okay to enter, and the parents greeted each other. Then Austin's dad walked over to the bedside and gently patted Briana on her head.

"Good to see you, Miss Robinson. How are you feeling?"

"I'm okay, Pastor Thomas. Thank you for asking."

"Your doctor tells us you're in a lot of pain and will need surgery for your injury. I don't want to keep you from your rest for long, but can we pray with you?"

"I would really like that, sir."

Pastor Thomas directed his wife, Austin, Briana's mom, and Jessica to join him at the bedside. They made a semicircle around Briana and prayed for her full recovery. Briana had closed her eyes during the prayer. When she opened them, her eyes fell on Austin for the first time since he and his family had come into her room.

He was standing at the foot of the bed, looking a bit timid. She thought, he's probably just embarrassed by that big ketchup stain smeared over the number 23 of his Lions basketball jersey he's wearing. She pointed to the smear. "Did you miss your mouth?"

In the few months she had known him, he always had a quick joke. Not this time. He simply touched her on the foot of her uninjured leg and smiled.

"Are you comfortable?" he said.

"Not so much."

"That was a dumb question. I just want you to be—"

"I am." Briana reached to pull the blanket up closer to her waist, but she couldn't stretch far enough.

"Can I get that for you?" Austin said.

Briana was frustrated that she was incapable of helping herself. For the next several months, she was going to be limited. She didn't like the idea of relying on other people to do things that she was accustomed to doing on her own. How could she go from being the strongest athlete on the squad to a broken-legged bowhead in the bed? With tears in her eyes, she dropped her head, admitting to herself, her family, and her friends the frailty caused by her broken leg. "Yes, I need your help."

"You got it." He walked from the foot of the bed to the right side where his parents were standing. They moved back so he could adjust the blanket for Briana. "Oh wait! I have something else for you too," he said, walking over to the chair where he'd placed his backpack. He pulled out a white wicker basket wrapped in hot pink cellophane paper. It had a cute plastic megaphone attached to the top. "Here you go," he said. She had never seen a basket decorated like that before. Inside the basket were her favorite treats—mini banana-nut muffins and lots of fruit. "Just what the doctor ordered," he said.

"Thanks, two-three," Briana said. "That's really sweet."

Ashley walked in just in time to keep Briana from trying to come up with something to say to avoid the awkward silence. She rushed over to the bed. "Hey, sister. How's the leg?"

"It's been better," Briana said.

"I'm sorry it took me so long to get here. I had to wait for the Fosters to get home. With all those people out there, doesn't look like you needed me though!"

"Yeah. I know, right? Dr. Sutton said it was pretty crowded."

"That's an understatement, Bree. It's packed. I had a really hard time getting in here. Have you thought about going out there just to let everyone know how you're doing?" Ashley looked at their mom.

"I don't know about that. Do you even feel up to it, honey?" said Mrs. Robinson.

"Well, wheeling me out there would be much easier than trying to get everyone in here two or three at a time." Briana slicked her hair back with her hand. "Even though I look ridiculous."

"Sweetheart, you look just fine," said Austin's mom. She turned to Mrs. Robinson. "Maybe you should call a nurse in here to see if she can go out?"

Briana's mom pressed the call light beside Briana's bed, and her nurse soon came in. Mrs. Robinson explained that they thought it would make more sense for Briana to greet everyone in the waiting room and requested permission to take her out. Within minutes, Briana was up and sitting in a wheelchair, with Ashley behind her ready to roll her into the waiting room.

After Ashley mashed the button, the huge double doors leading into the waiting area opened slowly. Briana reached her arm back over her shoulder, grabbing for her big sister's hand steering the wheelchair.

"You okay with this?" said Ashley.

"Yep. Just a little nervous about all eyes being on me and my big blunder."

"They're not here to kick you because you're down, sister. They're here to help you stand back up," she said. Then Ashley pushed her sister on through.

When the doors finally opened, the spectacle before Briana astounded her. Looking at the cheery faces of dozens of well-wishers welcoming her, she felt like the bright lights from the football stadium had made their way into the hospital waiting room. The sight of the massive gathering of friends, teachers, school officials, and church members flooded Briana's heart with gratitude. The painful misery of her injury evaporated among the black and gold balloon bouquets, the smell of yellow roses, and the sounds of her favorite cheer playlist streaming from the jam box. What mattered most, though, were her fellow squad members surrounding Isa who stood there uninjured, still in her Lions' cheerleading uniform, and holding a vividly decorated banner that read: Way to go Briana!

Briana's Box

Have you ever been to a hospital? You know it's one of the least fun places you can be, especially when you're the patient! Sicknesses, weakness, brokenness—like in Briana's case—are difficult conditions to endure. Here's why.

Do you remember how Briana felt when Austin had to help her with the blanket? Frustrated, right! She did not want people to think of her as a weak person who was unable to do simple things for herself. This is an attitude of self-reliance. To be self-reliant means that you believe you can do everything for yourself, without the help of anyone else. Girls who are self-reliant believe they have all the strength and power they need to get a job done by themselves.

Does this sound like anyone you know? The truth is, at one time or another, we all have demonstrated a self-reliant attitude! We dislike sickness, weakness, and brokenness because they force us to own up to the truth that we need help, destroying the wrong idea that as a human being you are enough all by yourself.

Father God actually goes against such proud, self-reliant people. On the other hand, do you remember what Briana finally said to Austin? That's right. She dropped her head and admitted she needed help. Faithgirl, when you bow your head and admit to Father God that you need his help, he gives you the special ability to accomplish everything he wants you to do. That powerful ability is grace, a treasured gift from Father God to his sons and daughters.

Like the coolest presents always do, Father God gives you the gift of grace in a unique package. Remember the gift basket Briana got from Austin? She had never seen anything like it before. The container was unique. Can you think of anything—or better yet, anyone—who is unique to Father God? That's right, you got it, girl! Jesus Christ.

Just as Briana's gift from Austin came in a unique package, God gives you his grace in his unique Son, Jesus Christ. Keep in mind that Father God pours everything that he is—love, goodness, compassion, fairness, and grace—into his Son, Jesus Christ. Jesus Christ, then, extends the grace of the Father to you.

Yet, not only to you! You are one daughter among many daughters and sons who are extended from Jesus Christ. Just like you, all God's children receive his grace. Grace works differently in each one. That is why it is important to accept your brothers and sisters. Father God has a plan, and every one of his children has a job to do to help finish the plan. The gift of grace is what God gives us to help each of us do our own part—a part that no one else can fulfill in quite the same way. Briana would not have received her favorite muffins, delivered with a joke and smile, if it were not for Austin!

> Just as each of us has one body with many members, and these members do not all have the same function, so in Christ we, though many, form one body, and each member belongs to all the others. We have different gifts, according to the grace given us.
>
> —*Romans 12:4–6*

Do you remember how Briana felt when she saw those doors to the waiting area open? Even though messing up in front of everyone at the half-time show bummed her out, Briana had an entire hospital waiting room full of people cheering her on toward recovery. You could say they are Briana's team, or family. In the same way, as a beautiful daughter of Father God, you have an entire family cheering you on through the game of life as you experience ups and downs, wins and losses, blessings and tough breaks. As you see your family in God show up in your life, may you be grateful, just like Briana, knowing God has sent you help. Are you ready to learn more about your relationships with brothers and sisters in Father God's family? Then read on, Faithgirl!

Believing with Briana

Who connected Briana with her family in the waiting room by rolling her out in the wheelchair? Right, her older sibling, Ashley! Ashley was the firstborn child of their parents. You have an older sibling—the firstborn—who connects you with the family of God too. What's his name? Jesus, you got it!

Jesus Christ is like Briana's sister, Ashley, in another way too. Do you remember that Ashley was unable to be physically present with Briana? She wasn't at the hospital at first. Likewise, your big brother Jesus Christ is not present physically in this world. Jesus lived as a man until his thirties. With his death, Jesus finished the job Father God had sent him to do in the world. Father God then used his mighty power to bring Jesus back to life and seat Jesus Christ at his right-hand side on his throne in the heavenly realm.

Though Father God wanted Jesus to be with him in the heavenly place, he also desired the work of his Son, Jesus Christ, to continue, so he could have as many daughters and sons as possible. While he was alive in the world,

Jesus went through all the towns and villages, teaching in their synagogues, proclaiming the good news of the kingdom and healing every disease and sickness.

— *Matthew 9:35*

To keep the good deeds of Jesus going, Father God decided that all daughters and sons working together would serve as Jesus's new physical body in the world. By following Jesus, you become a part of this body of Christ, learning his ways and doing what he did.

Whatever Jesus did, he did with a special attitude in his heart. Jesus' way of doing things was with an attitude of loving self-sacrifice. That same way of doing things — in giving yourself away for someone else's good — is how you and your sisters and brothers in the body of Christ will live now.

Having a heart committed to loving self-sacrifice meant Jesus endured some heart-wrenching conditions. Yet, he endured them because of how much he loves God the Father and you. Jesus Christ's loving self-sacrifice caused him to suffer:

- Rejection
- Sickness
- Pain
- Piercing
- Crushing
- Discipline
- Wounding

That's probably not an example you're excited about following, right? You don't want to be connected to a body that has to go through that! Well, hold on just a minute, Faithgirl. It's not the end of Jesus' story! Remember, he *endured*! Yes, he experienced it, but he also beat it in the end! Jesus was confident and reliant on Father God's love for him. He knew that if he would commit to loving self-sacrifice, in the end he would have great joy being with the Father.

For the joy set before him he endured the cross, scorning its shame, and sat down at the right hand of the throne of God. Consider him who endured such opposition from sinners, so that you will not grow weary and lose heart.

— *Hebrews 12:2–3*

Praise Prompt

Psalm 30 describes that though tough times do come, good times are up ahead for daughters who stick with God! As you read it, think about the people you love most in your life. Consider the conditions you would endure so they could be well. Thank Father God that because you're his daughter, your joy exceeds sorrow!

Psalm 30

I will exalt you, Lord,
for you lifted me out of the depths
and did not let my enemies gloat over me.
Lord my God, I called to you for help,
and you healed me.
You, Lord, brought me up from the realm of the dead;
you spared me from going down to the pit.
Sing the praises of the Lord, you his faithful people;
praise his holy name.

For his anger lasts only a moment,
but his favor lasts a lifetime;
weeping may stay for the night,
but rejoicing comes in the morning.
When I felt secure, I said,
"I will never be shaken."
Lord, when you favored me,
you made my royal mountain stand firm;
but when you hid your face,
I was dismayed.
To you, Lord, I called;
to the Lord I cried for mercy:
"What is gained if I am silenced,
if I go down to the pit?
Will the dust praise you?
Will it proclaim your faithfulness?
Hear, Lord, and be merciful to me;
Lord, be my help."
You turned my wailing into dancing;
you removed my sackcloth and clothed me with joy,
that my heart may sing your praises and not be silent.
Lord my God, I will praise you forever.

Now that you know that Jesus' way of loving self-sacrifice is temporarily brutal yet blessed in the end, you're probably beginning to understand the importance of accepting your siblings in the family of God. You need the grace that God gave them, and they need the grace that God gave you! Jesus Christ himself connected with others to help him complete the work Father God assigned to him.

While he was in the world, Jesus had followers whom Father God chose to help Jesus fulfill his purpose. In the same way, your brothers and sisters in the family of God are people he chose to assist you in getting your job done. As God's beautiful daughter, you have inherited a huge family who is committed to your well-being and success. Father God looks to your brothers and sisters as coworkers with him who make sure you receive your:

- Practice
- Provision
- Prayer
- Produce
- Prize

Now that's some good news! Briana's tidbits will help you learn more about these five functions of your siblings in God's family, so keep reading, Faithgirl. And hello there, sister! Welcome to the family of faith!

Briana's Tidbit #1: Practice

Do you remember when Mrs. Robinson, Briana's mom, wanted her to get some rest instead of seeing visitors? Like Briana, you probably wish that your mom would worry a little less about you, and allow you to make your own decisions. You are definitely becoming more responsible for yourself. Still, you want to make good choices that help you become the girl Father God intends, right? Then you need training and practice!

Father God will train you by giving you special members in your new family who function just like parents do. They are your brothers and sisters, yes. Yet, because they've been walking close to God longer than you have, they can direct and guide you the way that a mother and father do. They will gently serve you in the way a parent serves his or her own children.

Instead, we were like young children among you. Just as a nursing mother cares for her children, so we cared for you. Because we loved you so much, we were delighted to share with you not only the gospel of God but our lives as well.

— 1 Thessalonians 2:7–8

At times, you might feel that they are nagging. After all, you're no baby! Yet, they are teaching and training you so you will be well prepared to carry out the role Father God has for you in his plan. Training is a major part of parenting.

My son, keep your father's commands and do not forsake your mother's teaching. Bind them always on your heart; fasten them around your neck. When you walk, they will guide you; when you sleep, they will watch over you; when you awake, they will speak to you. For this command is a lamp, this teaching is a light, and correction and instruction are the way to life.

— Proverbs 6:20–23

Daughter Deed

Do you get tired of grown-ups constantly telling you what to do? Can you do this daughter deed, Faithgirl? In the space below, write how you feel about all the things the adults you live with ask you to do. Think about how doing those things is going to help you in the future. Do your responsibilities in your home really matter? Or do you feel like doing the same thing over and over again is just a big waste of time?

_____

_____

_____

_____

_____

_____

Through her accident, Briana learned that doing the same thing many times is good training. Do you remember when Dr. Sutton told her it was a good thing they had practiced that basket toss so many times? If Briana had not repeatedly practiced catching Isa, she would have dropped her on the floor. Not good. The accident would have been much worse than it was. Yet, because Briana had performed that same stunt many times, it was a habit. Catching Isa was her natural response, instead of letting her friend crash to the ground.

Faithgirl, without proper practice and training, your decisions and choices will leave you crashing down to the ground and your life spiraling out of Father God's loving control. You may think it useless repeating tasks and assignments that your older siblings in your faith family tell you to do. Does Bree's accident change your mind? Instead, remember that your family is actually helping you establish wise thoughts and ways that lead to life.

Most of all remember, they're doing it because they love you.

Briana's Tidbit #2: Provision

Do you remember when Briana was trying to get all cute before her visitors came in? Her mother had lovingly packed Briana's duffle bag, filling it with everything she would need while she was in the hospital. That's because loving you includes providing for you. It was important to Mrs. Robinson that Briana had the resources she needed.

Supplying what you need is one of Father God's top priorities too. He wants to meet all of your needs, both physical and spiritual. Often, your sisters and brothers in the body of Christ are his instruments for providing the resources you need. Sharing is one of the best benefits of belonging to the family of God.

Now the multitude of those who believed were of one heart and one soul; neither did anyone say

that any of the things he possessed was his own, but they had all things in common.

—Acts 4:32 (NKJV)

And you thought it was just a reminder for two-year-olds! Think again, Faithgirl! God wants his family members to share with one another, so that none of his children goes without the necessities of life. Let's face it, there are some basic things, like food, clothing, and shelter, that we all need to survive in our physical world. Father God expects his daughters and sons to distribute those resources to all people who are in need of them, and especially to people who are siblings in his family.

Daughter, You Decide

With so many choices these days, it's probably tough knowing the difference between a genuine need and a desire. A need is something you must have in order to exist. A want, or desire, is something you'd like to have, yet is unnecessary for your survival. What matters most to you? What matters most to Father God?

Do you have a responsibility to secure the resources you need to survive? Of course you do! When you talk about what you want to become when you grow up, it shows that God is already giving you ideas about how you will become a productive, resourceful woman. Not much longer and you'll get to it, girl! As you keep walking with Father God, you will become a mature daughter, who he blesses with so many resources that you have enough for yourself and to share with others. Until then, trust Father God. Remember he has adopted you into the family that includes your big brother, Jesus Christ, and deposited all you will ever need in him.

Briana's Tidbit #3: Prayer

Speaking of big brothers, Briana learned that having a big brother around can come in handy. Do you remember when Austin's dad, Pastor Thomas, walked into Briana's hospital room? He had little to say and assured Briana that he intended to stay briefly. That's because he was most interested in praying for Briana's recovery. He asked Father God to provide the healing that Briana needed in her leg, so she could return to the work of leading her squad.

In God's family, one of the most significant things your sisters and brothers will do for you is pray. You have sisters and brothers whose number one priority is to pray for you. Like Pastor Thomas, these siblings understand that when you walk closely with God, your prayers are powerful and they work! Pastor Thomas wasted little time but got right down to the business of communicating with Father God. Your praying siblings know that lengthy words are unimpressive to the Father. He sees you at all times, and he knows what you need before you utter one word anyway! The brother who loves praying for you more than any other, Jesus Christ, said you should pray like this:

> " 'Our Father in heaven, hallowed be your name,
> your kingdom come, your will be done, on earth
> as it is in heaven. Give us today our daily bread.
> And forgive us our debts, as we also have forgiven
> our debtors. And lead us not into temptation, but
> deliver us from the evil one.' "
>
> — *Matthew 6:9–13*

What else did Pastor Thomas do? Right! He directed everyone else in the room to encircle Briana and join in praying. Faithgirl, you can pray by yourself, and your heavenly Father will hear you and respond. He loves you just that much. But guess what? The force of praying sisters and brothers is greater. Father God's ultimate desire is for a family, a large community of children who love him. Though he starts with just one person, his hope is that the one will expand to include many, many more people. So when two or three of his kids get together to pray about things affecting the family, he gets excited! In fact, he's so thrilled that he uses all his power to do what they ask of him!

> "Again, truly I tell you that if two of you on earth
> agree about anything they ask for, it will be done
> for them by my Father in heaven. For where two or
> three gather in my name, there am I with them."
>
> — *Matthew 18:19–20*

Briana's Tidbit #4: Produce

Two-three was starting to become someone special to Briana. You do remember who that is, don't you? Yep, you got it, one Austin Thomas. Initially, she seemed to care little for Austin. But, through her unfortunate accident and hospitalization, she was learning that sometimes bad situations actually bring out the best of what is inside of you — and other people you thought you knew.

When Austin showed up in Briana's room, it taught her that she really didn't know him at all. It surprised her that he even cared whether she was all right. Yet, as she stared at him standing at the foot of her bed with that silly ketchup stain on his jersey, she realized Austin really was concerned about her. The compassion he showed her by bringing her a basket full of mini-muffins and fruit made her heart thaw from the frost that kept her from liking him.

Producing fruit is another thing brothers and sisters in the body of Christ help you do. Not the fruit that was in Briana's basket, though! The kind of fruit that comes from being God's daughter. It's called fruit of the Spirit. Fruit of the Spirit are the character traits God's presence in your life causes to grow inside of you and flow from your heart. You can most clearly see the fruit of the spirit in the way you relate to other people, especially during difficult times. That's why when Austin showed Briana compassion, she was able to treat him gently. Despite his stupid jokes and her tough exterior, he's a caring individual, and she's gentler.

Father God uses tough times like Briana's injury to highlight the areas in your heart that are unlike his. He also uses people who think and feel differently than you do to show you where there are weeds and rotten fruit instead of fruit of his spirit! Even during unpleasant circumstances with imperfect people (which all of us except for Jesus Christ are!) as his daughter, Father God is cultivating these nine qualities to flow from your heart to your brothers and sisters, and even those people who are not in the family of faith:

- Love
- Joy
- Peace
- Patience
- Kindness
- Goodness
- Faithfulness
- Gentleness
- Self-control

Got fruit? Fantastic, Faithgirl! Fruit of the Spirit is sweet indeed, but the prize of Father God is better! Read Briana's last tidbit to learn why!

Briana's Tidbit #5: Prize

Briana learned that having a big sister like Ashley around does come in handy. Do you remember when Briana grabbed her sister's hand before they went into the waiting room to see everyone? She was feeling uneasy about what was in front of her, looming on the other side of those intimidating double doors. Briana was embarrassed, thinking her accident a clumsy mistake. Ashley reassured Briana that no one was looking to belittle her, but that the waiting room was full of folks who were there to support her. Then Ashley pushed Briana through to the crowd— with all of their gifts and gratitude—on the other side.

Faithgirl, what it means to be Father God's beautiful daughter is that there's a reward for you too! You have an inheritance waiting for you in the heavenly realm where Father God is now. Like Ashley rolling Briana in the wheelchair toward the waiting room, you just need a change of perspective, some encouraging words, and a little push from a brother or sister to help you receive it.

Your new family helps you see things the way Father God sees them. Sometimes, especially when you're not feeling like your best, you can focus on all the wrong things. You may dwell on the pain or embarrassment you feel, instead of the goodness of God that is in every situation. In Briana's case, she considered herself a klutz, but she really saved Isa's life—truly, a phenomenal deed in God's eyes! Jessica and Dr. Sutton helped her see it that way. Because your brothers and sisters are also following Jesus Christ to the Father, they can help you see things as God does when your feelings are clouding your perspective.

Relying on your feelings is a surefire way to defeat. Seriously, Faithgirl! How many times a day do your feelings change? Exactly, too many to count! Sometimes you need some help silencing those negative, false thoughts about who you are. God can use your brothers and sisters to replace those wrong thoughts with his thoughts about you.

Father God gave you sisters and brothers in the body of Christ to speak encouraging words to you. While Briana's feelings caused her to mistakenly believe the visitors were judging her for taking a fall, Ashley shared the truth that they all wanted to see her stand up strong again.

Sometimes you might feel like you're the punch line of a cruel joke. Yet, in Father God's family, no one is laughing at you when you fall. Truth is, we all fall many times, Faithgirl! What distinguishes a daughter of God, though, is that she gets back up again and again, because she's got brothers and sisters telling her the truth.

So, get on up, girl! You're God's child, and with a little push from your siblings in the family of faith, you're on your way to get a marvelous prize. What was waiting on the other side of those doors? Gifts galore! Balloons, candy, flowers, fruit baskets! What more could Briana get? Much more. What mattered most was the love and grateful heart of another person, and the acknowledgement that Briana had done a great job.

Make no mistake about it; your heavenly reward is great when you're a daughter of God. But the greatest of them all is love. When in the heavenly place with Father God, on the other side of your disappointments, sickness, negative feelings, and hard circumstances of life, the part of your inheritance that means the most is the voice of Father God saying, "Well done, daughter!"

Beginning with Briana

Hopefully, you're finished trying to get things done with your own strength, and by yourself! Briana has given you many reasons to follow Jesus Christ and rely only on the grace of Father God instead. By now, you also know that as a part of the body of Jesus Christ, you have many brothers and sisters cheering you on to victory! So, what's next?

Start just like Briana did. Ask Father God to send you some help. Briana had suffered a humiliating tumble to the ground, but the ultimate result was good for her. Had she not hit the ground and broken her leg, she might not have cried out to God for help. That desperate cry for help from the Father set off a chain of encounters with Father God and the people in her life that blessed her in ways she could not have imagined. Here's why.

When you ask Father God to send someone to help you, he does. Father God loves us so much that everyone who asks gets what he or she asks! So when you ask Father God for someone to help you, that is exactly who you get—the person the Father has assigned to be a helper. That someone is his Holy Spirit.

As your advocate, the Holy Spirit starts teaching you and making things clear to you, especially the ways and thoughts of Jesus Christ. Gradually you begin seeing things differently, just as Briana did. In the end, you will find that by the power of his Holy Spirit teaching you, Father God is able to make changes in your heart that you never even dreamed about—like Briana being kind to a certain pesky newcomer to Live Oak Junior High!

Daughter, Declare Your Prayer

Father, thank you for my big brother, Jesus Christ! I am grateful for the love that you pour out on him and extend to me. Father, send me your help. I want to live by your grace. Teach me to rely only on you to accomplish my part in your plan. Please direct me to my sisters and brothers in your family. I'm excited about receiving them just as you received me!

CHAPTER 5

Resisting Your Father's Challenger

Briana stood there in disbelief. It took Jessica to remind her that everybody was scattering, and it was time to go.

"Let's go Briana," Jessica said. "The show's over."

"This isn't a show, Jess. Are we going to just stand by and let this happen? Doesn't this bother you at all? What if that was us in a few months?"

"That could never be us. No matter what happens, I will always be here for you."

Briana smiled and hugged her best friend. "I know you will. It just makes me sad to see them like this. And now, Taylor seems to be completely out of control. I can't do nothing while one of our team members is about to get hurt."

"What do you mean? I actually think Kaitlyn can take her, don't you? She's one of our strongest! Remember that time when we were working on the pyramid for the game against—"

"Jessica! This is no time to crack jokes. I think we really need to take this seriously."

Kaitlyn James and Taylor Dawson were the talk of the day. Everyone was anticipating Friday night after the eighth grade boys' football game. The two girls, once best friends, were set to fight. Kaitlyn had emerged from last spring's cheer tryouts victoriously, making the squad. Taylor did not.

Briana had heard of competition splitting up friendships before. Yet, she'd believed nothing could divide Kaitlyn and Taylor. The two had been inseparable their entire lives. That is until summer cheer camp. Kaitlyn connected with new friends from across the country, and she grew closer to girls right from Live Oak Junior High. Girls like Briana.

One day at practice after school, Briana noticed that Kaitlyn had less pep in her step than she typically did.

"Are you feeling okay, Kaitlyn?"

"Sort of. It's really cool that you're asking. I actually miss having someone to talk to on days like today."

"Well, you can talk to me if you want. I know I'm not Taylor, but—"

"No offense, Briana, but that's what I mean. I miss Taylor. She won't even talk to me now."

"Seriously?" Briana asked. Kaitlyn nodded her head. "Why not?"

Kaitlyn explained that when they'd returned home

from summer cheer camp, Taylor seemed critical about the stories Kaitlyn wanted to share. "It was like she had something bad to say about everything I tried to tell her," she said.

"Did you try listening?" said Briana. "It was probably hard on her trying to figure out what she was going to do without cheerleading."

"I really did, Briana. I asked her questions about what she had done while I was gone. I tried to make plans for us to spend time together. And I called her every single day, just like normal." Yet, nothing she'd done seemed to be enough to keep their friendship alive. Soon, their once rock-solid relationship became nothing more than a faded memory.

Briana's mind flashed back and forth between her conversation with Kaitlyn and the unfortunate incident occurring right before her eyes. Even knowing the girls' history, she felt they were without reason to fight. She thought, why didn't they fight to keep their friendship alive instead?

For weeks, she'd watched them casually greeting each other in the hallways when they passed each other. Silence followed that, and then Taylor's visible absence from the football games and pep rallies. Now finally, something more had brought the former friends to the point of wanting to actually exchange blows—well, at least one of them. Briana was there when Taylor issued the challenge after the morning pep rally.

"You know," Kaitlyn said, "you're jealous, Taylor.

You were never my true friend. Why couldn't you just be happy for me when I made it, even though you didn't?"

"Me? Jealous of you? I don't think so! If I'm not mistaken, you're the one going behind my back, sending notes to my real best friend about what a loser you think I am! You're so afraid you can't even say it to my face! What's the deal?"

The growing crowd waited for Kaitlyn to answer the question. Did she lack the courage to confront Taylor directly? During the pause, Briana prayed that somehow the scene would end. She hated seeing Kaitlyn and Taylor at odds, knowing that only a few months earlier they were the coolest pair of friends at Live Oak. Well, besides her and Jess.

Despite Briana's prayers, and spurred on by the antics of Austin Thomas, the argument kept heating up. Austin squeezed his way from the back of the crowd to the front, standing right next to Kaitlyn. He held his hand out like a talk show host, extending the microphone in front of Kaitlyn's mouth. "Yeah, so what's the deal?" Austin asked. "You too scared to tell it like it is to Taylor's face?" The crowd laughed, and Kaitlyn ended her silence.

"Anything I have ever needed to tell Taylor, I always have." Kaitlyn looked directly at her ex-bff. "And I always will. I'm not afraid of you."

"Then how do you explain this?" Taylor reached in the rhinestone studded back pocket of her jeans, pulling out a piece of folded notebook paper. She unfolded the paper, waving it in the air. Briana saw that cursive handwriting in neon pink ink filled the space between its light blue lines. Kaitlyn always signed everything in pink and used a heart shape to dot the I in her name.

Kaitlyn snatched the piece of paper from Taylor's hand and started reading the letter. "I don't know where you got this or who wrote it, but it wasn't me. I don't have time to waste writing notes about you, so go yell at someone else." Throwing Taylor's so-called evidence of Kaitlyn's betrayal up in the air, she turned her back and walked away. "This is stupid. I am so done."

Taylor yelled to make sure Kaitlyn would hear her. "How about after the game tonight? Will you have time then? Or will you still be too scared to own up to your words and face me then too? You are such a coward!"

Kaitlyn waved her hand, disregarding Taylor's insult. "Whatever, Taylor. It's like you're punishing me for something that isn't my fault," Kaitlyn said. "Don't you get it? I didn't write some stupid letter about you, and I'm not the one who cut you from the squad!"

"You never did know when to close that mouth of yours," said Taylor. "I know how to help you keep your mouth closed though. See you after the game."

The cheers of the crowd gathered around the girls was deafening to Briana. While most of the other kids seemed excited about the prospect of Kaitlyn and Taylor fighting, Briana was determined to keep the girls from battling it out. She thought, should I report Taylor for bullying? Maybe I can talk to Taylor myself. Who really wrote that stupid note? What can I do to help?

Daughter, You Decide

What do you think Briana can do to help? What would you do if you were in her situation? Do you think this is a case of bullying?

Okay, that's enough, Briana thought. She spoke up. "Taylor, maybe there's a better way—"

"Briana, this is none of your business. It's between me and Kaitlyn only."

"Kaitlyn is my business ... and so are you, remember? I know you're hurting too, but this is not—"

"Oh, I'm just fine. But you're about to be in a world of pain too, just like Kaitlyn, if you don't back off, Briana. I'll see you tonight," she said, before taking a couple of steps away from Bree. Taylor paused and then faced her former friend. "Besides, why should you care ... and what do you know anyway?"

Briana's Box

Wow! What in the world just happened! Have you ever been sandwiched in the middle of a bad situation between two people? No fun, right? Briana's goal was simply to be a good leader and friend by helping reconcile Taylor and Kaitlyn. Unfortunately, she encountered resistance as she became involved between the clashing of two warring Live Oak Lions!

By voting her cheer captain for the year, Briana's cheer peers had honored her with the role of leadership. To them, she exemplified the qualities of a strong leader. One of the primary characteristics of a good leader is her ability to encourage the team. A strong leader is one who builds up and motivates each member toward success. Here's why.

Briana has learned the power of one. After months of practicing cheer stunts and building pyramids, she has learned that if one of them is hurting, injured, or not doing well for any reason, the squad cannot build. On the other hand, if one of them is doing well and really excited about something, that joy spreads to the rest of the group! One person really can make a difference, for better or worse.

Did you know that you are a leader, just like Briana? When you become his daughter, Father God gives you a position of leadership. You may be leading your younger siblings in your family at home, the youth of the church, or a club at school. Whatever your leadership opportunity, Father God trusts you, by his grace and with love, to encourage and build up, not tear down, the people you lead.

Just as Briana learned, whether the family of God successfully builds and grows depends on the condition of each of the individual family members. When anyone of the family is hurting, ailing, or unable to do his or her part, the entire group suffers with that person. At the same time, when one of God's children is doing well and is happy, we're all happy! The attitude and condition of one person will ultimately affect the condition of the entire family.

Do you think Briana has a relationship to those people that she does not lead on the squad? You're right! She sure does. To those people, like Taylor Dawson, Briana is still a friend. Because Taylor failed to make the team, Briana was no longer Taylor's leader. Yet, she did attempt to help Taylor as a friend would, by trying to resolve her accusations against Kaitlyn without resorting to violence. Here's why.

Briana understood that Taylor's removal from the cheer squad hurt. More than that, Taylor also felt not being a part of the team would mean the loss of her best friend. That's enough to put any girl in a really bad mood! Briana realized that when it feels like you've been kicked to the sidelines of life, you can take the disappointment, anger, and frustration that you feel out on other people. Sometimes, even the people you actually love the most.

Father God trusts you with the people you do not lead as well, Faithgirl. Briana befriended Taylor, even though she wasn't a cheer family member. In the same way, God wants you to live friendly toward those people who are not a part of his family of faith. Like Briana did with Taylor, you can ask God to help you see beyond the way people are acting and try to understand how they feel. When you consider circumstances from someone else's perspective, and then take the action God gives you to solve his or her problem, it's called compassion. Compassion is a major attribute of Father God's character.

Praise be to the God and Father of our Lord Jesus Christ, the Father of compassion and the God of all comfort, who comforts us in all our troubles, so that we can comfort those in any trouble with the comfort we ourselves receive from God.

— 2 Corinthians 1:3

Initially, it might seem that your friendliness and compassion is unsuccessful. Do you remember how Taylor turned on Briana? It seemed like Taylor was uninterested in hearing what Briana had to say at all! Yet, Taylor paused to think about Briana's words. In that brief moment of thought, she questioned why Briana cared and what Briana knew.

When you care about hurting people like Taylor Dawson, and you take time to show it, those people want to know your reason for even caring. Curiosity about you, why you care, and what you know is good. Do you want to know why? You are your Father's daughter!

Being the much-loved daughter of Father God means caring about what he cares about. What Father God cares about most is hurting, broken people who are not following his Son, Jesus Christ, to him. They do not know him. When you become a compassionate friend to such people, and they start asking you questions, you have the chance to tell them that you care because Father

God cares. The truth that you know is that the Father loves them too!

> And he has committed to us the message of reconciliation. We are therefore Christ's ambassadors, as though God were making his appeal through us. We implore you on Christ's behalf: Be reconciled to God.
>
> — *2 Corinthians 5:19–20*

Daughter Deed

Bullying is serious business. Be sure to tell your parents, an adult counselor at school, or another grown-up you trust if you or someone you know is being bullied. Being a Faithgirl, you also understand that Father God makes the difference, even in a bad situation like bullying. Can you think of anyone you know who regularly bullies or picks fights with people? Have you ever thought about why she or he acts so mean? Spend a few minutes talking to Father God about that person. Ask him if he wants you to help him or her. Ask him how he wants you to do it. Then, will you do a daughter deed, and write that person a friendly letter? Include why you think they act that way. Tell them how much God loves them. Your letter is not for sharing with that person, it's between you and God. Each day, continue to pray for your friend. As Father God gives you grace, your chance will come to tell him or her why you care and what you know!

_____

_____

_____

_____

_____

_____

As you continue thinking about Briana's dilemma, you know that initially she was uninvolved in this whole mess! She was just passing through the last of the students lingering after the pep rally, happily mixing with the crowd, until Taylor and Kaitlyn's public dispute attracted Briana attention. Eventually though, Briana's loyalty to her relationship with Kaitlyn made it impossible for her to remain disengaged. Briana made a decision to defend the welfare and interests of the Live Oak Lion with whom she was connected — her fellow cheer mate, Kaitlyn. Here's why.

Briana knew that she and the squad have to stick together at all costs. As much as she understood how Taylor was feeling, she refused to start acting like her and adopting her unkind ways. Briana and Kaitlyn were a part of the same cheer family, and Briana had to prove her loyalty to the squad and its mission of spreading Live Oak Junior High spirit among the students.

God has a mission too, Faithgirl, and you have a role to play in its fulfillment! That mission involves conflict. As God's daughter, you are involved in a conflict that you didn't ask to be a part of too. Until now, you've pretty much just happily followed your family and friends along, being the best Faithgirl you know how to be! As God's daughter though, you'll soon recognize that you're just like Briana — right smack dab in the middle of a war zone asking yourself, Wow! What just happened?

What happened is that by the nature of your relationship with Father God and Jesus Christ, you inherited an enemy. Just as Briana engaged in the fight because she was Kaitlyn's cheer sister, you are now engaged in a battle because you are Jesus Christ's sister. Your big brother, Jesus Christ, also named the Lion of the Tribe of Judah, has an enemy, called Satan. Because he hates Jesus Christ, Satan goes after all Jesus's siblings — including you.

Be alert and of sober mind. Your enemy the devil prowls around like a roaring lion looking for someone to devour.

— 1 Peter 5:8

Yes, Faithgirl, becoming a much-loved daughter of Father God also means becoming a well-equipped soldier in an intense spiritual fight. For our struggle is not against flesh and blood, but against the rulers, against the authorities, against the powers of this dark world, and against the spiritual forces of evil in the heavenly realms.

So, you say, but I'm not looking for a fight. Increase the peace! Not an option, girlfriend. The fight is looking for you because you belong to the Father. Just like Briana ultimately had to step up and prove her loyalty to the squad by standing up for Kaitlyn, you have to be loyal to the family of faith by standing up for Jesus Christ.

Are you ready to rumble? Well hold on; slow your roll, sister! Maybe you could use just a bit more information about the battle, don't you think? As you read on, you will learn that the spiritual battle you are fighting with your Father God is:

- Invisible
- Interdependent
- Internal
- Intense
- Inevitable

Believing with Briana

The battle between God and the Enemy is invisible. Remember, the beauty of believing and having faith in Father God is that there is more to life than what your eyes can see. The things that you can see are actually fading away. It's the things that you cannot see with your eyes that are real. This is true of the battle daughters of God face too. You are unable to see the forces of darkness and evil working against you, but you will certainly experience their negative effects in your life if you fail to resist them.

Guess you had better learn how to resist then, you think? Follow the example of your big brother. If there's anybody who knows how to defeat Satan, it's Jesus Christ. He's the one the Enemy really hates anyway, not you. As much as you will struggle against the Enemy, it won't be to the same degree as Jesus. He resisted to the point of pouring out blood! The wounding of Jesus Christ on the cross was a bloody sacrifice unlike any other. Yet, the cross wasn't the only place Jesus dropped his blood.

One other place where Jesus bled gives you a clue on the importance of remembering that you're fighting a hidden, invisible enemy who must be resisted in a hidden, unseen way. One dark night, Jesus went up to a mountain he visited often, called the Mount of Olives, where he enjoyed spending time talking with Father God.

In that special time and place of prayer to his Father, Jesus shared how much agony he was experiencing, knowing that his bloody death on the cross was the only way he could defeat Satan. He prayed that if there were another way, Father God would allow him to do it that way instead. But he also prayed that the Father do what he wanted to do, not what Jesus himself wanted.

Knowing that his Son wanted to please him and complete his plan, Father God responded by sending helping angels to give Jesus the strength to pray even harder. Jesus prayed so hard, in fact, that his sweat and blood mixed and poured from his face as he reached up with all of his heart for Father God.

There, on that high, hidden mountaintop with Father

God and only a few disciples, Jesus Christ fought his adversary with heartfelt, agonizing prayer. That's how you will fight this invisible war too—with perseverant, unseen prayer, in a secret place, with a handful of your sisters and brothers who are following Jesus Christ.

And pray in the Spirit on all occasions with all kinds of prayers and requests. With this in mind, be alert and always keep on praying for all the Lord's people.

— Ephesians 6:18

Your sisters and brothers in the body of Jesus Christ are a critical part of the battle, because the fight is an interdependent one. If you want to maintain the victory that your big brother, Jesus Christ, won for you with his blood, then you have to depend on other sisters and brothers who are fighting with you. Here's why.

Though one may be overpowered, two can defend themselves. A cord of three strands is not quickly broken.

— Ecclesiastes 4:12

It is much easier for the Enemy to defeat you if you try to stand alone. Yet, if you stay connected and fight with your siblings in the family of faith, you can defend each other. When Father God first created human beings, he determined it was important for us to have help. Remember this, Faithgirl, no matter what it looks like or how you feel, you're never alone in the family of faith! But the Enemy of Father God sure will try to get you thinking you are alone and in this thing by yourself.

In fact, Satan launches a full-scale assault on the way you think, making the battle an internal one. The place where you have to fight the good fight is in your mind. That's why Father God calls his enemy the Father of Lies — because he tries to fill your mind with wrong information. Your protection against the false words of the Enemy is knowing and believing the truth of what Father God is saying instead. Father God has spoken in the past, and he continues to speak to his sons and daughters today.

In the old days, God spoke to our ancestors through a special, limited group of people he chose to hear him and then tell the rest of his people what God said. They recorded their experiences with God in writing, and you have much to learn from reading what they wrote in the Bible.

These days, God speaks to you, and all of his children, through the life and words of his Son, Jesus Christ. God is willing to speak and share truth with anyone who is willing to follow Jesus Christ to him! You can study and focus on the words and teachings of Jesus Christ in the Bible too.

As you pray for him to do it, God's Spirit will animate Jesus's words in your heart. They will become more than just printed words on a page. There will instead be a spark within you. That light lets you know God has just spoken to you! The words Jesus has spoken are full of the

Spirit and life. It's that life and those words that help you overcome the Enemy.

Still, the fight to overcoming is a hard one! This battle is intense, filled with extraordinary challenges and obstacles. Father God uses the battles to make your faith as strong as it can be. Satan uses them to try to accomplish the vicious goal he has for the people God created. That wicked purpose is to steal, to kill, and to destroy the spiritual life with Father God that walking with Jesus Christ makes possible.

If you are not already following Jesus Christ, Satan's first objective is to steal your spiritual potential. With God-limited and temporary influence in the natural world and circumstances around you, the Enemy tries to keep you distracted from the reality of the spiritual world, and your need for Jesus Christ and Father God. Yet, when your heart begins to think about God and his ways, you're on your way to new life!

The Enemy knows that the best way to ensure you never follow Jesus to Father God is to prevent you from thinking about God in the first place. In the mind of such a person, it's as if God doesn't even exist! This lack of consideration of God is a spiritually dead path you want to avoid.

As a Faithgirl, you are not even trying to go there! Thankfully, you're already following the way to life, Jesus Christ! Still, be aware, sister! The Enemy still has two other tactics waiting for you. Since his attempts to steal your spiritual potential were unsuccessful, now he works to kill your promise of reaching your full potential in God.

The Enemy slaughters God's promises and your life with him when subtle, wrong beliefs gradually fill your mind. After much time passes, these little thoughts grow so strong that they hold you back from moving ahead with your big brother, Jesus Christ. In the end, it's just as if a murderer has snuffed out the life of goodness that Father God promised you.

Sometimes attempted assassins are unsuccessful, though. Observant, alert people on the lookout for illegal activity often thwart their plans. You, Faithgirl, can be one of those people for Father God! When you are, there's only one thing left for the Enemy to do. When he's failed to steal from or execute you, Satan tries to destroy the abundant life that's yours when Jesus Christ is your escort.

What he could not steal or kill, the Enemy will lastly attempt to ruin. Faithgirl, what you don't know can hurt you. When you do not know what's on God's mind, the Enemy has a chance to sneak in and destroy the good work God is doing in your life. Father God knows everything about everything! If you learn what God knows, you can stop the Enemy from destroying your spiritual life!

Just as you do with any other person, you learn what God knows by asking him. As you invest your time in growing the relationship through prayer and quiet times alone with him, he sees that he can trust you. God wants to share information about his plans with his children.

> "This is what the Lord says, he who made the
> earth, the Lord who formed it and established
> it — the Lord is his name: 'Call to me and I will
> answer you and tell you great and unsearchable
> things you do not know.'"
>
> —*Jeremiah 33:2–3*

Know this, Faithgirl. Satan is cunning and covert, deliberately cloaking his activity in darkness, masking his evil as good. Yet, it's not his plans that are at work; it is what Father God has put in motion. On your own, it's impossible for you to know what God is planning and doing. But, you're not on your own anymore, are you? You're sticking with Jesus Christ, and he's leading you all the way to the Father. Because of your relationship with your big brother, Jesus, you can know.

> I no longer call you servants, because a servant
> does not know his master's business. Instead, I have
> called you friends, for everything that I learned
> from my Father I have made known to you.
>
> —*John 15:15*

Knowing what's on God's mind allows you to flip the script on Satan and ruin the ideas and plans that he makes in opposition to Jesus Christ.

> For though we live in the world, we do not wage
> war as the world does. The weapons we fight
> with are not the weapons of the world. On the
> contrary, they have divine power to demolish

**strongholds. We demolish arguments and
every pretension that sets itself up against the
knowledge of God, and we take captive every
thought to make it obedient to Christ.**

— 2 Corinthians 10:3–5

If you're starting to feel a little intimidated, rest
assured that allegiance to Jesus Christ is the result of all
this fighting. In the end, Jesus Christ and other sons and
daughters (yes, including you!) win! Yet, you still have
to endure the heated process of standing and fighting,
Faithgirl. You cannot avoid this war. As Father God's
daughter, your participation in this struggle is inevitable.
Here's why.

Father God is a fair Father. As he rules the world,
he desires to pour out justice on his creation, treating
all people alike. When Adam, the first human being
God created, decided to do things differently than the
way God had directed him, Adam experienced separation from God. Remember, paying more attention to the
cares of life than to God leads to spiritual death. Every
human being inherited Adam's tendency to live like God
doesn't exist, disobey God's directions, and do things our
own way instead of God's. So, one man's error made us
all error-prone!

In the beginning when Father God made Adam, his
nature was just like God's—no errors, slip-ups, mistakes,
or thoughts of himself whatsoever. But the Enemy caused
Adam's character to change.

A different man decided he wanted to correct Adam's error and get him back to the original condition in which God made him. Do you have an idea about who that man might be? You got it! The man who wanted to fix Adam's error was Jesus Christ. He loves us so much that he endured the punishment for Adam's failure that God required in his love for fairness.

Father God looked at the situation with fairness in his heart and mind. If the actions of one man caused the problem in the first place, then one man's actions could also solve the problem in the end. That is God's justice. So, as a relative of Adam, you took on his nature. Bummer, right? Well, here's the good news! In all his fairness, Father God promises that when you're a daughter following Jesus Christ to him, you take on Jesus' nature, and become newly made in the way Father God originally intended.

Therefore, if anyone is in Christ, the new creation has come: The old has gone, the new is here!

— *2 Corinthians 5:17*

And Jesus' nature is something fierce, Faithgirl! The firstborn Son of God is a warrior. Father God has declared that his Son, Jesus Christ, is the King of Kings! All great kings know what it takes to fight and win war. Jesus Christ knows this far better than anyone else does.

Who is this King of glory? The Lord strong and mighty, the Lord mighty in battle.

— *Psalm 24:8*

Praise Prompt

Psalm 18 describes how God helps his daughters fight! Read it in its entirety if you can, and pay close attention to the verses below. As you read it, think about learning how to win your struggles and challenges in life just like Jesus Christ did. Thank Father God that he teaches you how to fight like a Faithgirl and win!

Psalm 18:29–49

With your help I can advance against a troop;
with my God I can scale a wall.
As for God, his way is perfect:
The Lord's word is flawless;
he shields all who take refuge in him.
For who is God besides the Lord?
And who is the Rock except our God?
It is God who arms me with strength
and keeps my way secure.
He makes my feet like the feet of a deer;
he causes me to stand on the heights.
He trains my hands for battle;
my arms can bend a bow of bronze.
You make your saving help my shield,
and your right hand sustains me;
your help has made me great.
You provide a broad path for my feet,
so that my ankles do not give way.
I pursued my enemies and overtook them;
I did not turn back till they were destroyed.
I crushed them so that they could not rise;
they fell beneath my feet.
You armed me with strength for battle;

you humbled my adversaries before me.
You made my enemies turn their backs in flight,
and I destroyed my foes.
They cried for help, but there was no one to save them—
to the Lord, but he did not answer.
I beat them as fine as windblown dust;
I trampled them like mud in the streets.
You have delivered me from the attacks of the people;
you have made me the head of nations.
People I did not know now serve me,
foreigners cower before me;
as soon as they hear of me, they obey me.
They all lose heart;
they come trembling from their strongholds.
The Lord lives! Praise be to my Rock!
Exalted be God my Savior!
He is the God who avenges me,
who subdues nations under me,
who saves me from my enemies.
You exalted me above my foes;
from a violent man you rescued me.
Therefore I will praise you, Lord, among the nations;
I will sing the praises of your name.

Are you still feeling up to the fight? Good! Father God has given you everything you need to keep from losing. Come on now, Faithgirl! You know your daddy would never send you out to fight unless he knew your foe's defeat was a sure thing! Briana's tidbits show you the three principles you need to know to prevent the Enemy from stealing, killing, and destroying you. You're going to need:

- Faith
- Hope
- Love

You Ready? Okay! F-I-G-H-T! Fight, let's fight!

Briana's Tidbit #1: Faith

Do you remember what the Enemy's first strategy is? Right, to steal the potential for spiritual life by keeping your mind distracted from the existence of God. Remember, the world that we perceive with our five senses is like a shadow. It's not the real thing, but it suggests the real thing. Satan tries to keep your mind on the shadow that you see in this world, so you won't pursue the reality in God. Yet, Satan is so *not* in control! In his love for you, Father God gives you faith to squash the Enemy's efforts to divert your attention from spiritual life with God.

Faith is an enormous gift from God. When you receive faith from God, he's investing your heart with the holding capacity to acknowledge that Jesus Christ is his Son. But, faith that comes from God includes more than room in your heart to acknowledge that Jesus is God's Son. Faith from God also bends your heart toward confidence in everything else that is true *because* Jesus is Father God's Son. When you believe that Jesus is the Son of God, and you are entirely reliant on Jesus for your welfare and the quality of life you experience, you are walking in the faith of God. This faith is what causes you to rise above the natural world around you and emerge as a spiritual person.

This is the victory that has overcome the world, even our faith. Who is it that overcomes the world? Only the one who believes that Jesus is the Son of God.

— 1 John 5:4–5

Would you like to know why the belief that Jesus is the Son of God is powerful enough to overcome evil? Because by identifying Jesus as a Son, Father God made clear that Jesus was a reflection of himself. Throughout his life, Jesus referred to himself using various designations. Other people identified him by an assortment of names too. Yet, when God introduced Jesus Christ to humanity, he wanted to show that to see and experience Jesus was to see and experience a representation of himself. So, he said, "This is my Son, whom I love; with him I am well pleased" (Matthew 3:17).

Hopefully, your heart is feeling that spark, illuminating for you why it is so important to understand what it means to be God's beautiful daughter. The Father called Jesus "Son" because Jesus represented God to the world. Father God calls you "daughter" because as you follow Jesus Christ, you become a mirror image of him too.

In love he predestined us for adoption to sonship through Jesus Christ, in accordance with his pleasure and will — to the praise of his glorious grace, which he has freely given us in the One he loves.

—Ephesians 1:4–6

Above everything else, the Enemy wants to wipe out the conditions of daughterhood and sonship. After Father God announced that Jesus was his Son, Satan immediately challenged Jesus' sonship. He continues to dispute the relationships of daughters and sons to Father God today. Yet, when you receive God's faith, and believe and rely on the fact that Jesus is God's Son, you defeat the Enemy's plot to rob you. Instead, you receive an entire package of good benefits from the Father who loves Jesus and you!

Over time, Father God by his Spirit gently guides you through lifelong discovery and exploration of the riches you will inherit as his daughter and fellow beneficiary with Jesus. With faith from God, you have a deep treasure chest of everything you will ever need to conquer every obstacle the Enemy sets before you because you follow his Son. And Father God gave the Son all his own power and the permission to overthrow Satan once and for all!

So, by all means, receive the faith, girl!

Briana's Tidbit #2: Hope

Overcoming the thief means Father God turned your mind toward him and gave you the faith to prevent Satan from stealing your potential for a rich spiritual life. That is fantastic! The Enemy's no quitter, though. He may back off for a while, but he will return when he thinks he has a better chance of taking you down.

When he returns, he does it vigorously. This time, he'll be aiming to extinguish the spiritual life that you do have. He does it by targeting your mind with wrong beliefs about your future with God. Initially, these faulty expectations ignite your imagination, infusing you with excitement and anticipation about what is ahead. Eventually though, they burn your heart to a crisp, leaving you disappointed and wondering why a father who loves you would do something like that to you.

Dear sister, the Father who loves you is innocent of creating such disappointment. It is the Father of Lies who derails daughters from the destined future God has in mind. Rather than allowing the Enemy's false expectations to misdirect you, God gives you what you need to smother every faulty flame launched at your mind. Hope is what halts the Enemy's hurling of erroneous expectations.

Hope is confident expectation about what is going to happen in your future. With hope, you sincerely believe that something you're waiting for is going to occur in your life, although you have yet to see it. Think of it like this. Has one of your parents ever promised you something? When it did not happen immediately, what did you do? You kept asking them "When?" Right! After you kept begging (and they told you to stop whining, right?), you finally experienced exactly what they promised. That is hope.

Father God makes promises to you too. Remember, when Father God invited you to come and receive his gift of faith, it was an enormous package filled with promises. One of those promises is a hope, one single accomplishment you can eagerly anticipate is going occur in the future.

> **There is one body and one Spirit, just as you were called to one hope when you were called; one Lord, one faith, one baptism; one God and Father of all, who is over all and through all and in all.**
>
> — *Ephesians 4:4–6*

That one hope that God gives to daughters and sons along with faith is this: because Jesus Christ lives in you, you can expect that in the future when Father God displays his firstborn Son, Jesus Christ, to the entire world as the outstanding, excellent, and supreme ruler who God honors above all, God will honor you too. Sounds like an appointment worth keeping, right?

Then stay on track, Faithgirl, and avoid the disappointing false expectations of the Enemy. Embrace the one true hope that comes from Father God.

Briana's Tidbit #3: Love

When you've smoldered the attempts of the Enemy to snuff out your spiritual life, it's because you held on to the hope that comes from Father God. Way to protect your mind from false expectations! The Enemy still has one trick up his sleeve, though. Some tricksters just don't know when to stop!

Satan will stop at nothing to see you ruined. With this final tactic, his goal is to tear down the spiritual life that God has built in you. Hatred is what Satan feels for the Father and for Jesus, the Son. If the world around you seems to mistreat you because you are walking with Jesus, it is the Enemy reminding you that he hates your Father and brother. But, your brother said to keep this in mind about hatred:

> **"If the world hates you, you know that it hated Me before it hated you. If you were of the world, the world would love its own. Yet because you are not of the world, but I chose you out of the world, therefore the world hates you."**
>
> *—John 15:18–19 (NKJV)*

Jesus's words also tell you how to respond to and overcome the Enemy's painful reminders of his hatred for God. Do you want to know how a true daughter of the heavenly Father responds to hatred and persecution? She loves her enemies, she prays for those her mistreat her, and she does good even to people who hate her.

Love is graphic.

Love is patient. You wait until that person understands how much God loves you.

Love is kind. You are good to others because Father God is good to you.

It does not envy. You are grateful for how God has blessed you.

It does not boast. You accomplish nothing without God's help.

It is not proud. You rely on God for the strength that you need.

It does not dishonor others. You cherish all people God created.

It is not self-seeking. You give what God gave you to others.

It is not easily angered. You are peaceful because God's in control.

It keeps no record of wrongs. You forgive because you need God to forgive you.

Love does not delight in evil but rejoices with the truth. You are happy because God makes hearts free.

It always protects, always trusts, always hopes, always perseveres. You will fight to the finish for the faith!

Faithgirl, love never fails.

Beginning with Briana

In the past, maybe you've failed to see your journey of faith as a fight. Is Briana's experience with Kaitlyn and Taylor's scuffle making you think about God differently? Hopefully, you understand that there will be times of uncomfortable struggle in your life, yet God only uses those times to bring you closer to him.

If you want to fight like a Faithgirl right now, the first step is to enlist for combat. Remember, it's faith, hope, and love that defeat evil schemes to steal, kill, and destroy. Start by asking Father God to fill your heart with faith in his Son, Jesus Christ, and watch out! You're on your way to V-I-C-T-O-R-Y!

Daughter, Declare Your Prayer

Father, thank you for helping me trust in your Son, Jesus Christ! I want to fight with all the might you give me for the truth that Jesus Christ is the Son of God. When the battle gets tough and the Enemy attacks my mind, make my thoughts turn to your faith, hope, and love. Love never fails!

CHAPTER 6

Reflecting Your Father's Image

As they pulled up to their driveway of her home, Briana wondered why the porch light was off, and none of the house lights seemed to be on. Her mom always left at least one light on whenever they planned to arrive home after nightfall. "Did you forget to leave a light on, Mom?" she asked.

Her mother turned off the car. "I sure did. I guess we were in such a hurry when we left I just didn't even think about it. Anyway, Ashley should be in there. I can't imagine why she would just sit in the dark."

"She's probably watching a movie. You know, no lights give you the full movie theater effect."

She shook her head. "I guess so. Here. Take my keys. Go ahead and unlock the door for me, please. I'll start grabbing bags out of the back."

Briana walked up to the front door of her house and

struggled to get the keys in the door without any light. When she finally wiggled the key into the lock, she opened the door. She reached to turn on the entryway light and was shocked by what she heard and saw.

"SURPRISE!" her friends yelled.

"What are you guys doing here?" she said

Jessica, Ashley, and her closest friends from the cheer squad were standing in front of her with hot pink party hats on. The confetti and streamers they had thrown at her when she walked through the door lined the floor, and balloons floated across the ceiling, partially obstructing the banner that read: Happy 13th Birthday, Briana!

Her mother walked in behind her and then gave Briana a hug.

"Happy birthday, baby. I hope you enjoy your evening."

She squeezed her mom and then looked at Jessica. "I can't believe you guys got me like this! You totally lied to me! I thought we were going out tomorrow night!"

"Well, duh! They wouldn't call it a surprise party if you knew about it, right?"

Briana shook her pointer finger in Jessica's face. "That's alright. Just wait. Payback, my friend, payback!"

Jessica smiled. "I love you, girly. Happy birthday," she said, hugging Briana.

"Okay, okay. Attention, attention." Ashley jokingly cleared her throat. "Since our guest of honor has arrived, the party can officially begin." Briana stood beside her sister, holding her hand and beaming with excitement as she surveyed the twelve guests who had come to celebrate her birthday.

Ashley continued. "So here's how it's going to work. We're going to move from where we are now to the game room, which we have transformed for our special occasion tonight. We all know what a fashion diva Briana is, so if you don't have a flair for fashion, then this party is not for you!" The twelve girls screamed, giddy with excitement. "But if you are ready for this glam slam in honor of Bree's birthday, then let's hit the salon!"

"The what?" Briana asked, laughing.

Jessica grabbed Briana's hand and pulled her toward the upstairs game room. "Just come on! You'll see!" The rest of the pack followed them, and the blaring music Ashley turned on soon overpowered Jessica's words, forcing Briana to read her lips. "Are you ready?" Jessica mouthed.

"Ready!" Briana screamed.

Jessica pushed open the French doors to the game room.

Briana's jaw dropped in amazement. "Are you kidding me?"

The once plain game room was vibrantly decorated like a beauty salon! In the middle of the room was a lounging area with two swirl-shaped sofas and a glass table. The walls were lined with salon style hooded hair dryers. In two of the corners of the room were a huge round mirror, and a white table with all kinds of styling tools like hair spray, curling irons, and hairbrushes. One corner was decked out as a manicure station, and the other had a huge massaging chair with a foot spa at the base for performing pedicures. Sweet!

Briana's mom, Austin's mother, and their cheer coaches, Mrs. Hines and Mrs. Ward, were all dressed up like professional beauty stylists wearing fancy wigs, voluminous eyelashes, and white salon coats. Briana's mom had even thrown on a pair of crazy, colorful eyeglasses and a hot pink wig styled like a big beehive! She peeked over the top of her glasses and greeted the girls in a funny sounding French accent.

"Hello, ladies. Welcome to Salon Bree. We are happy to serve you today as you prepare for a night of fashionable fun." She looked at the other three grown-ups in the room. "Allow me to introduce my team."

Briana's mother introduced the women by their fake names for the night and explained that the girls would rotate through four stations in the salon—hair, makeup, nails, and feet. When they were runway ready, Bree's mom explained, they would choose a designer gown of their choice and walk the red carpet for a photo shoot. "So! Let the luxuriating begin!" she said with a wave of her hand.

Ashley got in on the fun too. She dressed up like a waitress in a café and served the girls chocolate-covered strawberries, sparkling fruit punch, dainty croissant sandwiches, and of course, Briana's favorite—banana-nut muffins! The older women treated them like royalty, styling their hair, and giving them relaxing facials, manicures, and pedicures. As far as Briana was concerned, it was the best salon in town!

When the girls' treatments were finished, Briana's mom directed their attention to a couple of wardrobe racks in the corner of the room. Beautiful dresses of various styles and colors filled the racks.

"Now, ladies," she said, "you are to pick one designer original to wear when you walk the red carpet." She still attempted to speak with that crazy French accent.

"The what?" Briana joked.

"The runway. Downstairs. Now shush, my lady. Anyone who has undergone such a magnificent makeover will appear before the crowds on the red carpet."

"And what will we wear, madame?" said Briana, playing along.

"You are to pick one gown. My assistant Ashley will help you dress in the bathroom down the hall. Understand?"

The girls giggled at Mrs. Robinson and said yes before rushing to the clothes racks. Each of them picked the dress of their choice and prepared to walk like a superstar down the makeshift red carpet in the living room downstairs. Briana went first.

Praise Prompt

Psalm 104 is an amazing picture of God's beauty in nature. As you read the verses below, think about how awesome the Creator is. Then celebrate! The same God that made the world also made you! Now *that's* a good reason to smile!

Psalm 104:1–9

Praise the Lord, my soul.
Lord my God, you are very great;
you are clothed with splendor and majesty.
The Lord wraps himself in light as with a garment;
he stretches out the heavens like a tent
and lays the beams of his upper chambers on their waters.
He makes the clouds his chariot
and rides on the wings of the wind.
He makes winds his messengers,
flames of fire his servants.
He set the earth on its foundations;
it can never be moved.
You covered it with the watery depths as with a garment;
the waters stood above the mountains.
But at your rebuke the waters fled,
at the sound of your thunder they took to flight;
they flowed over the mountains,
they went down into the valleys,
to the place you assigned for them.
You set a boundary they cannot cross;
never again will they cover the earth.

When Briana reached the bottom of the stairs, she saw that the photographer was Mrs. Hines' husband. "Hey, Mr. Hines! You're a photographer?"

"I am tonight, Miss Robinson. Happy birthday. Now, strike a pose!"

All twelve girls took their turn walking the red carpet. In fact, they were so excited about their new image, they each took two turns, changing outfits in between. When all the walking, squealing, eating, and gift opening was done, everybody was exhausted! Briana walked the last guest, Austin's mom, to the door. "Good night, Mrs. Thomas. Thank you so much for coming and for all of your help."

"You're welcome, sweetheart. My pleasure. Oh! Before I forget." She rummaged through her purse and pulled out a cute pink gift bag. "From the Thomas family, with love."

Briana pulled out the glittery pink Bible from the bag. Her name was inscribed in silver cursive in the bottom right-hand corner. "I love it, Mrs. Thomas! Thank you!"

After closing the door behind Mrs. Thomas, she ran to the couch and sat down, nestling against her own mother who had finally plopped down. "How in the world did you do all of this?" Briana said.

Mrs. Robinson rubbed Briana on the head. "It's a long story. I'll have to tell you all about it . . . later."

"Watch the do, Mom, watch the hairdo. I just came from the most exquisite salon in town."

Her mom laughed. "Did you have fun?"

"You know it. I feel like a queen, Mom. Thanks for everything." She leaned over and kissed her mom on the cheek. "I'm off to get some sleep." Briana got up and headed up the stairs to her bedroom. Before she went to bed though, she wanted to take one last peek in the game room, to look at the place of the best birthday party she'd ever had. There was one final surprise waiting for her.

Austin Taylor was in the game room sweeping up the floor. Briana interrupted his whistling.

"Hey, Austin. I didn't know—"

"Yeah, we're just cleaning up."

"Who's we?"

"Me, my dad, and Mr. Hines. They're loading up some stuff in the truck."

"So, you mean you guys are the ones who did all of this for me? Have you been here all night?"

"Yep. Between me, my dad, and Mr. Hines, you're looking at your videographer, your set designer, your chef, your security guard, and—"

" ... and my photographer. I never even noticed you guys were here working so hard."

"Well, it was kind of a girly thing you know, not really the place for a bunch of guys, know what I mean?"

"I get it, Austin. It's hard for me to believe that you'd be willing to give up your Friday night for this." She grabbed a bottle of pink nail polish and shook it. "Your dad must have forced you to do it."

"No, not exactly. My dad is cool. We have fun hanging out together."

"So how long have you known about this?"

"I've been in on it since the beginning. It was actually Dad's bright idea, but he wanted to keep it a secret. I promised him I wouldn't do or say anything to tip you off."

"No way! Why would he do all of this for me? Wait a minute. Did my mom pay you guys or something? I can't do enough chores to pay you for this!"

Austin shrugged his shoulders and kept working, not noticing the disbelief on Briana's face. "Don't worry about paying for it, Bree. The cost is taken care of." He stopped cleaning long enough to look at Briana. He smiled, and she noticed that he was starting to blush. He quickly looked away. "You look st—"

Briana was afraid to know what Austin thought about her makeover. Was he going to say stupid? Or straight up ridiculous? It could be stunning, but she didn't give him the chance to finish. "So uh, you and your dad, I mean, you really get along well?"

"Yeah. He's got mad love because I'm his first son and the only one. That whole thing."

"Must be nice."

"Yes and no." He grabbed a bottle of water and took a sip. "Yes, because everything he gives, he gives to me. Not just stuff. You know what I mean? It's like, he loves the things . . . the people . . . that I love."

"And the no?"

"I know he wanted more kids. He wanted a huge family and never meant for me to be the only child. I think that's why he does so much for my friends. If you're connected to me, then he treats you the way he treats me. It's like you become a part of us. I don't know. He's just cool like that."

Pastor Taylor walked into the game room, interrupting their conversation. "Who's cool like what?" He didn't wait for an answer. "Wow, Briana! You look fabulous. Now that's what you call a makeover, huh? You're destined for stardom young lady." He grabbed a couple of chairs and walked back out to go load them in the truck.

"I agree," Austin said, "Oh! Hey, I've got something for you." He grabbed a DVD and a long white envelope off the table. "Here you go. The video of your party."

"Awesome! I guess now I can have another party to watch the party!" She held up the envelope, ignoring the handwriting on the front. "And what's this?"

"Nothing much. Just a little something I wanted to share with you."

She read the small, scrawny cursive on the envelope: To Briana, Love Austin.

Briana's Box

Say what! No, Austin Thomas did not just use the *L* word! Okay, maybe he didn't actually say he loved Briana, but still! Briana felt a little strange, and yes, excited even, about the way Austin was talking. Knowing that he cared made her feel special. It had taken her some time to warm up to Austin, but since they had become friends, her life did seem to be changing for the better.

Daughter, You Decide

It sure sounds like Briana and Austin are headed in a special direction, don't you think? Their parents are so *not* about to let them date at their age! But she's not even sure how she's supposed to feel about it. And she surely doesn't know how to respond to him. Daughter, you decide. What would you do if a boy gave you a letter like the one Austin gave Briana?

Briana realized that her own situation with her father might not ever change. She had grown accustomed to seeing other girls with their fathers. Yet seeing Austin with his dad was teaching her new things about the way fathers love their sons, especially the one who was born first! That's important for you to understand too. Here's why.

Briana's experience with Austin and his dad is similar to your experience with Father God and his first Son, Jesus Christ. Remember why Austin said his father loved him so much? Right! Austin was his father's first and only son. As the only son, Austin was the recipient of all of his father's love, gifts, and energy. But, Austin knew that his father wanted more children.

Likewise, in the beginning, Jesus Christ was the first and only Son of Father God. Because he had no other children yet, Father God poured all of his love, gifts, and energy into Jesus Christ. Yet, the Father's desire and intention was always to have a large family full of daughters and sons that he could love.

Do you remember what Austin's dad did to meet his desire to have more children to love? Yes! He loved Austin's friends. Whomever Austin loved and cared about, his father loved and cared for too. Austin's father welcomed his son's friends, like Briana, into their relationship because Austin loved them.

This is exactly what Father God does as well. To fulfill the desire in his heart for a large family full of daughters and sons, he loves whomever his first Son, Jesus Christ, loves. Whomever Jesus loves, the Father loves. He welcomes friends of Jesus Christ, like you, into the loving bond that the two of them share.

The way people see the bond of love between Austin and his dad is when they work together. Because of how much they love each other, Pastor Thomas and Austin enjoy collaborating. They coordinated every detail to pull off Briana's party according to the original plan. Lastly, Austin was careful to do only what his father instructed him to do and say. Briana was astonished that Austin was in on it from the start, and that he kept quiet about it the entire time!

Just like Austin and his dad, Father God and Jesus have been joyfully working together from the start. They make every detail of God's plan flow together so it ends exactly the way the Father originally intended. Just like Austin, Jesus followed Father God's directions with diligence, carrying out the plan to perfect completion.

When the girls completed their makeovers, they walked downstairs like superstars to parade down the red carpet and shine in front of the camera. Aside from having great fun in the process, the highlight and purpose of the entire evening was transformation into an image that, as Pastor Thomas said to Briana, made her destined for stardom.

Your future and destiny from Father God includes shining like a star too. You might not see your name in the bright lights of LA, or a star on the Hollywood walk-of-fame might not be in your future. Yet, the red carpets of this world that we see with our eyes are fading, and there is honor in your future from Father God, which lasts forever.

Even though the girls had a blast celebrating her birthday, the point of Briana's party was to transform each girl into an image worthy of honor. That, Faithgirl, is also the point of everything God is doing in your life. The desire of Father God's heart is to transform you into the image of the one person suitable to be exalted, like a shining star. Do you know who that person is? You guessed it, girl! That person is Jesus Christ.

Believing with Briana

Your makeover into the image of Jesus Christ is a special piece of God's ultimate work of art. You could think of yourself as one line in the perfect love poem! Father God reproducing the life of Jesus Christ in us is accomplished:

- Discreetly
- Divinely
- Definitely

Do you remember where the celebration honoring Briana's birthday started? Upstairs in the game room, right! The privacy behind those closed French doors was just right for transforming ordinary young women into extraordinary models of perfection. The girls needed much help with their makeovers. After all, skilled artists who know exactly how a model is supposed to look do the best makeovers. Her mother, cheer coaches, Mrs. Thomas, and Ashley all contributed to the process. Before receiving the honor of walking the red carpet, they underwent treatment at five stations: hairstyling, facial, manicure, pedicures, and wardrobe.

Walking through the process of transformation could be embarrassing, so Father God begins discreetly, too. Before you're ready for the public, Father God prepares you in private. If you've ever seen a makeover, you know this is the loving thing to do! Makeovers get messy and ugly before they get pretty. Father God is not out to shame you in front of everybody else. A beauty queen in the Bible, named Esther, had a fabulous (and long!) makeover in private too, before she went public.

Before a young woman's turn came to go in to King Xerxes, she had to complete twelve months of beauty treatments prescribed for the women, six months with oil of myrrh and six with perfumes and cosmetics.

— Esther 2:12

Esther had people helping her too, just as Briana did. Father God does not leave you helpless either. Your makeover is divinely inspired. The best person for the job of reproducing Jesus Christ in you is the Holy Spirit. The Holy Spirit knows exactly what Jesus looks like, and the Spirit is skilled at re-creating that same look in you. He does it by guiding you through various circumstances of life and training you in those situations.

Briana's makeover consisted of stops at five different stations before she was fit for public display. At each of those five stops, the stylist formed some feature of Briana in a new way. Each girl was given a new look in relation to her hair, the features on her face, her hands, her feet, and the clothes she wore.

Likewise, the Holy Spirit will guide you to specific experiences and newly form the characteristics of Jesus Christ in you. The Spirit restyles your hair, or what is growing out of your head. If you're going to shine for your heavenly Father, then your mind has to change.

Who has known the mind of the Lord so as to instruct him? But we have the mind of Christ.
— *1 Corinthians 2:16*

You remember that your mind is where the battle is, don't you? So make sure you see your stylist, the Holy Spirit, to get the Jesus Christ cut!

Please keep it moving though, because there is more new styling on the way. The Holy Spirit will also attend to the features on your face. Your nose, eyes, ears, and mouth require major reconstruction to the pattern of Jesus Christ if you're going to light up the world with Father God!

Your nose, eyes, ears, and mouth let you know what's up in the natural world around you. That's exactly what they do in the spiritual world too. Your spiritual life is sensational! You don't think so? Well, think again, Faithgirl! The knowledge of Jesus Christ has a distinctive aroma, like a sweet-smelling fragrance you can detect with your nose. When the Holy Spirit makes over your eyes, you learn what it means to look good to Father God, the way Jesus does.

> **Do nothing out of selfish ambition or vain conceit. Rather, in humility value others above yourselves, not looking to your own interests but each of you to the interests of the others.**
>
> *— Philippians 2:3–4*

Ears are important too, because Jesus Christ made decisions based on what he heard Father God speak. And speaking of speaking! The matter of your mouth is urgent and powerful, dear sister, so the Holy Spirit must fill it with Christ's words of life.

The last two game room stations that Briana and the girls went to both involved large tubs filled with water. Don't you enjoy soaking your hands and feet in a bin of warm water all bubbly with soap? Briana's manicure left her hands feeling clean and rejuvenated. The pedicure, which was her last stop before wardrobe down the hall in the bathroom, made her feet feel brand new and ready to walk with some pep in her step!

Just as it was during Briana's makeover, warm water and cleansing are a major part of the Holy Spirit making room for the life of Jesus Christ to show up in you. Father God wants his children to worship him with uplifted hands that are clean, rather than unclean as if they've worshiped a false god. Jesus demonstrated what the touch of a daughter or son with clean, refreshed hands like his can do.

> When Jesus came into Peter's house, he saw Peter's mother-in-law lying in bed with a fever. He touched her hand and the fever left her, and she got up and began to wait on him.
>
> — *Matthew 8:14–15*

The Father looks for more than just clean hands though, so the Holy Spirit will also get your feet ready for you to walk out your life in the way that Jesus did. As the master artist who transforms you, the Spirit gives you the understanding and wisdom necessary to live a life that honors and pleases God in every way. The Holy Spirit uses the feet of Jesus as a mold for your own, setting you up to walk as he did. Here's how you get to stepping:

> Follow God's example, therefore, as dearly loved children and walk in the way of love, just as Christ loved us and gave himself up for us as a fragrant offering and sacrifice to God.
>
> — *Ephesians 5:1–2*

When it was time to get dressed in their beautiful gowns, Briana fell in love with the long white one embellished with beading and crystals. It was a good thing Ashley was there to assist her, because it would have been impossible for her to dress herself. She polished off her ensemble with simple, yet elegant jewelry and a classic pair of sateen ballet flats. The final adornment, which sealed her status as the center of attention, was a petite tiara that sat modestly on her beautifully styled head. Without a doubt, she definitely was flawless in her appearance.

A flawless appearance before him is what your heavenly Father has planned for you too. The model he uses to assess your completeness is the Son he loves so greatly, Jesus Christ. Briana was able to finish flawlessly with the help of Ashley, her assistant for the evening. Likewise, the Holy Spirit, your helper sent to you from Father God, will enable you to walk into your future as a daughter made over into the image of his Son, Jesus Christ. Before him you will stand in unsurpassed and flawless beauty.

There is no doubt about this, Faithgirl. This is the future and destiny of all daughters and sons of Father God. He definitely determined it before he even created the world! So, since it's a done deal, do you want to know exactly how you will look?

Then look no farther than your brother, Jesus Christ, and to Briana's tidbits that include three insights into Jesus' nature. Three statements Jesus made (yep, some more "I AM" thoughts) show what he is like, and what you are becoming by the work of the Holy Spirit. Jesus said,

- I AM Gentle
- I AM Humble in Heart
- I AM Generous

Just as Austin did for Briana, Jesus has left you a special letter telling you what he's like inside. Make sure you read it in a quiet place, when you have some time alone. Imagine that Jesus is sitting right there next to you, waiting for you to follow him to Father God.

Dear Faithgirl,

I am gentle. I know you've been hearing a lot about bullying lately, but I'm no bully. Other people may get rough or violent with you, trying to make you do things their way. Just as heaven is higher up than the earth, my ways are higher than yours are. Still, I will not use force to bring you near to me. I am kind and mild when I invite you to walk with me. My hope is that you will follow me because you love me, not because you are afraid of me. Sometimes you don't always recognize my voice because I am soft-spoken, but I'm constantly calling you. When I bring you to me, I do it with kindness. My kindness always works.

I am humble in heart too. I understand other people can make you feel nervous and afraid sometimes, with all of their rules and regulations: "Do this, don't do that." They act as if the entire world revolves around them. I am not like that. I'm very simple and don't claim to be so important and special that you can't approach me. When I see that life is weighing you down, it makes my heart heavy with sadness. So, I'll get down in the dirty, messy situations of life with you, no matter what other people think. After that, I'll make a swap with you.

I trade you because I am generous. I love to give. So, when I bend down to pick you up, you can give me the ashes of the mess in your life. Then, I will give you the crown of beautiful life spent walking with Father God. I understand you think you don't deserve it. Remember though, this life really isn't about you or what you think. It's all about Father God and what he thinks. He thinks that because I was willing to give my life, the most valuable thing that a person can give, you do deserve it. According to Father God, whomever I love and cherish deserves to receive good gifts. And guess what, daughter of God? I love you.

Daughter Deed

Jesus is always inviting you to spend time with him. He wants to take you to the heavenly Father in prayer. Now that you've read your letter from Jesus, will you do a daughter deed? Write a letter back to Jesus in the space below, telling him how you feel about his letter. Do you want the Holy Spirit to make you over into his image?

_____

_____

_____

_____

_____

_____

_____

_____

_____

_____

Beginning with Briana

In the natural world, salon visits and makeovers are
great! Still, the spiritual beauty that radiates from within
you matters most to Father God. Fancy clothes, blingy
jewelry, and hair whipped just right are not the things
that make you beautiful. In God's sight, a daughter's
gentle and peaceful spirit shining outwardly is priceless
and unfading.

> **Charm is deceptive, and beauty is fleeting; but a
> woman who fears the LORD is to be praised.**
>
> — *Proverbs 31:30*

 ## Daughter, Declare Your Prayer

Father, thank you for choosing to make me over! I
am grateful for the work of your Holy Spirit within
me. May I always be willing to learn from you.
I'm excited about becoming a reflection of Jesus
Christ, the one you love. It's by following him that
you accept me, and make me gentle, humble, and
generous!

CHAPTER 7

Representing Your Father's Interests

Social Studies was Briana's favorite subject in school. She enjoyed learning about different people and cultures around the world. Briana hoped to travel to other countries and explore the way other kids lived firsthand. Until she was able to do that though, she read tons of books and imagined herself traveling to the destinations she longed to visit.

Briana felt sad during class discussions about countries where kids experience war, hunger, and disease. Can you imagine a bomb going off in the middle of your street? Briana had even learned that there were places where people lived without running water. News like that bothered Bree and made the things she griped about seem, well . . . little. She was starting to get why her mom was always telling her to eat her food and be grateful.

Daughter, You Decide

There are people who need help in all parts of the world.
If you could go anywhere in the world to help make a difference, where would you go?

She didn't know how she could do it, but she wanted
to make things better. So, Briana went to the first person she always did when she needed answers—Jessica.
After all, that's what best friends are for, right? The girls
talked one day after cheer practice. "Jess, something's
been bothering me," she said.

"What's wrong?"

"You know how we've been talking about the villages
where the people don't have water and food and stuff?"

"Yeah. That reminds me, I forgot to label my map.
Did you finish yours?"

"Not yet. Some of that stuff is really starting to bother
me."

"It's just a map, Briana. It won't take more than fif-
teen minutes, tops."

"Not the homework, Jessica! The stories. I mean ...
the people. Look how blessed we are, and them, maybe
not so much."

"Well, I try not to think about it too much."

"That's just it; I can't stop thinking about it. I mean,
can you imagine what it must be like not to be able to just

go to the fridge and grab a bottle of water when you want it? Or what about not being able to take a shower after sweating all day in the sun?"

"Eww. That's disgusting."

"I'm serious, Jess. We have to do something."

"I understand how you feel, Bree. But what can we do? Nobody would take us seriously. We're too young."

"They will if we show them that we really want to help."

"Well, for starters, we have no money ... honey. And whatever you decide to do, you're gonna need lots of that to make it work."

"You stopped saying 'we.' So, I'm in this by myself then?"

"Of course not. You know I'm with you. I'm just saying we need to think it through. That's all."

"You're right about that."

"Tell you what, why don't we talk to Michael about it? He can probably help us."

Jessica's brother, Michael, was in college, and he was the leader of a group of students who are always serving people in the community. He'd let Briana and Jessica tag along once when they were building a new home for a family whose house was destroyed by a tornado. He would know what Briana could do.

That night when they talked, he had some great ideas about how the girls could get started. "Start small," he said, "but think big. You don't have to go to another country or even another city to find hungry people."

It was hard for Briana to believe it, but Michael told her that people not less than thirty minutes from her house didn't have meals sometimes. "Are you serious?" she said.

"Absolutely. And the list goes on and on." He showed Briana a list of all the service projects his organization was working on for the school year. "So you see, there is no shortage of people who need help right in your own backyard. It's just up to you to take the initiative. So, what's it going to be?"

Briana had no answer for Michael. How was she supposed to know what to do?

Briana's Box

Talking to Michael only confused Briana. She wanted to help, but now she was overwhelmed with options! What would you choose to do if you were in Briana's situation? Wow, you really are sounding like your heavenly Father's daughter now! The first thing to do is ask Father God. Here's why.

Father God loves the people of the world. He does not want to see them destroyed. His heart's goal, or mission, is reconnection with his human creation, removing the separation that Adam caused when he got off track. You do remember Adam, don't you? Then, of course, you remember what Jesus did! Jesus is the Son who solved the problem of alienation from Father God.

Praise Prompt

Psalm 47 is a joyful picture of all groups of people praising God. As you read it, imagine how exciting it would be to dance, sing, and leap with excitement before the Lord, along with billions of other people. Now that's what you call a celebration!

Psalm 47

Clap your hands, all you nations;
shout to God with cries of joy.
For the Lord Most High is awesome,
the great King over all the earth.
He subdued nations under us,
peoples under our feet.
He chose our inheritance for us,
the pride of Jacob, whom he loved.
God has ascended amid shouts of joy,
the Lord amid the sounding of trumpets.
Sing praises to God, sing praises;
sing praises to our King, sing praises.
For God is the King of all the earth;
sing to him a psalm of praise.
God reigns over the nations;
God is seated on his holy throne.
The nobles of the nations assemble
as the people of the God of Abraham,
for the kings of the earth belong to God;
he is greatly exalted.

Yet, Jesus is not the only problem solver. God chooses other daughters and sons to become problem solvers too. Yes, that means you! Yet, you don't get to decide which problem you get to solve. Father God has already done that for you.

You would feel just like Briana if you had to decide which problem to solve. Do you remember how she felt? Overwhelmed, right! When we are responsible for solving too many problems, we do our jobs poorly. Father God relieves us of the burden of trying to do it all by giving each of his daughters and sons specific deeds that complete his mission.

> **In the same way, let your light shine before others, that they may see your good deeds and glorify your Father in heaven.**
>
> *— Matthew 5:16*

Still, you do have a responsibility to identify your job in helping other daughters and sons complete the mission of your Father in heaven. As one of his daughters, you represent his business interest of reuniting the world with him.

> **We are therefore Christ's ambassadors, as though God were making his appeal through us. We implore you on Christ's behalf: Be reconciled to God.**
>
> *— 2 Corinthians 5:20*

The way you know what Father God has assigned you to do is to ask him in prayer.

Believing with Briana

Do you remember who Briana asked for help (well, besides her bff!)? A big brother, right! Just as Briana went to Jessica's big brother, Michael, you can turn to your big brother, Jesus. Like Mike, Jesus Christ had a list of things Father God called him to do. Jesus said,

> "The Spirit of the Lord is on me, because he has anointed me to proclaim good news to the poor. He has sent me to proclaim freedom for the prisoners and recovery of sight for the blind, to set the oppressed free, to proclaim the year of the Lord's favor."
>
> — *Luke 4:18–19*

In the towns and villages in which he traveled, Jesus did his part to complete the Father's mission by:

- teaching in their religious meetings,
- telling publically the good news that God's heavenly realm and authority was on earth,
- taking away every disease and sickness.

Now that's what you call good work! Are you ready to get in on the action? Your age is not a limitation. With some help from the adults in your community, you can start becoming a good leader right now, Faithgirl!

Daughter Deed

Think of your age as an asset, not a restriction, and start serving now. Girls like you can be the most compassionate and generous people in the world. Your energy is amazing! Can you do a daughter deed? In the space below, list the names of ten adults (please, Faithgirl, don't forget your parents!) that you know will help you serve in your community.

_____

_____

_____

_____

_____

_____

Look at Briana's tidbits. They share some great ideas for ways you can serve, based on the experiences you've shared with her in this book.

Briana's Tidbit #1: Host a Clothing Drive

Do you remember Briana's struggle to find an outfit to wear on her first day at Live Oak Junior High? There are many children with a much bigger problem than a new outfit for one day. Consider organizing a clothing drive in your community to help kids in need of clothing. Near to the beginning of the school year is a great time to do a clothing drive for school uniforms. Or, when the cold winter months are approaching, you could organize a clothing drive for warm articles of clothing.

Briana's Tidbit #2: Feed the Hungry

Banana-nut muffins anyone? Briana taught you a lot about a healthy spiritual diet, remember? Many people lack nutritious food to eat. Hunger is a crisis affecting millions of people throughout the world. You can help solve the problem in your area by hosting a food drive and giving the cans to the local food pantry. Or you could organize a group of parents and kids from your youth group to prepare and serve meals in the building of your local church.

Briana's Tidbit #3: Protect the Children

Briana introduced you to the adorable Foster twins, Madison and Mason, when she helped her sister, Ashley, babysit. Their parents wanted to keep them safe from the fumes while they painted the house, remember? It's hard to imagine that anyone would ever want to harm a child. Yet modern day slavery, also called human trafficking, endangers the lives of millions of children throughout the world. Many of the victims are girls your age. What can you do to help? One way is to raise money to support the work of large organizations that work to fight human trafficking. With the help of adults, you could organize a kids' night out program. Offer to provide safe, entertaining childcare for families in your community at a low cost. Then donate the money you earn to trustworthy groups fighting human trafficking.

Briana's Tidbit #4: Help the Hospitals

People of all ages dislike hospital visits. Yet, being in the hospital is a real bummer for kids. Briana's leg injury taught you just how important it is for young people to have a family of supporters cheering you on to recovery when you're sick. You can encourage a sick child by volunteering at your local children's hospital. Most hospitals would love to have you come and read to their young patients. Or you could coordinate a card-writing campaign and have your entire class, club, team, or cheer squad make bright, colorful get-well cards to send to sick kids.

Briana's Tidbit #5: Ban Bullying

Briana's ex-cheer mate Taylor was fierce! Even though Briana understood why Taylor was hurt, you learned that violence is never an acceptable solution to a problem. Still, bullying endangers the lives of countless children every day. You can help by speaking up if you know someone is being bullied, just as Briana did. More than that, you could host a rally or carnival to increase the peace in your community. Invite and include adult counselors, community leaders such as pastors, and well-known antiviolence organizations to your event.

Briana's Tidbit #6: Share the Good News

Briana's glam slam was a blast! To top it all off she got great gifts from her family and friends, including a Bible from Austin's mother. How cool was that? You can't be a Faithgirl without one! Yet, millions of people do not have a Bible translated into the language they speak. Can you imagine trying to read the Bible in German? Can you host a used book drive? Invite your family members, friends, and neighbors to donate their books. Sell them to your local book reseller, and then donate the funds to a trustworthy Bible translation ministry.

Beginning with Briana

As you ask Father God what your assignment is, he will bring more ways you can serve to mind. After praying and receiving directions from Father God, pray again! Never stop praying. Ask your parents, teachers, friends, and sisters and brothers in the family of Father God for help. Then get ready, Faithgirl! Before you know it, you'll be working with your heavenly Father to accomplish his mission!

Daughter, Declare Your Prayer

Father, thank you for choosing me to work with your Son, Jesus Christ! Help me to become the problem solver that you are calling me to be. Show me the gifts and talents you have given me to help fulfill your mission. Empower me to use them to draw people to you. I am excited about doing good deeds that honor you!